LONDON

2,000 years of a city and its people

LONDON

2,000 years of a city and its people

FELIX BARKER and PETER JACKSON

MACMILLAN PUBLISHING CO., INC.
NEW YORK

Macmillan Publishing Co., Inc.
866 Third Avenue, New York, N.Y. 10022

**Library of Congress Cataloging in
Publication Data**

Barker, Felix, 1917–
    London: 2,000 years of a city and its people.

    1. London — History.

I. Jackson, Peter Charles Geoffrey, 1922–
joint author.   II. Title.
DA677.B36   1974   942.1'2   74–10884
ISBN 0–02–507120–3

First American Edition 1974

Printed in Great Britain

Designed at The Curwen Press by
James Shurmer

CONTENTS

PREFACE

"I have often amused myself with thinking how different a place London is to different people. They, whose narrow minds are contracted to the consideration of some one particular pursuit, view it only through that medium. A politician thinks of it merely as the seat of government in its different departments; a grazier, as a vast market for cattle; a mercantile man, as a place where a prodigious deal of business is done upon 'Change; a dramatick enthusiast, as the grand scene of theatrical entertainments; a man of pleasure, as an assemblage of taverns, and the great emporium for ladies of easy virtue. But the intellectual man is struck with it, as comprehending the whole of human life in all its variety, the contemplation of which is inexhaustible."

James Boswell, 1763

Though not our direct inspiration, Boswell provides an apt text. The purpose of this book is very much to show London 'in all its variety'. The city's architecture is the background to high-spirited social life; great events rub shoulders with trivial curiosities; topography and popular entertainment are bed-fellows. But we have imposed some discipline on this happy confusion. As strict a chronology as possible has been observed so that London's growth may be seen at all its stages, and the reasons for its development understood. We have confined ourselves to contemporary illustrations, or those nearest in date to the event or building depicted. And we have chosen the London County boundary as it existed until 1965 as the limit of our study. This rule has been bent only once, I think—and then by only half a mile—to squeeze in Chiswick House.

Our general method has been to consider buildings, institutions and amenities like railways, roads and bridges at the time they were created, or at their most important stage of development. One possible drawback to this is that when a subject has been dealt with, or the first stage of a building completed, they are inclined to be forgotten unless there is a very pressing obligation to return to them. Doctors, for instance, might well protest that medicine has progressed since the eighteenth century, which is the only time hospitals are fully scrutinized.

Our strictness with the dates of illustrations is not pedantry, but to ensure as accurate a view of the past as possible, and show things as they looked to people at the time. For the same reason, quotations in the text when not attributed may be assumed to be contemporary. Scholarly topographical reconstructions, such as Sorrell's view of Roman London and Brewer's London in the Middle Ages, are used because they are helpful. But fanciful scenes, much favoured in Victorian histories, have been excluded. So you will not find Charles II chatting to Nell Gwynn over the wall of her house in St James's Park. This restriction has set problems, especially for the early and medieval periods before engraving. But manuscript illustrations, like those showing the Wat Tyler rebellion, have helped to fill gaps, as have photographs selected to avoid anachronisms.

As this is predominantly a pictorial history, we have, to a certain extent, let pictures determine the events and places dealt with. This is why important, but abstract, subjects like London's government have received rather less emphasis than perhaps they should. Sometimes the choice of pictures may seem rather arbitrary. Why, for instance, a picture of Brompton Oratory, but not Westminster Cathedral? The answer is that we have been governed partly by the way we have treated various subjects, and partly by the availability of pictures showing places at a particular date. We have had to be selective. We have also, quite unashamedly, played favourites.

A pictorial London history on this scale has not been attempted before because the undertaking would have been impracticable without one main source on which to draw. Our source has been Peter Jackson's collection. Built up over two decades, this is now probably the most comprehensive in private hands. As well as rare prints and original drawings, it contains ephemera that reflect the collector's delight in 'curiosities'. We gladly risk the accusation of frivolity by including a few of these, among them a handbill advertising a Singing Mouse which apparently performed in the Strand during the last century. Out of a total of 997 plates, 550 are from the Jackson London Collection. Our next largest source is the British Museum which supplied ninety. Foreign sources included Paris, Ghent, Arras, Basle, Utrecht, Stockholm and Farmington, Connecticut, U.S.A. Most of the fifty-five colour plates are from museums, institutions, and private houses. Acknowledgements and full attributions for every illustration will be found at the end of the text.

As the writer of the book, there is only one thing I would like to explain. History is full of contradictions; controversies abound. But in a book of this sort, and with so many subjects to be dealt with, often very briefly, it has not been possible to go into conflicting arguments. I have thought it better to accept the most authoritative and cautious view. I am thinking of the different viewpoints which surround the murder of the Princes in the Tower, and hope to have steered a centre course in events like the Gunpowder Plot which involve religious controversy.

Though I am solely responsible for the text and captions, these would be poorer without Peter Jackson's help. As an explorer with a sketchbook in every part of London, he has acquired an encyclopedic amount of little-known information. My knowledge of London comes largely from reading and research; his has the added vitality of being gained from the pavement. In the most happy of collaborations which has spread over fourteen years, we planned every section of the book together, decided on pictures and lay-outs and the proportion of text to illustration, favouring pictures wherever possible. When, occasionally, the text required illustrations, even the existence of which was uncertain, Peter Jackson's search for them was indefatigable. His finding of rare items makes publication possible, for the first time, of manuscript drawings of the theft of the crown jewels from the Chapel of the Pyx, the Hearth Tax record of the baker's shop where the Great Fire started, and a picture of the Berners Street hoax, believed to be unique. In the final stages, our lay-outs were modified to meet suggestions by James Shurmer of The Curwen Press who is responsible for the overall design discipline.

So many books have been consulted that to compile even a Select Bibliography would be difficult. So we simply list a few which have been found indispensable, and which may suggest further reading to those interested. Foremost is the *Survey of London* (now edited by F. H. W. Sheppard and published by the Greater London Council) which has reached thirty-seven volumes, and will eventually encompass all London. Among modern works, the next in importance are the two London volumes (1952 and 1957) in the Penguin *Buildings of England* series edited by Nikolaus Pevsner. Wheatley and Cunningham's *London Past and Present* (1891), and William Kent's *Encyclopaedia of London* (1937) are excellent reference works.

For original research, unlikely to be superseded for many years, the following have proved invaluable: *Old London Bridge* (1931) by Gordon Home; *The Growth of Stuart London* (1935) by Norman G. Brett-James; *The Great Fire of London* (1920) by Walter George Bell; *The Rebuilding of London after the Great Fire* (1940) by T. F. Reddaway; *The Early History of Piccadilly, Leicester Square and Soho* (1925) by Charles Lethbridge Kingsford; *Georgian London* (1945) by John Summerson; *The Thames in 1750* (1951) by Hugh Phillips; and *Records* of the London Topographical

Society (in progress). Nineteenth-century London is briefly but comprehensively dealt with by Asa Briggs in a chapter of *Victorian Cities* (1963). For the twentieth century, *London, Aspects of Change* (1964), Report No. 3 by the Centre for Urban Studies, is austere but extremely informative. Without Sydney Anglo's scholarly monograph, *The Great Tournament Roll of Westminster* (1968), the section on the tournament would have been impossible. And time and again we have come back to that great quarry of information, *Old and New London* (1873-78) by G. W. Thornbury and E. Walford. This was published by Cassell, and we are proud that, a century later, our book comes from the same house.

We can never thank sufficiently the museums and libraries which have been so helpful, or the learned societies, institutions and individuals who have given us specialized advice. Our debt to the British Museum, London Museum, Westminster Library, Guildhall, and London Library is considerable; several local libraries have been very co-operative; and so, too, have more scholarly institutions like the College of Arms and the Society of Antiquaries of London.

In his search for pictures outside his own collection, Peter Jackson would especially like to thank the National Monuments Record, the Librarian of the *Architectural Review*, and the photographic departments of the Victoria and Albert Museum, London Transport, the Department of the Environment, the Greater London Council and the Public Record Office. An important source of reference has been *A Catalogue of Maps, Plans and Views of London* (1878) which lists the great collections made by Frederick Crace in the nineteenth century, and now in the British Museum. Most of the photography of the prints and drawings at the Museum was done by John Freeman to whom special thanks are due for his skill and care.

Help has been given by owners of paintings and, to mention two among many, we are grateful to the Duke of Bedford and the Earl of Cadogan. Lord Cadogan opened up his Scottish castle, and, at his own expense, despatched a photographer there to provide us with a portrait of an eighteenth-century ancestor. The Duke of Bedford personally led us through the attic floors of Woburn in his enthusiastic, but unfortunately unavailing, search for a picture of the first Bedford House in the Strand.

Among scholars who went to exceptional trouble to answer queries, I wish to thank John H. Harvey, author of *Gothic England* (1947), for his help over difficulties arising from Wyngaerde's drawing of the Privy Stairs at Whitehall. On a more personal level, we remember with gratitude the enthusiasm of our agent, the late Peter Watt, which helped to launch this book; the patience shown over a long period by the directors and staff of Cassell's; and the fastidious work of their editor, Esther Eisenthal. I am grateful to my family for their forbearance during an excessively long gestation. It is impossible to thank adequately my wife for her research, especially for the early and later parts of the book. One special contribution was her analysis of the tricky population figures of London in the early years of the Census returns. She also brought her historical knowledge to many periods covered in the book, made valuable suggestions about the draft manuscript, and vigilantly read the proofs.

Peter Jackson

Felix Barker
Lindsey House, Blackheath

LONDON FROM THE BEGINNING

London from the air

Looking down on London from a height of three miles, we see the Thames tracing its serpentine course from Kew to the Estuary, and out into the inky blackness of the North Sea. Hazy sunshine bathes five counties in a strange, luminous glow. With roads and reservoirs, parks and playing fields, twenty-two bridges and an infinity of houses, this is the London of the twentieth century. But geographically it is also the Lower Thames Valley as it has looked for 2,000 years. This could be the London Basin in prehistoric times or when the Romans invaded.

At a point where the Thames could be forded (almost exactly in the middle of this view) the infant London was born and took shape during the first century A.D. It was among the earliest cities of northern Europe. A chronological table is dangerous because historical records are inadequate, and archaeological evidence often inconclusive. Paris is older than London by at least a hundred years, and a firm date for the beginning of Cologne – A.D. 50 – makes it at least four years older than London, if we accept London's foundation as coinciding with the second Roman invasion. Brussels, Lisbon and Geneva may well have been roughly contemporary, but London is centuries older than Amsterdam, Madrid, Moscow and Berlin, and is probably older than Prague, Warsaw or Vienna.

Medieval historians were not inhibited by probability. They cheerfully gave London a far earlier foundation. Trojan heroes (legendary builders of Rome, Paris and Lisbon) were fashionable founders, and Brutus was held responsible for London. 'Brute, lineally descended from the demi-god Eneas, the sonne of Venus, daughter of Jupiter, builded this city near unto the river now called Thames,' declared Geoffrey of Monmouth in the twelfth century. He said this New Troy had existed from 1108 B.C. Another legend prefers the mythical King Lud as the founder. Sixty-six years before the birth of Christ, he is said to have built walls and gates (including Ludgate) and to have given his city the name *Lud's-town*. Mythology also relates that King Lud was succeeded by his brother, and that he had been reigning about eight years when Julius Caesar arrived.

We shall examine the ascertainable facts in detail, but it is interesting to hear the Elizabethan historian, John Stow, on the reason why the Thames was preferred as the site of 'a royal city' rather than the Severn or the Trent. It reaches 'furthest into the belly of the land,' he noted, and 'openeth indifferently upon France and Flanders, our mightiest neighbours to whose doings we ought to have a bent eye and special regard'.

Aerial view taken 1934.

The Prehistoric Site

Through the wide valley ran the largest river in Britain fed by streams from the thickly wooded hills we now call Highgate and Hampstead, and from the heights above Camberwell. In prehistoric times this part of the Thames basin was wild, uncultivated territory. The extent to which it was affected by the river is uncertain. The imaginative reconstruction, left, supports the theory of marshy land flooded at high tide with islands – Thorn-ey, Chels-ea, Bermonds-ey, Batters-ea – emerging from a lagoon. More recent research, however, suggests that the river banks were not inundated, because the Thames ran about fifteen feet deeper than it does today. Whichever alternative we prefer, the twin hills on which the greatest city in the world was to grow – Ludgate Hill and Cornhill – were forty feet above water-level.

Geology determined why this, rather than anywhere else along the Thames, became the chosen spot. At this point for the first time it could be forded and eventually bridged. Here, forty miles from the sea, the river had a gravel bed. The gravel sub-soil also provided the earliest trading vessels from Gaul with a firm landing ground on either bank.

No records and no archaeological evidence allow us to build huts or see any tribal community here in the pre-Christian era. From axes, spearheads and knives that have been found, it is certain that hunters knew this territory; but there has been no trace of prehistoric pottery, which would be unassailable evidence of a camp or early town.

The idea that there was a pre-Roman settlement is based largely on the name. The first recorded name, *Londinium*, is Roman, but this is based on an earlier Celtic name, *Londinion*. This would suggest that a Celtic town existed when the Romans came, but it is not conclusive because the Romans often gave native names to places they founded.

Another reason for the persistent legend of a London before the actual occupation is the discovery of some pottery. A few pieces imported from Arezzo in Italy, and belonging to the early part of the first century A.D., have been found in the City and Southwark. They could have been brought there from somewhere else later, but they permit the cautious deduction that a few prospectors from the Roman world may have built a wharf and warehouses in a settlement near London Bridge a decade or so before the arrival of the Claudian legions in A.D. 43.

1

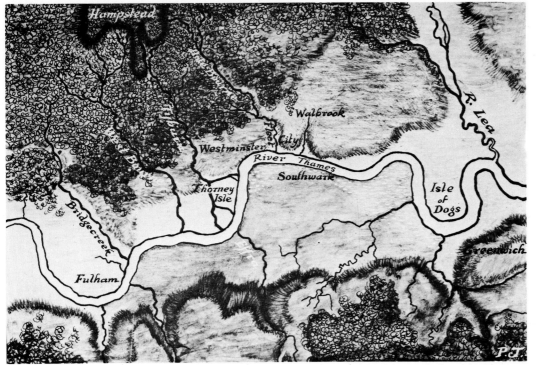

2

1. Site of prehistoric London – a reconstruction from the south-east

2. Map showing the valley where the city came to be built. Approaching from the heights above Greenwich, the Romans had a clear view of this sweep of the Thames, and marching on a straight course would have reached the river bank opposite Westminster.

The Roman Invasion

When Julius Caesar landed in 54 B.C. his invasion force of five legions and 2,000 cavalry met fierce opposition from the tribes of south-eastern England which harassed his advance from the coast near Deal. The territory of the Catuvellauni lay to the north of the Thames and west of the river Lea, and it was against them that Caesar ordered his main attack. The defenders, ill-equipped and unorganized in comparison to the Roman soldiers, still had a natural advantage–the river–which as Caesar himself records in his *Gallic Wars* 'can be forded only at one place and that with difficulty'.

Across the Thames the British forces were drawn up behind pointed stakes, and sending the cavalry into the water first, followed by the infantry, Caesar made the crossing. Unable to withstand the attack the Catuvellauni 'abandoned the banks and took flight'.

The exact scene of this incident is endlessly debated, for Caesar does not name it, and, in fact, makes no mention of the place his followers were to call Londinium. If there was a rough daub-and-wattle village, a river trading post, he does not record it. All we know is that at Westminster and Chelsea, on the direct line of his advance, were the hard foundations on which, at low tide, a crossing could be made through about five feet of water.

The question of whether Caesar left behind him some sort of embryonic London is uncertain. During his campaign he would have needed to keep open his line of supply from the south coast and this would have involved a bridgehead on the river, an advance base from which to direct operations north of the Thames. A bridge would have been a necessity, and it has been suggested that when Caesar returned to Gaul he may well have left a wooden pile bridge and that around this grew up a little trading community during the following century. There is, however, no evidence for such an idea.

Ninety-seven years after Caesar left, the Romans made their second invasion. In the reign of Claudius an army of 40,000 landed in A.D. 43. Again the Thames was the main defensive line. Some soldiers swam across, but this time a bridge was definitely built, and once on the other side the infantry 'assailed the barbarians from several sides at once and cut down many of them'.

From this time London may be said to have been founded. Within ten years it was a flourishing town built on the more easterly of two hills that were separated by the River Walbrook. In A.D. 60 there is the first definite mention of London by Tacitus who calls it a place 'filled with traders and a celebrated centre of commerce'.

1. Caesar's invasion required about 800 vessels, mostly shallow-draft barges. Remains of a Roman ship of this sort were found buried on the shore of the Thames near Westminster Bridge in 1910. Made of oak, it would originally have been 60 feet long and 16 feet wide. This particular Roman vessel appears to belong to a later period. It may well have been one of the ships in which Allectus tried to escape from London (page 15).

2. Roman trading ship–probably second-century–found at Blackfriars in 1962. It was a keelless, flat-bottomed barge, carvel-built. The most interesting feature was the mast-step, above, cut into a heavy transverse rib. In this was discovered a coin (arrowed) of Domitian's reign, with the goddess Fortuna holding a ship's rudder on reverse. It is assumed that it was placed here by the shipwrights for good luck.

3. Julius Caesar. Authentic bust found in the forum at Tusculum (Frascati) near Rome. The famous British Museum bust of Caesar is no longer believed to be genuine.

4. Cunobelinus (Shakespeare's Cymbeline), great-grandson of the king who opposed Caesar. He was principal ruler of south-east England between the Roman invasions. Cunobelinus kept peace with Rome during his reign of nearly forty years, and won Britain a degree of national independence. The rebellion by one of his four sons, who fled to Rome for support, led to the Claudian invasion in A.D. 43.

The City Wall

After the second Roman invasion, the British tribes in the west and north defied the legions and opposed the army of occupation. Revolt culminated in the action of Queen Boudicca (popularly, Boadicea). When her husband, the King of the Iceni, died, his will was ignored by the Roman officials, his territory (Norfolk) despoiled, and their daughters violated. She herself was flogged. All this goaded her to revenge.

While the Roman Governor, Suetonius Paulinus, was suppressing insurrections in north Wales, the Iceni and the neighbouring Trinovantes under the command of Boudicca descended on London. The unwalled city, which was not a main military post, stood no chance. Suetonius marched south, but had to decide either to save London or to prevent the revolt spreading throughout the province. Strategy forced him to sacrifice the city. 'Neither the tears nor entreaties of the stricken citizens bent him from his purpose,' Tacitus relates.

The inhabitants – Romans and 'friends of Rome' – were 'massacred, hanged, burned and crucified' by the Britons under their avenging warrior queen. How many died in the city is unknown, but the total killed in London, Colchester and Verulamium (St Albans) is given as 70,000. The ashes of the destroyed buildings still lie between ten and twenty feet below modern London. The fearful heat of the burning may be judged from a small heap of contemporary coins found near the north end of London Bridge; flames have partially fused them together.

Fortunately, by A.D. 61, the date of Boudicca's attack, London was already too well established as a port and commercial centre for the devastation to be more than a temporary setback. The city was rebuilt, and in the next half-century acquired an imperial scale. From the ashes of the rough Romano-Celtic town rose a basilica and forum, temples, shops and private houses laid out in the formal, square patterns of Roman town planning.

The military were not leaving anything to chance again. A fortress, about 200 yards square, was built in the north-west of the city in the present Cripplegate area. This served to guard the safety of the new London as building progressed. Then in about A.D. 120 a defensive wall was started round the whole city. This precaution may possibly have been instigated by that great builder of walls, the Emperor Hadrian, who came to Britain in this year and whose bronze head, above right, was to be found in the Thames.

The fortress caused the curious change that can be seen in the direction of the line of the wall. The re-entrant angle between Newgate and Cripplegate was a mystery until archaeological excavations after the Second World War revealed that two already existing walls of the fort had been incorporated in the new wall. Possibly 15 feet high, and in parts 8 feet thick, the Roman wall encircled 330 acres. This made London the largest city in Britain, and the fifth largest in the Roman Empire north of the Alps.

On a foundation of flint and rammed clay, the wall was built of Kentish ragstone with courses of brick bonding running right through horizontally at levels of about three feet. Outside the wall was a defensive V-shaped ditch. The bastions, twenty-one of which are definitely known to have existed, were probably additions built about a century after the wall was finished. Six main gateways punctuated the walls at intervals and led out to the great Roman roads radiating from London.

3

1

4

2

5

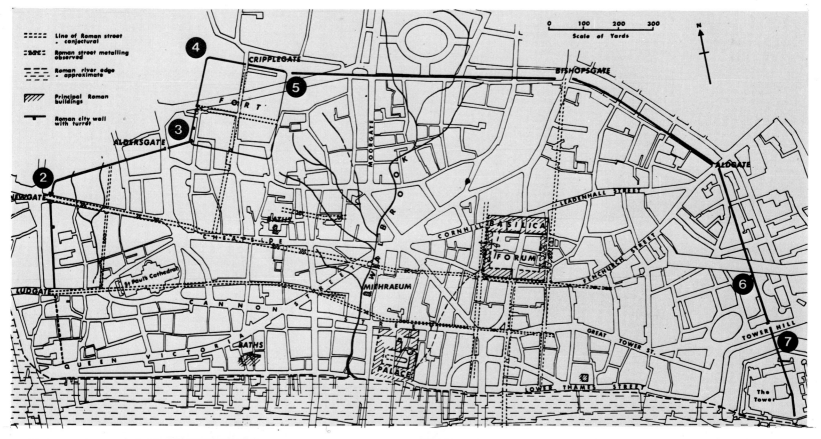

Legend:
- Line of Roman street – conjectural
- Roman street metalling observed
- Roman river edge – approximate
- Principal Roman buildings
- Roman city wall with turret

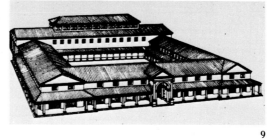

6

7

8

9

1. The Emperor Hadrian. This bronze head was part of a statue which may have stood in the Forum. This would have been appropriate as there is evidence that the Forum was built during his reign. The head, sixteen inches high, was dredged from the Thames near London Bridge in 1834. A bronze hand, possibly part of the same statue, was found in Lower Thames Street. Both are in the British Museum.

2. Roman Newgate – the only gate for which there is enough archaeological evidence for a confident reconstruction.

3. Foundations of the south-west corner of the Roman fort. They lie in the basement of a bombed building in Noble Street. Visible are: the curve of the fort wall (A); the rectangular corner turret (B); the junction of the City wall and the fort (C); and a small part of an inner, thickening wall which was added when the City wall was incorporated with the older fort wall (D).

4. Corner bastion at Cripplegate (Roman origin disputed).

5. Wall at St Alphage's – medieval top, double Roman (fort and city) walls at base.

6. Wall at Trinity Place – lower part Roman.

7. Tomb (partially restored) of Classicianus, appointed Procurator of Britain after Boudicca's revolt. The upper portion was found in a bastion of the Roman wall near Tower Hill in 1852.

8. Excavations in the same area in 1935 produced this upside-down stone bearing the bottom three lines. The central portion is missing, but the inscription, translated, may be presumed to read: 'Sacred to the memory of G. Julius Fabius Alpinus Classicianus . . . Procurator of the Provinces of Britain [this monument was set up by] his wife Julia Pacata Indiana, daughter of [Julius] Indus.'

9. The Basilica – reconstruction of the principal public building, based on discoveries in the Leadenhall Market area. Combining the functions of a town hall and law courts, the Basilica was just over 500 feet long, considerably larger than similar buildings in any other Romano-British town. From the foundations of walls, excavated in 1888, on either side of Gracechurch Street, it is possible to see that it roughly conformed to the pattern of basilicas in other Roman provincial towns. There was a large hall, offices and courtrooms, and to the south it looked out over the Forum – the enclosed courtyard which was colonnaded on three sides. In this administrative centre, the senate of Londinium would have met.

The Temple of Mithras

Our picture of Roman London derived from Latin historians and the semi-legendary accounts of Anglo-Saxon chroniclers is richly supplemented by archaeology. An idea of everyday domestic life can be built up from a hundred fragmentary finds, from locks to cooking utensils, from scent bottles to mirrors, from a leather bathing slip to a bronze fibula brooch, from an ear pick to a folding foot-rule. A minute green tablet provides an unexpected sidelight. It tells us that Caius Silvius Tetricus, possibly London's earliest oculist, sold ointments for rough eyelids and lotions for 'attacks of bleariness'. A wax writing tablet from the bed of the River Walbrook bears the evocative inscription: 'Take good care you turn that slave girl into cash.'

Tessellated pavements indicate that the colonists tried to establish something of the same standard of luxury that prevailed in Rome. In the foundations of a building in Lower Thames Street came evidence in 1848 of a central heating system for a public baths or a well-to-do private house. A hypocaust provided hot air which came up through the floor to warm the room above.

Bombing during the Second World War gave the London archaeologists unprecedented opportunities for finding traces of the Roman occupation. By chance the worst hit area was the very centre of what had been the ancient city, the place where the River Walbrook flowed into the Thames. Bulldozers probably swept away three-quarters of the evidence before anyone could see it, but there were still some notable finds among the thirty acres of debris.

In the summer of 1954, digging on the west side of the Walbrook revealed the foundations of a building which the archaeologists soon recognized as a pagan temple. Trenches were cut and the foundation of its walls, triple apse, and a double row of pillars were revealed. This was the first and only Roman building in London of which there was a complete plan.

In September came the discovery of the marble head of the god Mithras. This was conclusive evidence of the already suspected idea that the temple was dedicated to the Sun God who had followers all over the Roman world. Mithraism, which rated strength higher than gentleness and made a special virtue of courage and action, had a particular appeal for the Roman soldiers who brought it to Britain. Here was the London shrine of the god whose religion was to perish in the struggle with Christianity in the third century. A series of other important discoveries were made in the Temple of Mithras during the following few weeks.

1. One of the 1954 discoveries in the Temple. Central figure in the marble group is Bacchus. On his right is Silenus seated on an ass. A workman's pick-axe fractured the group, probably decapitating the figures on the left, an attendant Satyr and Maenad at whose feet crouches a panther.

2. 1869. A tessellated pavement was found near Bucklersbury and the Walbrook when Queen Victoria Street was being excavated from the Mansion House to Blackfriars. It was visited by 30,000 people in three days. The site was about ninety yards from the Temple of Mithras.

3. The marble head of a river god. About sixty-five years before the discovery of the Temple of Mithras this head, in white marble and probably belonging to the second century, was found near the Walbrook. It now seems certain that it was one of the many idols in the temple.

4. Mithras slaying the bull – the epic struggle symbolic of man's journey through life. Relief found in 1889 at the same time as the river god. Clearly it once belonged to the temple. Inscription suggests it was dedicated to the god by Ulpius Silvanus, a retired soldier of the Second Legion.

5. The bearded Serapis, Egyptian god of the harvest, identified by the corn measure on his head. Found sixteen days after the head of Mithras, Serapis was one of the gods which might have been expected in the temple.

6. The discovery made on 18 September 1954 which established the Walbrook temple as that of Mithras. The god is wearing the Phrygian cap with which, legend says, he was born. The head probably formed part of an important statuary group in the temple.

7. Queues of people stretched all the way into Cannon Street when the Temple of Mithras was opened to view shortly after its discovery in 1954. There were about 100,000 visitors in five days. The unprecedented interest led to demands in Parliament and by the Press for its preservation *in situ*. This was virtually impossible, as a fourteen-storey office block, Bucklersbury House, was planned for the site. There were structural difficulties, the cost prohibitive, and, having extracted their data, the archaeologists did not consider it essential. It was decided to demolish the temple systematically so that it could be rebuilt. The bricks and stones were numbered and stored for eight years. They were then reconstructed, only a few yards from the original site, in a forecourt in Queen Victoria Street where the temple may be seen today.

3

4

5

6

7

13

At the beginnin
half-way throug
Roman occupati
the height of its p
capital, had lo
London was n
province. With
45,000, it was t
name.

The three mi
complete, and a
a drawbridge to
stretched across
On to it conve
Canterbury and
from Chicheste
southern wall wh
running the leng
have had a com
piles, it may ha
mined by the eb
wall must have
no trace of it ha
gate a road wou
the buildings wl
Basilica and the

The Basilica,
crowned the hig
contained within
Market stands t
we can estimate t
long from east t
it consisted of a
dimensions are
which served as
exchange was
Basilica in Rome
and attached to
building, most p
in the Forum
arcaded shops. I
fort built for pro

The layout o
jectural, inferre
Basilica, the gat
have been foun
major diagonal s
the bridge to A
led to Colcheste
Ermine Street, t
width of the st
from thirty feet
different sorts fa
houses were of st
of timber becaus
is no suggestio
houses; rather th
even shacks sid
which can be se
built round ope
streets were 'lo
with their narrov

'The Mart of Many Nations'

For six hundred years after the Romans left, London's story is fragmentary. There was no reason for a general exodus with the departure of the legions, but slowly the city fell into ruin and became largely deserted. Some people lived on among the crumbling buildings and overgrown streets, and when the Saxons invaded the country in 467, Britons, defeated at the Battle of Crayford, took refuge there.

It was sufficiently important in 604 to merit a Christian mission. Mellitus, a monk from Rome, was ordained Bishop of London by Augustine, and on the easterly hill of the city he founded the cathedral of St Paul. But after twelve years Mellitus was driven out; the capital of the East Saxons relapsed into heathenism; and the seat of the Primate of England, intended for London, was established at Canterbury where it has remained.

The Thames brought trade to the city so that by about 730 we learn from Bede that it was 'the mart of many nations resorting to it by land and sea'. But the river also brought the dragon-prowed ships of Danish invaders. From 834 until 1016 the Vikings were a constant menace. Their attack in 851 left the city a black, smouldering wreck and was accompanied by terrible slaughter. Thirty-five years later King Alfred recovered the lost city from the invaders, repaired the breached walls, and trapped the next fleet of Viking invaders in the River Lea. During the peace of the following century London became the largest city in the kingdom.

In 980 the Vikings were back, and, in the confused period of occupation that followed, they were dislodged and London recaptured by King Ethelred in about 1014. If the Norse sagas are to be trusted, Ethelred's return was dramatic. He sailed up the Thames with the Norseman, Olaf, who brought his ships right up to a heavily defended London Bridge. Cables were thrown round the piles, and the oarsmen rowing hard downstream pulled down the bridge. Ethelred was succeeded after two years by the young Danish king Canute (Cnut) who was proclaimed King of All England. London paid him heavy tribute, but had its reward. During his reign the city grew so in importance that it was to replace Winchester as the capital of England, a position which it was never to lose.

1. Viking ship. This early manuscript drawing depicts the sort of carved prow which, seen in the Thames, must have struck terror in the tenth-century Londoner.

2. Viking tombstone discovered near a human skeleton in St Paul's Churchyard in 1852. Roughly two feet square, it is of the tenth or eleventh century. Relief shows a strange beast with interlaced limbs and either antlers or lappets. An inscription reads: 'Konal and Tuki caused this stone to be laid'.

Founding of the Abbey

Among the buildings plundered by the pagan invaders during the ninth century was the little timber church of St Peter on Thorn-ey, the island of brambles. Here the Christian Church had been founded in 785. Legend claims a more ancient and miraculous beginning, but the charter still survives to tell us that in this year, Offa, King of Mercia, granted lands and privileges 'to St Peter and the People of the Lord dwelling in Thorney in the terrible place [i.e. sacred place] which is called Westminster.'

The small band of Benedictine monks attached to the church late in the tenth century believed that the place where they worshipped had been consecrated by St Peter himself. No further reason was needed to encourage the pious king, Edward the Confessor, to replace the little Saxon building with a great cruciform church. In a palace built nearby he was able to watch the work go forward, and from this time Westminster became the traditional residence of English kings. A contemporary chronicler calls it a pleasant situation 'among the fruitful fields and green ground with the principal river running near.'

King Edward was determined to outdo all other churches in England and Normandy, and one tenth of his property 'in gold, silver, cattle and all other possessions' went into the work. In fifteen years the rough church of timber beams had been replaced by a building with a stone roof and pillars occupying almost the whole area of the present abbey. In 1065 his church was ready, and, says the *Saxon Chronicle*, 'At Midwinter King Edward came to Westminster, and had the minster there consecrated, which he had himself built'. But three days before the ceremony – Christmas Day – he fell ill, and was too weak to attend. He rallied sufficiently to sign the charter of the Foundation, but his Queen presided in his stead. On 5 January 1066, the Confessor died, and the next day he was laid to rest before the high altar of the abbey he had created. That same day with urgent speed his successor Earl Harold was crowned.

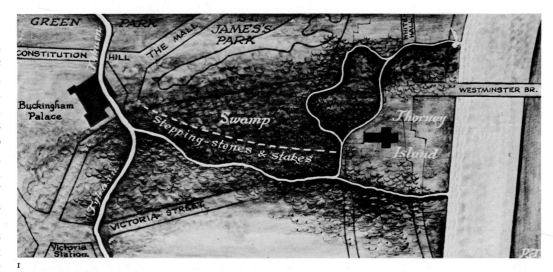

1. Thorney Island, where Westminster Abbey was built, was bounded by the Thames, Tyburn and swamps, its approach possible only by boat, ford and stepping stones. The ancient site is imposed on a modern map.

2. Edward the Confessor's shrine attracted pilgrims from earliest times. This thirteenth-century drawing shows seven blind men receiving their sight at the tomb. A priest sings the *Te Deum* while one man climbs right under the tomb, as was the custom, so that he might receive a cure from the sacred corpse of St Edward.

3. 'The body of King Edward is taken to St Peter's Church' – the scene from the Bayeux tapestry. A workman, left, fixes a weathercock standing on a ladder which stretches from the adjoining palace of Westminster to the Abbey. The Hand of God pointing down from Heaven indicates that the Abbey had been consecrated. Pall-bearers, right, bring the King's body to its rest.

The Norman Occupation

On the death of Edward the Confessor, the national council—the Witan—hurriedly chose Earl Harold as King. The choice was sound, but trouble inevitable. In Normandy Duke William maintained that his cousin, the Confessor, had promised him the crown, and that Harold had sworn to support his claim. Victory at the Battle of Hastings did not lull William into thinking that London would fall easily to his 10,000 men. The city's defences were being strengthened. So he approached only as near as Southwark, which he burnt, and then struck west. He crossed the Thames at Wallingford, and outflanked the capital. The countryside which supplied London's food was laid waste, and within a few weeks a deputation consisting of Edgar Atheling, the uncrowned king-elect, the Witan, and London's leading citizens came to meet him at Berkhamsted to offer him the crown.

On Christmas Day 1066, William went to Westminster and was crowned before the high altar – standing on the grave of the Confessor. In almost solitary splendour he took the royal oath and promised to treat his new subjects with the same justice as those of Normandy.

Even if he carried oppression to other parts of the country, William the Conqueror seems to have been determined to win London's favour. Early in his reign he granted the city a charter which, translated, reads: 'William, King, greets William, Bishop and Godfrey, Portreeve, and all the burghers within London, French and English, friendlike. And I will that both be worthy of all the rights of which ye both were worthy in King Edward's day. And I will that every child be his father's heir after his father's day. And I will not suffer that any man offer you any wrong. God keep you.'

Ostensibly for defence against Danish invasion, but more probably from a sense of insecurity and knowing that much of his time would be spent out of London, William built three strongholds in his capital. Immediately after his coronation he moved to Barking while, a Norman chronicler tells us, 'certain strongholds were made in the town against the fickleness of the vast and fierce population'. Undoubtedly this refers to preliminary work on the Tower of London, building of which started the following year.

The other two strongholds were Baynard's Castle built by Ralph Baynard, its first custodian, who came over from Normandy with the Conqueror, and Montfichet Castle, probably named after another of his followers. Baynard's was on the river a mile west of the Tower. Montfichet, a moated keep, is thought to have been near Ludgate, but it did not survive long and no view exists. By

1

2

1272 it was already 'old and ruined'. These three strong points were linked into a defensive whole by the wall of the city.

The first part of the Tower to be built was the central White Tower, started in 1078 on William's orders by Gundulph, Bishop of Rochester. The massive keep of white Caen stone, ninety-two feet tall, and with walls up to fifteen feet thick, was basically designed to accommodate the King, his family, royal household and treasure. From the dungeons a winding staircase in one of the four corner turrets led to the various state apartments and the sternly beautiful Norman Chapel of St John. Successive kings added the surrounding features that still survive. The inner curtain wall with its dozen small towers was largely the work of Henry III. Edward I added the outer defences including the Traitors' Gate in St Thomas's Tower, the moat, and the Middle Tower which guards the outer entrance.

Although the main royal residence was the palace at Westminster, the Tower was the king's refuge in times of crisis, and Henry III preferred to live there. To London down the centuries, the Tower was to become something more – a symbol of authority and strength as well as a place of imprisonment, torture and execution, the name of which inspired fear.

1. William the Conqueror–from the Bayeux tapestry. The only portrait of historical value.

2. The charter granted by William to the city, now preserved at the Guildhall. This politically important document, written in Anglo-Saxon, is only six inches by one inch in size. From fragments of the original seals its date is reckoned to be 1066 or shortly after.

3. This late sixteenth-century view shows, in broad outline, the Tower much as it looked in Norman and early Plantagenet times. The clusters of smaller pitch-roofed buildings and the Chapel of St Peter ad Vincula, however, belong to a later period.

4. The White Tower as it looks today.

5. A Norman builder, from an early manuscript.

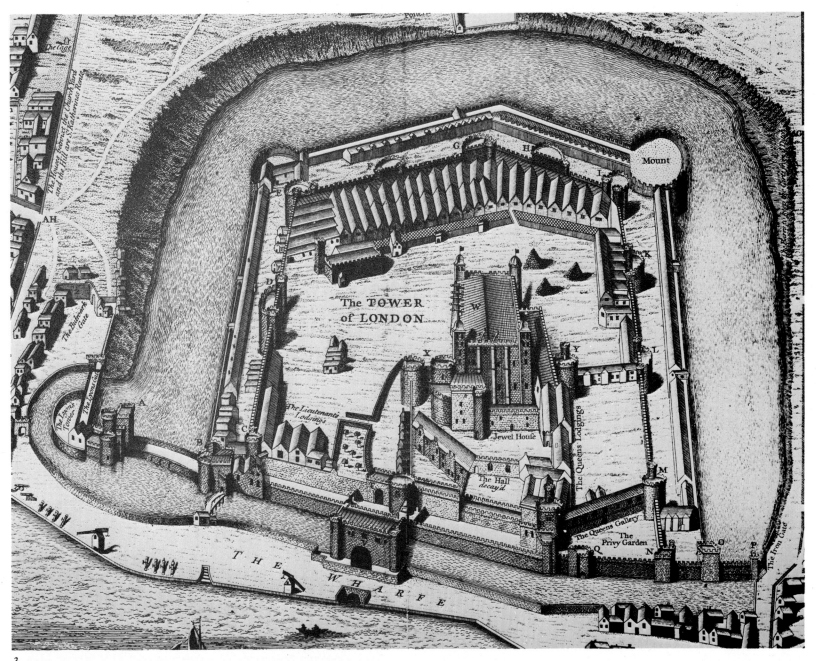

3

4

5

Growth of the Norman City

For the first twenty years after the Norman Conquest London probably changed very little from the walled city of Anglo-Saxon times. But between 1077 and 1136 a series of devastating fires raged through the houses of thatched roofs and timber frames. Four times in those sixty years London had to be rebuilt, and in November 1090 its citizens faced another catastrophe when a violent south-east gale blew down 600 houses, tore the roofs off several churches including St Mary-le-Bow, and caused such a torrent on the Thames that the wooden bridge was almost entirely swept away.

So began the building of narrow streets – among them Corn Hill, Thames Street and East and West Cheap – roughly on the same lines (and many with the same names) we know today. But the great achievement of William and his Norman successors was not so much domestic as ecclesiastical. By 1183 William Fitz Stephen in his *Descriptio Londoniae* records: 'Also as concerns Christian worship there are both in London and the Suburbs thirteen great Conventual Churches and one hundred and twenty-six lesser Parochial'.

This means that London had a parish church to every three acres and with a population of 40,000 a place of worship for every 300 inhabitants. So formidable a building programme would not have been possible without the heavy taxes imposed by William II, or without some forced labour. Another stimulus was the change at court which followed the death of Henry I's son in the *White Ship*. Frivolities were abandoned for religious devotion, and to this period belong the foundation of the priories of Holy Trinity by Aldgate, St Mary Overy just across London Bridge in Southwark, and the church and priory of St Bartholomew the Great.

In the more carefree days before his son was drowned, Henry had a jester and organizer of revels named Rahere. The jester turned solemn with his king. On a journey of penance to Rome he fell ill and made a vow that if his life were spared he would establish a hospital for the poor on his return. St Bartholomew appeared to him in a vision and named Smithfield as the site.

Near this place used for executions (and destined to be famous for the fair on the feast of St Bartholomew) Rahere began building in 1123. To the south of the church was the small priory where, now dedicated to monastic life, he lived as prior with thirteen Augustinian companions. By the time of his death twenty-one years later, Rahere had probably seen the completion of the choir with its massive Norman columns and groin-vaulted ambulatory.

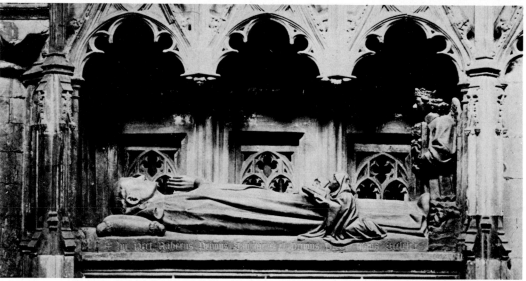

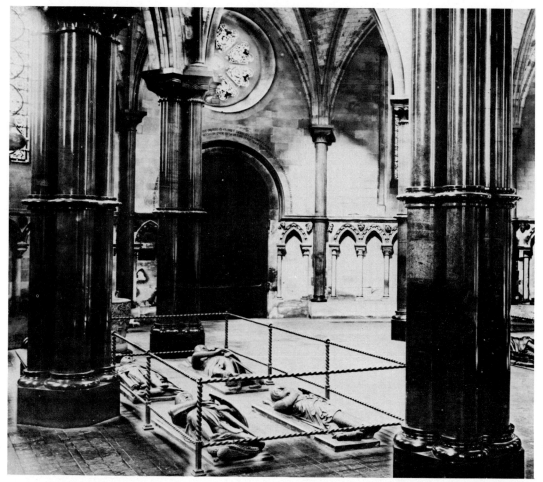

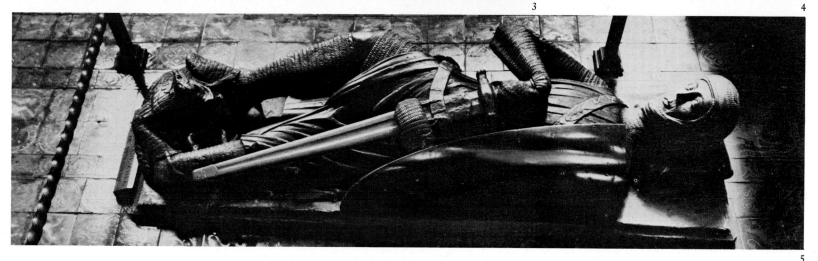

The Temple

Of the thirteen monasteries existing in London by the end of the twelfth century, two were dedicated to military action. They belonged to the Order of St John of Jerusalem founded in Clerkenwell about 1100 and the Knights Templars established in Holborn some thirty years later.

The Templars (named after the palace they occupied in Jerusalem on the site of Solomon's Temple) moved from the northern end of Chancery Lane to a site between the Strand and the Thames where they built what is thought to have been a large monastery about 1160. Their tilt-yard, testing ground for battle with the Saracen, lay just to the north of the Strand boundary.

When not on a Crusade, the Templars lived a life of extreme austerity. Perpetual chastity and self-denial were demanded, and there was a penitents' cell in the wall of the church. But these high standards were corrupted by great wealth and power in the thirteenth century, and in 1307 the monastery was suppressed on the orders of the Pope.

All that is left is the round church, shaped like the Holy Sepulchre. The oblong part of this late Norman and Early English church was added half a century later. In the floor lie the effigies of eight knights of the Order, among them the Earl of Pembroke, Henry III's boyhood guardian, and his son, Gilbert Mareschel, also Earl of Pembroke.

1. St Bartholomew the Great. View from the south transept looking into the choir where the founder's tomb can be seen on the north side.

2. Rahere's tomb. 'When he attained the flower of his youth, he began to haunt the households of noblemen and palaces of princes where, under every elbow of them, he spread their cushions, with apings and flaterings delectably anointing their eyes, to draw to him their friendships. And yet he was not content with this, but haunted the king's palace, and among the noisefull press of the tumultuous Court enforced himself with jollity and carnal suavity....' From a description written by one of Rahere's canons soon after his death.

3. The Round Church of the Templars dedicated in the presence of Henry II in 1185 with its circular nave surrounded by six columns of Purbeck marble. Gilbert Mareschel, fourth Earl of Pembroke, was killed in a tournament at Ware in 1241 and his body brought to the Temple for burial beside his father and brother.

4. A Knight Templar from a thirteenth-century manuscript.

5. The Earl of Pembroke – one of the eight effigies.

The First Mayor

A few weeks before King John was forced to seal Magna Carta at Runnymede, he granted a charter to the City confirming its right to choose a mayor by annual election. It stipulated that a 'discreet and fit person' should be elected and 'presented to us or our justices if we are not present and shall swear fealty to us'. The date was 9 May 1215, and this was the foundation of the municipal autonomy which the City has always guarded so jealously. It made the mayor supreme in the City, and within the City's limits second only to the king. Archbishops and even the king's brothers had to follow him.

The first Mayor of London had been elected some twenty-five years earlier. He was Henry Fitz Elwin, possibly a draper, of 'Londonstone' (implying residence near the Roman stone in Cannon Street). Elected in about 1189, he held the position until his death a quarter of a century later. Little is known of him, and his portrait is a romantic reconstruction, but it is on record that he was one of the collectors of the ransom for the kidnapped Richard I.

Apart from the mayoralty, the City won its rights as an independent 'commune' through John's attempt to usurp the power of his absent brother. While Richard was in the Holy Land in 1191 a meeting of barons and Londoners took place in St Paul's Cathedral at which it was decided to recognize John as regent on condition that he accepted the rights of the commune.

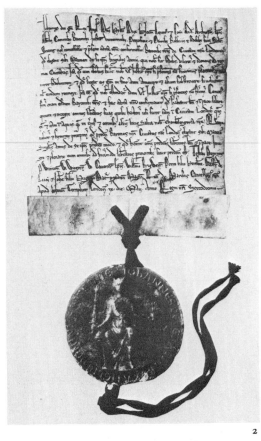

1. Henry Fitz Elwin.

2. King John's Charter.

3. The thirteenth century saw the formation of a royal menagerie at the Tower. 'The King to the Sherriffs of London, greeting,' came the edict of Henry III in 1256. 'We command you, that of the farm of our city ye cause, without delay, to be built at our Tower of London an house of forty feet long, and twenty feet deep, for our Elephant.' The appearance of this rare animal is preserved for us in this contemporary manuscript drawing.

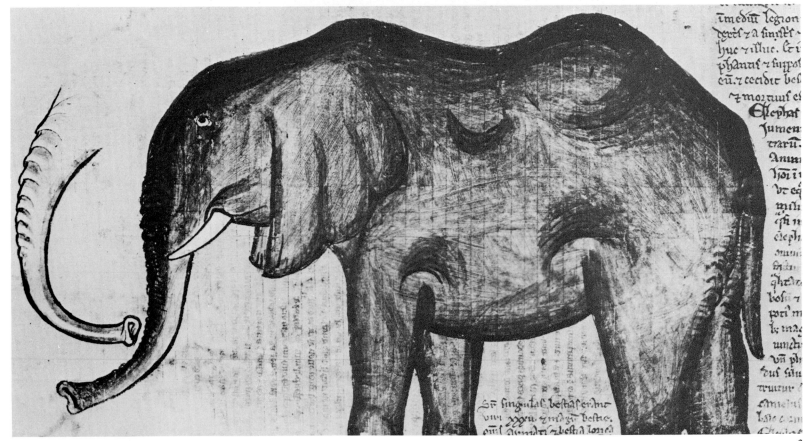

Westminster Assemblies

'What touches all should be approved by all.' This democratic pronouncement by Edward I led to two important assemblies at Westminster. The first was in 1275, the second twenty years later. Archbishops, bishops, abbots, seven earls and forty-one barons were summoned by name to discuss with the king how 'common dangers should be countered by measures agreed upon in common'. The basic idea of the English Constitution was born. Though this Parliament was in no sense yet a ruling body, Westminster Hall became the seat of administration.

Much of Edward's long reign was spent away from his capital in his struggle against the Welsh and the Scots. In his father Henry III's time, a captured Welsh prince, Gruffydd ab Llywelyn, had died while attempting to escape from the Tower. Thirty-nine years later Edward brought the head of Gruffydd's son back to London as a trophy. It was set on the turret from which Gruffydd had tried to escape, and, crowned with ivy, was an ironic fulfilment of the old Welsh prophecy that a Llywelyn should wear a crown in the market place of London. From Scotland Edward returned with a heavier prize, the Stone of Scone.

1. Edward I's Parliament.

2. Edward I's Queen, Eleanor of Castile, died in 1290 at Harby, Nottinghamshire, and the cross erected at Charing was the last of twelve such monuments that marked her funeral progress to Westminster Abbey. Destroyed during the Commonwealth in 1647. The present Charing Cross dates from 1863.

3. Until Edward I captured it in 1296 and brought it to London, the Stone of Scone was preserved in Scotland at Scone Abbey. It is of reddish-grey sandstone and has a long legendary history. Edward had the oak chair built round it in 1300 at a cost of 100 shillings, and it has been used at every Coronation since 1308.

4. On the night of 1 March 1244, the captured Welsh prince, Gruffydd ab Llywelyn attempted to escape from the Tower where he had been kept a prisoner for three years by Henry III. His great weight snapped the rope down which he was climbing and he broke his neck.

Expulsion of the London Jews

In the summer of 1290 a long-feared decree was issued to the Jewish population of England. All 16,000 of them were to leave the country. London's Jews left on 9 October – St Denis's Day – three weeks ahead of the general exodus. Their treasure and such property as they could remove went with them by ship from the Thames to Flanders and a less hostile continent. In the City the sheriffs read the royal proclamation that they should not be harmed or robbed, but their synagogues and cemeteries were forfeit. Their houses and shops in the district near Guildhall known as Old Jewry were left empty and boarded up, soon to be confiscated by Edward I.

Since their immigration from Rouen soon after the Norman Conquest, Jews had grown rich and had suffered severe persecution. Their protection had depended on royal favour and the amounts which the king could raise from them by loans or fines. Thus in Henry II's reign the Jews had enjoyed more or less complete immunity, for, in 1188, they had raised about a twelfth of the Crown's annual income.

Preferring to keep apart from the general community, the Jews made their first London settlement in Broad Street, but trade attracted them towards the great market of West Cheape. The homes of the richer merchants of Old Jewry were among the finest mansions in the City, and their ever-increasing prosperity caused envy among Christians who were forbidden by the Church to make money by usury. By the middle of the thirteenth century the Jews had acquired through mortgages a hold on so much land that their power was alleged to be a threat to the Crown. Popular prejudice fed on anti-Jewish propaganda and wild stories that at Passover Jews murdered Christian boys for ritual purposes.

Persecution had grown in impetus throughout the century. In John's reign they were harried, tortured and imprisoned, and London Jewry was sacked. In 1262 their quarter was again attacked and 700 were killed by Simon de Montfort who also destroyed records of money due to them for debts. Ten years later Edward I so restricted Jewish activity that many faced starvation. On suspicion of coin-clipping the whole Jewish population of England was imprisoned in 1286, and in London alone 293 were sentenced to be hanged and drawn. This was the twilight of their existence in England. Having squeezed them dry the Crown decided that England had no further use for them. Within a decade came their expulsion. It was to be 365 years before they returned.

1. English Jews, wearing horned cowls and distinctive markings on their dress. This manuscript drawing shows them being attacked. 'To prevent likewise the mixture of Jewish men and women with Christians of each sex, we charge, by authority of the General Council, that the Jews of both sexes wear a linen cloth, two inches broad and four fingers long of a different colour from their own clothes, on their upper garment, before their breast.' – The decree of Stephen Langton, Archbishop of Canterbury, issued by a synod at Oxford in 1222. One reason for the decree may have been that shortly before, a deacon who had fallen in love with a Jewess had been converted to Judaism. For this he had been sent to the stake.

2 *and* 3. In an attempt to turn Jews into Christians, two houses for the reception of the converted were founded, one in Southwark in 1213 and the other in New Street, now Chancery Lane. Henry III paid for this latter 'Domus Conversorum' which was adapted from the house of a rich Jew which had come into Crown possession. The Chancery Lane chapel is shown in the manuscript drawing (2), and part of an original arch (3), is still preserved in the wall of the Public Record Office, now on the site.

'Most Noble City'

In the crude yet evocative manuscript drawings of the thirteenth and fourteenth centuries we see for the first time 'the most noble city' of which the monk Fitz Stephen wrote. To his enthusiastic eye London 'pours out its fame more widely, sends to farther lands its wealth and trade, lifts its head higher than the rest. It is happy in the healthiness of its air, in the Christian religion, in the strength of its defences, the nature of its site, the honour of its citizens, the modesty of its matrons; pleasant in sports; fruitful of noble men.'

From the gabled, half-timbered buildings that cluster inside the crenellated walls, below, project inn signs including the common one of the ivy bush which was to give rise to the saying that good wine needs no bush. Fitz Stephen speaks of these taverns, and relates that among them was 'a public cook shop' selling 'viands, dishes roast, fried and boiled, fish great and small. . . .'

The St Paul's faintly and variably depicted in these drawings was probably the fourth building on the site. The first cathedral, built by King Ethelbert in the seventh century, was destroyed by fire in 961; the next cathedral, burial place of early kings, was burnt down in 1087; and the rapidly built Norman one 'had great hurt' in the 1137 fire. Well might Fitz Stephen say: 'The only pests of London are the immoderate drinking of fools and the frequency of fires.' The fourth St Paul's, the great cruciform cathedral with its 245-foot spire, was completed in 1221 and towards the end of the century the surrounding great wall, first built in 1109, was strengthened. An order made by Edward I gives the reason: 'By the lurking of thieves and other bad people in the night time within the precincts of the churchyard, divers adulteries, homicides, and fornications had been committed therein.'

1. This is the first known view of London, and comes from a road map prepared by Matthew Paris in about 1252. The sketch, marking the start of an itinerary from London to Rome, depicts, on the left, Westminster Abbey, on the right, the Tower, and centre, St Paul's. Six gates are shown in the wall, and the wavy lines indicate the Thames. Paris, a monk at St Alban's Abbey, knew London well as he frequently went to Westminster on behalf of Henry III.

2. Close study of the faint drawing of London from the fourteenth-century *Historia Regum Britanniae* reveals Westminster Abbey, left, the Tower, right foreground, and St Paul's, centre background, with spire next to right-hand banner.

3. Spire of St Paul's with weathercock from a 1307 MS. This vane predates one in gilded copper put up after the spire was struck by lightning in 1444. Robert Godwin was winding up the vane when 'the rope brake and he was destroyed on the pinnacles and the cock was bruised, but Burchwood the King's plumber set it up again' (Stow).

4. The walled city from which the dancers appear in a well-drilled chorus line with pipe and tabor is arbitrarily called Constantinople by the monk who illuminated the Luttrell Psalter in which it appears. That this formalized view is really London is suggested by, among other things, the weathercock on top of the central building, which is meant to be St Paul's.

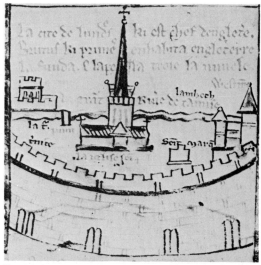

1

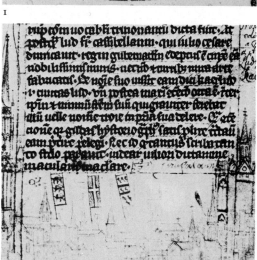

2

3

4

Robbery in the Abbey

Towards the end of April 1303, while Edward I was absent from London on his Scottish campaign against Wallace, a daring robbery took place at Westminster. The Royal Treasury, housed in the virtually impregnable Chapel of the Pyx, was broken into. Thick walls and double oak doors secured with seven locks did not prevent the crime in which 'chests and coffers [were] broken open and many goods carried away'. The King's Crown and three other crowns were left scattered on the floor. Apparently they were abandoned as too difficult to

dispose of. A travelling merchant, Richard de Podlicote, carried out the robbery with the assistance of ten monks. It was carefully planned to the extent of growing a thick clump of flax in the cloister garden in which the treasure could be hidden until it was conveyed in leather-covered panniers to a boat and carried across the Thames. A linen draper in St Giles was one of the receivers and hid his part of the haul, gold and silver vessels, in Kentish Town. Podlicote was caught with about £75,000 worth of the King's jewellery still on him. The monks, including the sub-prior and sacristan, were imprisoned, and Edward's vengeance on the

ringleader is said to have included nailing his skin to the chapel door.

Just over half a century later a moated Jewel Tower was built as part of the Palace of Westminster, about a hundred yards from the scene of the crime. Standing in the angle of the wall at the south-west corner of the royal garden, it encroached considerably on land owned by the Abbey of St Paul's, Westminster. The official responsible for this purloining was William Ussheborne, Keeper of the King's Privy Palace, who stocked the moat with freshwater fish for his own use. To the delight of the monks, divine retribution overtook him when he choked to death on a pike from his 'fishpond' and died without absolution.

The new Jewel Tower was not used for the official Coronation regalia, but was a repository for the sovereign's private treasure and jewellery. In Tudor times, when the Court moved to Whitehall, it became the Royal Wardrobe.

1. Theft from the King's chest – manuscript drawing.

2. The arrest of de Podlicote, and breaking into the Treasury.

3. In this reconstruction of the Abbey precincts, the Jewel Tower, moated on two sides, is on the south-west corner of the gardens of the old Palace of Westminster. Behind the Tower in the reconstruction is the round Chapter House. This obscures a view of the eastern part of the cloisters in which is the entrance to the Chapel of the Pyx.

4. The Jewel Tower today, seen from the opposite side.

5. The Chapel of the Pyx. The scene of de Podlicote's crime was the royal treasure house, protected by the inviolable sanctuary of St Peter from Norman times. It is a relic of Edward the Confessor's time and is perhaps the oldest surviving chamber in the Abbey.

6. The door of the chapel on which, according to tradition, de Podlicote's skin was nailed.

5

6

1. 'The Black Death', 'The Pestilence', 'Sweating Sickness' – were the terms used indiscriminately during the Middle Ages to cover a variety of epidemics. Leprosy was another scourge. Determined efforts were made to prevent the spreading of disease. The City voted as much as £100 for the cleaning of putrid ditches. Porters and watches on the city gates were (as shown left) under oath to exclude lepers.

2. There were leper hospitals at St Giles, Knightsbridge, and St James. Sufferers, like this woman, permitted to beg in the street, had to carry a warning bell.

3. To mitigate and prevent the spreading of epidemics, infected clothes were burnt.

2

3

The Black Death

'The pestilence, which originally started in the country occupied by the Saracens . . . started in England in the region of Dorchester about the time of the Feast of St Peter [29 June] A.D. 1348,' wrote Robert of Avesbury, a contemporary chronicler of the Black Death. 'It allowed scarcely anybody whom it wanted to die to live more than three or four days . . . and around about the Feast of All Saints [November 1] it reached London and every day it took away the life of many people; and it increased so much that from the Feast of Purification [2 February] until after Easter in a newly made cemetery next to Smithfield more than 200 bodies were buried almost every day. . . .'

During the seven months that the Black Death swept through London, fourteen London rectors died as well as the Abbot and twenty-six monks at Westminster. The parish churchyards could not cope with the burials. A cemetery was opened in the Minories, and another, of thirteen acres, to which the chronicler refers, was given by Sir Walter Manny to meet the emergency. It was to become the site of the Charterhouse. By the end of May 1349, when the worst of the bubonic epidemic was over, about half the population had died, a total, it may be reckoned, of at least 30,000 people.

Chaucer's Pilgrims

In an age of pilgrims and many scattered shrines, no tomb attracted more penitents and miracle-seekers than that of Thomas à Becket. His relics might be seen elsewhere – at Bury his boots were preserved, at Verona in Italy one of his teeth – but it was to Canterbury that pilgrims travelled in their thousands from all over England to see the altar steps where he had been martyred in 1170 and where traces of his blood were said to be still visible.

London was both a starting place and a stage on the road to Canterbury. In St Paul's Churchyard pilgrims could see where St Thomas's father and mother were buried, and on London Bridge was the tall, graceful chapel dedicated to the Archbishop, part of whose boyhood had been spent in the city. In Southwark there were, doubtless, monastic hostels for the poorer pilgrims, and for the more well-to-do a night on the way could be passed pleasantly at the Tabard Inn.

From the Tabard one April day in a year sometimes presumed to have been 1388, a group of twenty-nine pilgrims set out. Fact and poetry here become indivisible. Geoffrey Chaucer brings these men and women so fully to life that he seems part imaginative poet, part actual reporter. Can we not name the Shipman as John Piers? Is not the Canon the real-life William Shuchirch, and the fat, tongue-tied 'Geoffrey', Chaucer's self-deprecating portrait of himself? The Host of the Tabard we may fairly identify with Harry Bailly, Southwark publican and Member of Parliament.

The Canterbury Tales, mostly completed by 1393, was the culminating masterpiece of a man who only began to write poetry in the middle of a worldly career. All his life, from boyhood in Thames Street where his father was a vintner, Chaucer mixed with every class and sort of person. He served as a page to Edward III's son Clarence; probably encountered Dante and Boccaccio during a visit to Italy; and as Comptroller of Customs met all types of Londoners. For twelve years he lived in rooms in the gate-house over Aldgate. He was in the secret service abroad; came under the patronage of John of Gaunt; and in 1389 was created Richard II's Clerk of Works. He was responsible for maintaining the Palace of Westminster, the Tower, the Mews for the King's Falcons at Charing Cross, and royal manors at Kennington and Eltham. Yet another responsibility was the repairing of the banks of the Thames between Woolwich and Greenwich where, at one time, he had a house.

This varied career as a public servant does not appear to have been remunerative. Throughout his life there were interludes of near-penury from which he was relieved by small pensions. His output of poetry was considerable, but, before printing, the financial returns for a writer were limited. It was only in the last few months of his life that Chaucer seems to have been free of financial worry. An extra pension from the new king, Henry IV, enabled him to buy the lease of a house at Westminster, on the ground where Henry VII's Chapel now stands.

He died nine months later, in 1400, aged about sixty, and was buried in Westminster Abbey. This was not necessarily a mark of position or esteem; more probably his right as a tenant of the Abbey grounds. For 150 years only a plain slab marked his grave, but during the reign of Elizabeth I, when his fame was fully established, a far more elaborate tomb was raised to him in the east aisle of the south transept which we now know as the Poets' Corner.

1. 'To putte other men in remembraunce of his persone, I have herre his lyknesse.' – wrote Thomas Hoccleve, a fellow poet, as a note to the portrait of Chaucer which he commissioned a miniaturist to paint in the margin of one page of *The Regiment of Princes*.

2. About 1400 a copy of Chaucer's *Troilus and Criseyde* was produced showing as its frontispiece the poet reading his work to a noble company in a setting which reveals Italian influence.

3. The Tabard Inn from which the pilgrims started was at No 85 Borough High Street. The earliest mention of it is 1306. It has twice been pulled down – in 1629 and 1875 – and the present building is modern.

1

2

3

The Troubled Reign of Richard II

As he went through the City on the way to his Coronation, Richard II passed under a triumphal arch in Cheapside on which was set an unusual effigy. It was the grotesque figure of a man vomiting. He was recognizable as Sir Robert Belknap, and London was delighted. Sir Robert, Chief Justice of Common Pleas, had tried to deny the Mayor and Aldermen their traditional privilege of serving as royal cupbearers at the Coronation banquet. This was the City's satirical revenge.

The rough jest went deeper. In 1377 when Richard, a boy of ten, came to the throne, many of the City's ancient rights were being contested – a process referred to darkly as 'taking the City into the King's hand' Richard told a deputation headed by the Mayor that he would protect the City's interests as if they were his own.

This satisfied the deputation, but in the country revolution was brewing for a quite different reason. To raise money for the French wars, a tax of a shilling a head had been levied. This Poll Tax fell disproportionately on the poor. Serfs, labourers, small craftsmen and apprentices were goaded into action.

On the night of 12 June 1381, a great concourse of men camped on Blackheath. Behind them were two weeks of rioting and serious incidents at Rochester, Canterbury and Dartford. At Brentwood in Essex there had been trouble under the leadership of a far from meek and humble priest named Jack Straw. At Maidstone the ever-growing army had elected as their leader a veteran of the French wars, a powerful mass orator and firm disciplinarian. His name was Walter, and by trade he was a tyler, or tiler, of roofs.

Blackheath was the last resting place of the thousands of men – one chronicler puts the number at 60,000 – who with 'Wat Tyler' at their head were marching on the capital to settle their grievances. Before they moved off on the following morning, John Ball, a priest who had escaped from Canterbury prison, delivered a sermon on human equality, taking as his text a couplet:

> *When Adam delved and Eve span*
> *Who was then the gentleman?*

Fired by the message, the ragged army set out for Southwark.

1. The oldest contemporary representation of an English king, this portrait of Richard II is almost life-size. Painted on a panel which hangs in the nave of Westminster Abbey, it shows the young King in the robes in which he probably appeared at the Feast of St Edward the Confessor, whom he particularly venerated. ('By St Edward!' was his favourite oath.) The portrait is attributed to Adrian Beaunevene of Valenciennes, court artist to Charles V of France.

The Peasants' Revolt was not simply a rural affair. Inside London the rebels had strong allies, and not only among their fellow labourers. It was an alderman, Walter Sibil, who made the success of the invasion certain by letting down the drawbridge to them on London Bridge; and another, William Tonge, who, out of either fear or treachery, opened Aldgate to the Essex men led by Jack Straw.

While merchants barricaded themselves in their houses, Wat Tyler moved on to the Strand and ransacked the Palace of the Savoy, home of the King's uncle, John of Gaunt. In the Temple, lawyers' records were burnt. Newgate and Fleet prisons were opened. That night, Thursday, the rebels camped outside the walls of the Tower where Richard and his counsellors had taken refuge defended by 600 men-at-arms. The morning brought a message. The King would meet them at Mile End. 'My good people,' he is on record as saying, 'I am your King and your lord. What is it that you want?' To this Wat Tyler made his demands: all serfs to be freed; forced service to be stopped; the removal of trading restrictions; and a general amnesty. Richard replied that charters of freedom would at once be prepared.

But even while these pledges were being made, a group of independent rebels stormed the Tower and dragged out and beheaded the Archbishop of Canterbury and the Treasurer. When Richard returned from Mile End he found his stronghold plundered, and took refuge for the night in the Royal Wardrobe near Blackfriars.

The climax of the revolt was reached the next day, Saturday. Again Richard went to meet the rebels, this time at Smithfield. Backed by only a handful of soldiers and the prestige of kingship, a boy of fourteen faced the murderers of his counsellors. Exactly what happened was not clear even to many present, but it seems that William Walworth, the Mayor, who accompanied the king, called

5

out for 'Wat Tyler of Maidstone'. Mounted on a pony, the rebel approached Richard. 'Be of good cheer, brother,' is supposed to have been his insolent greeting, and one royalist chronicler has it that he drank a pot of ale while talking to his sovereign. There were angry words and a threatening gesture which, rightly or wrongly, the Mayor interpreted as directed against the King. He drew his dagger and struck Wat Tyler who was unsaddled and died shortly afterwards.

There seems little doubt that this would have been the signal for Richard's death had he not acted at once. Ignoring the shout of rage that went up, and heedless of the drawn bows, he acted as befitted the son of the Black Prince. Turning his horse, he faced the threatening mob with the cry, 'I will be your chief and captain!'

Meanwhile London was belatedly stirring

to deal with the situation. Sir Robert Knolles, a celebrated soldier of fortune, assembled a thousand men. Faced with organized pikes, their leader dead, and believing their cause was won, the rebels dispersed, marched through the City, over London Bridge, and back to their homes by way of the Old Kent Road. But the hopes they took with them soon died. Once the danger was over, the King's word was forgotten, his promises overruled by Parliament. Jack Straw was beheaded at Smithfield. John Ball was brought to trial and hanged, drawn and quartered in the presence of the King.

London quickly settled down. Walworth was knighted. Knolles was rewarded with the right to build a house near the Tower for an annual tribute, payable each Midsummer Day, of a red rose. John of Gaunt started to repair his ravaged palace.

After a few months little remained to show that the Peasants' Revolt had ever taken place. But, on Walworth's death he was succeeded as Mayor by John of Northampton, member of the lesser 'non-victualling' Drapers. His election was almost certainly the direct result of fears prompted by the Peasants' Revolt. For two years he fought to break the trade monopolies of the City, reduced the price of fish, and won the good opinion of the poor.

2. 'When Adam delved and Eve span, Who was then the gentleman?' – illustration of John Ball's text from a manuscript drawing.

3. In his sermon John Ball incited the peasants to attack the principal lords of England and the lawyers.

4. Simon of Sudbury, Archbishop of Canterbury, seized by Wat Tyler's men in the Tower. John Ball was among the rebels in this incident.

5. In the manuscript painting there is a simultaneous representation of the slaying and of Richard appealing to the rebels immediately afterwards.

The Deposition of Richard II

The reign which started so courageously at Smithfield ended in ignominy with Richard II's deposition in the Tower. Splendour at Court had only been made possible by fines and loans extorted from the City. In the summer of 1399, the exiled Henry Bolingbroke, Duke of Lancaster, landed with an army from France, and Richard was captured at Flint Castle and brought to London.

The story of the last months of his reign is told in the richly illuminated chronicle of Sir John Froissart. This wandering French historian was in England in Edward III's reign and again four years before Richard's death. The mysterious circumstances of the King's end at Pontefract – was it natural death, starvation, or murder by smothering? – eluded Froissart as they did all chroniclers. 'I could not learn the particulars of it,' he admitted, 'nor how it happened.' He was even under the impression that Richard had died in the Tower.

When he became Henry IV, Bolingbroke had Richard's body buried at Kings Langley. His son, Henry V, who as a boy had been treated with kindness by Richard, removed it to the present tomb in Westminster Abbey. This was, in a way, fitting, because, by arranging for the burial of two bishops in the Abbey, Richard had begun the practice which made the Abbey a national mausoleum.

1. 'The king, not knowing how to act in his distress, and fearing the Londoners would put him to death, yielded himself to [the Duke of Lancaster] . . .' – Froissart.

2. 'The Duke disbanded a great part of his army, saying . . . "We will carry him and his advisers to London and securely place them in the Tower". . . . It was resolved that the king should be deprived of all his state and outward marks of royalty. Froissart.

3. 'Intelligence was carried to the Duke of Lancaster that Richard of Bordeaux had a great desire to speak with him. The king received him with great kindness and humbled himself exceedingly . . . He addressed him – "Cousin of Lancaster when I look back I am convinced I have behaved very ill to you and other nobles of my blood. . . . All things therefore considered, I am willing freely to resign to you the crown of England, and I beg you will accept the resignation as a gift." ' – Froissart.

4. Coronation of Henry IV. 'The procession entered the church [Westminster Abbey] about nine o'clock, in the middle of which was erected a scaffold covered with crimson cloth and in the centre a royal throne of cloth of gold. When the duke [of Lancaster] entered the church he seated himself on the throne. . . . The archbishop of Canterbury . . . then asked the people if they were consenting to his being consecrated and crowned king. They unanimously shouted out "Ay!".' – Froissart.

5. 'Richard of Bordeaux, when dead, was placed on a litter covered with black, and a canopy of the same. Four black horses were harnessed to it, and two varlets in mourning conducted the litter, followed by four knights dressed also in mourning. Thus they left the Tower of London, where he had died, and paraded the streets at a foot's pace until they came to Cheapside, which is the greatest thoroughfare in the city, and there they halted for upwards of 2 hours. More than 20,000 persons, of both sexes, came to see the King who lay in the litter . . . his face uncovered.' – Froissart.

The Building of Westminster Hall

Richard II left London one great memorial. Six years before the end of his reign he set about rebuilding the royal Palace of Westminster. Its main feature was the Great Hall, probably the finest timber-roofed building in Europe. For this, oaks were ordered from the King's wood at Petley near Battle in the summer of 1393. Some may have come from Lord Courthorpe's Estate at Wadhurst, Sussex; and 200 trees were felled in Stoke Park near Kingston-on-Thames. Seven months later the Clerk of Works – the second after Chaucer – received instructions 'to repair the Great Hall within the Palace of Westminster, to take masons, carpenters and other workmen and set them to the said repairs; and also to take such stone as should be necessary for the work.'

The word 'repair' is misleading. Richard was planning something far more radical. It was little short of a complete transformation of the Hall which William II had built at the end of the eleventh century. William Rufus, working on the foundations of a pre-Conquest Palace, is said to have described the original Hall as 'a mere bedchamber' compared with what he intended to build. Now Richard was determined to improve on the Norman work with a Hall which would be a really worthy setting for great banquets and Parliamentary sittings.

Henry Yevele, the King's Mason, and one of the master craftsmen of the Middle Ages, worked on the plans for two years in collaboration with his friend Hugh Herland, the chief carpenter; and in 1394 building began. Richard had decided that the cost should be met by a tax on rich foreigners living in England. Yevele's main architectural contribution was the design for the North Front of the Hall which was set back between two flanking towers and which, with its window and Gothic doorway beneath, remains today largely unchanged. Only the fabric and certain details have given way to restoration over the centuries.

Herland's part was the hammer-beam roof, the Hall's great glory. The previous roof had relied for support on a double row of inconvenient wooden pillars. Herland wanted a roof which would span the whole sixty-seven feet of the Hall's width. His solution was huge carved arches strengthened by an intricate combination of subsidiary braces. These were made of timbers, two feet thick and up to twenty-three feet long. Much of the work was prefabricated away from the site, the timbers being shaped and fitted together in workshops near Farnham in Surrey, taken apart, and brought to Westminster for assembly. As a final triumphant touch of

1

2

3

ornamentation, an angel holding a shield was carved on each of the hammer beams. Although neither Yevele nor Richard lived to see the Hall completed, and in all its splendour, it was sufficiently far advanced at Christmas 1396, for a series of great banquets to be held and for jousts to take place down the 240 feet of its length. Richard presided over these celebrations in robes of gold, silver and precious stones. Less than a year later he was in the Tower, and his renunciation of the Crown, depicted in the scene opposite, was read in the Hall he had built.

1. The main entrance in the north front seen from New Palace Yard much as it appeared in Richard II's time except for the small buildings with casement windows, and the lamps.

2. The south end of the Hall showing the window which, during nineteenth-century reconstruction, was replaced by the present archway opening on to a corridor.

3. One of the twenty-six angels carved on the hammer beams. It carries a shield on which the royal arms of France are quartered with those of England. The carver was Robert Grassington.

St Stephen's

A private chapel was an important feature of a royal palace, and in 1292 Edward I decided to build something more impressive than the one which had existed at Westminster since Norman times. The style was influenced by the beautifully tall and slender Sainte Chapelle in Paris built half a century earlier. Height was gained by putting one building above another, and in St Stephen's this took the form of a main chapel above a vaulted undercroft with a clerestory above that. Thus the chapel, only 90 feet long and 28 feet wide, was 100 feet high. The chapel adjoined the south end of Westminster Hall and was set at right angles to it. The great East window faced out to the river, and to give an added vertical grandeur, the window mullions outside were brought down almost to the ground.

St Stephen's was not completed for seventy years, and Edward I was never to know that his inspiration had given London one of the first two Perpendicular buildings in England. The other was the Chapter House of St Paul's. An octagonal building set in a quadrangle of cloisters on the south side of the cathedral, this was the weekly meeting place of the Dean and canons for the administration of the cathedral. It was started in 1332. The same architectural trick was repeated of bringing the external mullions below the level of the inside window sills and filling in the blank lower spaces with a pattern of ornamental arches. Significantly, the same master builder worked on both. After spending six years on St Stephen's, William de Ramsey, Chief Surveyor of All the King's Works, appears to have shifted his main attention to the Chapter House. So that there should be no interruption to his work, the Mayor gave orders 'that Master William de Ramsaye Mason who is Master of the New Works at St Paul's and is giving his whole attention to the business of the said church shall not be placed on juries and inquests'.

Neither building survives to justify the claim that Perpendicular, long thought to have originated in Gloucester Cathedral, had its English genesis in London. But Wyngaerde's panorama (page 48) shows St Stephen's in the sixteenth century, and Hollar's engraving, above right, the Chapter House in 1647. Of the medieval St Stephen's, only the undercroft chapel survived the 1834 fire when the upper chamber was gutted. It could have been restored, but the chance was not taken.

1. The East end of St Stephen's Chapel – an early nineteenth-century reconstruction showing the Perpendicular treatment similar to St Paul's Chapter House. The chapel was given to the Commons in 1547 and was used as their chamber for nearly three centuries.

2. St Paul's Chapter House.

3. Undercroft chapel beneath St Stephen's, completed 1327, with lierne vaulting – short intersecting ribs.

4. Illuminated manuscript drawing of medieval builders at work.

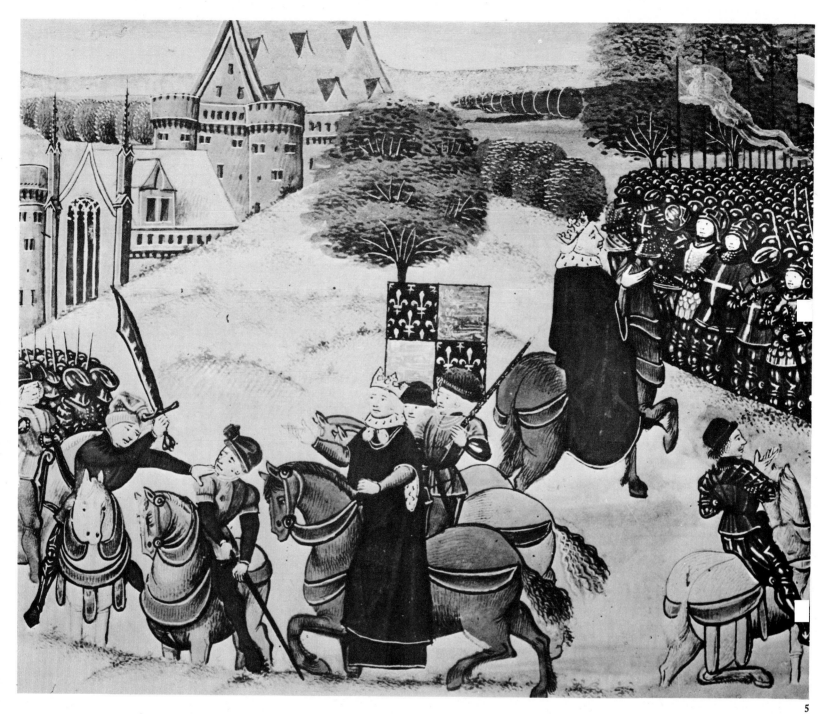

5

LONDON OF THE GUILDS

(1) St Katherine's .   (2) The Tower and moat   (3) All Hallows Bark

The Medieval City

'To this city, from every nation that is under heaven, merchants rejoice to bring their trade in ships,' wrote Fitz Stephen, and he might have added that the flow of goods was not all one way. In warehouses along the Thames were piled wool, cloth and corn, chief sources of England's wealth, ready for export in empty holds. By 1400 the city had become one of the greatest ports in western Europe. Its commercial prosperity lay largely in the hands of the trading guilds and of associations like the Merchant Adventurers and Merchants of the Staple formed to promote trade abroad.

As the merchants' ships came up the Thames, the stone bridge, built 200 years before, straddled the river barring immediate entry. To reach such wharves as Queenhithe they had to pass under the raised drawbridge. This was over the seventh arch from the Southwark side, and the bridge-master charged a toll of 6d. every time he wound up the stiff and rusty bascule.

At the beginning of the fifteenth century the Tower, alternative royal palace to Westminster, also guarded the entrance to London. From it, the wall, enclosing a square mile of congested houses, a hundred churches and nine monasteries, formed a defensive ring that stretched right round to the Fleet. Thirty feet high, London Wall followed the line of the Roman wall built twelve centuries

before, but which now had a crenellated medieval top.

Six gateways pierced the wall. Beyond them lay the fields of East Smithfield and the Moor, and the gardens of the outlying monasteries. Five hundred yards north-west of the Tower was Aldgate, in a room over which Chaucer lived and wrote for twelve years until 1386. Bishopsgate, the upkeep of which was the responsibility of the Bishop of London, was the same distance farther on. Then the wall ran an unbroken half-mile to Cripplegate and nearby Aldersgate. Newgate, rebuilt in the fifteenth century out of the fortune left by Whittington to the City, led out to Holborn and the north-west. Finally came Ludgate through which poured the carts and wagons to and from Westminster, a journey which took them along Fleet Street, described then as being 'in the suburb of London', and the Strand which was paved as far as the manor of the Savoy.

In this city of growing wealth even the houses of ordinary tradesmen were not small and primitive. From prints made before their early nineteenth-century demolition we can see the timber frames, gabled roofs, and overhanging eaves of those in the Minories and Butcher Row. According to a building account of 1308, a furrier's house consisted of a hall with a large bay window, upper rooms, and a stable with rooms and garrets above it. The hall would be a smaller version of the lofty, timber-roofed halls which were

a feature of the homes of rich merchants such as Sir John Crosby.

The panorama from the east, above, is a reconstruction made by H. W. Brewer in 1887. Even though it is very accurate, it can be faulted in detail. Land contours, for instance, make it unlikely that the moat which encircled the Tower could be connected with the City ditch.

2

(4) East Minster   (5) St Clare of the Minories   (6) Aldgate   (7) St Mary's   (8) Bishopsgate   I

1. Late medieval London – reconstruction by Brewer.

2. Most of London's medieval houses were swept away in the Great Fire. These in Butcher Row near St Clements in the Strand survived as tumbledown tenements until 1813 when they were demolished. The street derived its name from the 'foreign' butchers, that is, those who did not have the freedom of the City, and traded there.

3. Eltham Palace, then an hour's ride into Kent, now within the boundaries of modern London, was rebuilt in its present form on an older site by Edward IV thirteen years after Sir John Crosby's house in Bishopsgate. So similar are they, that the one in Bishopsgate might well have served as a model for the larger building at Eltham started in 1479. It was probably completed before the king's death three years later. The Hall deteriorated into a barn, but was restored in 1931.

4. Crosby Place (which may be seen immediately to the right of the tower of St Mary's in the panorama) was built in 1466 on the east side of Bishopsgate with a frontage of 240 feet to the street. Crosby was a rich merchant, soldier, warden of the Grocers and member of the Woolmen's Company. After his death it served as a palace for Richard III who, as Lord Protector, lived there through the six months of intrigue and bloodshed that ensured his succession. The great banqueting hall with its minstrels' gallery and richly carved ceiling fell into disuse after the Civil War. It became successively a chapel, warehouse, evening institute, and restaurant, until bought by the Bank of India. The hall was then carefully demolished, every stone and beam numbered, and rebuilt in Cheyne Walk, Chelsea, in 1910. As can be seen below, it shows no trace of its change of site.

3   4

rules of professional conduct. Broadly, they were divided into the trade guilds and craft guilds, and the usual admission was by apprenticeship. Only by years of practice, the craft guilds maintained, could workmanship reach the high standards which would make London's goods famous the world over. So a boy of twelve or fourteen would be apprenticed to a Master Craftsman for a term of seven years to learn the 'mistery' of his craft. At the end of his indenture he became a freeman of his Guild; free, that is, to serve any master or set up on his own.

The city was divided into twenty-five districts or wards whose elected representatives might, after the manner of other cities, be expected to have charge of administration; but so powerful were the Guilds that in 1376 they were given the right to elect all members of the Common Council, the city's parliament. This was modified to include both ward and Guild representatives, but the election of the Mayor, Sheriffs, and Chamberlain remained, as it still does, in the hands of Companies. To the Court of Aldermen sitting in Guildhall fell the tasks of keeping law and order, seeing to sanitation, street paving and water supply, looking after public morals, regulating prices, and countless other duties.

Great rivalry existed between the Companies, and by the end of the fourteenth century an order of precedence was settled for the twelve Great Livery Companies, confirmed by the Court of Aldermen in 1515. That order, still nominally maintained, is shown in their arms, bottom right. In terms of age, priority goes to the Merchant Taylors (1326) followed by the Goldsmiths and Skinners (1327). Altogether, there were about a hundred craft guilds.

When the new Guildhall came to be built the City Companies contributed to the cost, helped by bequests and subscriptions from individual wealthy citizens. Henry V granted a free passage for four boats and four carts to bring lime, ragstone, and building materials to the site. But funds dried up after two years, and the Common Council decided that to raise money taxes should be imposed on apprenticeships, deeds, wills, and letters patent. All fines were to be contributed to the new work. The revenue from London Bridge was also to be used. Even so, it was not until about 1422 that the great hall, second only to Westminster Hall in size, was ready for transacting municipal affairs, electing the Lord Mayor, Sheriffs, and the City's Members of Parliament, and the holding of banquets and important receptions.

1. Two apprentices who have served their term and saved enough money to start on their own, first submit a 'proof piece' of their handicraft to their Guildmaster. After a payment of fees, they may then hope to be admitted to 'the livery', the elect of the Guild.

The Guilds

In 1411 work started just north of the great commercial thoroughfare of Chepe on the building from which the City was to be governed. 'In this yere,' wrote the chronicler Robert Fabyan, 'was ye Guyld Halle of London began to be new edyfied, and an olde and lytell cottage made into a fayre and goodly house as it now apppereth.' Significantly it was called the Guildhall, not the Town or City Hall. By this time nearly a hundred Guilds or Companies existed, and so dominated the whole life of the City that inevitably the administration fell on them.

A Guildhall of sorts had probably existed on the site since the reign of Edward the Confessor, and from Saxon times merchants and craftsmen had organized themselves into 'gilds'. Originally social and religious fraternities, they developed into organizations for the promotion of trade and the protection of the members' interests. They did not lose their connection with the churches in their district or their patron saints, but they also built halls in the various centres of their work. These centres were well defined. In Cordwainer Street were the shoemakers; in West Chepe the saddlers and goldsmiths; further east the mercers; in Bread Street the bakers; and the tailors were in Birchin Lane and Threadneedle Street.

Self-governing, with their own traditions, ceremonies, and dress, the Guilds had strict

2. The only view of architectural value showing the south façade of the fifteenth-century Guildhall with its Gothic entrance. By masking out the roof, upper windows and the Renaissance top to the porch (all post-Fire accretions), we can visualize it as it was in 1425.

3. The only original and complete window of the Hall is in the south wall. It may have been one of those glazed with stained glass under a bequest by Whittington but destroyed during the Commonwealth as idolatrous.

4. Under the eastern half of the Hall is an imposing crypt, vaulted and supported on columns of Purbeck marble. This was probably the foundation of the fifteenth-century building, but may possibly have been the undercroft of an earlier chapel.

5. Company arms. *Top line* (from left to right): Mercers; Grocers; Drapers; Fishmongers; Goldsmiths; Skinners; *Lower line*: Merchant Taylors; Haberdashers; Salters; Ironmongers; Vintners; Clothworkers.

2

4

5

Election of the Mayor

From the day that King John had given the city the right to elect a Mayor each year, all kings had recognized the importance of the London merchants. They had to come to the City for loans to fight wars, and the merchants granted them, knowing that trade was affected by England's strength abroad. Henry V borrowed for his French campaign, and when he returned victorious from Agincourt he was given a great banquet at the Guildhall. Legend insists that at the end of the meal, Richard Whittington, the Mayor, took the royal bonds against which he and his associates had lent £60,000 and threw them into the fire. Even if the story is untrue, it indicates the value, in hard cash, that the City placed on a successful war.

The King also knew that the country's prosperity depended a great deal on the efficiency of the Companies and the quality of their goods. So the Companies were given privileges and monopolies. The Weavers were granted a charter by Henry I in about 1130, and they were the first of many to trade under royal licence. During Edward III's reign the Goldsmiths, Skinners, Drapers and others received exclusive trading rights.

By the end of the fifteenth century twenty-five Companies had received charters of incorporation, and these gave them more than prestige and trading advantages. They bestowed an inalienable right of existence which could not be threatened from reign to reign or by changing powers within the City.

Each year in October the Masters and Wardens of the Companies summoned their Liverymen to the Guildhall to elect the Mayor for the coming term. Custom, stretching over the centuries, has set the ceremony in an inflexible mould.

On the hustings at the east end of the great hall, strewn with sweet-smelling herbs, the City dignitaries gather while the Common Crier intones: 'Oyez, Oyez, Oyez. You good men of the Livery of Several Companies of this City, summoned to appear here this day, for the election of a fit and able person to be Lord Mayor of the City for the year ensuing, draw near and give your attendance'.

The names of the Aldermen who have served as Sheriffs are read out one by one, and voted for by a show of hands. To the Aldermen then falls the duty of selecting the Mayor from the two who have most votes. In the following month the Mayor – the term *Lord* Mayor came into use only after 1414 – is shown to the citizens. This is done in a procession through the streets which dates back to 1378 and probably before. At first the processions were simple, with the Mayor on horseback accompanied by the Aldermen and chief citizens. Then, in 1401, there is the first mention of minstrels. Fourteen years later, John Wells, Grocer, was one of the first Lord Mayors to introduce a touch of pageantry when he set up three fountains running with wine at Cheapside conduit. The wine was served to the public by three virgins representing Mercy, Grace and Pity. From 1422 the Lord Mayor's Show took the form of a cavalcade by water to Westminster, and it gained in splendour over the years.

After the Show there is a banquet in the Guildhall, a tradition dating back four centuries which replaced feasts previously held in the halls of the livery companies. At the banquet, as on every occasion inside the City, the Lord Mayor takes precedence over everyone but the Sovereign.

In June 1397 the Mayor in office died and Richard II accepted the interim choice of 'our well-beloved Richard Whityngetone, in whose fidelity and circumspection we do repose full confidence'. This was the first of one short and three full terms of office of London's most famous Lord Mayor. The known facts of his life are meagre, and while there is a lot of scoffing at the legend, it is possible, because of the gaps, to weave the story on their framework. If never a poor scullion, he was a third son and so hardly likely to have started life well-off. He was born in 1360 and his father appears to have been Sir William Whittington of Pauntley, Gloucestershire. He came to London and was apprenticed to a member of the Mercers Company. Legend is helped by the curious fact that when he was only twenty-one, and his apprenticeship just over, he was sufficiently wealthy to subscribe to a city loan. He married an Alice Fitz-aryn whose father, if not Whittington's master, was a rich man.

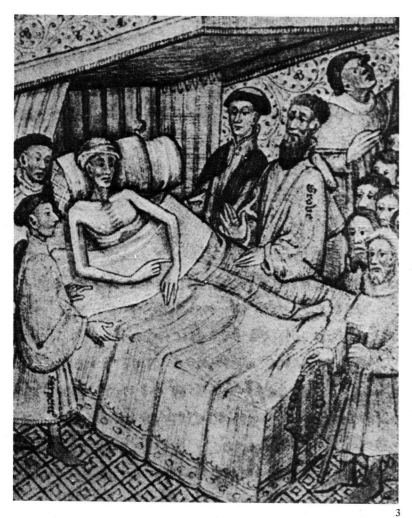

3

4

1. In response to an application in 1444 by the 'Men of the Mistery of Leathersellers in our City of London', Henry VI granted them a royal charter. It confirmed their ordinances, granted them, their heirs, and successors 'One Body and one Community perpetual and corporate', forbade fraudulent work, gave the Wardens the right of search for bad work in 'Cities, Vills, Boroughs, Places, Fairs, Cheapings, and Markets,' and permitted the granting of liveries. The illumination on the left of the Latin text shows the Leathersellers in blue robes kneeling to their royal patron chanting, '*Domine Salvum fac Regem*'.

2. A fifteenth-century Alderman in his robes of office. Simon Eyre was an Alderman in 1444 and Lord Mayor the following year. His career was an unusual one. He was originally apprenticed to an upholsterer and served his term under the impression he was a draper. In 1419, and at some expense, he transferred himself to another master, a full member of the Drapers Company.

3. On his deathbed in 1423 Whittington dictates his will to John Carpenter, Clerk of the City and his executor. Among his bequests was money to improve the Guildhall and to help found the Guildhall Library. He also left money to repair St Bartholomew's Hospital and to build almshouses, later removed from the City to Highgate, where they still exist.

4. 'Whittington's Palace' in Hart Street near the corner of Mark Lane. Leases definitely state this to be his house, according to the *Gentleman's Magazine*, 1796.

5. The 'Dick Whittington' legend appears to be based on a lost play of 1605, *The History of Richard Whittington, of his lowe byrth, his great fortune, as yt was plaied by the prynces servants*. Mention of his cat appears in a song published seven years later, and the cat is shown in a seventeenth-century engraving of him. The story that he heard Bow Bells ring out 'Turn again Whittington!' belongs to the eighteenth century. The stone on Highgate Hill, supposed to mark the spot, existed before 1795 when it was removed. The present stone, the third, was put up in 1869. There is no record that he was knighted or actually ever had a cat.

Whittington at Holloway hearing Bow-bells ring.

"Turn again, Whittington — Lord Mayor of Great London".

5

Attack on the City

The nearest that London came to being actively involved in the Wars of the Roses was the skirmishing attack made by Thomas Fauconberg in May 1471. 'The Bastard Fauconberg', Vice-Admiral of the Channel, and self-styled 'Captain of King Henry's people in Kent' brought a squadron up the Thames and demanded a passage for his army through London so that he could go to the assistance of Henry VI against 'the false usurper' Edward IV.

The Mayor refused. He would hold London for King Edward and for none other. It was anyway, he told Fauconberg, a lost cause; the Lancastrian army had been defeated at Tewkesbury. Fauconberg's reply was to bring his ships up the river from Sittingbourne and range them between the Tower and London Bridge. His insurgents, numbering several thousand, occupied Southwark. London rallied and its defenders hauled up the drawbridge on the bridge and raised a novel protection against 'the wild fire' of the Kentishmen in the form of large canvas sheets soaked in vinegar.

The attackers fired the Southwark end of the bridge, but as there was no way of spanning the drawbridge, Fauconberg ordered an outflanking attack from the north-east. Five thousand men, ferried across the river, broke into the city through Aldgate, as shown above, but the portcullis was lowered and they were trapped. A cannonade against the bridge by his ships made no impression, and, when he received news of the débâcle at Aldgate, Fauconberg decided to retreat. It was the end of the sortie against London.

Many of the Kentishmen were pursued and slain but their leader escaped for two months before he was captured and executed and his head sent to London. In a letter dated 28 September 1471, Sir John Paton noted: 'Item, Thomas Fauconbrydge hys hed was yesterdaye sett uppon London Brydge, lokyng into Kent warde.'

Caxton Prints at Westminster

For eight centuries the scribe remained the unchallenged recorder of the past and present, the only maker of books. Then, during the last peaceful years of Edward IV's reign, there arrived at Westminster a man bringing with him a revolutionary new craft from the Low Countries. In the autumn of 1476 William Caxton set up the first printing press in England at a house near the Chapter House of the Abbey. Caxton came originally from the Weald of Kent, but for the previous twenty-five years had lived abroad and had perfected his craft of printing in Bruges; now he returned to his native country with the machine which, magically as it must have seemed, was able to reproduce over and over again the pointed black letters which cost the scribe so much labour.

Caxton was already in his fifties when he started work in London near the Chapter House and later at 'The Sign of the Red Pale' by the Abbey Almonry. But his industry was prodigious. In the fifteen years before his death he produced ninety-six books or separate editions, many of which he himself translated and which involved 18,000 pages of hand-set type. The earliest, England's first printed book, was *The Dictes and Sayinges of the Philosophers*. The only surviving copy is dated 18 November 1477. This book was presented to Edward IV six weeks later, and a probable record of the event is a manuscript drawing, above right, at Lambeth Palace.

On one knee, Earl Rivers, the Queen's brother, is presenting the book of which he is the translator, and the whole group is of special interest. Behind the King is the Queen, and on his left the young Prince of Wales destined within six years to be murdered with his brother in the Tower. It is the only known portrait of the boy. His supposed murderer, the Duke of Gloucester, is the standing figure in cap and robes of state. The kneeling man in black is identified as Caxton. It has been objected that this appears to be a monk with a tonsure, but against this it can be argued that Caxton, nearing sixty, could have been bald, and that the gown, edged in fur, is hardly monastic.

From the time he came to live in the parish of St Margaret's, Westminster, he was a man of standing, and audited the parochial accounts for eight years. He was buried in the churchyard of St Margaret's, and right up to the time of his death in 1491 continued with his work. On his last day he was busy on a translation which his assistant, Wynkyn de Worde, subsequently printed. He left a legacy of books, set in eight different types, which ranged over history, chivalry, religion, etiquette, poetry, the lives of the saints, and Chaucer's *The Canterbury Tales*.

1. Presentation of *The Dictes* to Edward IV.

2. The handbill in which Caxton advertises a 'pye' or priest's guide to service ritual, obtainable 'good chepe' at Westminster.

3. The house in the Almonry, Westminster, where oral tradition has it that Caxton worked. It fell into disrepair, and disappeared in 1846. The site of the printer's workshop has always been a matter of controversy. In seven of his books he described himself as printing and translating in Westminster Abbey. This has led to a suggestion that he worked in the scriptorium of the Abbey, but there is no evidence for this. In other books he says only that they were printed at Westminster. In the advertisement, above, Caxton invited purchasers to come 'to Westmonester in to the almonesrye at the reed pale'. This is interpreted as being at a house bearing the sign of a red pale (in heraldry a vertical stripe on a shield) in the Almonry. This was an enclosure of almshouses, built by the mother of Henry VII, which stood to the west of the Abbey on a site where Victoria Street now joins Tothill Street.

The Princes in the Tower Mystery

The sudden and unexpected death of Edward IV in 1483 led to a brief but ruthless battle for power. It also produced the most famous mystery in London's history. The King's heir, Prince Edward, was a pale, studious boy of twelve, and the conflict centred round him and his brother, Prince Richard, three years younger. An immediate bid for control was made by their mother, Elizabeth Woodville, who assumed the role of Regent. Her formidable opponent was the late king's brother, Richard, Duke of Gloucester, whom the dying Edward had appointed Lord Protector.

Richard was in the north when news reached him of Edward's death. He hastened south with his ally, the Duke of Buckingham. During preparations for the Coronation, Prince Edward was installed in the state apartments of the Tower where he received visitors, and for a while there was nothing sinister about this arrangement. His uncle stayed vigilantly near at Crosby Place. At the other end of London, his mother, foiled in her plans and with three of her supporters under arrest, took sanctuary in the precincts of Westminster Abbey with her younger son. In a single month Richard had four powerful leaders of the Woodville faction executed on charges of treason; the Bishop of Bath and Wells came forward with a story that Edward IV's marriage to Elizabeth Woodville had been bigamous; Parliament accepted the Bishop's evidence, set aside the claim of the princes, and invited Richard to mount the throne; the younger prince was forcibly removed from Westminster and joined his brother in the Tower.

For a while the princes continued to be seen on the Tower greens practising archery, but then they simply disappeared. The one contemporary account (by Dominic Mancini, an important Italian visitor) records: 'He [Edward] and his brother were withdrawn into the inner apartments of the Tower proper, and day by day began to be seen more rarely behind the bars and windows until at length they ceased to appear altogether.'

What was their fate? That they were murdered at midnight by Richard's hired assassins who smothered them by forcing 'pillows hard unto their mouths' is the unproved assumption of Tudor historians. Two hundred years later the skeletons of two children were found walled up at the Tower, and this has been taken as conclusive evidence of the murder. These bones may well be those of the wretched children. Richard may have ordered their deaths. But it cannot be proved, there is a certain weight of probability against it, and other alternatives exist. One suspect is Buckingham, who for his own ends may have arranged the deed during Richard's absence from London on a Progress in the late summer. Just possibly, but not probably, the boys lived on elsewhere, closely confined, to die of natural causes or at the hand of Henry VII. To this day the mystery has resisted all probing.

1. Richard III.

2. Perkin Warbeck. So completely did the princes vanish that a pretender to the throne was able to appear within eight years. Perkin Warbeck, son of a poor Flanders burgess, maintained that he was Prince Richard, confident that no one could bring forward the real prince to refute his preposterous claim. Arrested and compelled to confess publicly at Westminster and Cheapside. Executed 1499.

3. The 'Princes' Room', legendary scene of the murder in the Bloody Tower, so called for this reason.

TUDOR LONDON

Henry VII's Chapel

The Tudors were great builders, and the first of the dynasty, Henry VII, bequeathed a sumptuous and beautiful addition to Westminster Abbey. Originally 'Henry VII's Chapel' was proposed as a memorial to Henry VI who had died in the Tower during the Wars of the Roses and had been buried at Windsor. His nephew, Henry Tudor, saw the shrine as a final triumphant gesture by the House of Lancaster. Permission for the 'holy body' to be brought to the new resting place was granted by the Pope who also promised to canonize the dead King.

These elaborate plans, however, were abandoned by 1503 when 'on the 24th day of January at a quarter of an hour before three of the clock' – it is Holinshed who is so precise – the Abbot, John Islip, laid the foundation stone. By then Henry had decided that the chapel should honour the Virgin Mary and that he should be buried there. For the salvation of his soul masses should be sung there 'as long as the world shall endure', and, so that these chantry ceremonies should be carried out, virtually a second establishment of monks was installed at the Abbey.

Robert Vertue was probably the chief designer, but as he died three years after its start, the work would have been carried on by his brother, William, the King's Master Mason, who had just vaulted St George's Chapel, Windsor. With its magnificent interior sculpture and the lacework delicacy of the fan-vaulted ceiling, it was one of the supreme achievements of the late Middle Ages. It was to be the resting-place of Henry and many English sovereigns.

Work on the chapel was still unfinished when Henry died in 1509, and during his last hours on his deathbed at Sheen he arranged for sufficient funds to be available for its completion. His funeral procession from Richmond approached Westminster by way of St Paul's where John Fisher, Bishop of Rochester, preached a sermon. In the Abbey a change was made in custom. He was not placed in a raised tomb but in a vault under the chapel floor. His Queen, Elizabeth of York, who had died in childbirth in 1503 was already there, so they would lie side by side.

Murmuring the plea for forgiveness, '*absolvimus*', the archbishops and other dignitaries of the church struck the coffin covered in black velvet with their croziers, and the body of King Henry VII was lowered to rest in the chapel he had created. The heralds removed their tabards to give formal voice to the announcement that the King was dead; then they resumed them to cry in unison, 'Vive le noble Roi Henry VIII!' To the young King, still in his teens, was left the duty of completing an architectural masterpiece.

1. This illuminated drawing of Henry VII giving the Abbot of Westminster the indenture for building the King's Chapel is from the indenture itself.

2. A tract to commemorate the funeral sermon on Henry VII preached at St Paul's by the Bishop of Rochester was printed with this woodcut by Caxton's apprentice, Wynkyn de Worde, at 'The Sign of the Sun', Fleet Street, 10 May 1509. The figure of the King has simply been inserted in an already existing block.

3. The Chapel – seen on the left of the Abbey.

4. Interior of the Henry VII Chapel.

5. A detail of the ceiling. A contemporary antiquary, John Leland, called the chapel one of the wonders of the world.

6. 'A comely personage a little above just stature, well and straight-limbed but slender . . . his countenance reverend and little like a churchman . . . neither was it winning or pleasing but as the face of one well disposed.' – a near-contemporary description of Henry VII whose effigy in black marble over his tomb was the work of Pietro Torregiano, a Florentine rival and fellow-student of Michelangelo.

London about 1550

In the middle of the sixteenth century an artist from the Low Countries drew the first panoramic view of London that exists. Anthony van den Wyngaerde enables us to see the whole stretch of the river from St Stephen's Chapel, Westminster, to Greenwich Palace. He brings Tudor London wonderfully to life; but little is known about him, and it is uncertain when he made his pen and ink sketches. We know that he was in London in 1558, but various buildings suggest that the view is as early as 1543. Buildings of conflicting dates appear side by side. Possibly Wyngaerde made preliminary drawings on an early visit (the panorama is clearly pasted together from a sketch book) and then returned at the end of Mary's reign or the start of Elizabeth's when he noted some changes but not others.

Behind the long roof of Westminster Hall is the Abbey, oddly orientated and surrounded by a confusion of towers. In the foreground of Palace Yard can be seen the medieval fountain and conduit head of the palace. To the right is the Clock Tower for which the clock – the earliest in England – was made in 1288. On a calm day the striking of the hours could be heard in the City.

Where Whitehall Palace should be is a blank. Wyngaerde made a separate sketch of this, right, perhaps intending to include it in the finished panorama. He shows magnificent river stairs which is interesting as they are not depicted in any other view of London, and are ill-defined in contemporary building accounts. The stairs may have been built in 1530 by Cardinal Wolsey when this was still York Place, or in 1548 after it had become a royal palace. If the artist's perspective is to be trusted, this 'great bridge' is not, as has previously been supposed, the Public Stairs or the New Privy Stairs. It is a third entrance lying between them.

Standing at the junction of the Strand and Whitehall is Charing Cross, the twelfth and last of the Eleanor Crosses, and on the river's edge can be seen the tall chapel of St Mary Runceval, the thirteenth-century Augustinian hospital for the poor which escaped suppression until 1554 when it became a private house. From about 1530 onwards the half-mile of riverfront from here to Arundel House became increasingly popular with the nobility. They took over most of the great episcopal palaces which had been the luxurious town residences of the bishops during the previous century and prior to the Reformation.

Identification of these new homes is extremely difficult, perhaps impossible. It seems that a fragment of Wyngaerde's sketchbook is missing, and with it Norwich House (acquired by the Duke of Suffolk in 1536), Durham House (home of Edward VI, the Princess Elizabeth, and Lady Jane Grey, 1536–1553), and Carlisle House (leased to Lord Russell, 1539). If so, the turreted gatehouse in the Strand is not, as attributed, that of Durham House, but is the entrance to Savoy Palace. The large building on the waterfront is the Savoy itself; next comes Somerset House (built by the Lord Protector on the site of the houses of the Bishops of Chester, Llandaff, and Worcester, 1549); and, a little back from the river, stands Arundel House (transformed from the home of the Bishop of Bath and Wells, 1549).

Beyond the Temple, where we can see the round Templars Church and the monastic buildings of the Whitefriars, is another blank space. Here should be Bridewell Palace, no Tudor view of which exists. With three courtyards fronting on the Thames and the Fleet this sumptuous palace was built by Henry VIII at great cost. He is said to have found it too noisy, and Edward VI granted it to the City thirty years later as a workhouse for the poor and a House of Correction 'for the

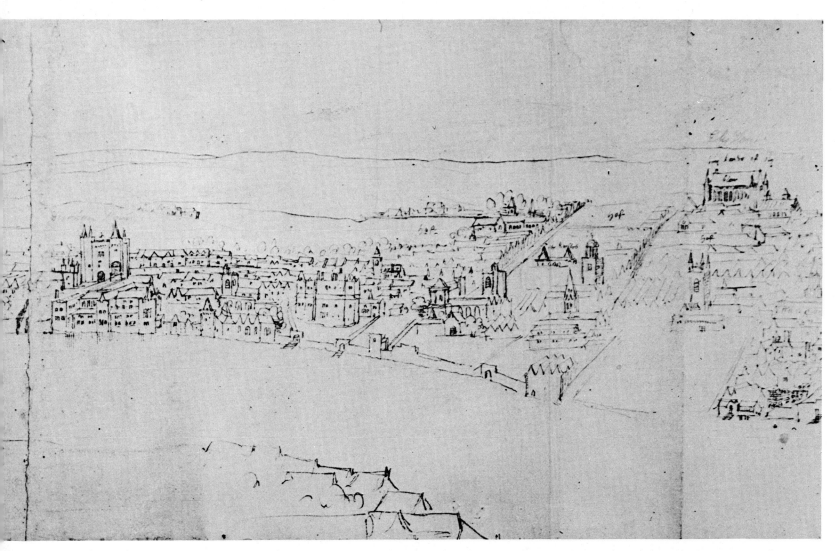

strumpet and idle person, for the rioter that consumeth all, and the vagabond who will abide in no place'. If Wyngaerde made a separate drawing of Bridewell, as he did for Whitehall, it has not survived.

Standing sixty feet above river level, Ely Place with its thirteenth-century chapel and great hall, had been one of London's most impressive buildings in the Middle Ages. Here the Black Prince stayed and John of Gaunt died. Its spacious gardens were famous for their roses, and when, during Elizabeth's reign, the Bishop of Ely was forced to leave part of the mansion to the Queen's favourite, Sir Christopher Hatton, he retained the right to walk there and to gather twenty bushels of roses annually.

On the two following pages we see the main part of the City from Baynard's Castle, fronting onto the river, in the west, to London Bridge in the east. In the foreground are the roofs of Southwark, and Borough High Street, lined with taverns like Chaucer's Tabard Inn. This was the end of the highway into London from the Channel ports.

Whitehall Stairs.

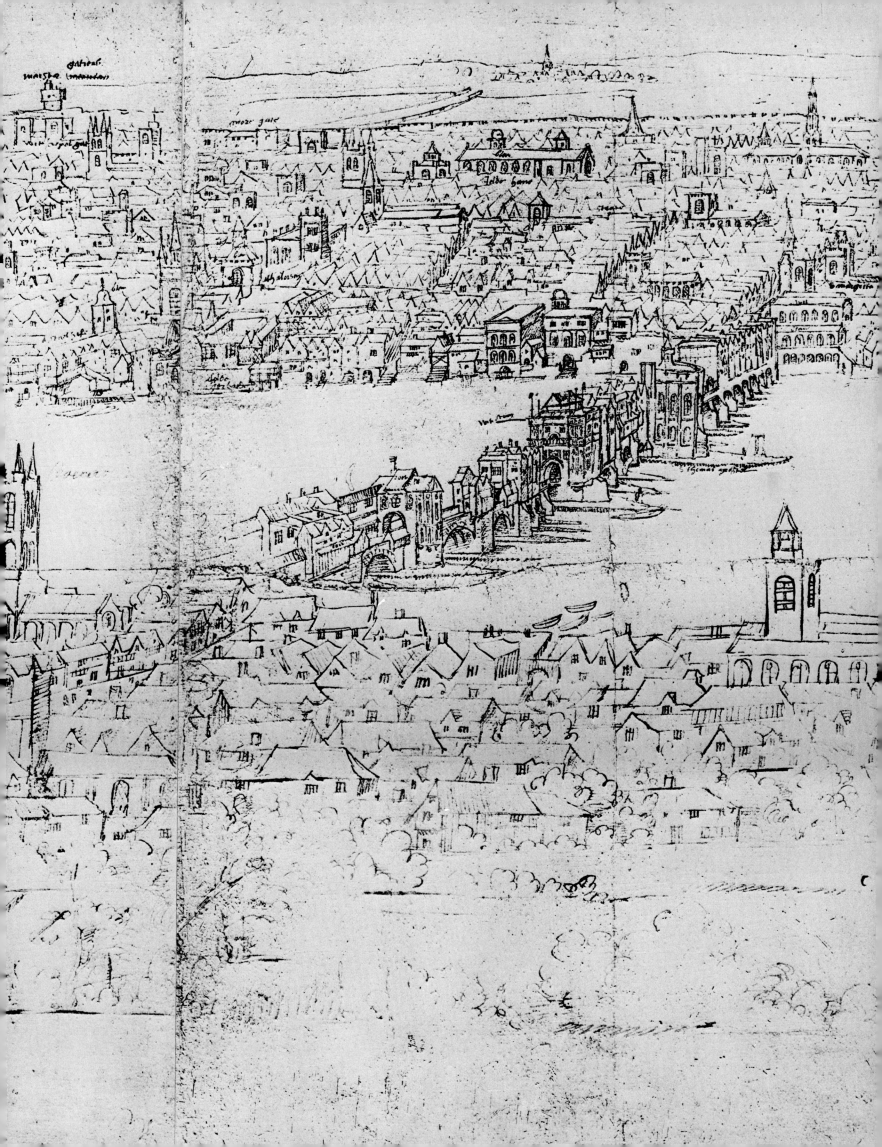

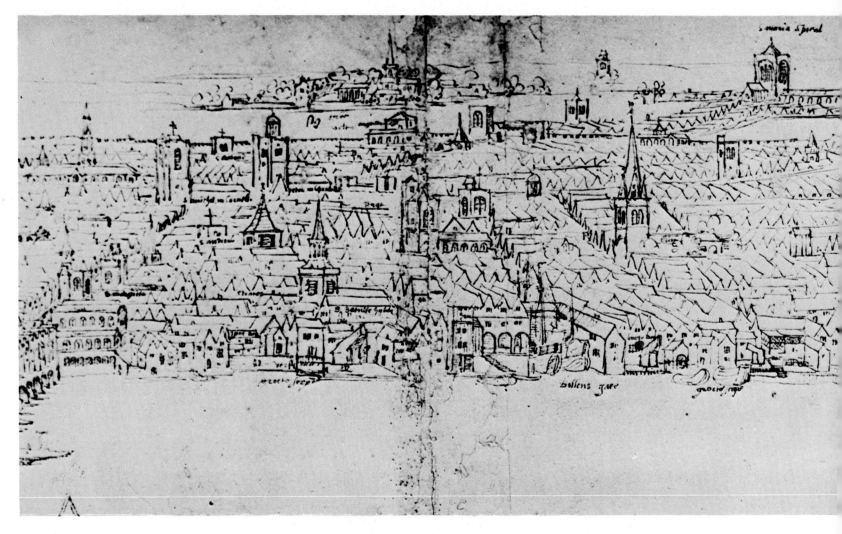

On the river's edge, and the extreme left of the section of Wyngaerde's panorama seen on the previous two pages, stands Baynard's Castle, the history of which goes back to Norman times. It was yet another royal palace. Henry VII made the castle his principal London residence in 1501 and 'repaired or rather new builded this house, not embattled or so strongly fortified castle-like, but far more beautiful and commodious'. With so many London homes Henry VIII used it only occasionally; but he found it a convenient place for his wives, all of whom lived here at some period.

Behind Baynard's Castle stands the glory of London, the great Gothic cathedral of St Paul's. Its soaring wooden spire was not long to survive after Wyngaerde's drawing. In 1561 it was struck by lightning or was burnt due to a careless workman – there are two theories – and though plans for a new spire were prepared it was never rebuilt. Just free of the east end of the cathedral can be seen the bell tower with its steeple. Here hung four bells which Henry VIII gambled away in a game of dice with his courtier, Sir Miles Partridge.

South, on the near side of the river, we come upon yet another magnificent palace. Closely surrounded with smaller houses, and with one façade overlooking Southwark High Street, Suffolk Place is a reminder that in Tudor London many great houses or inns resembled the fortress palaces of an Italian city. Hemmed in by streets and houses, they stood secure behind massive gates that led to sumptuous courtyards. Suffolk Place with its fine Renaissance towers had only a short history. Largely rebuilt about 1522 by Charles Brandon, Duke of Suffolk and boyhood friend of Henry VIII, it was to be pulled down before the end of the century. So fine a mansion on the threshold of London was ideal for receiving people of importance. It was used by the newly married Queen Mary and Philip on the night before their state entry in 1554. The Spanish King was Wyngaerde's patron, and it is not impossible that the artist was in the royal entourage.

London Bridge is the only link with the northern shore. Over it every traveller must pass. On our left is the tower of St Saviour's, which, with Winchester House just to its left, formed the Augustinian priory of St Mary Overy until the Dissolution. There are gabled houses on the bridge, and the narrow causeway between them goes under a stone gateway on the second pier from the shore. It carries the arms of the City, and is the formal entrance to London. But even more imposing is the great turreted gateway farther on. From its battlements rise poles carrying the heads of executed felons. Beyond, but not visible, are shops and stalls, and then we come to the tall chapel of St Thomas. It is built out on a pier which is the size of a small island, and on it someone is operating a wooden crane.

In the section of the panorama seen above we are looking at the busy commercial stretch of the river east of London Bridge as far as the Tower. This is the port of the City, and on its bustling waterfront are Botolph Wharf, the Custom House, and Billingsgate (marked *bullens gate*). With Queenhithe on the other side of the bridge, Billingsgate was the chief City wharf for fishing vessels, and as early as 1559 was declared 'an open space for the landing and bringing in of fish, corn, salt stores, victuals and fruit (grocery wares excepted)'. The sterns of two ships protrude from the wharf, and to save himself the trouble of drawing all the vessels anchored along here, the artist has just made a note – '*Grote scepe*', big ships.

A little farther east, but not clearly identifiable, is the Custom House. Built by John Churchman, grocer and Sheriff, in 1385, it is used for the weighing of all wool brought into London. Churchman was given a life-

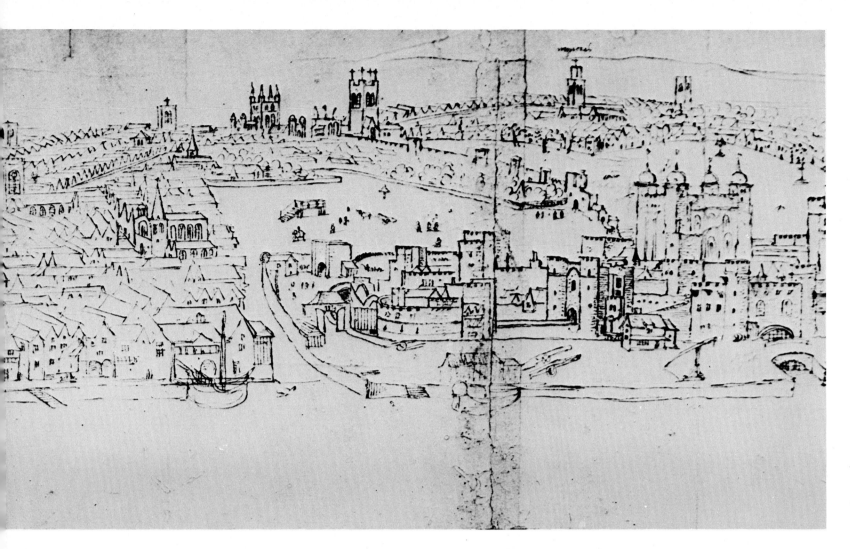

time grant by Richard II of a house and an adjoining warehouse in which wool was stored, weighed and after an excise had been levelled on it, was sold. The wool tax enabled Henry II to contribute to the building of London Bridge.

On the skyline is the square tower of the priory church of St Mary Spital, set in the open country but connected with the City by a narrow isthmus of houses that stretches north from Bishopsgate. Wyngaerde shows the church in seemingly good state although in 1540 its roof fell in—perhaps as a result of twenty-five tons of lead being pillaged for the repair of Westminster Hall.

Beyond the outline of a ship, the riverside houses peter out just short of the Tower, and what looks like a wide slipway leads up to Tower Hill. There stands a scaffold which Stow says ominously was 'always readily prepared'. The scaffold and the timber gallows are kept at the charge of the City 'for the execution of such traitors as are delivered out of the Tower, or otherwise, to the sheriffs of London by writ, there to be executed'. About the time of this drawing, its most notable victim was Lord Protector Somerset. Arraigned for treason while entrusted with the upbringing of his nephew, the boy king Edward VI, he was executed on Tower Hill early in 1552.

Conveniently close to the scaffold, and just to the west of it, is the church of All Hallows Barking, in the large cemetery of which were buried the headless bodies of many who were executed. Among them, in Henry VIII's reign, had been Bishop Fisher, though subsequently he was to be reinterred at Oxford. The church was founded by Richard I, and legend had it that his heart was buried under the high altar. The curious name is derived from the fact that the church originally belonged to the Abbess and Convent of Barking in Essex.

There is another chill reminder of death in front of the Tower itself. An inlet marks the water entrance, and behind it can be seen the grille of the Traitors' Gate through which Sir Thomas More and Bishop Fisher, Anne Boleyn and Lady Jane Grey made their last journeys. When, after the Wyatt rebellion, Anne Boleyn's daughter, the Princess Elizabeth, aged twenty-one, passed through the gate one wet Sunday morning in 1554 she was filled with foreboding. 'Bear me witness,' she said to the soldiers and her warders, 'that I come as no traitor.'

On the north side of the Tower four figures are approaching the Postern Gate in the City wall which leads out into the open space of East Smithfield, at one time the haunt of river pirates and their place of

execution. On the City side of the wall are garden plots and tenements which have encroached on Tower Hill. On the East Smithfield side, but hidden from sight, is a wide ditch, remnant of ancient fortifications. It was deep enough, Stow reports, for a man watering his horse to be drowned along with his mount. By the end of the century it was filled in except for a shallow channel.

The medieval wall with its intermediate bastions curves away to the north-west, following the line of the Roman foundations, until it reaches Aldgate. Lack of clarity and accurate perspective make it impossible to be certain, but it is fairly safe to assume that the actual gateway is the building shown between the two imposing church towers. These belong to St Botolph's in Aldgate High Street, outside the walls, and the Priory Church of Holy Trinity, which is inside. Wyngaerde shows the tower of Holy Trinity with its four corner turrets still standing, though at the Dissolution the surrounding priory—second only to Westminster—was pulled down by Sir Thomas Audley who sold off the materials at 6d a cartload. Aldgate had four towers on which, as on the gateway of London Bridge, the heads of traitors were placed. The artist appears to depict three heads on poles in a conventionalized way.

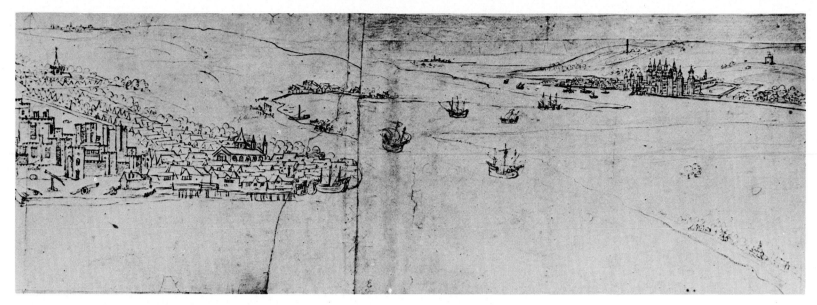

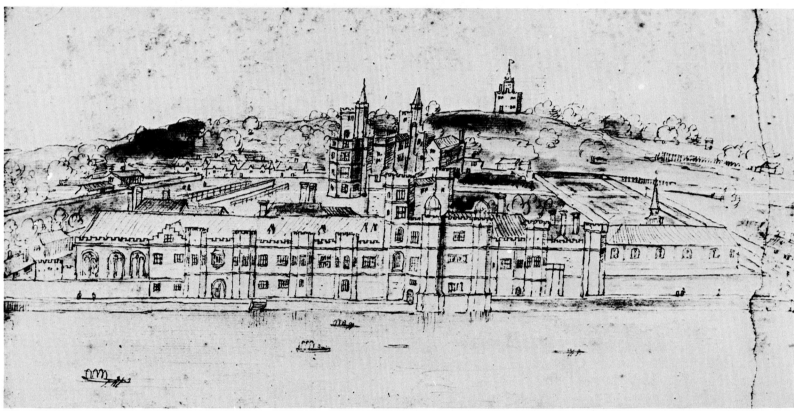

In the last section of the panorama, at the top of the page, the river curves away towards Greenwich. On the left is the south-eastern section of the Tower, that part of the otherwise sombre fortress which has a Privy Garden, Banqueting Hall, King's Gallery and Queen's Lodging. These and other domestic features of a royal palace were to be destroyed, probably in Cromwell's time.

On the left bank, as the river turns, are the hospital buildings of St Katharine's, one of the few religious houses to escape the Dissolution. The eastern fringes of London stop abruptly, for Wapping Marshes are inundated at high tide. The first village is Stepney with its medieval church of St Dunstan where, from 1538, all baptisms at sea were registered.

After this the Thames makes the large southern loop round the Isle of Dogs, so named, according to one story, because the royal kennels were just across the water from Greenwich Palace. We are faced with two conflicting views of the palace itself. In the panorama, the birthplace of Henry VIII, Mary and Elizabeth, lives up to the name Placentia, or Bella Court, as it was called by Humphrey, Duke of Gloucester, when he built it in 1443. As John Leland, the Tudor antiquary, wrote:

How bright the lofty seat appears!
Live Jove's great palace paved with stars.
What roofs, what windows charm the eye!
What turrets, rivals of the sky!

But most of those dreaming pinnacles seem to have disappeared by 1558 which is the date of Wyngaerde's detailed drawing of Greenwich, above, though Duke Humphrey's Tower still stands on the ridge of the hill.

With a battlemented front in brick, the creation of Henry VII, Placentia resembles Hampton Court, and is almost as large. On the left, three ecclesiastical windows suggest that here is the chapel. On the right, the long low building with a spire appearing above the roof may be the quarters of the Friars Observant, the Franciscans who baptized Henry at Greenwich but were the first to suffer the full blast of his anger. The palace has a tennis court; there is a hall for banquets and revels; and in the area behind the main river front on the left, Wyngaerde shows the tiltyard, scene of so many Tudor jousts.

Three additional pages from Wyngaerde's sketchbook, now pasted together in the Ashmolean Museum, Oxford, provide a more detailed view of the City waterfront. Unlike the main panorama, they are drawn from ground-level, and this has imposed a greater discipline on the artist. In the panorama he often cheerfully ignores perspective to show a church in the distance as large as one miles nearer. The Eleanor Cross at Charing towers above surrounding buildings. But here we get a real idea of a cluttered waterfront consisting of small gabled buildings and old warehouses. Looking across the river from the Southwark shore, the artist shows an area of trees, top left, which may be presumed to be Temple gardens, and extends his view, bottom right, to a point just west of London Bridge. At sometime during the half century before this drawing, a Venetian, who accompanied his ambassador to England, wrote in a letter: '. . . at present all the beauty of this island is confined to London, which, although sixty miles distant from the sea, possesses all the advantages to be desired in a maritime town; being situated on the river Thames, which is affected by the tide, for many miles . . . [and] . . . so much benefited by this ebb and flow of the river that vessels of 100 tons burden can come up to the city, and ships of any size to within five miles of it; yet the water in this river is fresh for twenty miles below London. Although London has no buildings in the Italian style but of timber and brick like the French, it appears to me that there are not fewer inhabitants than at Florence or Rome. It abounds with every article of luxury, as well as with the necessaries of life: but the most remarkable thing in London is the wonderful quantity of wrought silver. . . . In one single street, named the Strand, leading to St Paul's, there are 52 goldsmith's shops, so rich and full of silver vessels, great and small, that in all the shops in Milan, Rome, Venice and Florence put together, I do not think there would be found so many of the magnificence that are to be seen in London.'

York Place becomes Whitehall

North of the Palace of Westminster there existed from the thirteenth century a group of houses with a chapel and gardens called York Place. This was the official London residence of the Archbishops of York, and when Thomas Wolsey succeeded to the See in 1514 he set about making improvements. He renovated the chapel, and built a Great Hall near the river. But the Cardinal's star was already declining. Within a year of building the Great Hall the palace had been confiscated by Henry VIII. By Act of Parliament 1530: 'The entire space between Charing Cross and the Sanctuary of Westminster ... shall henceforth be the King's whole Palace of Westminster.'

The name of 'Whitehall', a hall for festivities, dates from this year. Henry made his own additions. He wanted to join the riverside buildings with those overlooking St James's Park, but was faced with the difficulty that the street from Charing Cross to Westminster was a public thoroughfare. The solution was a gatehouse under which the public could pass and across which he could go at the first floor level. This gatehouse (later to become known as the Holbein Gate because the artist lodged there) was demolished in the eighteenth century along with the less imposing King Street Gate farther south. Of Wolsey's York Place nothing remains except the vaulted wine-cellar, round the walls of which are the brick sills which were used to support the wine barrels.

1. Sixteenth-century Whitehall. The actual white hall – that is the Great Hall built by Wolsey in 1528 – can be identified in this detail from Agas's *Civitas Londinum*. It is the building with a pitched roof, seen end-on and showing three windows, under the 'C' of Court. The Hall was about 70 feet long and 40 feet wide with an exterior of stone and a battlemented parapet. It had, in fact, not small windows but a large mullioned window at each end.

2. Wolsey's wine cellar. This was under a building adjoining the Great Hall on the west side. The one remaining feature of the Tudor palace was threatened with demolition in a rebuilding scheme in the late 1940s. But it was preserved by an extraordinary engineering feat. The whole crypt weighing 800 tons was moved sideways on rollers a distance of 43 feet, lowered 18 feet vertically, and then rolled back into a position almost immediately below its original position. Moved one-sixteenth of an inch at a time, the operation was managed without a brick being disturbed.

3. The 'Holbein' Gate.

4. A similar gate built by Henry VIII which survives at St James's Palace.

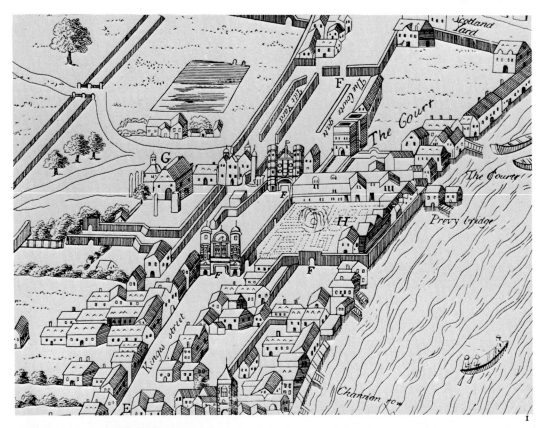

The Earliest Painting of London

About half a century before Wyngaerde, an unknown artist illuminating a volume of poems painted what may be regarded as the first real view of London. The Tower, London Bridge and the City as they appeared about 1500 are conventionalized in the medieval manner, but show various buildings in detail. The White Tower lives up to its name; behind is the grassy slope of Tower Hill Green; and beyond an imposing colonnaded building which is either Billingsgate or the Custom House. On London Bridge can be seen the Chapel of St Thomas à Becket. In the far distance are St Paul's and the City churches.

This miniature was painted in England in Flemish style for Henry VII or his son Prince Arthur, and is the decorative frontispiece to a volume of poems collected and composed by Charles, Duke of Orleans. The Duke, joint commander of the French forces at Agincourt, was taken prisoner on the field, brought to London and held to a ransom of 300,000 crowns for twenty-five years. He is shown in the White Tower writing home in 1440 just before his release: 'My brother and my comrade. If you wish to hear news of me from Albion, you must know that I have received good news on this side of the sea and that I shall return shortly.' The Duke is also seen looking from an upper window, greeting his ransomer, and leaving on horseback under the Byward Tower.

57

Court of Wards and Liveries

One of the most curious and indirectly corrupt of Tudor legal institutions was the Court of Wards and Liveries over which Lord Burghley, here presiding, was Master from 1561 to 1598. It was created by Henry VIII to deal with the estates of the large number of children who, by a feudal technicality, became royal wards. The court, sitting round the table in a small room in Westminster

Palace, is considering applications from people to take over these wardships. On the Master's right sits the Chief Justice of the King's Bench; on his left the Chief Justice of Common Pleas. He is faced by three clerks. On the extreme right, holding his brief and gesturing with his hand, is a lawyer pleading on behalf of a potential guardian. Sometimes adoptions are made for disinterested motives, but secretly everyone knows that taking on a child's welfare is often far from being an act of

high-minded charity; it is part of a mercenary traffic. The ward has to be bought from the sovereign, and if the child has a rich inheritance it is generally done by the guardian with the long-term hope of making a good thing out of it. The whole process is hedged around by lengthy formalities whereby lawyers and countless officials (and sometimes even Burghley) grow rich before they grant letters patent to a prospective guardian for a valuable wardship.

Elizabeth's Navy

Three years after she came to the throne, Elizabeth began to carry out the advice given by Sir Nicholas Bacon at her first Parliament. Building up her Navy 'against all evil haps', she made it 'the strongest wall and defence that can be against the Enemies of this Island'.

The enemy was not to threaten that wall until the Armada, but during the first two decades of her reign the Navy which the Queen fostered was to bring her renown. Adventurers like Drake, Hawkins, and Raleigh won her the title of 'The Queen of the Seas', and, back from the Spanish Main with their holds full of treasure, her ships saluted as they sailed past her palace at Greenwich. That title was gained not only at the point of a cutlass, but in shipyards round England and the dockyards which lined the Thames from the Medway to London Bridge.

In 1577 John Hawkins, the slave raider of the Guinea coast, was made Treasurer of the Navy, and for the next seventeen years he was in charge of the whole programme of building and equipping new ships and the refashioning of old. The land job was irksome, but he petitioned the Queen in vain for relief from the 'importable care and toil' of his office. Elizabeth had picked her man for his practical knowledge. In the Royal Dockyards at Deptford and Woolwich, and in private yards at Ratcliffe, Limehouse, and a dozen Thames-side villages keels were soon being laid down to a new, revolutionary pattern. Hawkins scrapped the main features of the old heavy men-of-war, and gave them more speed and a greater broadside of guns.

One of these new Thames ships, the *Repulse*, was taken by Drake into Cadiz harbour on his famous raid. Another, the *Victory*, built at Deptford under Hawkins's supervision, had Hawkins as her captain when she sailed against the Armada. When Raleigh decided to build a ship as a personal venture, he approached Richard Chapman, who had his own yard at Deptford near the Royal Dockyard. The ship which came off the stocks and into the Thames about a mile up river from the royal palace at Greenwich was the eight-hundred-ton *Ark Raleigh*.

She was subsequently bought by the Queen, a purchase approved by Lord Howard of Effingham, High Admiral of the Fleet. On board her, in the February of Armada Year, 1588, he wrote to Burghley: 'I pray you tell Her Majesty for me that her money was well given for the *Ark Raleigh*, for I think she is the odd ship in the world for all conditions, and truly I think there can be no great ship make me change out of her. . . .' Renamed the *Ark Royal*, she was Howard's flagship in the battle against the Spanish five months later.

4. John Hawkins – 'He had malice with dissimulation, rudeness in behaviour, and was covetous in the last degree.' This unflattering description by a contemporary ignores his service in the London shipyards and against the Armada, and the valour of the West Indies expedition on which both he and Drake died. Hawkins lived for thirty years in the parish of St Dunstan-in-the-East, Lower Thames Street, and on his death in 1595 left bequests to the poor there and at Deptford.

5. The *Ark Royal*, built at Deptford. She weighed 800 tons, her keel was 100 feet and she was 32 feet in the beam. She was manned by 268 sailors, and carried 32 gunners and 100 soldiers.

6. Shipwrights at work.

London Faces the Armada

On 15 June 1588, messengers rode out of Greenwich Palace carrying dispatches from the Privy Council to the Lords-Lieutenant of the counties. Spanish ships, forerunners of the Armada, had been reported off the Scilly Isles. After two years of preparation, the critical moment had arrived. The whole country must be alerted.

The Thames was ready for the defence of London. If the Spanish fleet sailed up the Estuary, it would be faced with a boom across the river at Tilbury, on which was mounted a battery of guns. It was also a pontoon bridge to move the Earl of Leicester's army, encamped at Tilbury, across to Gravesend if the Spanish landing was made in Kent. Nine batteries were mounted at bends of the river capable of raking almost every yard of the Thames with gunfire up to Blackwall, where a second boom was raised.

In London, all citizens capable of service had long since been registered and grouped into fighting units. Officers of the City's *corps d'élite*, the Honourable Artillery Company, were helping to train men all over England. A force of 10,000 London irregulars, backed by 14,000 men from the shires, were ready 'for the safeguard and defence of her Majesty's person'.

Lord Hunsdon, the Lord Chamberlain and the Queen's cousin, was in command of the London army, and by 27 July (the day the Armada reached Calais) his men were formed up behind barricades in villages from Brentwood to Stratford-atte-Bow along the natural defensive line of the River Lea. Elizabeth, it appears, was secretly intent on being with her forward troops when the invasion landed. But, dissuaded by Leicester, she moved with the Privy Council to St James's Palace and this was her headquarters through the tense, first week of August.

From here on Thursday, 8 August, she went to Tilbury to review the troops and made her famous speech. It was while at midday dinner at Tilbury that she received dispatches announcing the Armada's defeat. On her return journey, the Queen went to Greenwich by water, and by land through Deptford to Lambeth Stairs where the Royal Barge took her across to Westminster. Churchwardens at Lambeth disbursed three shillings 'for ringing when the Queene's Majestie came from the campe'.

To celebrate the victory, a silver medal was minted in Holland; a military review and tournament was held at St James's; banners and ensigns from captured Spanish ships were displayed in the City; and at St Paul's 'On Sunday, 24th day of November 1588, Our Sovereigne Lady Queene Elizabeth . . . gave God's publicke thanks for that triumphant and ever memorable victory over the Spanish Fleet proudly called the Invincible.'

1. The Armada victory medal.
2. The English army on the march.

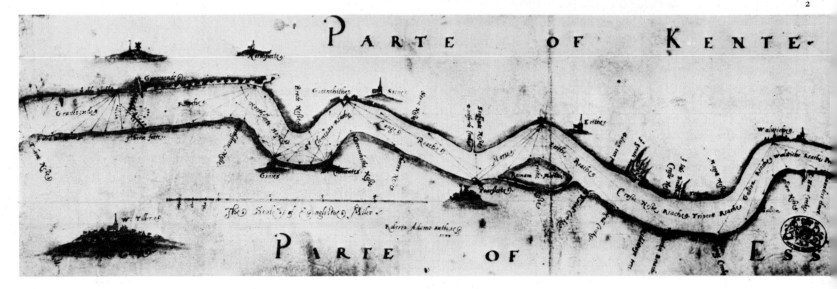

Voyages from the Thames

'Ever since I could conceive of anything [I have] been delighted with the discoveries of navigation,' wrote Robert Dudley, the Earl of Leicester's son. The explorer of Guiana spoke for all England. From the middle of the sixteenth century the urge for discovery set eyes on far horizons; and, backed by City merchants, many adventurers started on journeys down London's river. The brothers Stephen and William Borough weighed anchor at Ratcliffe at the start of the first passage ever made by an English vessel to Russia. From Blackwall, Frobisher's three ships set out on his second attempt to find a North-West Passage to China. Hundreds watched the great farewell from Greenwich of Sir John Willoughby who was to die in the frozen wastes of Lapland, while his companion, Richard Chancellor, got through the White Sea and reached Moscow.

But, of all the great voyages, none could compare with the one which ended at Deptford in 1581. Three years and four months after he had left England, Drake came up the river in glory. For the first time an Englishman had sailed round the world – a feat accomplished only once before in the world's history, by Magellan's expedition. Drake's was the first English ship to have been in the Pacific or the Indian Ocean. She had left Plymouth as the *Pelican*: on that April day in 1581 when she dropped anchor off Deptford she was the *Golden Hind*. Her rechristening, made in the Straits of Magellan, was Drake's impulsive tribute to a man who, in London thousands of miles away, had helped to make his voyage possible. Sir Christopher Hatton was one of a syndicate who had financed the expedition, and Drake adopted Hatton's emblem – '*a hind statant Or*'.

Not only had he charted the unknown: he had returned with Spanish plunder in his hold. Burghley, the diplomat, received Drake with caution; so did the City, fearful of reprisals on English goods in Spain. But the Queen, eager for her share of the gold, travelled down to Deptford, dined aboard the *Golden Hind*, and had Drake knighted in her presence. On her orders the ship was repaired and put in an enclosed dock at Deptford where she remained as a memorial to the great age of seafaring endeavour, until broken up eighty years later.

3. '*Thamesis Descriptio*' – sketch-map of the Thames at the time of the Armada drawn by Robert Adams, Architect and Surveyor of the Queen's buildings. The two booms and guns with their lines of fire are shown. Peter Pett and Chapman superintended the construction of the Tilbury boom which was made up of 120 masts, 40 anchors, and cables 9 inches thick.

4. Below London Bridge, and with the Tower in the background, high-prowed Elizabethan ships ride at anchor, while one, under sail, heads for the ocean on the ebb tide. The view, looking north-east, is from the Bermondsey shore, probably at the entrance of St Saviour's Dock. Across the water lies Wapping where pirates and sea-rovers were hanged at low-water mark, 'there to remain', writes Stow, 'till three tides had overflowed them'.

5 *and* 6. Sir Christopher Hatton, and his emblem – '*a hind statant Or*' – enlarged (6).

3

6

1

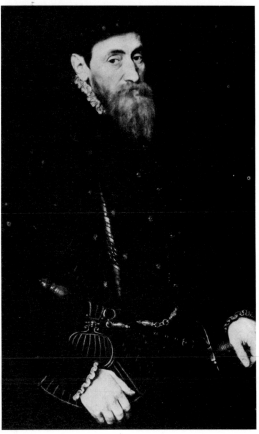

2

The Royal Exchange

Until the middle of the sixteenth century Antwerp was the commercial centre of the world. One reason for this seemed particularly clear to Thomas Gresham, mercer, member of a famous business family, and greatest financier of his day. In his role of Crown Agent in Antwerp, Gresham was frequently in Flanders, and he saw how the trade of all nations was attracted to Antwerp's Bourse. By contrast London traders in Lombard Street had to 'walk in the rain when it raineth, more like pedlars than merchants'.

In 1565 Gresham decided that London should have its own bourse where English and foreign merchants could trade. Ground was purchased in the centre of the City between Cornhill and Threadneedle Street by 750 leading citizens. Then, at his own expense, Gresham built the Exchange. Flemish materials and Flemish workmen were used, and, on the day the foundation-stone was laid, aldermen gave gold to the builders as an incentive. The Exchange was built in record time. The great open piazza, closely modelled on the bourses at Antwerp

and Venice, was completed in seventeen months. Towering over the colonnaded loggias was a tall column with a bell to summon merchants twice a day, and, surmounting it, Gresham's emblem, a grasshopper.

On the first floor above the colonnade were a hundred shops, but at first conservative merchants hung back, and for a while Gresham had to offer premises rent free to any who would keep them lighted and full of goods. But by the time the Queen visited it in 1570 and, says Stow, 'caused the same bourse by an herald and trumpet to be proclaimed the Royal Exchange', the place was a thriving centre for goldsmiths, apothecaries, and traders in materials, glassware, armour, and books. As Gresham had visualized, overseas trade was attracted to the sign of the grasshopper, and by the time of his death in 1579 London led the commerce of the world.

The building was to last until the Great Fire; its successor, designed on the same plan, until another fire in 1838; and in the third, and present, Royal Exchange are some of the paving stones first laid down by Gresham.

With the competition of the Royal Exchange, trading company after trading company came into existence for the expansion of overseas trade. Among them were the Muscovite Company, the Turkey Company, the Hudson Bay Company. Another, the Levant Company, fostered the East India Company, destined to be the greatest of all, virtually an empire in itself. Incorporated in 1600, the East India Company traded in Leadenhall Street where early in the seventeenth century East India House, below right, came into existence. It survived until 1726.

A rival to the Royal Exchange in the City appeared in the Strand within five years of Elizabeth's death. This was the New Exchange, below, built by the Earl of Salisbury on the site of buildings destroyed by fire at the back of Durham House. Its position was between the Strand and what is, today, the east end of John Adam Street. This collection of small traders selling a wide variety of goods on two floors was the modern department store in embryo.

1. The first Royal Exchange.

2. Sir Thomas Gresham. On his death he bequeathed most of his property to his widow, stipulating that when she died, his house in Bishopsgate Street and the rents from the Royal Exchange should be left in trust to the Mayor and Corporation and the Mercers Company. They were to be used to found Gresham College.

3. Billingsgate in 1598. 'A large water-gate, port or harborough for ships and boats commonly arriving there with fish, both fresh and salt, shell fishes, salt, oranges, onions and other fruits and roots, wheat, rye and grain of divers sorts for the service of the city. . . .' – Stow.

4. 'East Cheap. Now a flesh market of butchers there dwelling on both sides of the street: it had sometimes also cooks mixed amongst the butchers, and such other as sold victuals ready dressed of all sorts. For of old times, when friends did meet, and were disposed to be merry, they went not to dine and sup in taverns, but to the cooks, where they called for meat what they liked. . . .' – Stow.

5. East India House – an engraving of what is believed to be the first offices of the East India Company in Leadenhall Street. Earlier the Company is said to have transacted business in a Bishopsgate inn. Then, following its incorporation, the Company moved to Leadenhall Street, and in this seemingly fanciful building surmounted by a square-cut mariner and flanking dolphins began Britain's two and a half centuries' rule of India.

6. The New Exchange off the Strand.

3

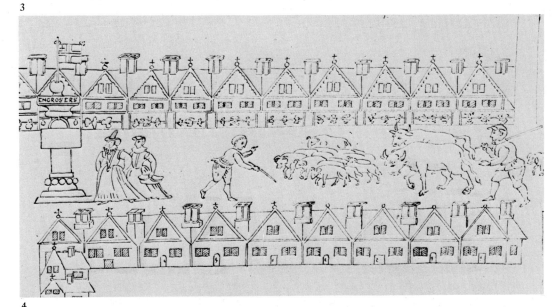

4

THE OLD EAST INDIA HOUSE IN LEADENHALL STREET 1648 TO 1726.
FROM A PAINTING IN THE POSSESSION OF Mr PULHAM OF THE INDIA HOUSE. 12 INCHES BY 8.

5

6

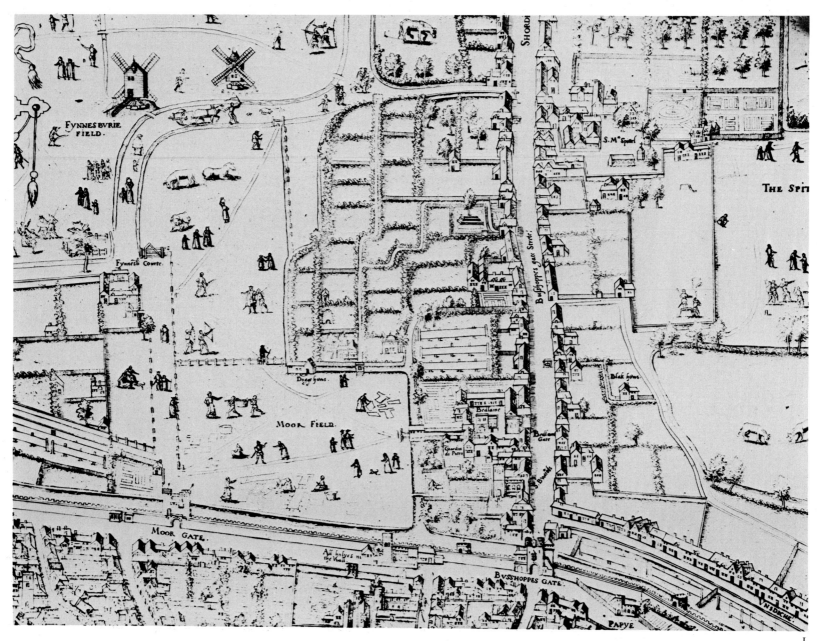

Moorfields in 1559

The view of the Elizabethan City (pages 70–71) is extended northwards by this map of the rural suburbs 'without the walls'. It shows us Moorfields and part of the Manor of Finsbury as they looked in 1559, as well as Bishopsgate Street, the main artery out of London to the north. The street is lined with houses, but almost at once there is a sense of being in the country. Behind the houses are hedged gardens, some ornamentally laid out with elaborate flower beds. Summer houses for banquets look out over pleasant meadows, artificial streams crossed by small bridges and two windmills.

It is an invaluable topographical record, but the human activity is equally fascinating. Laundresses lay out washing on the Moor; people promenade; milkmaids carry pitchers on their heads; and men practise archery (as they are bound to do if able-bodied and between the ages of seven and sixty). In the Artillery Ground, just west of *The Spit(el)*,

enclosed by a brick wall for safety, gunners from the Tower try out muskets forged in the Houndsditch gun factory. On the evidence of this map and an Elizabethan notebook which gives a list of 'marks' (possibly hoops in the ground like the one by the man holding an arrow in the north-west corner), it has been deduced that the archers are taking part in an Elizabethan form of golf with bows for clubs, arrows for balls, and the marks for holes.

This map is reproduced from one of two copper plates that have come to light only in the last ten years. With the other one (of the City), it becomes clear that they were part of a set, the rest of which are still lost, depicting the whole of London. The artist may have been Wyngaerde, and the engraver's style suggests Franciscus Hogenberg. One of the clues for dating it is the cross – not shown on any other map – in the churchyard of St Botolph's (*S. Buttofs*), just north-west of Bishopsgate. An Elizabethan undertaker, Henry Machyn, describes in his diary a bon-

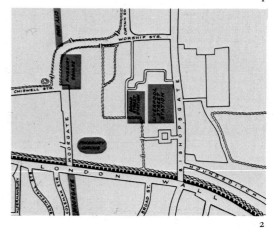

fire of Catholic books lit round the cross in August 1559, when the cross, built of wood, was itself destroyed.

In 1606 Moorfields was laid out with trees and walks, and became London's first park and place of recreation open to the whole public.

1. Part of the earliest known map of London.

2. The same area to-day showing modern features.

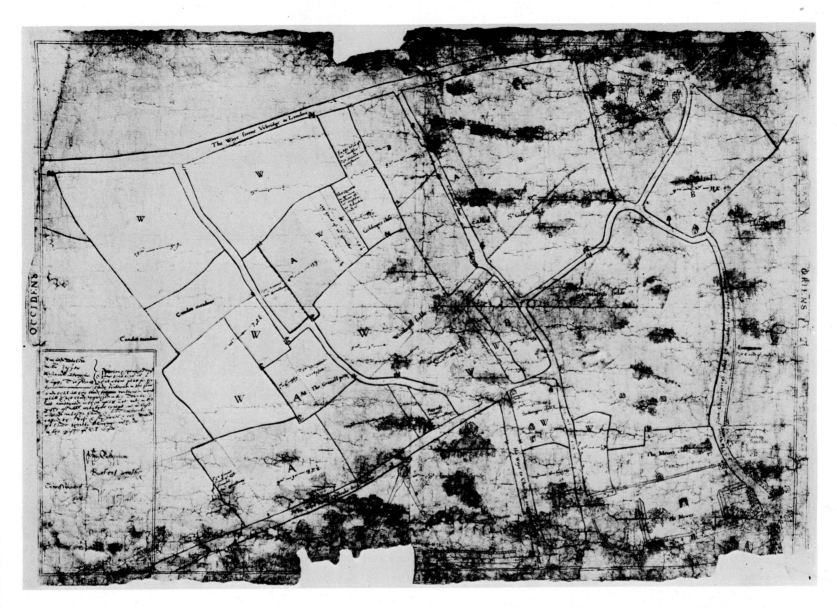

The West End in 1585

In 1585 London north-east of Charing Cross was still meadowland with only a few scattered farmhouses. The churches of St Martin and St Giles were quite literally 'in the fields'. Yet already in the rough, rutted lanes between hawthorn hedges the pattern of the modern West End had taken shape.

In that year a legal action was fought by a Bethnal Green brewer to establish pasturage rights for his horses in Geldings Close, south of the Uxbridge Road (Oxford Street). To help the courts, a survey of the whole surrounding area was made, covering about three quarters of a square mile. Most of this land had been acquired by Henry VIII some fifty years before; but once he had gained control of the water conduits (in *cunditt meadow*) for his new Palace of Whitehall, the king had been happy to lease the fields. By 1585, this gently rising hillside was being used for farming, brickmaking, quarrying of gravel, and the grazing of sheep, cattle and horses.

From the village of Charing, in the bottom right-hand corner, a road runs uphill to another small village, St Giles. This road is St Martin's Lane, the name and direction of which has remained unchanged for more than 360 years. When an Elizabethan, walking north, came to the junction of *Marshland* and *Long Acre*, he was faced with a sharp left-hand turn, just as we are today at West Street. Another few hundred yards brought him to St Giles with its church and houses in a tri-angle of roads which we now know as Shaftesbury Avenue, Charing Cross Road, and St Giles High Street.

A traveller wanting to go more directly north from Charing would prefer the next road. This led from modern Cockspur Street up Wardour Street to Oxford Street (*The Waye fromme Uxbridge to London*). Behind a brick wall, to the right of this road, is *The Mews*. At this time, it was the royal stables, but had originally been the place where the king's falcons were caged, or 'mewed'. A little farther north, also on the right, is a gap in the hedge, the entrance to the large expanse of *St Martin Fielde*. It is on a line with the south side of modern Leicester Square.

People heading north and west would take the next, parallel, road, *The Waye to Charing*

Cracked, badly stained, and preserved in the Public Records Office, this is one of the two earliest plans of London based on a careful survey. The other is of the City and Moorfields. Its modern limits are: on the north, Oxford Street; east, St Martin's Lane; south, Pall Mall; and west, Bond Street.

Cross from Colebrook (now Haymarket) which makes a right-angle turn to the left into *The Waye from Colebrook to London* (later to be called Piccadilly). At this junction (corner of Haymarket and Coventry Street) is a *Gun-powder House* in safe rural isolation, and in *Windmill Fielde* we see the mill which gives modern Windmill Street its name. Immedi-ately to its south, thirty years later, a house was built by one Robert Baker. Baker made his money from the manufacture of shirt frills, or 'pickadills', and, as a result, his house was nicknamed 'Piccadilly Hall'. From this, the street and the whole locality is believed to have derived its name. A little farther west, approximately where the map shows a gap in the hedgerow, is modern Piccadilly Circus. From here, the curving road follows very closely the line of Regent Street today, and the L-shaped kink in its route to Oxford Street is exactly where it would be affected by modern Glasshouse Street.

THAMESIS

Shakespeare's London

More than half a century after Wyngaerde, another artist from the Low Countries, Nicholas John Visscher, shows us the London where Shakespeare lived and worked. The view is dated 1616, but when he made his engraving in Amsterdam, Visscher probably relied on earlier maps and perspectives. He himself may never have been in London. It spans a quarter of a century of Shakespeare's life. This is much how the City looked when he arrived from Stratford-upon-Avon about 1586. Somewhere in the row of houses in the foreground, it may be assumed, he took lodgings around 1600. And this is the London from which he retired in 1610.

St Paul's, as ever, crowns the scene, principal church in the City which, despite the Dissolution, still has a hundred places of worship. The wooden steeple burnt down in 1561 has never been renewed. 'Divers models were devized and made,' writes Stow, 'but

little else was done; though through whose fault God knows'. The square tower remains, however, and visitors pay one penny to climb its stairs for a magnificent view. Below them in St Paul's Churchyard, and, crowded between the flying buttresses, bookstalls sell broadsheets, poems, translations and learned texts. More than half Shakespeare's plays were first sold here. Inside the cathedral services are now in English, publishers use the vaults for a store, and the main aisle is a distinctly secular thoroughfare. Coming up Ludgate Hill from Fleet Street people walk straight through instead of going round by Carter Lane. Like the galleria of some Italian city, it serves as a meeting place, a promenade, and a place for informal business.

Silhouetted against the sky we see the pagoda-like tower of the Royal Exchange, the soaring pinnacle of the Dutch Church, and the ornate lantern of St Mary-le-Bow. The windmill is probably on Saffron Hill. But the eye is drawn to the waterfront where the

informal jumble of varied buildings justifies the description of William D'Avenant – 'Here a palace, there a woodyard; here a garden, there a brewhouse; here dwelt a lord, there a dyer. . . .'

On the extreme left is part of Baynard's Castle, home of William Herbert, 3rd Earl of Pembroke, the playwrights' patron. Hidden from our view behind the castle lies the Blackfriars Gatehouse which Shakespeare bequeaths to his daughter.

Rising above the gabled rooftops of Queenhithe Dock, and carrying Queen Elizabeth's coat of arms, is one of London's earliest water-towers. Built in 1594, the tower has water pumped into it from the river, and its height provides enough pressure for the water to be carried by lead pipes to houses in West Cheap and Fleet Street.

The three wooden cranes which give Three Cranes Yard its name are clearly visible, and further east is the Steelyard (*The Stilliarde*) which has reached a critical moment in its

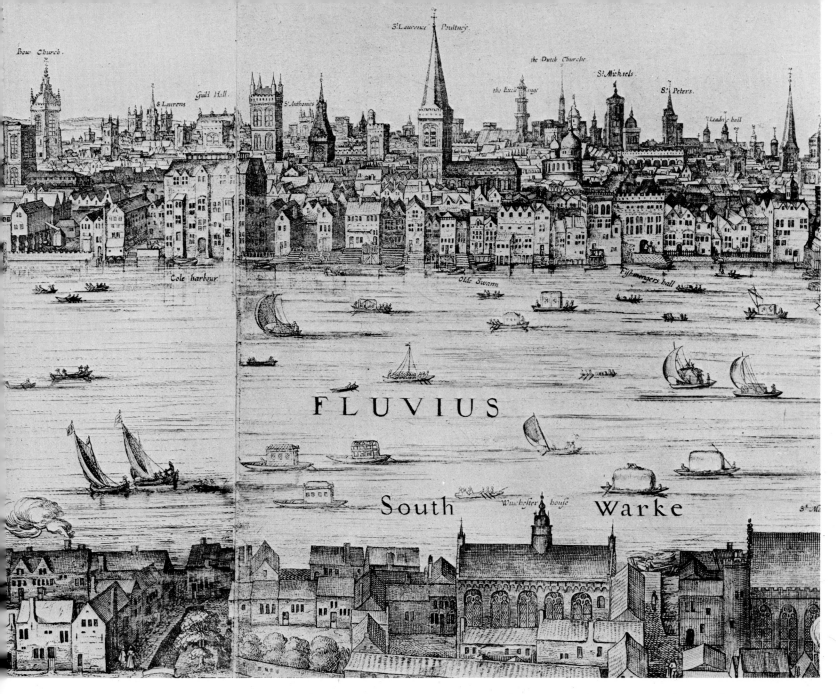

history. For nearly three hundred years it has been in the hands of the German merchants of the Hanse, importers of wheat and grain. Now it is being confiscated by the Crown, and is to be taken over by the Navy Office.

This is a period of rapid growth. A city of one hundred thousand people is overflowing. A buyers' market at the start of Elizabeth's reign (when so much confiscated Church property was available) has gone. At Cold-harbour (*Cole harbour*) we see the new trend. This tall, rambling fourteenth-century house is to be replaced by its owner, the 7th Earl of Shrewsbury, with small tenements let at high rents. In vain the City and the Crown try to restrict growth by imposing fines. Thousands from the country are coming to live here and are settling along the river. Intent on making their names, and enjoying life to the full, they are attracted by the magnet of Spenser's 'merry London' and 'Sweet Thames'. Shakespeare is only one. In a great company are Marlowe from Kent, and Drake

up from Devon with a house in Dowgate, a street running down to the river by the Steelyard.

Fishmongers Hall has steps leading down to the water in the Venetian manner, and in this one-mile stretch of the river we can count forty stairs, private and public. Round Swan Stairs *(Olde Swann)* are moored rowing-boats which take people across the Thames for a penny. Cries of 'Eastward Ho!' or 'Westward Ho!' indicate if a waterman is plying down stream or up. About 2,000 boats are in fierce competition, their disgruntled owners only permitted to charge fares fixed in Queen Mary's time. The watermen live mostly in Southwark. They form more than a third of the population of the Clink Liberty, a district which takes its name from one of its five prisons.

The seventy acres stretching from Paris Garden, just out of view, left foreground, to Winchester Palace, right, are now the playground of London. 'A continual ale

house' is how Dekker describes the buildings along Bankside. As well as taverns, there are theatres, the Bear Garden, and brothels. The back windows of the tenements look out over land cultivated by market gardeners, irrigated by canals, and with three pike ponds (two just visible to the left of the Bear Garden) for keeping fresh fish.

Most exciting of all, Visscher gives us a view of Shakespeare's Globe Theatre. With the opening of the Globe in the summer of 1599, and the Swan, Rose and Hope already existing (but not shown), Bankside has become the natural home for actors and playwrights. Shakespeare is among them by 1600, for he is paying taxes to the Bishop of Winchester in that year. Most of the Clink Liberty comes under the jurisdiction of the Bishops of Winchester, and we see the great hall of their medieval palace with its five tracery windows, built about 1400.

The Church does not seem over-fastidious about the source of its income. It draws

revenue indirectly from alehouse keepers, ladies nicknamed 'Winchester Geese', and from actors who, by legal definition, are rogues and vagabonds. Despite their reputation, the theatre people take part in the parish life of St Saviour's (the present-day Southwark Cathedral). Philip Henslowe, owner of the Rose Theatre, was vestryman and warden. Edward Alleyn, the actor, is another vestryman. And here Massinger, under contract to Henslowe, is to have a tomb.

In 1607 the bell in the tower of St Saviour's brings mourners to the funeral of Edmund, Shakespeare's younger brother, whose lodgings were in Maid Lane. All we know of this brother comes from the record in the parochial account: 'December 31. Edmund Shakespeare, a player, buried in the church with a forenoon knell of the great bell.'

1. Visscher's view of the bridge, dated 1616.

2. The bridge was built on nineteen piers, or starlings, made by driving wooden piles into the river-bed, each in the shape of a boat. Below water-level, these were rammed full of loose rubble with strength added by cross sleepers. The starlings reduced the Thames to one-sixth of its normal flow, and a fall of water of as much as five foot was created.

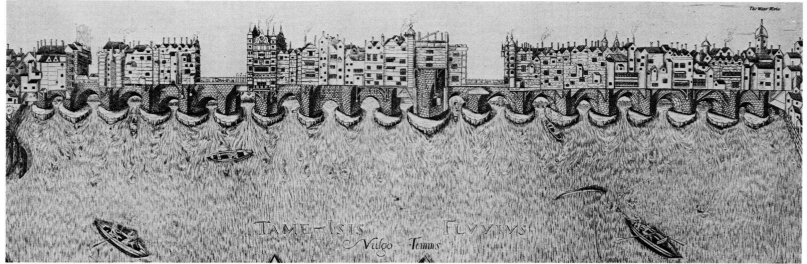

Old London Bridge

London Bridge is now at its period of greatest glory and most elaborate ornamentation. Four hundred years after its building, it is justly regarded as one of the wonders of the world. Nowhere else does a bridge of similar scale span so wide a river. 'A beautiful long bridge with quite splendid handsome and well-built houses which are occupied by merchants of consequence', wrote a German visitor in 1592 who also noted the grisly spectacle of the thirty or more traitors' heads that rotted on the Great Gateway. John Norden, the Royal Surveyor who engraved his meticulously accurate view of the bridge at the end of Elizabeth's reign, said it was 'comparable in itself to a little City'.

Of all the sumptuous buildings, the most remarkable was Nonsuch House which Stow called 'a beautiful and chargeable piece of work'. Four storeys high, of ornate Renaissance design with flagged cupolas at each corner and a typically Dutch gable, its imposing south façade is shown by Visscher in the second open space just beyond the drawbridge. Nonsuch – literally No-other-such-house – was prefabricated in Holland, shipped in sections to London, and erected on the bridge in 1577 allegedly without nails and with only the use of wooden pegs. Curiously little is known about the owners of this great building or to what use it was put, but it may have been the residence of the Lord Mayor.

From shore to shore, London Bridge was nearly three hundred and fifty yards long, and much of the central roadway was made dark by the tall houses that flanked both sides of it with overhanging and, in places, completely spanning roofs. The thoroughfare between the shops was only twelve feet wide, and was cluttered with stalls selling everything from hats and gloves to food and drink. Once on the bridge, a person felt as if he were walking along one continuous bustling street.

He only occasionally had a glimpse of the river or was conscious of the water racing through the arches below. Wheeled traffic forced him into doorways, and Norden talks of 'certain void places reserved from buildings for the retire of passengers from the dangers of cars, carts and droves of cattle'.

Congestion was inevitable, for, when its building was started in 1176, the bridge was only called on to fulfil the needs of a far smaller, medieval London. Built in Kentish Ragstone to replace a succession of timber bridges destroyed by fire and flood, the bridge was the brainchild of a parish priest, Peter de Colechurch (of Mary Colechurch, Cheapside). He gave it a religious significance by building a beautiful little chapel to Thomas à Becket (on the ninth pier from the north), and was himself buried in its crypt. But by late Tudor times, as we see in Norden's view, the beautiful Perpendicular Gothic exterior (shown by Wyngaerde, page 51) had been transformed. Another victim of the Reformation, it had been turned into a dwelling-house.

The bridge was thirty years in the building, and by the time it was finished plans were already made for houses, the rents of which would pay for its maintenance. By the middle of the fourteenth century there were one hundred and ninety-eight of them, but the bridge also had another source of revenue. All trade from the Continent was channelled over this, the only bridge across the Thames, and brought prosperity to the City. With a nice blend of piety and commercial gratitude, a number of merchants made bequests in their wills to 'God and the Bridge'. Not only London Bridge, but all subsequent City bridges have been maintained from these early endowments.

At the northern end of the bridge the power of the water was harnessed in 1580 by a waterwheel which pumped up river water for use in the City. This scheme was devised by a Dutchman, Pieter Morice, a servant of Sir Christopher Hatton. Though violently opposed by the City water-carriers, Morice obtained permission for his waterworks (*The Water Worke* in Norton's view, above) after demonstrating to the Lord Mayor and his officers that he could direct a jet of water over the tower of the Church of St Magnus. He was given a lease of the first arch for an annual payment of ten shillings and conveyed water, says Stow, 'into divers men's houses' at every tide. The Morice family ran the enterprise for 120 years, and the waterworks survived until 1822 when it was removed. As the City had given a 500-year agreement, the heirs in this venture still receive £3,750 a year in compensation from the Metropolitan Water Board.

3. Norden's view which is from the opposite direction to Visscher's – east looking west.

4. Nonsuch House. This detail from Hollar's view shows the rich decoration of the building. All the ornamental woodwork was brilliantly painted, and the house was crowned with carved gables and onion-shaped cupolas.

4

Birth of the Theatres

In April 1576, a plot of land was leased in Shoreditch, half a mile north of Bishopsgate, by a carpenter turned actor named James Burbage. Here, with the financial help of his brother-in-law, a grocer, Burbage built London's first playhouse. No picture of the Theatre, as it was called, has survived, but it was built of timber and was probably circular or polygonal. In its three tiers of galleries and unroofed central yard, up to a thousand people could watch the play.

Burbage's Theatre owed its design to the public inns where plays had been performed in the courtyards from the reign of Queen Mary and probably before. The trestle stages of the Boar's Head, Aldgate, and the Saracen's Head, Islington, were the setting for the first recorded performances in 1557. These inn-playhouses of the City kept up a running battle with the civic authorities until an impossibly restrictive law in 1574 prompted Burbage to build the Theatre outside the jurisdiction of the Common Council, but within reasonable walking distance for the public.

It was a big step towards improving the dignity of plays and playgoing. From its opening in August 1577, the new Theatre

with its permanent stage, tiring-house or dressing-room, and facilities for presenting serious plays immediately attracted companies of actors under wealthy patronage.

The success of the Theatre encouraged another speculator to build a second theatre within a year. Only a few hundred yards to the south, Henry Lanman, gentleman, erected the Curtain (named after the estate on which it was built) to a similar pattern, and apparently with equal success. 'Mark the flocking and running to the Theatre and Curtain . . .' exclaimed a Puritan critic who called the playhouses 'Venus palaces'.

We know what the Curtain looked like, thanks to an anonymous, probably unique, engraving of London. In contrast to most views, it shows a panorama of the City from the north. The date is about 1600. Obtained by an agent of the Dutch East India Company living in London about thirty years later, the engraving is preserved in his manuscript journal now in Utrecht.

The success of Burbage's Theatre and of Lanman's Curtain led to a merger. Eight years after their opening, the two managers signed a seven-year agreement to pool profits, and Burbage's company, now joined by Shakespeare, acted in both playhouses.

For an idea of the inside of these theatres we must refer to a drawing of another Dutchman also from Utrecht, a priest called Johannes de Witt. A pen-and-ink copy of a sketch he made is the only authentic and contemporary view of the interior of an Elizabethan playhouse. This was the Swan built in Paris Gardens on Bankside in 1595 by Francis Langley, goldsmith. London's fourth theatre, and the second erected on Bankside (the first was the Rose in 1588), the Swan was run in the teeth of opposition from the City Corporation who called it a meeting-place of 'thieves, horse stealers, whore-mongers, cozeneres, connycatching persons, practicers of treason and such other like'.

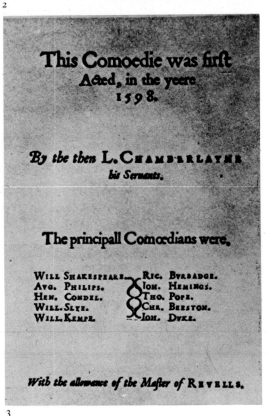

This Comoedie was firſt Acted, in the yeere 1598.

By the then L. Chamberlayne his Servants.

The principall Comœdians were,

Will. Shakespeare.	Ric. Burbadge.
Avg. Philips.	Ioh. Hemings.
Hen. Condel.	Tho. Pope.
Will. Slye.	Cha. Beeston.
Will. Kempe.	Ioh. Dvke.

With the allowance of the Maſter of Revells.

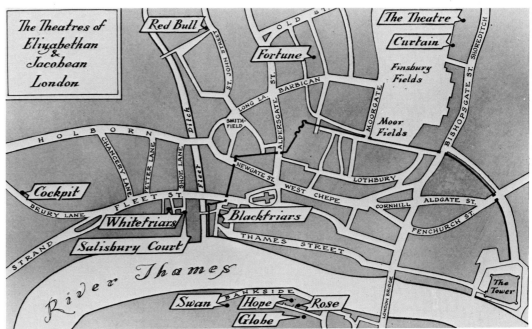

The Theatres of Elizabethan & Jacobean London

1. 'The View of the Cittye of London from the North towards the Sowth', c. 1600. The tall, octagonal building on the extreme left of the panorama, behind the L-shaped barn, is the Curtain. The enlarged view reveals two flanking wings which contained staircases to the public galleries and to the gabled hut over the roof of the stage. The flag signals a performance—perhaps *Romeo and Juliet* which 'won Curtain plaudities', or *Everyman in His Humour* which made Ben Jonson famous.

Another enlargement, above, of a part of the panorama slightly to its left, shows a square building which may be identified as the Fortune Theatre. Alleyn's playhouse (see next page) was built between Whitecross Street and Golden Lane north of Cripplegate in the first half of 1600—the year of the 'view'. Only two storeys are shown (it was to have three) so may have been under construction when the artist made his drawing. It has more windows and larger ones than the Curtain or the second Globe. The Fortune was destroyed by fire 1621, rebuilt 1623, finally dismantled 1649.

2. The Swan theatre on Bankside—De Witt's sketch.

3. Title page of Jonson's *Everyman in His Humour* naming an all-star cast including Shakespeare and Burbage's son, Richard.

4. A modern map of the Elizabethan and Jacobean playhouses.

5. Bear-baiting Pits were rough rivals to the theatres. Paul Hentzner, a German traveller, wrote in 1598 that both bulls and bears 'are fastened behind and then worried by the great English bull-dogs; but not without great risk to the dogs. . . . To this entertainment there often follows the whipping of a blinded bear which is performed by five or six men . . . without mercy. . . . He defends himself with all his force and skill, throwing down all who come within his reach. . . .'

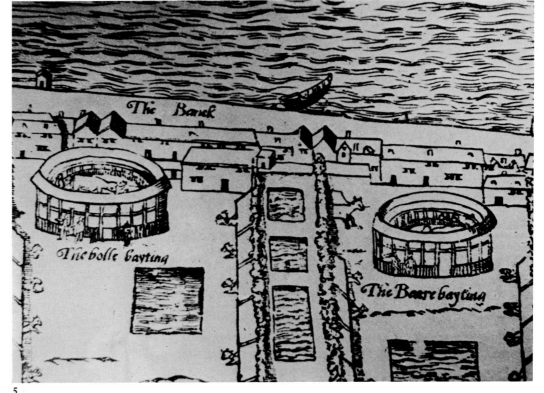

5

The Lord Admiral's Men

Harassed by the City Corporation, censured by the Puritans, often driven into the country by plague, and treated as rogues and vagabonds, the actors had need of powerful friends. Patrons were essential, and one of the most influential of these during the last quarter of the sixteenth century was Lord Howard of Effingham. He helped to create and maintain the Company known as the Lord Admiral's Men.

Lord Howard, Admiral of the Fleet which destroyed the Armada, gave his support and name about 1583 to the troupe whose guiding spirit was Philip Henslowe and the chief actor Edward Alleyn. Henslowe, who became the greatest theatrical manager of his day, started life with little money or education and had no trade. He is described as being a 'servant', but he married his employer's widow–Agnes Woodward of Southwark–and so came into considerable property. In 1587 he leased a small piece of ground, ninety-four feet square, on the corner of Rose Alley and Maid Lane. There he built a theatre in partnership with a grocer (who naturally had the refreshment rights).

The Rose, a circular building with galleries, was like its prototypes in Shoreditch. The first theatre on Bankside, it was the home of the Lord Admiral's Men for six important years, 1594 to 1600. In a year free from plague, they acted at the Rose every weekday from Easter to Midsummer and from about October to the beginning of Lent. In their three busiest years, they gave 728 London performances and produced fifty-five new plays, several by Marlowe.

The Rose's success was largely due to Alleyn, then in his mid-twenties, a star actor whose name guaranteed full houses. After Alleyn married Henslowe's step-daughter Joan, Henslowe made him a partner. From then on, Alleyn managed the company, selected and produced the plays, including Marlowe's *Tamburlaine* and *Faustus*, and acted the leading roles.

With several managerial and property interests–he was not above having a financial stake in the rival Beargarden–Alleyn gave up acting for three years after 1597. This weakened the company, and he returned to the stage at Queen Elizabeth's request in 1600, the same year in which the Privy Council authorized him to build a new theatre north of the river. This was the Fortune, outside Cripplegate (seen in the panorama on the previous page, and in symbolic cartographical form, right), for which the Admiral's men forsook Bankside. Puritan and local objections were overcome by Alleyn who tactfully made a weekly contribution to the poor of the parish.

1. Lord Howard, patron of the Lord Admiral's Men.
2. Lord Hunsdon, the younger, patron of the Lord Chamberlain's Men.
3. The Fortune Theatre, just outside the City limits.

The Lord Chamberlain's Men

The most famous Elizabethan acting company was the Lord Chamberlain's Men, briefly partners of the Lord Admiral's and then their rivals. They took their name from the first Lord Hunsdon, the Queen's cousin, and retained it after they were taken over by his son who was also Lord Chamberlain. Shakespeare joined them in 1594, and so did Richard Burbage, Alleyn's only serious competitor as a star actor.

Mergers with other companies secured their pre-eminence, but the decisive factor in the fortunes of the Lord Chamberlain's Company was the move from Shoreditch to Southwark.

Twenty-one years earlier, Burbage's father had built the Theatre in Shoreditch, and, though it had been used by various other companies at different times, the Lord Chamberlain's Men were occupying it in 1596 when the ground lease fell in. The landlord kept postponing renewal, and the Burbage family decided that new premises had to be found.

An attempt to convert an old monastic building at Blackfriars into a playhouse was defeated by local opposition, and the Burbages next planned to try their luck south of the river. Richard Burbage formed a syndicate with his brother and five actors, one of whom was Shakespeare, to raise the money, and they settled on the Liberty of the Clink on Bankside as a place which would be free of City interference.

Building a theatre was costly, and Burbage determined to use materials from the old Theatre, even though the ground landlord insisted they were his property under the terms of the 21-year lease. The Lord Chamberlain's Men chose Christmastide 1598, when the landlord would be safely away at his home in Essex, to dismantle the playhouse. The timbers were carried from Shoreditch to the river and ferried across to Bankside.

The ground was marshy and required heavy piles for foundations, but otherwise the work of reconstruction went ahead smoothly, and the Globe (so-called because its sign showed Atlas carrying the burden of the world) was ready by the following summer. Cylindrical in shape, open to the sky, and with tiered seats round a jutting stage, this was the 'wooden O' to which Shakespeare referred in the Prologue to *Henry V*, possibly the opening play.

The new home of the Chamberlain's Men was communally owned. The two Burbage brothers held a half share, and the other half was owned in five equal parts by Shakespeare and his four fellow players. Here were to be presented nearly all Shakespeare's thirty-seven plays.

4. The first Globe Theatre. This enlargement from Visscher is the only contemporary view. John Norden's map, below, shows that the theatre was actually several hundred yards farther south-east.

5 Edward Alleyn, principal actor-manager of the Lord Admiral's Men, and founder of Dulwich College.

6. Joan Alleyn, Henslowe's step-daughter – 'my good sweet mouse' as she was affectionately called by Alleyn whom she married in 1592.

7. Their star actor, Richard Burbage.

8. Nathan Field, one of the twenty-six 'Principall Actors' of Shakespeare's plays listed in the First Folio.

9. The rival theatres of the two companies – The Lord Admiral's Rose (misnamed *The Stare* in this 1600 view by Norden) and the Globe, to the south.

In 'The Quick Forge'

Shakespeare came to London when he was about twenty-three, and lived in what he called 'the quick forge and working-house of thought' until his middle forties and his retirement to Stratford-upon-Avon. The first irrefutable evidence of his presence in London is dated March 1594, when, along with Burbage and Kempe, he was paid for a performance at Court the previous Christmas. By this time he would have been working in London for several years and was living in the parish of St Helen's, Bishopsgate, conveniently near the Theatre. His move across the river more or less coincided with the building of the Globe on Bankside.

No record exists to show that he ever bought or rented a town house for himself, and his third London home, by Cripplegate, was in lodgings. His landlord in Silver Street was a Huguenot, Christopher Mountjoy, who may have been a theatrical wigmaker. Our knowledge is based on a lawsuit heard in 1612. Shakespeare was a witness, and it appears that he stayed at the house some time between 1602 and 1604. So it is possible that *Othello* may have been written here.

The Coronation of James I gives us another of our rare glimpses of Shakespeare. The Lord Chamberlain's Books state that he and eight other members of the King's Men received four and a half yards of scarlet cloth for suits from the Royal Wardrobe in Blackfriars.

His one recorded property deal in the City took place three years before he died when he bought a house two hundred yards from the Blackfriars Theatre in which he had held an interest since 1608. This 'Blackfriars Gatehouse' (adjoining what is now Ireland Yard) was inherited by his daughter Susanna after his death in 1616.

1. Tentative pinpointing (on John Agas's map) of Mountjoy's house on the corner of Mugle Street and Silver Street, Cripplegate.

2. Extract from Act I, Scene IV, of Shakespeare's *Henry VIII* which was being played on the June afternoon in 1613 when the Globe caught fire. *Chambers discharged* is thought to have been a salute of cannon which accidentally hurled a smouldering wad into the theatre's thatched roof. Wolsey's startled, '*What's that?*' and the Lord Chamberlain's '*Look out there, some of ye!*' would be the actors' spontaneous reactions which somehow found their way into the printed text. The theatre was burnt down in two hours, but a packed audience escaped safely except for one man whose breeches caught fire and were extinguished by a bottle of ale.

3. One of Shakespeare's six known autograph signatures on this mortgage deed, dated 11 March 1612, related to his purchase of the Gatehouse of Blackfriars Priory.

4. In the churchyard of St Mary Aldermanbury Shakespeare's bust stands as a memorial to John Heminge and William Condell, joint editors of the First Folio. Both lived in the parish for more than thirty years and were buried here.

5. After the Globe was burnt down in 1613, a second, slightly larger theatre with the same name was built on the site. This sketch of it by Hollar is the artist's original drawing for his engraved panorama (p. 125).

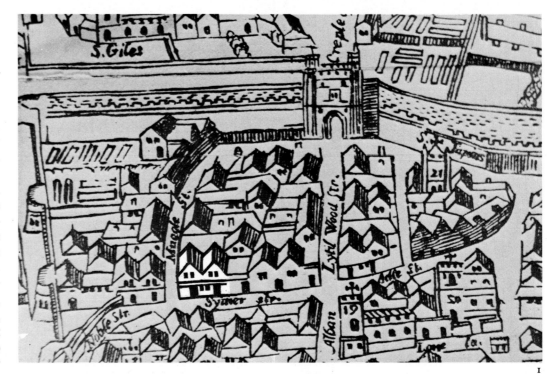

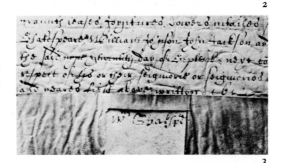

Two Marriages

A marriage in Elizabethan London culminated in a great reception. Stow describes how, after the wedding of the daughter of the London Bridge Master in 1562 'all the Company went home to the Bridge House to dinner: where was as good cheer as ever was known, with all manner of Musick and Dancing all the remainder of the day; and at night a goodly Supper; and then followed a Masque till midnight'. Some thirty years later, a comparable marriage-feast was held at Bermondsey half a mile down river from the Bridge. The bride and groom are not known in this painting by Joris Hoefnagel who gives the buildings a Flemish look and whose topography presents difficulties.

London is given so incredible an appearance by Marcus Gheeraerts in his picture of the ceremony which took place at Blackfriars in June 1600 that it can be considered only as a stylized, High Renaissance background. This was the marriage of Anne Russell, one of Elizabeth's Maids of Honour and Henry Somerset, Lord Herbert.

The bridegroom, Lord Herbert, who was twenty-four, is presumed to be the nobleman in white satin who is supporting the pole at the back of the litter in which Queen Elizabeth is being carried. Anne, his bride-to-be, is likely to be the girl on the extreme right, wearing a pendant, towards whom his hand is outstretched.

1. In Bermondsey, against a background of the Thames and the Tower, preparations are made for a marriage-feast. Servants are at work in the improvised kitchen, and a long table is laid out in an open-ended barn. The procession comes from the church on the right which could be either St Mary's or St Olave's. The bride, in Puritan or widow's black and wearing rosemary, walks between two men. They are preceded by men and women carrying large bride-cakes, by two fiddlers, and by a Malvolio-like attendant holding aloft a bride-cup decorated with rosemary.
2. As Gheeraert's picture shows, the Queen attended the Russell-Herbert marriage. A guest of Lord Cobham, whose house was near the bride's, she was met at the waterside and carried to the house of the bride's mother, Lady Russell, where she dined.

Preaching at Paul's Cross

Paul's Cross, in the churchyard to the north-east of old St Paul's, was the open-air pulpit which existed for two hundred years not only for Sunday morning sermons but as a centre of information. From the octagonal wooden pulpit beneath the ornamental cross, bishops gave thanks for war victories or thundered against decadent dress; news was read, laws proclaimed, and appeals launched. It was a place for penance and a public forum for all the great controversies of the day. As many as 6,000 people could gather round the

pulpit, and in the angle formed by the choir and north transept of the cathedral were built galleries and boxes for the Bishop of London, important visitors, the City fathers and their wives.

The above picture, dated 1616, and showing King James I and his queen, Anne of Denmark, listening to a sermon, is not a record of an actual event. In the last years of Elizabeth and early in James's reign the cathedral was in very bad repair, and this painting seems to have been made in the

nature of an advertisement for a restoration fund. The artist's idealized scene was, in a way, prophetic because four years later James came to the cathedral to launch an appeal for its restoration, and he heard the Bishop of London preach from the Cross. But events had outrun the artist's conception. By 1620, Queen Anne was dead. Paul's Cross, long the preserve of strictly Anglican preachers, did not survive the rising tide of Nonconformity. The last sermon was preached there in 1633, and ten years later it was demolished.

John Stow's 'Survay'

During the last decade of the sixteenth century an endlessly inquisitive old man made his way through the streets of London. Tall, lean, and approaching seventy, he explored all the City Wards. He visited every church and made notes on their monuments. With courteous mildness, he questioned old residents, and picked up curious scraps of information from innkeepers. He asked the City companies to let him see their records, and searched those in the Tower and every parish. From the muniment rooms of the dissolved monasteries he salvaged invaluable documents.

This task occupied John Stow, retired tailor and self-taught historian, for eight years, and in 1598 he published *A Survay of London*, the first detailed, comprehensive history of the city. This unsurpassed work, dedicated to the Lord Mayor and citizens of London, was the outcome of a perfect marriage between writer and subject. In writing it, he said he had 'attempted the discovery of London, my native soil and country'. Born in 1525, in the parish of St Michael's, Cornhill, Stow had in his youth talked to old men who remembered Richard III; he lived through the entire reign of Elizabeth, and saw James I come to the throne. His survey was the record of a London emerging from medievalism and taking modern shape, painstakingly accurate, enlivened by personal reminiscences, and written by an antiquary who hated the way beautiful things were being destroyed by greedy men.

It was Stow's claim that he never wrote out of malice, fear or favour. His only form of spite was to exclude from his book those (like the Vintners Company) who rebuffed him in his research. His devotion to history brought him into some poverty. As he himself said 'It hath cost me many a weary mile's travel, many a hard-earned penny and pound, and many a cold winter night's study.' The publisher of the *Survay* gave him only £3 (and forty free copies). At the age of seventy-nine, he was forced to obtain a royal licence to beg. This, issued by James I, described him as 'a very aged and worthy member of our city of London, who hath for forty-five years to his great charge and with neglect of his ordinary means of maintenance, for the general good as well as posterity of the present age, compiled and published divers necessary books and chronicles.' Stow put begging bowls out in the street, without much success. But his habitual cheerfulness remained unclouded. Walking one day with his friend Ben Jonson, he sardonically enquired of two cripples what he must pay to enter their order.

On his death in 1605, John Stow, citizen of London, was buried in St Andrew Undershaft, 200 yards from his home by Aldgate Well, and a monument was raised to him by his widow, Elizabeth. His effigy, originally coloured, shows him seated in a chair and writing his history. In his alabaster hand he holds a quill pen, and each year to mark the anniversary of his death, the Lord Mayor renews it as a tribute to the author of London's greatest written monument.

1. Stow's monument, erected by his widow in his parish church of St Andrew Undershaft. It shows him with the 'pleasant and cheerful countenance' ascribed to him by Edmond Howes, his literary executor.

2. Title page of the first edition of the *Survay*, published in 1598 when Stow was over seventy.

3. In about 1547 Stow established himself as a tailor in a house 'by the well within Aldgate' between Leadenhall Street and Fenchurch Street. He lived there for nearly thirty years, and St Andrew Undershaft where he was buried is nearby. This detail of Agas's map shows the immediate locality, Aldgate, and the well. Stow's house may be the shaded building at the division of the streets.

Printers, Books and Patrons

A century after Caxton, more than fifty printers were working in London. 'Buy a new book, sir!' was a familiar cry round St Paul's where most of the publisher-booksellers had their stalls. To advertise particular works, extra copies of their elaborate title pages were run off for display. In this way a master printer, Richard Field, with a press in Blackfriars, could tell all London in 1593 that Shakespeare's *Venus and Adonis* was on sale 'in Paul's Churchyard'.

Printers and most publishers were members of the Stationers Company which took its name from the bookstalls or 'stations' at the crosses of Cheapside and St Paul's. Among the Company's responsibilities was the suppression of books ruled illegal by the Bishop of London, and these were burnt in the kitchen of Stationers' Hall which lay to the west of the Cathedral. To help the printers, the Company insisted that no edition must exceed 1,250 copies. After that, the type had to be broken up and reset. So books were expensive and poorly-paid writers were forced to rely on patronage.

Edmund Spenser was one of many authors helped by the Earl of Leicester. Ben Jonson, who claimed he never made more than £200 from all his plays, lived five years in the house of Lord d'Aubigny to whom he dedicated his favourite books. Before he took orders and became Dean of St Paul's, John Donne made his home in the house of Sir Thomas Egerton, and later wrote some of his finest poems in an apartment of the large house in Drury Lane provided by his patron, Sir Robert Drury – after whose family the street was named.

Royalty were patrons of books. In his preface to his *History of the World*, Sir Walter Raleigh, himself a patron, acknowledged his debt to 'the inestimable' Prince Henry, son of James I. It was in hope of preferment by Queen Elizabeth that George Gascoigne, soldier and poet, made a flamboyant gesture. When he presented her with his *Hermetes the Heremyte* it contained an optimistic frontispiece of the scene, below, in which the author on one knee, and holding a lance, is handing her his book. A laurel wreath hovering over his head, mutely requests royal permission to descend.

1. Frontispiece of Gascoigne's book.

2. John Donne, poet and preacher – his monument in St Paul's. Prepared during his lifetime, it depicts him as he posed for it, in his study, his feet on an urn, his eyes closed, and naked under a winding sheet. Charcoal fires kept him warm as the sculptor, Nicholas Stone, worked. The effigy stood by his bed until his death, and then a marble version was set up in the cathedral. This was the only monument completely to escape the Great Fire.

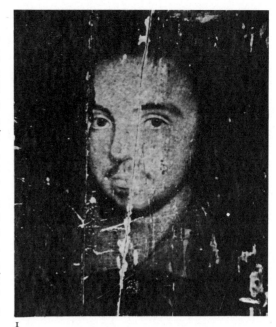

Murder at Deptford

It may never be known what drew Christopher Marlowe to the riverside village of Deptford on the last Wednesday in May 1593. But at a house kept there by a widow, Eleanor Bull – possibly a tavern on the water's edge – the playwright spent the whole day with three men. They were Ingram Frezer, servant of Thomas Walsingham, Nicholas Skeres, servant of the Earl of Essex, and Robert Poley, a Government secret agent. They talked and drank 'in quiet sort together', took a turn in the garden about six, and then had supper. At the end of the meal, it was said, tempers flared up about 'the reckoning'. There was a brief struggle, and within minutes Marlowe, most brilliant of Shakespeare's contemporaries, lay dead. Over his right eye was a wound, two inches deep inflicted by Ingram Frezer's '12d. dagger'. He was twenty-nine.

All this was set down by Her Majesty's coroner, William Danby, Gentleman, after an inquest held two days later when a jury of sixteen viewed the body. He was buried in the churchyard of St Nicholas's, Deptford. The church record, with the clerk's error of Francis for Ingram, still exists and reads:

Christopher Marlow slaine by ffrancis ffrezer; the · I · of June.

The explanation of a quarrel and self-defence apparently satisfied the jury, and within a month Frezer was pardoned by the Queen.

It was a verdict which very well suited the Government, but has been much queried by history. To the Privy Council, Marlowe was not 'the Muse's darling', the author of *Tamburlaine* and *The Passionate Shepherd*. He was an atheist, blasphemer and pervert. Only ten days earlier he had been before the Council to answer for certain of his atheistic writings found in the lodgings of his friend and fellow-playwright, Thomas Kyd. But to nail him was not easy. Marlowe had a powerful patron in Thomas Walsingham of Chislehurst, cousin of Sir Francis Walsingham, the Queen's spymaster. Also he had done the state some service. Six years earlier, and while still a student at Cambridge, he seems to have served as a secret agent abroad.

His sudden death and rapid burial in an unmarked grave in Deptford was so convenient, that his murder on secret government orders must be reckoned a possibility. Such devious methods are well in keeping with Elizabethan security work. Knowing that he might be arrested at any moment, Marlowe would have made for Deptford to hide while waiting for a passage to the Continent. But, before he could slip down the Thames, hired assassins led by Frezer would have caught up with him. They would have posed as drinking companions, perhaps agreed to be confederates in his escape. Only after supper would Marlowe realize that their smiles were counterfeit, that, with the approval of the Privy Council, they were really his gaolers and his executioners. But by then it would be too late.

1. Marlowe – a supposed portrait found in the wall of Corpus Christi, his Cambridge college, when renovations were being carried out there in 1952.

2. Wyngaerde's view of sixteenth-century Deptford.

3. Prematurely old and sick, Raleigh worked on his world history during his thirteen years' imprisonment in the Tower. King James ordered the Stationers to suppress it. Though this was rescinded, the first edition appeared without the author's name and portrait.

4. In Jonson's collected *Works* were nine of his plays, each dedicated to a different person. *Sejanus*, written in his patron's house, was flatteringly offered 'To the No Less Noble by Virtue than Blood: Esme L.[ord] Aubigny'.

The Chariott drawne by foure Horses vpon which Charret stood the Coffin conued w.th purple veluett and vpon that the representation. The Canopy borne by six Knight.

Vale! The Funeral of Queen Elizabeth . . .

'Then there was an open chariot, drawn by four horses, trapped with black velvet, beset with the Arms of England and France, wherein lay the body of the dead Queen, embalmed and enclosed in lead. . . .' So wrote John Clapham, a former member of Lord Burghley's household. He was an eyewitness of the procession from Whitehall to Westminster Abbey when Queen Elizabeth was carried on her last journey at the end of April in 1603.

After a reign of 44 years, the Queen had died in the previous month at Richmond. Her body had been brought in the royal barge to Whitehall where for five weeks it had been watched over each night by her ladies.

The picture above shows the horses, caparisoned almost to their fetlocks, and with pennants on their manes and tails. Over the body a canopy is borne by six knights. Gentlemen pensioners in black, with pikes reversed, walk beside the coffin. The twelve emblazoned banners depict the Queen's descent from the house of York. Bringing up the rear are four footmen, but the Queen's own horse, riderless, or the 266 poor women who followed the coffin, are not shown.

The Queen had outlived many of her great subjects. Her chief minister, Lord Burghley, Mr Secretary Walsingham, and her favourites, Sir Christopher Hatton and the Earls of Leicester and Essex had all predeceased her. But Raleigh was present as Captain of the Guard.

John Stow who, as an old man of nearly 80, could have seen the funeral, leaves us this description: '. . . there was such a generall syghing, groaning and weeping as the like hath not been seene or knowne in the memorie of man, neyther doth any historie mention any people time or state to make such lamentacyon for the death of their soverayne.'

. . . et salve! The Welcome for King James I

This was the first of eight triumphal arches which greeted James and his Queen, Anne, on their procession through London. The great welcome took place on 15 March 1604, nearly a year after the Scottish King's accession.

On Elizabeth's death James had immediately come south, but all ceremonial had been postponed because of plague which, during 1603, accounted for the lives of 30,000 Londoners, one-fifth of the population. But by the following March the plague had gone, and London made up for the delay with so much pageantry, oratory, and music that it took the King and Queen six hours to travel from the Tower to Whitehall.

The sumptuous double arch, left, surmounted by a model of the City was set up in Fenchurch Street. The whole frame was covered with a silk curtain painted like a cloud – symbolic of sorrow that had gathered over the city in its prolonged wait for the new King's arrival. Now, at his approach, it instantly fell away. So began the reign of the man whom a contemporary French statesman was to call 'the wisest fool in Christendom'.

STUART LONDON

The
High and mighty
Prince, IAMES
KING of great
Britane, Fraunce
and Ireland. &c:

The Gunpowder Plot

In March 1604, James I, first of the Stuarts, rode through streets lined with Londoners, cheering and curious to see their King. Even then, if official records are to be trusted, his death was being plotted by Papist malcontents. Thomas Percy, cousin of the Earl of Northumberland, was already discussing with Robert Catesby, a Warwickshire gentleman, 'a most sure way' of assassinating him. Our knowledge of what eventually occurred is based on suspect testimony, perhaps partly contrived to make anti-Catholic propaganda, but the main outline of the Gunpowder Plot seems tolerably clear.

Actual steps towards the King's violent end began soon after April 1604, when another of the chief conspirators, Thomas Winter, returned to England from Flanders where he had been vainly trying to obtain Spanish aid for overthrowing the throne. With him came a soldier of fortune, a tall, red-bearded fellow in his thirties called Guy Fawkes, who was to be the main instrument of the crime.

Surrounding the southern end of the Parliament buildings in Westminster were a number of private houses, and one of them, only a matter of yards from the House of Lords, was rented by Thomas Percy. He took up his tenancy attended by Fawkes who, in a servile white smock and false name, acted the role of his servant.

The conspirators' first idea was to dig a tunnel under the House, but this difficult operation was abandoned when the ground-level crypt immediately beneath the Peers' Chamber became available. In March 1605, thirty-six barrels of gunpowder were ferried secretly by night across the Thames, and hidden in the cellar under pipes of winter firewood.

All was now ready for action, but a severe outbreak of plague that year postponed the opening of Parliament until 5 November. The conspirators dispersed, and during the summer some of them developed qualms. Quite apart from the King, were they not sending about 500 innocent men to their death? As a result, ten days before Parliament assembled an anonymous letter was sent to a peer, Lord Monteagle. Delivered by an unknown messenger to his Hoxton house, it contained a warning to avoid Parliament, which was to receive 'a terrible blow'.

For some reason the King was not informed of the threat until 4 November, the day before the opening. This delay was either to catch the assassins red-handed or (as some Catholic interpreters hold) to ensure the greatest outcry by a dramatic, eleventh-hour discovery. King James ordered the building to be searched, and this was carried out by Sir Thomas Knyvet, a Westminster magistrate, at midnight. He found the gunpowder under the faggots, and immediately arrested Fawkes who, it seems, had been left behind to fuse the charge.

The King was roused and Fawkes hauled before him. Calmly, he gave as his explanation that 'a desperate deed requires a desperate remedy'. Later in the Tower he withstood 'uttermost' torture for three days while his confederates escaped to the North. Catesby and Percy were killed and Winters wounded in a round-up at Holbeach, Staffordshire. The trial of the eight survivors was held in Westminster Hall the following January. Sir Edward Coke, the Attorney General, spoke of the frustrated plan as one of 'the greatest treasons that ever were plotted in England'. The sentences of death were a foregone conclusion.

MISCHEEFES MYSTERIE: OR, Treasons Master-peece, *The Powder-plot.*

Inuented by hellish Malice, preuented by heauenly *Mercy : truely related.*

And from the Latine of the learned and reuerend Doctour HERRING *translated, and very much dilated.*

By IOHN VICARS.

The gallant *Eagle,* foaring vp on high : Beares in his beake, *Treasons* difcouery. MOVNT, noble EAGLE, with thy happy prey, And thy rich *Price* to th' *King* with speed conuay.

LONDON, Printed by E. GRIFFIN, dwelling in the Little Olde Bayly neere the figne of the Kings head. 1617.

2

1. The eight conspirators – 'gentlemen of good houses of excellent parts, of very competent fortunes and estates' but, Coke insisted at their trial, 'most perniciously seduced, abused, corrupted, and Jesuited.'

2. The warning is received! A satirical cartoon on the title page of a book published twelve years later shows Robert Cecil taking the letter from (Mont) Eagle.

3. Before bringing the gunpowder across the river, the conspirators stored it in this house on the Lambeth shore. It was demolished early in the nineteenth century.

4. The old House of Lords, setting for the plot, prior to its nineteenth-century demolition, showing the door by which Fawkes reached the crypt.

5. The cellar, 75 feet long and 24 feet wide, in which barrels of gunpowder were hidden under firewood was on the ground floor immediately below the House of Lords. Formerly, it served as the kitchen of the Palace of Westminster, but in 1605 was let to a coal-merchant named Bright. When he gave up his lease, Percy rented it. There was no further need for the deeper tunnel on which the conspirators were working.

6. The conspirators went to the scaffold, five in St Paul's Churchyard on 30 January 1606, three in Old Palace Yard, whence they were drawn on wooden sleds the following day. The last to die was Guy Fawkes who, weak from torture, could hardly mount the ladder. Their heads were then cut off, and, as Coke predicted with some relish at their trial, were 'set up in some high and eminent place, to the view and detestation of men, and to become a prey for the fowls of the air.'

3

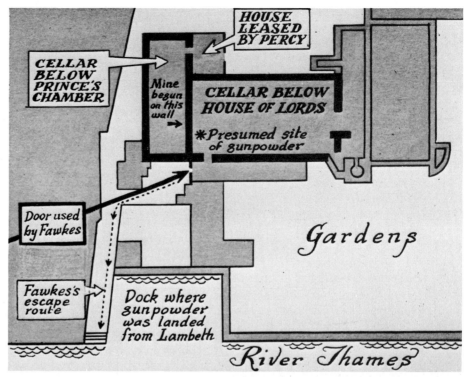

CELLAR BELOW PRINCE'S CHAMBER

Mine begun on this wall →

HOUSE LEASED BY PERCY

CELLAR BELOW HOUSE OF LORDS

＊Presumed site of gunpowder

Door used by Fawkes

Fawkes's escape route

Dock where gunpowder was landed from Lambeth

Gardens

River Thames

4

5

6

The City's Water

At the beginning of the seventeenth century, London's population was probably about half a million. It had multiplied by five since Henry VIII's reign. But its water came from the same sources and by much the same methods as served the far smaller medieval city. Famous wells like Goswell and Clerkenwell were often polluted, and the Thames, Walbrook, and Fleet had long since ceased to be clear rivers from which people were willing to draw drinking water. The main source of fresh water were conduits supplied from outlying springs. From Highgate, the Tyburn flowed down to a waterhead (where Stratford Place, Oxford Street, is today) from which it was channelled through three and a half miles of leather pipes to Cheapside. Another built by William Lamb (remembered by Lamb's Conduit Street) supplied Holborn.

The conduit system dated back to 1285, but the number of public taps at conduit heads had not kept pace with the population. There were fewer than twenty in 1600, and insufficient pressure of water to supply more. Members of the Honourable Company of Water Tankard Bearers–about 4,000 strong– who delivered fresh water to the door were in such fierce competition that an order had to be issued forbidding the use of weapons to secure a place at the taps.

A water tower at Queenhithe (page 94) and another supplied by a waterwheel at London Bridge helped to bring piped river water to houses for domestic use and for anyone enterprising enough to install a flushing water closet, the recently invented device of Queen Elizabeth's godson, Sir John Harington. But when it came to fresh drinking water, even someone as influential as Lord Burghley had difficulty in getting a private lead off a conduit to his house in the Strand. And even this was cut off when demand outran supply in a drought.

There were constant complaints and Parliament issued numerous instructions, but nothing practical was done until 1609. In that year Hugh Myddelton, a Welsh businessman, engineer and goldsmith, put forward a revolutionary plan. A friend of Raleigh's who lived in Basinghall Street, he had studied the whole problem closely. His solution was to find a good source far out of London and bring the water in by aqueduct. He offered to finance and build the river which would stretch nearly forty miles from springs at Amwell and Chadwell in Hertfordshire.

Myddelton said he could complete the work in four years. But he was hampered by landowners, and the task of cutting an open channel, ten feet wide and four deep, following the contours of the land, proved harder than

he had reckoned. In 1611 when his river had reached Enfield, money ran out, and he was forced to ask for more time. Financial help came from James I. The King who had seen the New River pass close to his palace at Theobald's offered to pay half the cost in return for half the profits.

A year later the great enterprise was finished. Pure Hertfordshire spring water flowing down a gradient of two inches in the mile, was carried into London across dips and valleys by more than a hundred wooden bridges. The longest of these aqueducts was just over a quarter of a mile, and another seventeen feet high. The flow, controlled by forty sluices, was augmented by thirteen wells from which water was pumped. The end of its winding course was a circular reservoir in Islington named New River Head.

On Michaelmas Day, 29 September 1613, the Lord Mayor delivered an heroic poem beside the reservoir to an assembly which included labourers who had worked on the river and were decked out in Green Monmouth caps in honour of Myddelton. To a fanfare and the cry of, 'Flow forth precious spring!' the floodgates were opened.

From New River Head the water was subdivided in large wooden pipes to different parts of London, and from these by smaller pipes to private houses. But this latter development took time, and Myddelton, who had locked up his capital in the project, was soon forced to form the New River Company and sell shares. It paid no dividends until 1633, two years after Myddelton's death. But from then on, prosperity grew with the needs of the city. When taken over, with seven other private water companies, by the Metropolitan Water Board in 1904, its value was more than £5,000,000. Today New River ends at Stoke Newington, and the Board offices are on the site of the original reservoir.

1. A water-carrier. Despite the difficulties of their job water-carriers fought all attempts at improving supplies, which they saw as a threat to their livelihood.

2. A seventeenth-century pump in the yard of the Leathersellers Hall near Bishopsgate. As well as supplying water, it could be adapted so that fountains of wine poured from the breasts of the mermaid on special occasions.

3. New River Head, Islington – view looking south showing the Waterhouse on a circular island in the reservoir. In the background is St Paul's.

4. A waterwheel works a pipe-boring machine. Pipes, of two to ten-inch bore, were scooped from solid tree trunks, usually elm. Joints were made by driving tapered ends into larger ends. At one time the New River Company had 400 miles of wooden pipes in use.

5. Before the New River, the City's water was mostly brought from the Tyburn to various waterpoints. One of these was 'The Little Conduit in West-Cheap by Paul's Gate', built in about 1441 and attached to the Church of St Michael-le-Quern (destroyed in the Great Fire). The pipes, which are shown, continued on to serve the Great Conduit (built 1285) at the east end of Cheap. Three-gallon tankards for carrying the water surround the conduit.

6. Sir Hugh Myddelton, builder of the New River.

1

2

3

4

5

6

Patron of the Arts

In 1608, the year after he came of age, Thomas Howard, 2nd Earl of Arundel bought back his family home between the Strand and the Thames. Arundel House (pages 74, 137) had been forfeited to the Crown eighteen years before when his father was attainted for Catholic conspiracy. But now the young Earl was in royal favour, his title restored, and a marriage dowry made it possible to raise the £4,000 indemnity for the house. During the next few years, Arundel was to become the greatest art patron of the times, and the gardens and galleries of his mansion the setting for an astonishing collection of sculpture and paintings.

Arundel spent much of his life travelling abroad, and, in Italy especially, he caught the Renaissance enthusiasm for classical antiquities. At the watergate of Arundel House, ships from abroad began to unload crates packed with Greek and Roman sculpture, then virtually unknown in England. Thirty-seven statues (some of which are seen in Daniel Mytens's portrait of the Earl, above) were displayed. Seeing these glistening white marble statues for the first time, Francis Bacon started back in mock-alarm exclaiming, 'The Resurrection!'

There were 128 busts (including the head of Homer now in the British Museum), 250 inscribed marbles, as well as altars, sarcophagi, and antique fragments. The great and varied collection also contained gems and paintings, mostly by Holbein. During the Civil War nearly half the 'Arundel Marbles' were to be destroyed, and by this time the man who had acquired them had died abroad in Padua.

Outwardly austere and unbending, Arundel was, nevertheless, invariably friendly to foreigners. He was responsible for bringing to England the engraver who provides us with the most beautiful and detailed views of seventeenth-century London. He discovered Wenceslaus Hollar in Prague, and sometime after 1635 the artist arrived in London. At Arundel House, Hollar not only began his great record of the capital but settled down domestically by marrying Lady Arundel's waiting-woman. 'He was a very friendly, good-natured man as could be,' recorded the antiquary, John Aubrey, 'but shiftless as to the world, and died not rich.'

1. The Earl of Arundel with his marbles – portrait by Mytens.

2. Wenceslaus Hollar.

3. View from the roof of Arundel House by Hollar.

4. Courtyard of Arundel House, another view by the artist of his patron's home. Facing towards the Strand is a building with a large dormer window which may well be the artist's studio. Propped against the wall are two pictures. Working here, he engraved many London views. During this time Hollar was also drawing master to Prince Charles, afterwards Charles II.

Inigo Jones

When the Earl of Arundel visited Italy in 1613, he was accompanied by the perfect guide, a man with an unrivalled knowledge of Italian art and architecture. Inigo Jones was a Londoner. Son of a City clothmaker, he was born in Smithfield; but his spiritual home was Italy where he had steeped himself in the Renaissance and had become a disciple of the Vicenzan architect, Palladio.

Until he was forty-two Inigo Jones's reputation rested on 'rare Devices', masques for the Court, many of which he evolved with Ben Jonson. Then, on his return from his year's tour with Arundel, he was appointed Surveyor-General to the King. It was an appointment destined to change the Gothic face of London. In the next twenty-seven years leading up to the Civil War, Jones was to bring about a revolution in English architectural taste. Within a month of taking up his duties in September 1615, he was making sketches for a small palace at Greenwich which could have passed for an Italian villa.

This was at the request of Queen Anne who found Placentia, the Tudor royal palace, too extensive for her. Anne's death brought work on the Queen's House to a temporary halt, and long before it was completed the first strictly classical building in England – and Jones's masterpiece – had gone up in Whitehall. This was the Banqueting Hall.

It was built on the site of an Elizabethan banqueting hall and another burnt down in 1618. Inigo Jones drew on Palladio for his inspiration and added his own touch of genius. The interior proportions were those of a double cube. On the outside was a perfectly symmetrical placing of windows set between columns and pilasters. The total effect was, and remains, 'masculine, solid, simple' – Jones's three tenets of style. Classical severity is given visual interest by subtle variations of detail.

1. Inigo Jones, from the original drawing by Vandyke.

2. A sketch by Jones shows his early idea when, as Surveyor-General, he designed a classical west front for St Paul's Cathedral in about 1634. With its triple doors, pilasters and scroll brackets, the façade is clearly modelled on the Gesù Church in Rome. In fact (as may be seen, page 138) most of this design was abandoned in favour of a large Corinthian portico, the first of its kind in Britain.

3. The Banqueting Hall, Whitehall. This preliminary drawing from the architect's sketchbook reveals that he toyed with the idea of a triangular pediment over the three central bays. But a ghostly pencil line behind it shows the design as it was finally to emerge, with the pediment discarded.

4. In his design for a masque, Jones incorporated a view of London and St Paul's from the south.

2

3

4

It is uncertain whether the Banqueting Hall–the setting for State receptions, Royal banquets and Court masques–was conceived by Jones as a complete entity or as part of a greater plan. Drawings survive of a grandiose Whitehall Palace in which it is incorporated. But some of these are by John Webb, who was Jones's pupil and assistant, and were drawn after Jones's death. The vast scale of this proposed palace may be judged by the front elevation, below, right, designed to overlook the Thames. In this, *two* Banqueting Halls, balancing the design, are dwarfed by the main central block. Behind this façade there was to have been a magnificent Renaissance palace stretching from the Thames to St James's Park. These plans were ordered and laid aside by Charles I, reconsidered after the Restoration, but finally discarded by Charles II because of the cost. Whether Jones or his assistant made the actual drawings, it is clear that they followed a scheme worked out in detail between them.

With the accession of Charles I, work was resumed on Jones's small palace at Greenwich, bottom left, which had stopped at the first floor. In 1629 it went ahead for Henrietta Maria, the new Queen. The design was ingenious, the result of Jones's determination to get the best of two worlds for his royal patron. At that time the public road between Greenwich and Woolwich divided Greenwich Palace from its grounds south of the present road. It was on a line with the colonnade of today. So that the Queen should have un-impeded view and access to both park and main palace, he built half the house on one side of the road, half on the other. A central bridge joining them spanned the road. In 1661 two further bridges were built at either end which changed the plan of the Queen's House from an H-shape into a square.

Inigo Jones was also influential in the lay-ing out of Covent Garden. The fourth Earl of Bedford whose house was in the Strand wanted to build on his land which stretched north to Long Acre. A Commission on Buildings, under royal patent and with the Earls of Arundel and Pembroke among its members, strictly controlled all such develop-ment. The Earl was granted a conditional licence, but only on payment of £2,000 to Charles I. To Jones as the executive head of the Commission fell the task of reconciling the King's aesthetic demands with Bedford's financial speculation. His solution, which he worked out with Isaac de Caus, was a large piazza, formal, and classical in character.

On the south side of the Covent Garden Piazza were the gardens of Bedford House (see Hollar's aerial view, top, far right). To the north and east were houses behind a colon-nade. On the west there was only one main

5

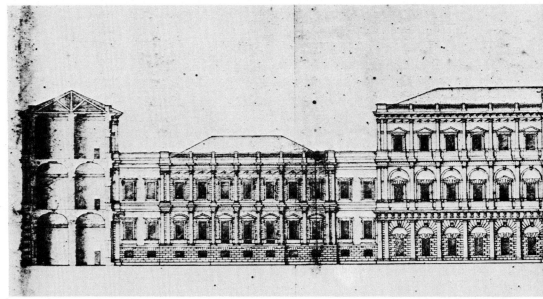

8

9

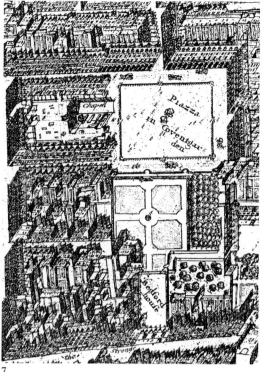

building, a church. As the church would not produce a revenue, Bedford stipulated that it should be kept simple – 'not much better than a barn'. This prompted Jones's celebrated reply that he would design a barn, but it would be the handsomest barn in Europe.

The Church of St Paul (below, right) was gutted by fire in 1795, but the portico with its large Tuscan columns survived and the massive roof with projecting eaves was restored to Jones's design.

5. The Banqueting Hall in about 1690.
6. Interior of the Queen's Chapel, St James's, now Marlborough House Chapel. Jones's first ecclesiastical building, it was completed in 1627. With Venetian window, coffered ceiling, and Palladian detail, this domestic chapel for Henrietta Maria was an architectural innovation for England.
7. Covent Garden and Bedford House.
8. Design for Whitehall Palace.
9. Queen's House, Greenwich.
10. St Paul's, Covent Garden, by Hollar.

6

7

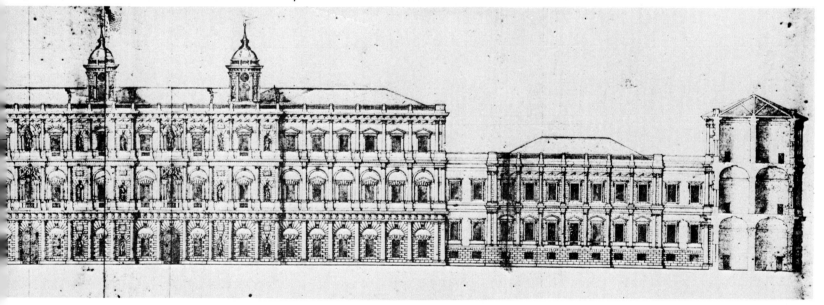

10

Prospect of Lincoln's Inn Fields.
from E.N.E.

South Side   Duke Street   Lindsey House   Newcastle House   Gt. Q

Lincoln's Inn Fields

The Italian hand of Inigo Jones stretched beyond Whitehall and east of Covent Garden. In 1617 the Surveyor-General was asked by King James to prepare a plan for turning three meadows called Lincoln's Inn Fields into a place of 'public health and pleasure'. This followed a petition from the Inns of Court and surrounding parishes that these Crown pasture lands should be laid out with walks in the manner of Moorfields.

James died before the idea took shape, and no specific plan by Jones survives. The next, somewhat contrary scheme of which we hear, came in 1629 when William Newton, a Bedfordshire man, obtained a licence to build houses on the edge of the Fields. Newton, London's first speculative builder, was opposed by the members of Lincoln's Inn who said the houses would annoy them 'with offensive and unhealthful savours'. But he won the day, and started work on the west side of the square, farthest from the Inn.

Under the control of the Commissioners on Buildings and the influence of Inigo Jones, the style of the façades was consistently Italian. The houses were faced with Ionic pilasters, and Jones himself is credited with the design of one of the most distinguished, Lindsey House, built in 1640. Nothing else of the seventeenth century survives, but the classical style was to be echoed in the eighteenth century by Palladian admirers. Immediately next to Lindsey House is another which, though the style is almost identical, was built nearly a hundred years later. The early flavour of Lincoln's Inn Fields is also to be found in Newcastle House on the north-west corner, though this is a modern copy of the 1685 original.

The west side of the square was originally pierced by Duke Street (briefly Sardinia Street between 1878 and 1912). It passed right through one house in the terrace by means of a curiously shaped arch on ground-floor level. Early maps indicate that this street was part of an ancient way that crossed the Fields diagonally. It went past a small building used for the storage of gunpowder and into Holborn through Great Turnstile, then a revolving gate which prevented horses entering the fields or grazing cattle from escaping.

Hollar's prospect, looking westwards from Lincoln's Inn, shows the square in its full glory. But it is difficult to know when it was drawn. The costumes suggest the two decades after 1640, but even by 1658 – tentative date for the artist's bird's-eye view (page 136) – houses on the north side of the square were not nearly so advanced, and there are other discrepancies. It is probably a drawing made soon after the start of building (c. 1638) which could have been used by Newton as an advertisement to show what his houses would look like eventually.

Extending westwards from the north corner of the square ran Great Queen Street, another of Newton's speculations. Spoken of in the eighteenth century as 'the first uniform street', its 'stately and magnificent' terraces of houses built about 1635 were to serve as a model for the whole Georgian style in formal, classical street architecture. With their regular brick façades, and Corinthian pilasters

3

4

rising from first floor to cornice, these houses again show Newton, the speculator, conforming to the ideas of Jones, the planner.

The building of Kingsway (page 348) in 1905 cut right through this important street, and all other examples of what Newton called 'fair dwelling houses' have since disappeared.

1. Hollar's view, probably prophetic, of Lincoln's Inn Fields.

2. The archway, also seen in the panorama, and Duke Street (then Sardinia Street) disappeared in 1912. Another Sardinia Street was created on the south-west of the square.

3. Lindsey House, the square's one surviving original building.

4. Late seventeenth century Newcastle House.

5. Great Queen Street with its uniform, terraced houses.

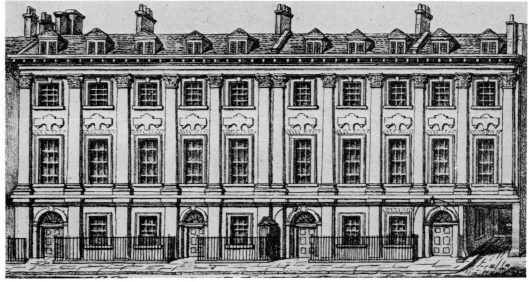

5

The Civil War

In 1633 when the Lord High Treasurer commissioned an equestrian statue of Charles I for his Roehampton garden, there was still no open breach between King and Parliament. London was not yet a divided city of 'roundhead' apprentices and Whitehall 'cavaliers'. But Westminster was soon to become the arena for a momentous struggle between popular will and a monarch resolved 'to live of his own' without Parliament. It started in the Great Hall with the trial of Charles's chief minister, the Earl of Strafford (executed on Tower Hill, 1641) and culminated in the attempted arrest of the Five Members in St Stephen's (January 1642).

During Christmas 1641, the Trained Bands were at the alert and everyone at Court wore his sword, for Whitehall was full of anti-Catholic demonstrators and revolution was in the air. When Charles found 'the birds had flown'–the five Members of Parliament escaped down the Thames by boat–he knew the tide of rebellion had risen too high. A few days later he left London for a more loyal York.

When he came south in the following autumn, an attack by 15,000 Royalist troops was anticipated by Parliament which put London into 'a posture of defence' by erecting barricades on the main roads into the city. Fearing 'furious assault' by Prince Rupert, even more formidable defences were put up the following year. One hundred thousand Londoners were pressed into digging trenches and building fortifications. Puritans worked on Sundays and engineers were imported from Holland. The Common Council ordered that servants and children should help. Oyster wenches were among the women whom the satirist, Samuel Butler, reported helped 'to dig like moles'. The result was a series of forts at strategic points and eighteen miles of ramparts encircling the perimeter of London. All the forts were sited within view of each other so that, wherever attack came, troops could leave the forts and man the defences. The number of troops at any one fort was considerable. The ironically named Fort Royal in St George's Fields (21 on the map, top right, and present site of the Imperial War Museum) held 3,000 soldiers. The earthworks were nine feet wide, and, with the outer ditch, eighteen feet high. The muzzles of 212 cannons awaited the mounted assault of the Cavaliers. In the City, John Milton preferred a private form of defence. He pinned a poem on his front door in Aldersgate asking that his house should be spared.

Neither powder nor poem was needed. London's Lines of Communications were never tested. Brentford was the nearest

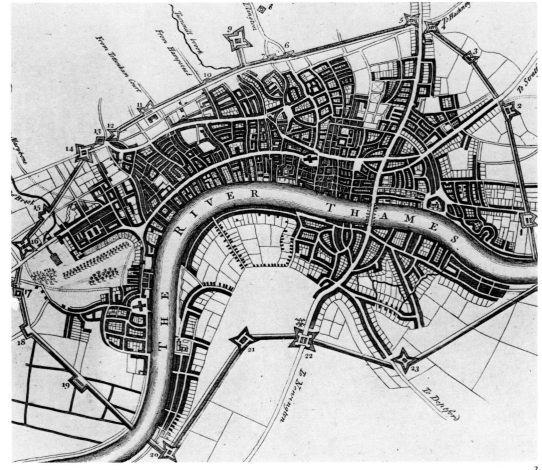

3

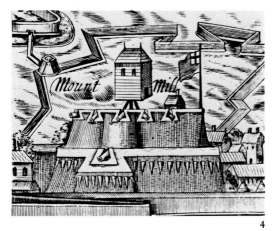

4

5

6

Royalist troops came to the capital. One dramatic Sunday morning 24,000 men were drawn up in defence at Turnham Green. They were a mixture of raw recruits and Edgehill veterans, but though not very impressive, they outnumbered the King's army by two to one. So the attack was not launched. After firing some cannon, the King made a tactical withdrawal during the afternoon, and at Kingston the gates were opened to him by Royalists. These matters were to be settled not in London but at Naseby.

1. The equestrian statue of Charles I, ordered by Lord Weston for his garden, and now in Whitehall, was not set up until 1676, forty-three years after it was cast. During the Civil War Royalists hid it in the crypt of St Paul's, Covent Garden. When Cromwell's men discovered the statue in 1655, they gave it to a Holborn brazier, John Rivett, to be destroyed. But Rivett preserved it, disguising his action by selling souvenirs said to be made from the melted-down brass. The sculptor was Hubert Le Sueur for whom the King sat. The pedestal is probably by Wren.

2. The execution of the Earl of Strafford.

3. 'A Plan of the City and Suburbs of London as fortified by Order of Parliament in the Years 1642 & 1643' drawn by George Vertue for Maitland's *History of London* (1738). It is said to be based on a lost map by Hollar. A battery and small redoubt (17) was on the present site of Buckingham Palace. Other important forts were at New River Head (9), junction of Oxford Street and Wardour Street (14), Hyde Park Corner (16), in Tothill Fields (19), Vauxhall (20), and spanning Newington Road at its juncture with Borough High Street (22). Contemporary accounts name additional forts at Rotherhithe, Nine Elms, and in St George's Fields (half-way between 20 and 21).

4. The only contemporary and authentic view of the fortifications is a woodcut from a 1643 broadside. It shows Mount Hill Fort (6), Finsbury (present site: the intersection of Goswell Road and Seward Street). The first fort to be erected, it was two storeys high and commanded Finsbury Fields. A trench dyke connected it with the next battery to the west at St John Street.

5. The fortifications passed about 300 yards north of Southampton House (11), Holborn, and when it was rebuilt as Bedford House, Bloomsbury Square, after the Civil War, the breastworks were incorporated as a natural feature of the gardens. With the final demolition of the house in 1800, the fortifications disappeared under what is now Russell Square.

6. An anti-Papist demonstration in Cheapside, May 1643, when the thirteenth-century Eleanor Cross was pulled down. A Cromwellian Troop of Horse and two Companies of Foot stood guard over the operation. As the actual cross fell from the summit, trumpets sounded a fanfare, and applauding spectators threw their caps into the air.

The Trial and Execution of Charles I

As London lay under a black frost in January 1649, Charles I was brought a prisoner to St James's Palace. The three and a half years of uncertainty and intrigue since the Royalist defeat at Naseby were over. Across the Park, the Great Hall of Westminster was being cleared of booths and tradespeople, and prepared for the King's trial. The next day, 20 January, he was carried by sedan chair to Whitehall Palace, and then by water to Westminster to avoid the possibility of Royalist demonstrations in New Palace Yard.

Defiantly wearing his hat, and resolutely refusing to plead or even acknowledge the court, Charles faced the charge of treason for levying war 'against the parliament and kingdom of England'. He sat aloof in an armchair of crimson velvet, facing his judges and with his back to the spectators from whom he was separated by a wooden barrier.

The trial lasted four days. Of the 135 Commissioners ordered by Parliament to serve as the jury, only 68 answered the roll. Among the absentees was Lord Fairfax, Cromwell's Commander-in-Chief of the Army. He was utterly opposed to any trial which might result in the King's death, and, when his name was called, Lady Fairfax shouted down from a gallery, 'He has far too much wit to be here!'

The judicial challenge to the divine right of the monarchy cut deep into the conscience of a divided nation. Its outcome – the pre-determined verdict of an armed minority – had neither justice nor the will of the nation behind it. When John Bradshaw, the presiding judge, pronounced sentence of death, the King's guards, under orders, chorused 'Execution!' and blew tobacco smoke into the royal face. 'Poor souls,' observed Charles with magnanimity, 'for sixpence they would do the same for their commanders.' As the news of the verdict passed through the streets, his subjects wept.

So that he should not hear the hammering of the scaffold going up outside the Banqueting Hall, Charles spent his last two nights not in the Palace of Whitehall, but at St James's. On the morning of his execution, Tuesday, 20 January, he slept peacefully until about 5.30 a.m. when he drew back his bedcurtains. 'Though it has not long to stand on my shoulders, take all the care you can of my head,' he said to his barber. He decided to wear three shirts lest the crowd should mistake shivering for cowardice.

At ten o'clock, accompanied by Dr Juxon, the Bishop of London, and Col. Tomlinson, his gaoler, Charles set out, walking briskly between a double line of infantry, through St James's Park to Whitehall. He crossed the already crowded street by way of the long corridor in the Holbein Gate that served as a bridge between the two halves of the palace. In his bedroom he received the Last Sacrament, passed through the Banqueting Hall and out through a first-floor window on to the scaffold.

Whitehall was packed. Every window was filled. Spectators clambered on roofs for a view. But the King saw that they were being kept too far away to hear the speech he had prepared. So he addressed his last words to the fifteen or so persons on the scaffold. The winter sun was shining brightly at two o'clock when the King removed his cloak and doublet. With the final mysterious admonition to Juxon – the one word, 'Remember!' – he placed his head on the low block.

The axe fell, and, as one young man in the crowd recorded, 'There was such a dismal universal groan amongst the thousands of people who were in sight of it, as it were with one consent, as I never heard before and desire I may not hear again.'

1. King Charles I faces his judges.

2. In hat and dark suit, and wearing the insignia of the Garter, the King as he appeared at his trial.

3. All impressions of the execution, even if contemporary, take artistic liberties. The scaffold could not possibly have come up to the top floor windows of the Banqueting Hall, as shown. It was built at first floor level, probably at the north end and extending only as far as the second window down Whitehall. Which window did the King use? The second window from the north – the Charing Cross end – is traditionally known as 'King Charles's window'. But in 1649 a narrow two-storey building abutted the north end of the Banqueting Hall (as shown in 5), and it was through the first floor window of this annex that Charles probably approached his death.

4. Lord and Lady Fairfax, the King's ardent supporters.

WHITE HALL

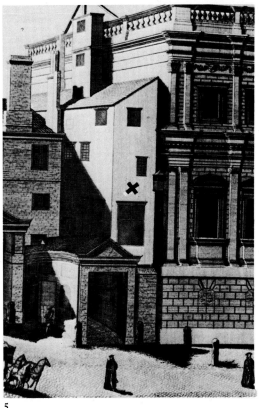

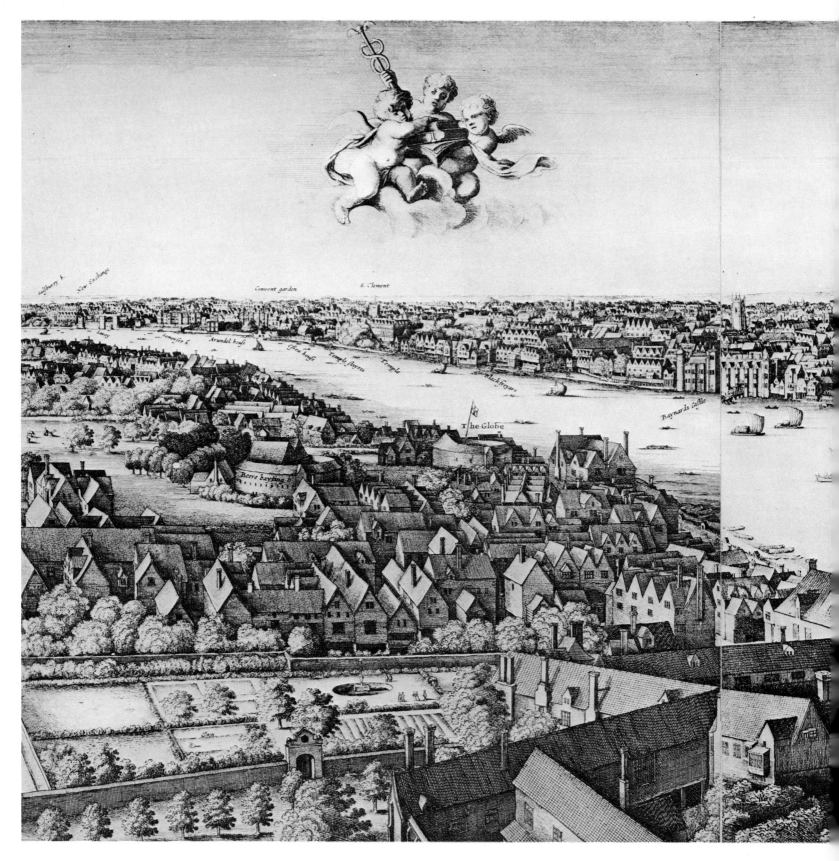

Hollar's View

From the tower of St Saviour's – now Southwark Cathedral – Hollar looks north-westwards over mid-seventeenth-century London. He follows the southward curve of the river as far as Salisbury House (site of Shell-Mex House today) and the New Exchange in the Strand. Immediately below us is Winchester House, the rambling remnant of the historic bishops' palace. No

bishop has lived there for twenty years, and in 1642 it was converted into a prison. Next door to the Clink, it provides yet another gaol for a rowdy neighbourhood. The palace has acquired outbuildings since we saw it in Visscher's panorama, and application has been made to convert the quadrangle and stables to the south into a riding school. The episcopal property is soon due to be broken up completely, but Hollar shows a walled and well-kept garden still existing.

Bankside is now crowded with quite imposing houses, a distinct improvement on the rows of alehouses and watermen's lodgings of Tudor times. The detail with which they are drawn is typical of Hollar's meticulous, realistic style. Where Visscher conventionalized his panorama with a straight riverfront and extravagantly soaring spires, Hollar is concerned with perspective and correct proportions. There are minor topographical mistakes, probably because the

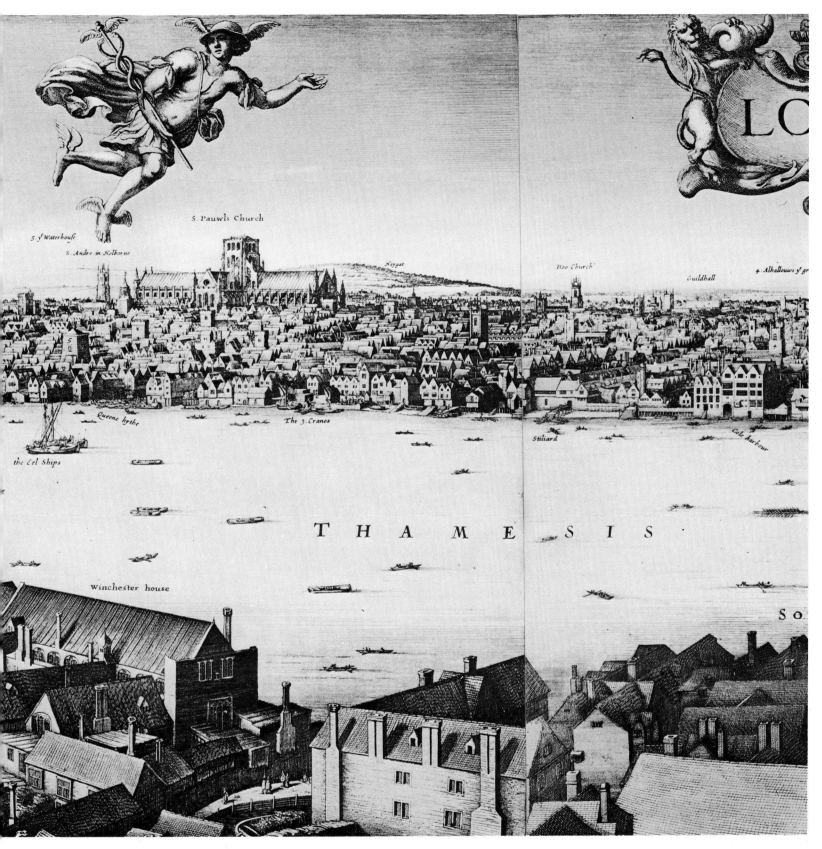

S. of Waterhouse

S. Andre in Holborne

S. Pauwls Church

Heygat

Boo Church

Guildhall

4. Alhallouws of gr

LO

Queene hythe

The 3. Cranes

Stiliard

Cole harbour

the Eel Ships

T H A M E S I S

winchester house

So

panorama was published in Antwerp in 1647 at which date the artist who had fought with the Royalists had been banished from England for four years. His long view (of which this is only the easterly section) must have been based on sketches he made before his exile and partly on memory. This would account for the appearance of the second Globe though it had been pulled down in 1644, and for confusing it with the Bear-Baiting pit (*Beere bayting h*). The Globe lay to the south-

east of the Bear Garden, and the nearer building has a double-gabled tiring house, or dressing room, essential for a theatre but not wanted for a bear pit. Obviously the two inscriptions should be transposed.

As in Visscher, two eel ships are anchored off *Queene hythe*. As early as 1224 there were Dutch eel boats in the Thames, and by this time they were obviously an accepted part of the river scene. According to legend, the Dutch were given perpetual rights to

river moorings for their eel ships by Charles II after 1665 because they brought in supplies during the Plague. This is improbable as England was then at war with Holland. But certainly in 1699 William III granted his fellow-countrymen exclusive foreign landing rights for fish at Billingsgate. Though they had no charter to prove this, the Dutch held tenaciously to these rights, and until the Second World War kept two ships moored off the Customs House.

When the House was to let

Four years after the execution of Charles I, another trial of strength took place at Westminster between the country's leader and the country's Parliament. It was now Cromwell's turn to learn the stubborn opposition of the House of Commons to individual power; and, just as Charles went into St Stephen's to arrest the Five Members, so Cromwell entered the chamber in April 1653, to expel the Rump Parliament.

The evening before, the Lord General had held a large, informal conference of politicians and soldiers at his house in Whitehall. He had received, as he thought, an undertaking from the Members not to go further with their Bill designed to extend the Long Parliament in a way which gave the existing members a monopoly of power. But the next morning messengers hurried up Whitehall with the news that the Bill was being rushed through at once.

Considering himself betrayed, Cromwell went down to the House at the head of a file of troops. He left the soldiers outside, strode through the door in Westminster Hall (then the only access to the Commons) and into St Stephen's. Grimly he sat down to listen to the debate until, with the whispered aside, 'This is the time I must do it', he rose and denounced the House. In the ensuing hubbub, Cromwell violently accused members of being drunkards and whoremongers who had trifled with the nation. 'You are no Parliament, I say you are no Parliament; I will put an end to your sittings!' he shouted, and signed to his lieutenant to let in the troops.

The Speaker and the more defiant Members were jerked from their seats. The mace—emblem of the House's authority—was seized from the table and thrown down. 'What have we to do with this bauble?' said Cromwell. 'Take it away!' Disregarding, like Charles, outraged cries of 'Privilege!' he turned out all the Members by force. Then he locked the door of the empty House and put the key in his pocket. Next day someone pinned a notice on the door—'This house to Lett now Unfurnished.'

At the time of Cromwell's dramatic move, the House of Commons had been occupying the medieval chapel of St Stephen (page 34) for just over a hundred years. The secular conversion, which took place in Edward VI's reign, had been easily made. The Speaker's chair replaced the altar under the great East window. The choir stalls became benches for members. Where the screen had divided choir from nave was the 'Bar of the House'. The small nave became 'the Lobby'. Though St Stephen's was to be rebuilt and has been replaced, the form of the House has not altered essentially to this day.

Hollar's 1647 etching, right, shows *Parlament House* at right angles to Westminster Hall. Because the chapel was too lofty for parliamentary comfort, a false ceiling was put in below the upper range of windows. Tapestries covered the walls, and the lower windows were partially plastered up. The Star Chamber was in the house with six gables which stands between Westminster Hall and the river.

The Great Seal of the Commonwealth, above, bearing the inscription, 'In the Third Year of Freedome by God's Blessing Restored 1651', depicts the Long Parliament in Session. It is valuable in presenting an unexaggerated impression of the size of the chamber, then hung with tapestries. The tapestries were replaced by panelling early in the eighteenth century.

Be gone you rogues
You haue Sate long enough

C: Caper   C: Lam   G. O Cromvel   This is an Oule.

4

Ciuitatis Weſtmonaſterienſis pars

Parlament Houſe   the Hall

5

1. Oliver Cromwell – the portrait by Peter Lely, showing a wart under his lower lip, perhaps painted in the artist's studio in Covent Garden. The Lord Protector's famous injunction was recorded by Horace Walpole: 'Mr Lely, I desire you would use all your skill to paint my picture truly like me, and not flatter me at all; but remark all the roughnesses, pimples, warts and everything, otherwise I will never pay a farthing for it.'

2. In this house, tradition has it, Cromwell lived with his family for six years prior to 1654. Houses in many parts of London have been popularly ascribed to Cromwell, and the position of this one cannot be pinpointed with certainty. But it was probably on the St James's side of Whitehall. Four months after he was made Lord Protector, he moved into Whitehall Palace. Attempts to cope economically with their vast new home and the palace servants constantly frustrated the thrifty Mrs Cromwell.

3. The Great Seal of the Commonwealth.

4. The dissolving of the Long Parliament, as depicted in a satirical Dutch engraving of the period. Cromwell, in cloak and plumed hat, accompanied by other army officers, arrives at the bar of the House and says, 'Begone you rogues, you have Sate long enough.' (There are numerous variations of the words.) Four obey. General Worsley at the table directs clerks to remove books. In the background Major-General Harrison with soldiers pulls the Speaker from his chair. The mace has been picked up by an officer on the right of the Speaker. The little dogs may be caricatures of the British lion enforcing order. The owl, a figure of learned solemnity, probably satirizes all men who sit in committee – here the Parliamentary body.

5. Hollar's view from the river.

The Restoration

All fountains in the City ran with wine on 29 May 1660, the day that Charles II rode into his capital and monarchy was restored to England. Cannons were fired from the Tower. Decoration hung from every window. For eleven years the country had been without a king, but now the Lord Protector was dead, and on this fine sunny day which was also the King's thirtieth birthday Puritan black gave way to coloured silks.

The reception began at Blackheath whence Charles had travelled on the long journey back – via Breda, Dover and Canterbury – from his enforced exile. After inspecting the whole army, he started towards London. At Greenwich there was a great bonfire; in Deptford girls danced ahead of his white horse scattering spring flowers; and at Lambeth the Lord Mayor surrendered his sword of state–symbol of the City's jealously guarded rights of independence–and Charles returned it.

Bowing to all the enthusiasm in the crowded streets, the King remarked ironically that he now realized that he should have come back sooner. Watching in the Strand, the diarist John Evelyn thanked God that the Restoration had been achieved without a drop of blood being spilt. It might so easily have been otherwise; for many who were cheering the King had been his father's enemies. In a plumed hat, and riding behind the Lord Mayor, he approached the Royal Palace of Whitehall with an escort of five regiments of cavalry. The street was lined on both sides with leading citizens in velvet coats and gold chains, but their cheers could not completely drown reminders of the bitter past. Outside the Banqueting Hall, women sat in tiered stands erected on the very spot where Charles I had been executed.

Both Houses of Parliament had been waiting for many hours to kiss his hand, the Commons in the Banqueting Hall, the Lords in the Great Hall of the Palace. He had hoped to be there by midday, but so great had been the welcome, that he did not arrive until seven in the evening. It had been a long day, one too charged with emotion to sum up in a speech of thanks. 'I am so disordered by my journey,' he said, 'and with the noise still sounding in my ears (which I confess was pleasing to me because it expressed the affections of my people) as I am unfit at present to make such reply as I desire.' Then, with a promise to restore freedom and happiness to the nation, the King closed the door on a still celebrating London.

1. Charles II's arrival at the Banqueting Hall.
2. Triumphal Arch erected in Fleet Street for the Coronation procession.
3. The King in his Coronation robes.

1

3

2

4. The ceremony in Westminster Abbey. There was a lapse of a year after his return before Charles II was crowned, sitting on a great scarlet dais before the altar in the Abbey. The traditional progress from the Tower and the Coronation service were carried out with full medieval splendour for the last time. The delay made it possible to replace the Crown Jewels which had been seized during the Commonwealth and 'totally broken and defaced'. The regalia are mostly those used to this day.

4

The Royal Park

To the west of Whitehall lay St James's Park, a walled royal precinct which Charles developed in the style of the gardens at Versailles. To the menagerie of exotic animals installed by James I, and the small landscape improvements made by his father, Charles now added the Canal. This long rectangular strip of ornamental water (page 166) was similar to one laid out by Le Nôtre at Versailles, and there is some evidence that the King invited the French architect to London to design it.

Charles enjoyed exercise and was a great walker. The park, so convenient to his palace, was the scene of almost daily promenades. Surrounded by courtiers, he might visit the Royal Aviary to feed the birds. Moved from the palace and enlarged, the Aviary was on the south side and gave rise to Birdcage Walk. A brisk 'constitutional' in the direction of Hyde Park would take him up what, in consequence, is now Constitution Hill. Sometimes he had an entourage, as seen left. Sometimes a foreign emissary panted in the wake of his quick stride. But often he walked unattended, pleased to be seen by his subjects, who had permission to use the grounds. His brother, James, whose official residence was St James's Palace on the north side of the park, once chided him about the dangers of this practice. Charles brushed it aside. 'They will never kill me,' he replied, 'to make you king!'

In the tree-lined walk in front of the gardens of St James's Palace was played the game which gave the Mall its name. 'Pelemele' was how Pepys spelt it, and when he first saw it in April 1661, the Duke of York was playing. It was also a popular sport with the King. In their father's time, and perhaps earlier, it had started on the site of the road we now call Pall Mall. But for greater convenience the long alleyway was moved into the park. For a while this was also called Pall Mall, but then, presumably to avoid confusion, this was shortened to the Mall. Curiously little is known about the game itself. In France, where it originated, it was called 'paille-maille' (from *palla*, a ball, and *malleus*, a mallet), and seems to have been a cross between golf and croquet. It was played on a ground of crushed shells in an alley which, as can be seen, above right, has wooden sides. It was about 850 yards long, there was a hoop at each end and several balls appear to be in play simultaneously.

Walking in the park in 1671, Evelyn saw Charles 'in very familiar discourse' with 'Mrs Nellie as they cal'd an impudent comedian, she looking out of her garden on a terrace at the top of the wall and [the King] standing on the greene walk under it.' This

was the garden of the house which the King gave Nell Gwynn on the south side of Pall Mall backing on to the park. At first the gift was only on lease, but the story goes that she returned the conveyance to Charles saying that, as she had 'always conveyed free under the Crown', she would not accept it save as a freehold. This she was granted, and lived there until her death in 1687 when the house passed to the Duke of St Albans, her son by Charles. The house has been swallowed up, but the site (the present No 79) remains the only freehold on the south side of Pall Mall which does not belong to the Crown.

The only surviving house associated with Nell Gwynn is in Fulham. This is Sandford Manor, below right, between the King's Road (i.e. King Charles II's road) and the Thames just to the west of Stanley Bridge. The tradition of her ownership–there is no printed reference before 1812–is based on a plaster medallion found on the estate, a thimble with the initials N.G. on it, and a Freemason's badge, supposed to have belonged to Charles II, discovered under floorboards. Nell Gwynn's mother may also have lived there, for she is known to have resided in Chelsea and was drowned in the Thames in 1679.

4

1. Accompanied by his courtiers, and by his pet dogs which caused him to be nicknamed the 'King of Curs', Charles II strolls in St James's Park. In the background is that part of the royal palace which lay on the West side of Whitehall. The covered, external stairway led to a long straight corridor on the first floor by which Whitehall could be crossed above the arch of the Holbein Gate (the turrets of which are seen), to the right of the Banqueting Hall, and so into the main part of the palace. The cow, which shows such lese-majesty by turning its back on the King, must be descended from the herd which Mrs Cromwell introduced into the park so that the palace should enjoy fresh milk.

2. 'Pale Maille, a game wherein a round bowle is with a mallet struck through a high arch of iron (standing at either end of an alley) which he that can do it at the fewest blows, or at the number agreed on, wins. This game was heretofore used in the long alley near St James's and vulgarly called Pell-Mell.' – from *Glossographia* (ed. 1670) by Thomas Blount. This detail is from an early eighteenth-century print.

3. Another view of the game being played, in a detail from Kip, c. 1710. Comparison between Rocque's (1746) map and the modern Ordnance Survey suggests that the alley ran from the Victoria Memorial to the Duke of York's Steps and was on the line of the present tree-lined walk on the north of the Mall.

4. Nell Gwynn when she was about twenty. After her death in 1687, seventeen years later, she was buried in the chancel of St Martin-in-the-Fields when a funeral sermon 'much in her praise' was preached by a future Archbishop of Canterbury.

5. Sandford Manor. A photograph taken about 1960. Then owned by the North Thames Gas Board, and situated in unromantic proximity to its gasholders, the house has survived demolition threats. In 1972 it was bought by a firm which plans to include it in a new housing scheme.

3

5

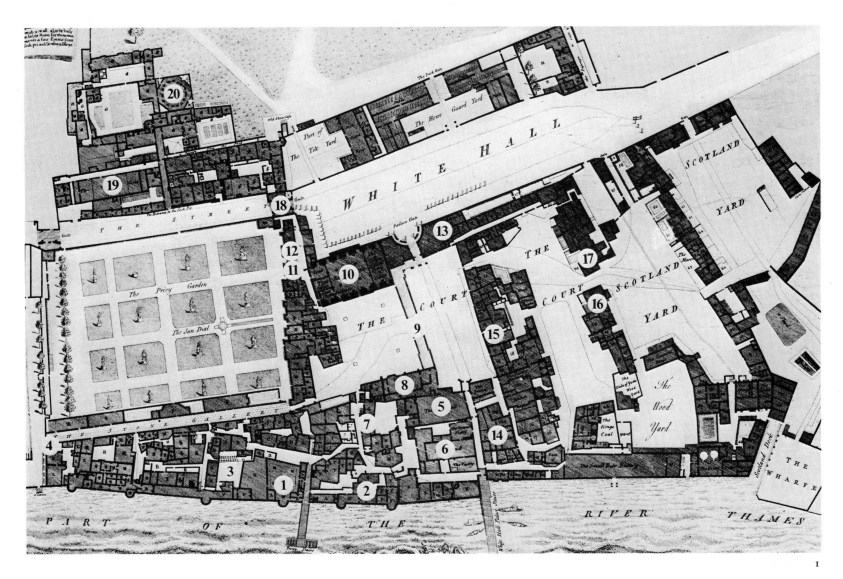

Whitehall Palace

Charles II inherited a palace which a French visitor described as 'ill built, and nothing but a heap of houses erected at divers times and of different models'. More like a small village, Whitehall was a maze of irregular courtyards and narrow passageways. It provided 2,000 rooms for officials and courtiers as well as riverside apartments for the King (1) and Queen (2) and homes for Charles's mistresses, at least five of whom lived there openly. A few impressive buildings like the Great Hall and the Banqueting Hall gave the palace some dignity. But it was most inconveniently pierced by two public rights-of-way, one running north to south from Charing Cross to Westminster, the other from the street of Whitehall to the Thames at Whitehall Palace Stairs.

The above plan, based on a survey of about 1670, shows two sides of the King's Privy Garden flanked by buildings. These were given a unity by two long galleries at first floor level. The Privy Gallery, at least a hundred yards long, stretched south from the Holbein Gate (18 and below right) almost to the Privy Stairs. Off and below it were some of the chief rooms of the palace. It was joined at right angles by the Long Gallery which was over the Stone Gallery. On the west, the Privy Garden was screened from the public in *The Street* by a high wall.

John Evelyn tells how one October day in 1664 he met the King in the Privy Gallery and was taken by him to a window. Charles asked for paper and crayon, and then, 'laying it on the window-stool he with his own hand design'd to me the plot for the future building of White-hall, together with the roomes of State and other particulars'. Lack of money meant that Webb's overall plan (page 116–17) had to be discarded for piecemeal improvements. The King refashioned the main entrance from *White Hall* into *The Court* and erected a gallery (9) which divided the public way to the river from the royal precincts at the back of the Banqueting Hall. He built a chemical laboratory (12), converted the Great Hall (5) into a theatre, and redesigned his own apartments. Indulging his passion for games, he built an indoor tennis court (19) where Pepys was amused to note he climbed on to scales before and after each game to see how much weight he had lost.

His mistress, the Countess of Castlemain was lodged above and near the Holbein Gate, but for her successor, the Duchess of

1. King's Apartments.
2. Queen's Apartments.
3. Apartments of Maids of Honour. Courtyard used for King's Aviary (moved to St James's Park, 1668).
4. Site of Duchess of Portsmouth's apartments (built 1671 and subsequent to this survey, improved 1678, burnt down 1691).
5. Great Hall (built 1528, burnt down 1698).
6. Chapel Royal (date unknown but probably pre-Tudor, burnt down 1698).
7. Presence Chamber.
8. Wine Cellar (Tudor, extant but lowered 19 feet during 1950 rebuilding scheme).
9. New Gallery (built 1669).
10. Banqueting Hall (built 1622, extant).
11. Treasury.
12. King's Laboratory.
13. The Wardrobe.
14. Block containing pantry, buttery, and cellars.
15. Kitchen and domestic offices.
16. King's Music House.
17. Lord Chamberlain's Office.
18. Holbein Gate (built 1532, demolished 1759) and Countess of Castlemain's lodgings.
19. The Tennis Court (built 1662, still in use 1768, demolished by 1812).
20. The Cockpit (built 1533, converted into theatre 1632, demolished 1675).

Portsmouth, the King built really imposing apartments–virtually a mansion–at the extreme southern end of the Stone Gallery (4). Two other favourites, 'La Belle Stuart' and Winifred Wells–both Maids of Honour–had lodgings round the courtyard which housed the King's Aviary (3).

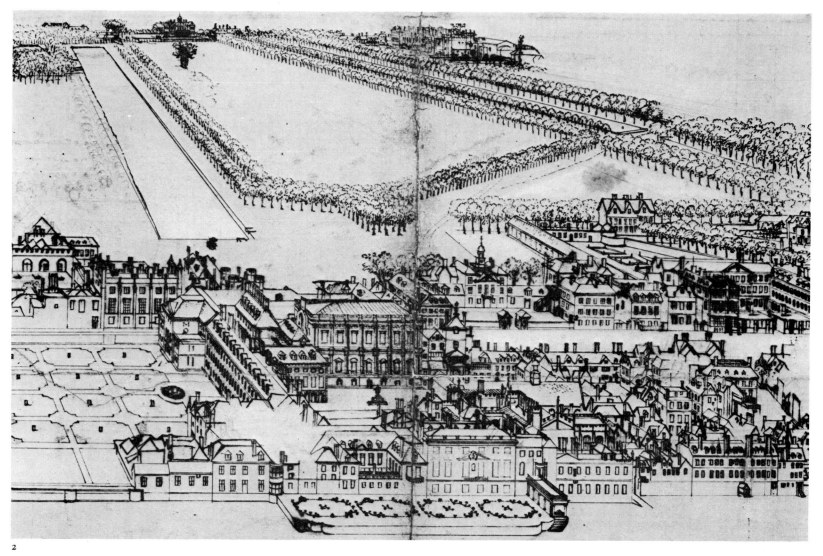

2

3

4

Charles supped at the Duchess of Portsmouth's on the February night in 1685 when he had an apoplectic fit which led to his death five days later. In her apartments, too, started the fire which severely damaged the south-east of the palace in 1691. The drawing, above, compared with the plan, opposite, shows the extent of the damage. Again, by comparing this view, drawn about 1695, with Hollar's of 1645, left, we can see the changes brought about by Queen Mary whose riverside garden and apartments were designed by Wren. This 1695 view also shows the new Privy Gallery block built by Wren for James II. It is the last look we have at the palace, for in 1698 an even greater fire was started by a Dutch laundry girl who, drying some linen in an upper room, carried up an extra load of charcoal and carelessly left the clothes hanging near the fire. She died in the flames, and nearly every building was reduced to ruins. Whitehall ceased to be a royal palace and became simply a topographical expression.

1. Plan of Whitehall about 1670.
2. Whitehall looking west. Pen and ink drawing possibly by John Kip, c. 1695.
3. Hollar's 1645 view, based on his slightly earlier drawing.
4. Whitehall Palace from the street, looking south.

Theatre Revived

The theatre, moribund during the Commonwealth, received new stimulus from the King and his Court. With the Whitehall Cockpit so conveniently near the Palace, playgoing became an almost daily royal diversion. For some years, however, the monopoly of producing plays was granted to only two men, Thomas Killigrew and William D'Avenant. To Killigrew, who had shared his exile, and was his Master of the Revels, the King granted a patent for the first Theatre Royal. For three years this had its temporary home in a converted tennis court in Vere Street, Clare Market–the address and site now lost under Kingsway. Then, in 1663 Killigrew's Theatre Royal was built a few hundred yards farther west. It stood on the site of the present theatre at the corner of Russell Street and Brydges Street (now Catherine Street), but no picture of the original building survives.

To Charles, accustomed to seeing actresses on the stage in France, boys in girls' parts were absurd, and his charters for the new companies expressly required the employment of actresses. For once the King was on the side of the moralists. They were particularly critical of one boy actor, Edward Kynaston, who not only made an exceptionally beautiful woman on stage but went driving in the park in female costume. There were seven women in Killigrew's company, and one of them, probably Margaret Hughes, gave the first public performance by a woman on the stage when she appeared as Desdemona in 1660.

The other licensee, William D'Avenant, had staged masques for Charles I, and had kept the flame of the theatre at least flickering during Cromwell's time with private performances in the City. Now he opened in Salisbury Square, off Fleet Street, at a playhouse which had surreptitiously been used during the Commonwealth. A year later he moved to Lincoln's Inn Fields where he took over and converted Lisle's Tennis Court (identifiable in Hollar's bird's-eye view, top right) into the Duke's Theatre. This is said to have been the first public theatre to have a proscenium arch and the facilities to set and strike scenery during a play.

Ten years later D'Avenant moved from Lincoln's Inn Fields to Dorset Gardens by the Thames where Wren built him a fine theatre seating 1,200 people (top, far right). A scene from *The Empress of Morocco* (above right), produced there in 1673, gives us the earliest view of the interior of a Restoration theatre with picture-frame stage and realistic scenery. As Ogilby and Morgan's map shows, right, Dorset Gardens Theatre was just to the west of the Fleet, and had its main entrance facing the river.

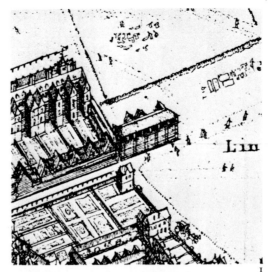

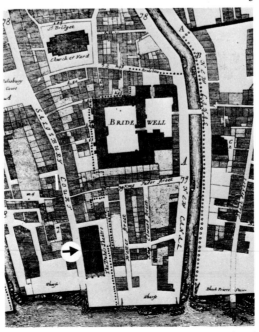

1. The tennis court in Lincoln's Inn Fields which D'Avenant converted into the first Duke's Theatre.

2. View of the Dorset Gardens Theatre, as it would be seen by a playgoer arriving by boat. This theatre, to which D'Avenant's company moved after leaving Lincoln's Inn Fields, had a fine classical facade in Wren's best manner.

3. Interior of the Dorset Gardens Theatre in 1673 showing a performance of a tragedy, *The Empress of Morocco*. The leading players were Thomas Betterton and his wife, who ensured the theatre's success after D'Avenant's death.

4. Margaret Hughes was a famous Desdemona for several years, but left the stage about 1670 when she became accredited mistress of Prince Rupert and was given a fine country house in Hammersmith. She gambled away all the money left her by the Prince and was then forced by necessity back to the stage.

5. 'Our trusty and well beloved' Thomas Killigrew, as the King called him, was dramatist as well as manager. Even Pepys blushed at his comedy, *The Parson's Wedding*. Nell Gwynn was in his company, and he opened a school for young actors in Barbican.

6. The exact position of Dorset Gardens Theatre, near Bridewell (on the present site of the City of London School), is arrowed on the Ogilby and Morgan map of 1676.

Samuel Pepys Esq., Londoner

Seventeenth-century historians fall back on Pepys as gratefully as they do on Stow or the drawings of Hollar. His diary, over a million and a quarter words long, which he kept from 1660 to 1669, is not only a mine of diverting gossip. It is an essential source book for Restoration London. Its writer was peculiarly equipped to keep it, for London dominated Pepys's whole life. He was probably born in Salisbury Court, off Fleet Street, and was brought up there over his father's tailoring shop. He was baptised at St Bride's, educated at St Paul's School, then near the Cathedral, and married at St Margaret's, Westminster. As Navy clerk and secretary to the Admiralty, Pepys was at the centre of public affairs and had an entrée nearly everywhere.

These qualifications were combined with a diarist's nose for scandal and occasion. As a boy of fifteen he was in Whitehall to see Charles I's execution. Twelve years later he was on the ship which brought Charles II back from exile, and in the Abbey for the King's Coronation. He courageously stayed in London during the Plague, and noted how grass grew in Whitehall. A reporter for posterity, he climbed the walls of the Tower and up the belfry of All Hallows, Barking, for a good view of the Fire.

This complete Londoner sat in Parliament as a Member, was briefly a prisoner in the Tower (accused of Papacy), and became President of the Royal Society. He died in Clapham and was buried in the City. Though not primarily an historian, or as concerned with topography as Stow, Pepys accumulated a valuable collection of London books and prints including many engravings by Hollar. When he moved in to No 14 Buckingham Street, the official Admiralty residence near Charing Cross, in 1688, he housed his library in a room overlooking the Thames. He bequeathed it to his nephew, John Jackson, for his life; and when Jackson died, it was sent to Pepys's old college at Cambridge, Magdalene, as he had asked. The library consisted of over 3,000 volumes and manuscripts, among which was the diary written in shorthand in six notebooks. It took four years to decipher and the major part of it was first published in 1825.

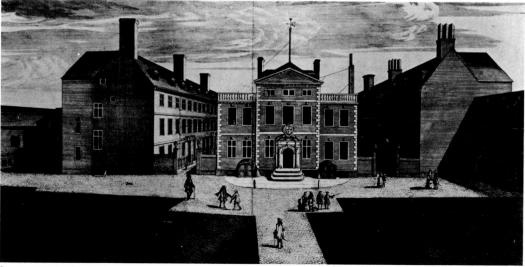

1. The diarist, aged thirty-three.

2. Pepys's library – a drawing from his London collection.

3. The Navy Office in Seething Lane, off Tower Hill, built to replace a previous Office burnt down in 1673. It was designed by either Wren or Robert Hooke, the City Surveyor. Pepys lost his house in the Fire, but most of the Navy records were salvaged and he saved his diary and books. To reduce fire risk the new Navy Office was built in the middle of a courtyard. As Secretary to the Admiralty, Pepys then moved farther west and nearer Whitehall. He set up house at No 12 Buckingham Street (later incorporated with No 14).

West Central London, 1658

'What will be the end of it, God knows!' exclaimed Pepys, as he contemplated the development of London in the middle of the seventeenth century. We can get an idea of the changes which prompted his remark from this astonishing bird's-eye view of the west-central area as it looked in 1658 or shortly afterwards. In a hundred years, rural meadows with grazing cattle and the Strand, which was only a thin line of small houses, have been transformed into a city where blocks of buildings, terraces, and houses four storeys high fill a maze of streets. Speculators have clearly defeated all the laws passed against overcrowding.

The invaluable Hollar reveals the growth that took place between Chancery Lane and St Martin's Lane – the great mass of it after 1600. His imaginative eye, hovering high above the Thames, looks north to Holborn. Running east to west, the street curves south by St Giles passing out of view just beyond an embryonic Tottenham Court Road. The straight section of New Oxford Street which cut out the loop from the top of Drury Lane to St Giles Circus was not built until 1847.

Dominating the centre of the view is Covent Garden Piazza (p. 117), completed about twenty years earlier, and the most important feature of the Bedford Estate. In this period of development the revenue is enormous from these forty acres, bounded by Long Acre, Drury Lane, the Strand and St Martin's Lane. Most of the estate is owned by the Earl of Bedford, and he was on the spot to manage it. At the time of Hollar's drawing, the fifth Earl is living in Bedford House (built 1586) which has a tower, a timber framed frontage with seven gables, and gardens stretching up to the Piazza.

During the Commonwealth, forty-five rooms of the Earl's house had been stripped and the contents sold because of his vacillating loyalties. But his business acumen remained completely consistent. Into a large Dutch chest, kept in Bedford House as a family bank, went rents from all the leased land and the income from his houses round the Piazza.

The property was to yield even more in the next century. The fifth Earl died at Bedford House in 1700, and shortly afterwards his son moved the family home from the Strand to Bloomsbury (p. 158). Bedford House was demolished and on the site were created the present Tavistock Street and Southampton Street (which gave the Piazza its first access from the Strand).

To the east of Bedford House, and built partly on ground acquired from the Bedfords, is a towering mansion, Exeter House (demolished 1676). Londoners of this period are still inclined to think of it as Burghley House because, in the previous century, it was the home of William Cecil, Lord Burghley, Queen Elizabeth's minister. But now · it belongs to his descendant, the Earl of Exeter.

The Bedfords must sometimes have felt themselves hemmed in by their close neighbours, the Cecils. Presumably because his son, Thomas, was heir to Burghley House, old Lord Burghley had built another smaller dwelling just to the east of it for his favourite second son, Sir Robert Cecil. But, very early in the century, Robert – by then he was Lord Salisbury – decided he wanted something grander, and created Salisbury House, centre foreground, on the other side of the Strand. This, in turn, passed to his son who erected the 'many gentle fair houses in a row' on the west side of St Martin's Lane.

Still notably vacant are the ten acres of marshland called St Giles's Fields, though the footpaths trodden by little figures anticipate Earlham Street and Monmouth Street which were to cross at Seven Dials when they were built in 1693. West of what is now Charing Cross Road is so barren it seems possible Hollar did not complete this part of the engraving.

In this pre-Kingsway period, Drury Lane provides the main diagonal artery to the north-west. It had been paved early in the century because so many carriages became bogged down in the mud. The name is derived from the Drury family whose house, rebuilt by the Earl of Craven, faces onto Drury Lane with a garden backing onto a street behind. We see Craven House just about the year the Earl is living there with Charles I's sister, the exiled Queen of Bohemia.

Between Drury Lane and Lincoln's Inn Fields lies Clare Market (*New Market*) built in 1657 by Lord Clare whose princely house, described as a palace, is somewhere in the immediate neighbourhood. The two buildings with colonnades, where meat and fish are sold three days a week, are in the middle of the small piazza. South-east of the market can be seen the gardens of New Inn and Clement's Inn ('where I think they will talk of mad Shallow yet'), now built over. This is an area Hollar knew intimately for he had lodgings by Clement's Inn at about this time.

The obelisk-shaped tower on the river by Arundel House (*Ye Waterhouse*) narrows down the date to the decade between 1655 and 1665, while the state of building round Lincoln's Inn Fields make 1658 the most likely year. But it also incorporates some seemingly post-Restoration features. This suggests that the artist may have spread the laborious survey that would have been necessary over a number of years. The view is almost certainly part of a larger plan, though no other sheets have survived.

A Last Look at Old St Paul's

For more than 400 years a part-Norman, part-Gothic St Paul's dominated London. But now we are looking at the great medieval cathedral for the last time. Its destruction in September 1666 meant the passing of a famous landmark, and the disappearance of the nave (right) which from early times had served London for secular as well as religious purposes. It was used as a meeting place, promenade, shopping centre on wet days, and as a thoroughfare for those wanting a short cut between Ludgate and the City.

But the Fire also solved a headache for the authorities. The fabric had never completely recovered from the Elizabethan disaster when the spire was struck by lightning, collapsed, and set fire to the roof. Foundations and vaulting were cracked, and the upper walls of the nave thrust out of true.

Charles I had raised a fund of over £100,000 for restoration, and Inigo Jones encased the west part of the Cathedral in ashlar masonry, a fabric which, as can be seen, far right, seems unsympathetic for a Gothic building. He then indulged his classical fancy by grafting a Roman portico (fig. 4) on to the west front. During the Commonwealth, St Paul's was treated as a symbol of papacy. The Repair Fund was confiscated and the interior destroyed. Cavalry mounts were stabled under its massive arches. Some of the scaffold shoring up the central tower was removed and sold to provide a colonel with arrears of pay. As a result, part of the roof fell in and the south transept was reduced to ruins.

To see what could be done to save the crumbling, desecrated St Paul's, a Royal Commission was set up at the Restoration. One member was a rather surprising choice. He was an Oxford professor of astronomy, Christopher Wren, who at that date had not a single building to his name. Wren's suggestions were radical. The central tower must come down. It should be rebuilt not with a spire but a dome. This idea, backed by his own drawings, had a very mixed reception, and to give Wren a chance to explain it to an expert committee, the Dean, Dr William Sancroft, arranged a meeting in the Cathedral. This took place on 27 August 1666.

Everyone was a little tense on the hot, dry day, when the committee started on its tour of inspection accompanied by workmen with plumblines and measuring rods to take readings at Wren's requests. Wren, carrying his plans, knew that he had John Evelyn, the diarist, to back him up, and that the Dean was half on his side. His adversaries were a fashionable architect, and another man whose main concern was economy. Under the tower with its cracked pillars he unrolled the

NAVIS ECCLESIÆ CATHEDRALIS S. PAVLI. PROSPECTVS INTERIOR.

1

ECCLESIÆ CATHED S. PAVLI. A MERIDIE. PROS

2

3

drawings of his proposed dome. It would, he insisted, make St Paul's an even greater landmark.

His suggestions were closely argued, but by the time the tactful Sancroft was steering his party across the road to the Deanery for refreshments, the committee had been more or less won round to Wren's dome. Six days later, however, all these deliberations were to be confounded by the outbreak of the Great Fire.

1. The Norman nave, looking eastwards towards the choir, as it appeared two years before the Fire. Its twelve bays and plain Early English vaulting show no signs of the dilapidation causing so much concern in other parts of the Cathedral.

2. South view of St Paul's.

3. All that remains of old St Paul's – the foundations of the cloisters and chapter house on the south side, charred and blackened by the Fire.

4. 'For a structure comparable to any in Europe' was Evelyn's description of Inigo Jones's portico of Corinthian columns. It was built sometime after 1633. Charles I paid for it out of his own purse. This post-Fire view shows the portico without the statues of James I and Charles I which stood on the two middle pedestals in the balustrade.

4

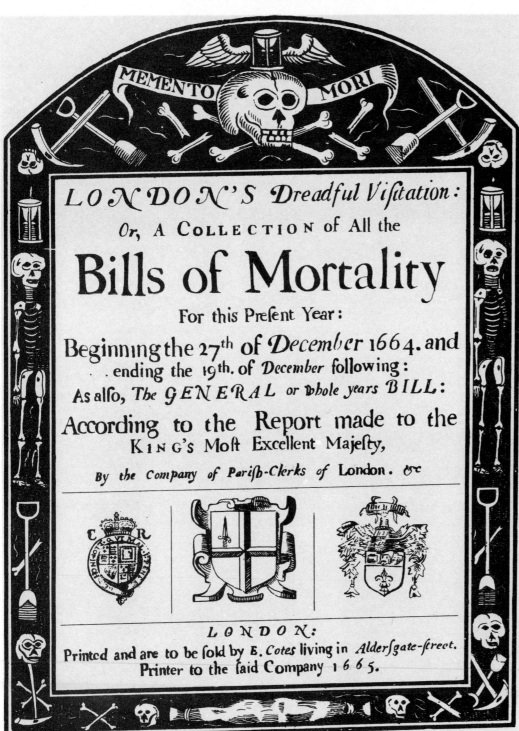

1. Londoners fleeing from the plague arrive in the country – woodcut from a broadside exhorting country people to give them help during an earlier outbreak in 1630.

2. Title page of a special edition of the Bills of Mortality. Parish clerks sent weekly lists of deaths and their causes to the Company of Parish Clerks which co-ordinated and printed them. This provided warning of plague epidemics. The Bills were sold to the public for 1d. or for an annual subscription of 4s.

3. A red cross on the locked door marks a London house visited by the plague. Over it is a notice on which would be inscribed: 'Lord have mercy on us'. With a raised stick, a dog killer is about to strike. Dogs, like cats, were widely thought to carry the disease wrongly supposed to be contagious. Black rats, real harbourers of infected fleas, were not suspected.

4. In a single room are seen all the horrors of the plague when houses were sealed and families cooped up together in fatal proximity. Plague quarantine (first imposed under an order of Henry VIII's time) was forty days. Two victims together in the bed on the right are approached by a doctor. A woman, lame with plague sores, carries a stick. A coffin lies ready for one body that is laid out.

5. The very first case in the Great Plague appears in the burial register of St Paul's, Covent Garden, seen here as the background to the pall-bearers. They are preceded by a man carrying a warning bell and two women searchers whose white wands mark them as official 'searchers' for plague victims.

6. As churchyards overflowed, plague pits had to be dug in open ground in many outlying parishes. Near the church at Aldgate, perhaps depicted here, 1,114 corpses from this parish and Whitechapel were thrown, according to Defoe, into one 'dreadful gulf' in a fortnight.

7. As the plague subsided, people trickled back to London. By December (when the first week's mortality roll was down to 210) country coaches and carriers' waggons were loaded with returning refugees. Here they are seen coming into the City from the north.

The Great Plague

When Margaret Ponteous, a doctor's daughter, was buried at St Paul's, Covent Garden, on 12 April 1665, the cause of death was given briefly. 'Pla' was all the clerk wrote in the church register. The symptoms of bubonic plague were all too well known. Inflamed blotches, purple, black or scarlet on the body, swelling in groin or armpit. Since 1603 there had been only four years without some deaths from the dreaded and familiar scourge. Margaret's death gave no clue to suggest the start of the worst epidemic in London's history.

The next plague death came a week later, this time in St Giles-in-the-Fields. Attempts by the parish officer to seal the infected house were frustrated. Neighbours wiped the red cross off the door, and released the inmates. Deaths in this district of crowded tenements multiplied rapidly – over a hundred in the second week of June – and infection, carried by fleas, spread along Holborn and down Chancery Lane to the Strand. In the City the worst affected parish was Cripplegate which lost 6,640 people during the three months, July, August and September.

In the hot, rainless weather, the death roll mounted alarmingly. Plague carts rumbled through the streets carrying naked bodies to quickly dug pits. All who could fled. Probably two-thirds of the population went into the country, and the Court moved to Oxford. In Whitehall the sole representative of the Government was George Monck, Duke of Albemarle, and in the City Sir William Lawrence, the Lord Mayor, stayed behind to organize relief.

During the worst week in the middle of September over 12,000 died, and bodies lay about the streets or in houses because burials could not keep pace with death. Quack remedies abounded. Doctors were brave but helpless. The streets glowed with fires lit in the vain belief that they would purge 'the infectious air'. There was a final spasm of horror during this month before things improved. The disease suddenly became more virulent: victims died in forty-eight hours instead of four to five days. But as autumn gave way to freezing winter the mortality figures fell. By Christmas many refugees felt it safe to come back, though the King did not return until February.

How many really died will never be known. Many deaths were concealed by families fearful that they would be locked up with the victims. Thousands were shovelled into mass graves without record. In the official Bill of Mortality 68,596 deaths are attributed to the disease. The true figure is probably nearer 110,000. If so, the Great Plague claimed one person in three who remained in London.

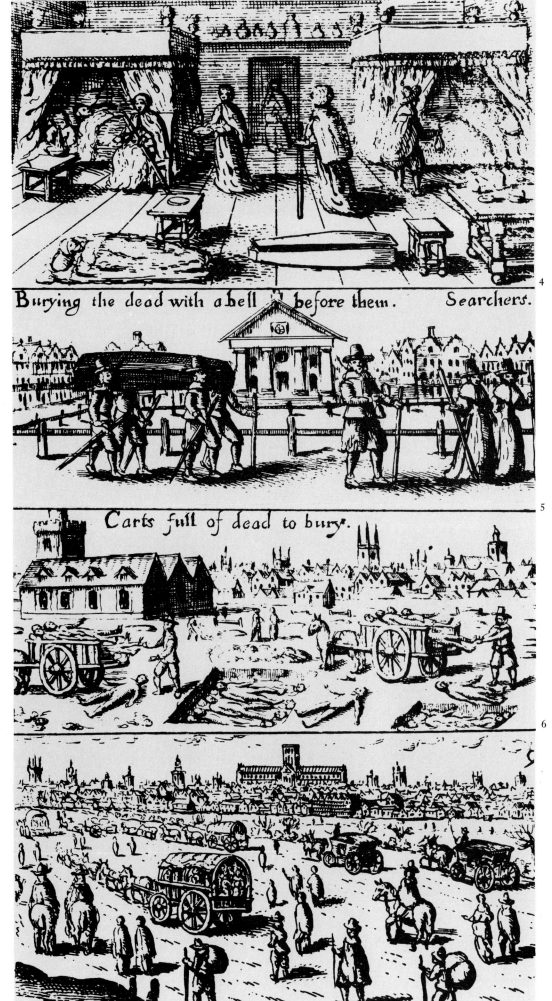

Burying the dead with a bell before them. Searchers.

Carts full of dead to bury.

141

Abbildung der Statt LONDON, sambt dem erschröcklichen brandt daselsten, so 4. tagen lange gewehrt hatt. A: 1666. im 7bris.

1

Diary of the Disaster

Sunday, 2 September   Fire broke out in Pudding Lane between 1 a.m. and 2 a.m. By morning 300 houses reported on fire. North end of London Bridge alight by 8 a.m. Flames reported creeping north uphill from Thames Street. The Steelyard blazing all afternoon. During the night the City Halls of the Companies of Plumbers, Parish Clerks and Joiners caught fire.

Monday, 3 September   Fine sunny day. Fire burning on half-mile of river front west of London Bridge and on a line with Cannon Street to the north. Reaches Baynard's Castle by 9 a.m. By 3 p.m. whole of Lombard Street and Royal Exchange consumed. Merchants refuse to allow demolition. Billingsgate, only 150 yards from outbreak, catches at 6 p.m.

Tuesday, 4 September   The worst day. Fire north of Threadneedle Street. Cheapside destroyed. St Paul's caught at 8 p.m. Organized demolition started. Guildhall catches. Flames burst through City wall into Liberties by way of Ludgate. Over Fleet Ditch. Prisoners in the Fleet released. Salisbury Theatre and Inner Temple on fire. Wind rose in evening before subsiding.

Wednesday, 5 September   Five-sixths of City destroyed. Fall of wind and demolition effective and fire checked by midnight. Fears of fresh outbreaks from sparks blown from smouldering buildings. Royal Proclamation for Relief.

Thursday, 6 September   Two hundred soldiers brought in to prevent further outbreaks. But fire decisively halted at Fetter Lane, Cock Lane, and All Hallows, Barking. King addressed refugees at Moorfields and scotched rumours that outbreak the result of Papist or foreign plots.

The Great Fire

Hardly had the last victims of the Plague been shovelled into their mass graves than London was struck by the disaster of the Great Fire. The author of the contemporary pamphlet *God's Terrible Voice in the City* linked the two events. As he saw it, the Fire was divine retribution on a sinful population who had not heeded the previous warning. This time there was no escape for the wealthy. Rich and poor suffered in the Fire which broke out in Pudding Lane near London Bridge in the early hours of 2 September 1666 and engulfed practically the whole City.

As with the Plague, the start of the Fire seemed insignificant. The King's baker, Thomas Farrinor, whose premises in Pudding Lane were ten doors from Thames Street, apparently left a pile of faggots too near an oven. He insisted that he had thoroughly 'drawn' the fire, but the coals could not have been fully extinguished. At 10 p.m. on the Saturday night he went to bed 'leaving his providence with his slippers'. Within three hours his house was full of choking smoke. Awakened by his manservant, he escaped with his wife, daughter, and the servant from a garret window and along a gutter to a neighbouring house. A maid left behind was the first of the Fire's few fatal casualties.

The Lord Mayor, Sir Thomas Bludworth,

was awakened, but thought it just a typical minor outbreak, and Pepys, roused from his bed in Seething Lane, did not watch the flames for long. But a strong east wind was fatal. A spark from the timbers of the baker's burning shop ignited a pile of hay in an inn yard. The inn caught and the flames passed into Thames Street which was lined with warehouses stacked with tallow, oil and spirits.

In the narrow streets of pitch-coated timber buildings, instant action against fire was essential. Buckets of water, hand-squirts, and long-handled fire-hooks (to pull down blazing framework) could deal only with outbreaks. After this, demolition in the path of the fire was the only remedy, and, fearing the compensation that might have to be paid, Bludworth failed to give the orders that might have saved London.

Pepys who took a boat on the sunny Sunday morning recorded utter confusion – 'everybody endeavouring to remove their goods, and flinging into the river, or bringing them into lighters which lay off; poor people staying in their houses as long as till the fire touched them, and then running into boats, or clambering from one pair of stairs by the water-side to another.' He saw pigeons that also remained till the last moment fall with singed wings. Because no one was acting, he went to Whitehall to warn the King.

Houses, he said, must be pulled down, and Charles told him to return to the City and give the Lord Mayor specific orders. But Bludworth seemed powerless in the face of what Evelyn calls 'tenacious and avaricious men'. 'Lord, what can I do? I am spent. People will not obey me,' he said to Pepys.

1. The Fire seen from Southwark – a German or Swiss view.

2. Refugees flee from the burning City on the night of the outbreak. The building at the north end of London Bridge still stands, and the roof of St Paul's is intact.

3. Only a few days before the outbreak of the Fire, a tax collector, John Webb, made this entry in his record of hearths to be taxed in Pudding Lane. The oven under the name 'Thomas Farrinor Baker' is the one in which the Fire started. The Hearth Tax, first imposed in 1662, was levied at the rate of two shillings a hearth.

4. Fire-fighting in the seventeenth century.

Not until the King had put the Duke of York in supreme command on Monday was decisive action taken. Stations were then established in an arc round the path of the fire as it was fanned westward by the wind. Each was under the command of a Privy Councillor or nobleman who had a fire-fighting squad of five justices of the peace, the parish constable, thirty soldiers, and a hundred other men. The King himself moved from point to point on horseback. He distributed guineas to encourage workmen, and, bespattered with mud and water, personally fought the fire among the falling buildings. Seamen, drafted in from the dockyards, began systematic destruction of whole streets with gunpowder, and this, combined with the dropping of the wind on Tuesday evening, at last checked the holocaust. In the west it was halted in Fleet Street at the corner of Fetter Lane; to the north-west in Cock Lane near Smithfield; and to the east at the tower of All Hallows, Barking.

As explosions grew fewer, and smoke drifted away, there was revealed what Pepys called 'the saddest sight of desolation that I ever saw'. In four days, 13,200 houses had been destroyed, and 100,000 people made homeless. Four hundred streets, alleys and courtyards were a mass of rubble and smouldering timbers. Five-sixths of the area within the walls had been laid waste. The medieval City had gone for ever.

But there was no great loss of life. Only eight people were killed as a direct result of the fire. Evacuation had been chaotic but successful. Carrying their valued possessions, and desperately offering 'Forty pounds for a cart!' nearly everyone was able to escape. This was managed even though London Bridge, the City's lifeline to the south, was blocked. That the bridge escaped total destruction was, ironically, due to a previous fire. Thirty years before, buildings had been burnt down at the north end, and this had left a space extending over five piers. By 1651 one large building had been restored at the point where the bridge joined Fish Street, and this quickly went up in flames. Falling timbers crashed on to the water-wheels. They also impeded the escape route. But the gap saved the rest of the bridge.

The catalogue of destruction was appalling. The Guildhall, the heart of the City's administration, was gutted. Without windows, doors or gallery, only the stone walls still stood. The great timber roof was charred beyond salvage. Thanks to the strength of the vaulted crypt, however, the City records, most complete of any in the world, were saved. Gresham House (fig. 167 on map, page 147) off Bishopsgate Street became the temporary home of the City Council, the Lord Mayor, and other homeless officials.

The commercial heart of the City, the Royal Exchange (166), was also a ruin. The flames had run through the galleries of shops, and only the scarred tower rose above the rubble. Billingsgate fish market had been an early victim; but the poultry market of Leadenhall (168) escaped thanks to the resource of an alderman who, like the king, had gone among those fighting the flames with a hatful of coins. The walls of Leadenhall were the first point where the spread of the fire was halted.

The ancient halls of the City Companies were a terrible loss in terms of both history and architecture. Forty-four of these buildings were destroyed, many of them converted private palaces of great magnificence dating back to early medieval times. Only seven escaped, and, except for such details as the

fourteenth-century crypt of the Merchant Taylors Hall (133), nothing of the pre-Fire buildings now survives. Off Ludgate Hill, the burning of the early fourteenth-century hall of the Stationers resulted in a great loss of gold and silver plate. But for the bookseller members of the Company there was an even worse disaster. The Stationers used St Faith's, a chapel in the crypt of St Paul's, as their parish church, and as the fire had crept up the hill they moved their wares into it for safety. Each bookseller made his own pile of books on the chapel floor. Doors and windows were strengthened so that no spark could get in. But in the inferno that was St Paul's at the height of the fire, the roof fell in and, says Evelyn, crashed through the cathedral floor into the crypt. Accounts of the cause vary, but the result was the same: the incineration of hundreds of thousands of precious volumes.

After burning for two days and nights, St Paul's was a gaunt skeleton, roofless and without windows. 'Only a huge heap of stones cemented together by the lead with which the church was covered,' was one description. Evelyn estimated that six acres of lead from the roof had been melted, and

fighting the fire in the cathedral had been made impossible by the river of molten metal. Inigo Jones's portico, though still standing, was cracked and discoloured, and his casing of Portland stone had not saved the nave. Workmen salvaging in the rubble found fragments of statuary and broken tombs including that of a fourteenth-century Bishop of London whose mummified body was revealed. Only Donne's monument (page 106) was intact.

Out of a total of 109 parish churches, 84 were destroyed. Thirty-five of these – many of them fine examples of Norman and early Plantagenet work – were never rebuilt. To this list of destroyed buildings has to be added the Custom House (169), the Herald's Office (161), prisons such as Bridewell and the Fleet, three of the City gates – Ludgate, Newgate and Aldersgate – Salisbury Court Theatre, a large part of the Inner Temple (though the hall and the church of the Knights Templars escaped), and schools such as Christ's Hospital whose 200 'Bluecoat' pupils were evacuated to Islington.

Immediate relief was needed for the thousands of homeless people. With everything lost, they camped in the fields round

5. 'A ruinous heap' was how London appeared to one eyewitness after the Fire, and this detail of a view by Hollar shows the measure of the disaster. Rubble lies so thick that the ground level is raised by four feet. In this section of the City alone, a dozen Company Halls are so ruined that we cannot identify them. But a number of the roofless, gutted churches with skeleton towers can be named. Travelling, left to right, from Baynard's Castle (A) to Coldharbour (K), we come to:

B. St Bride's, Fleet Street. Built c. 1222. Tomb of the printer Wynkyn de Worde destroyed. Rebuilt (fig. 94 on map, see over).

C. St Benet, Paul's Wharf. Built c. 1111. Bells referred to by the Clown in *Twelfth Night*. Rebuilt. Now the Welsh church (fig. 7 on map).

D. St Peter, Paul's Wharf. Built c. 1170. Not rebuilt (fig. 8).

E. St Nicholas, Cole Abbey. Built c. 1241. Largely attended by fishmongers. Rebuilt (fig. 10).

F. Possibly Trinity the Less, Little Trinity Lane (fig. 35).

G. St Martin Vintry, Thames Street. Built c. 1107. Parishioners largely in the wine trade. Not rebuilt (fig. 56).

H. St Mary-le-Bow, Cheapside. Built c. 1091. Most important church in the City after St Paul's. Meeting place of ecclesiastical Court of Arches. Probably derived name from the 'bows' or arches of the Norman crypt which survived Fire. Rebuilt (fig. 18).

I. All Hallows the Great. Built c. 1235. Set up arms to greet Charles II a month before his Restoration which Pepys called 'a great eyesore'. Rebuilt (fig. 53).

J. All Hallows the Less. Built c. 1240. Not rebuilt (fig. 54).

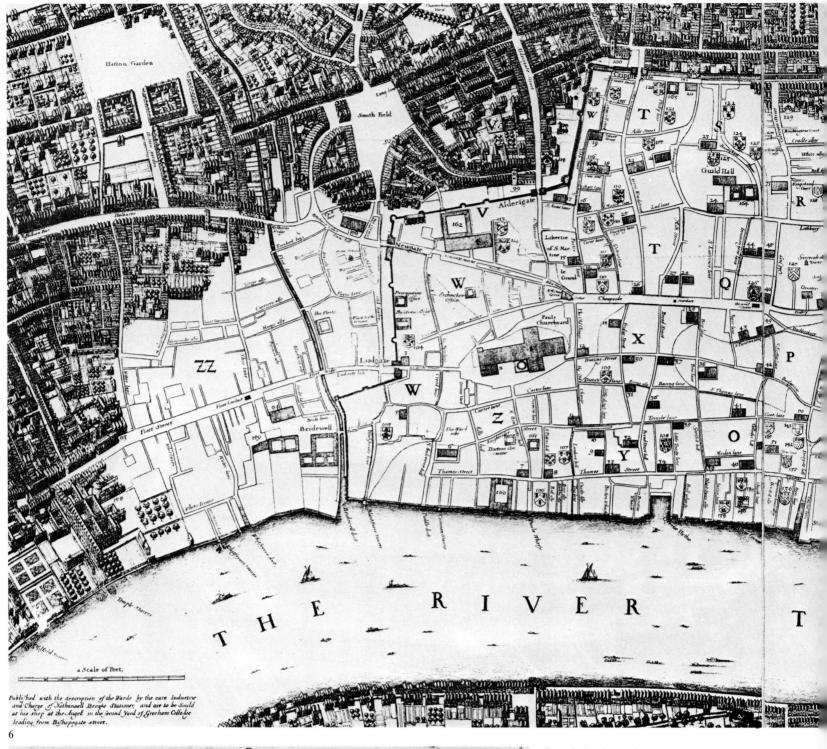

6

London where there were emergency arrangements for the distribution of bread and other provisions. The justices of the surrounding counties were ordered to find free storing places for people's goods. All towns and cities had to receive refugees and allow them to ply their trades. As has become a tradition, the Lord Mayor administered a disaster fund and subscriptions came in from all over England.

During the long process of rebuilding London, 80,000 were forced away from the City, and some even emigrated to St Helena at the invitation of the East India Company. Many who did not go so far failed to return. Six years after the Fire 20,000 had still not come back.

7

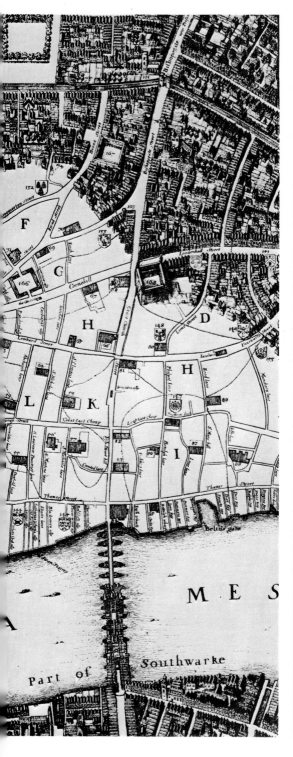

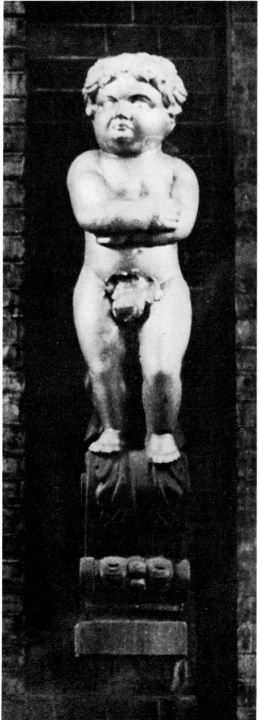

8

Everything points to the negligence of Farrinor, the baker, as the cause of the Fire, but a French Huguenot, Stephen Hubert, confessed to deliberate arson. Hubert, who was almost certainly mad, said at his Old Bailey trial that he had put a fireball through the bakery window on a long stick. Even Farrinor, anxious to be absolved from responsibility, said this story was absurd. So did the Lord Chief Justice. But the jury found Hubert guilty, and he was hanged at Tyburn.

So many wild rumours circulated of Papist and foreign responsibility that there was a Parliamentary post-mortem. It found nothing very sinister. The Fire, the report concluded tamely, was due to 'the hand of God upon us, a great wind, and a season so very dry'.

6. Hollar's map based on 'a exact surveigh' made in December 1666, on the order of the Lord Mayor.

7. Receipt sent by the Lord Mayor to the small village of Cowfold, near Horsham, Sussex, which collected 53s. 9d. for the relief of Fire sufferers. Subscriptions came in from all over the country. York sent £398. Lyme Regis collected £100 within a week.

8. The Fire's end is marked only by the small wooden figure of the Fat Boy. It is in Cock Lane, near Pie Corner, West Smithfield. The convenient summary that the Fire 'began at Pudding Lane and ended at Pie Corner' inspired a Nonconformist preacher to air the theory that the Fire was 'occasioned by the Sin of Gluttony'.

9. By a curious inversion of values, the main memorial to the Fire is not where it mercifully ended, but where it began. The Monument, built in 1677, was sited 202 feet from the Pudding Lane house, and this is also the height of the column. Plans for surmounting it with first a symbolic phoenix and, then, a 15-foot statue of Charles II were discarded for the present vase of flames. Wren designed the Monument in collaboration with Robert Hooke, the City Surveyor.

9

Rebuilding

On the base of the Monument, Charles II in Roman costume is seen coming to the rescue of a fallen and languishing London. The rescue took time. Though an inscription says that the City's rebuilding was completed in 'three short years', thirty would be nearer the truth. There was no delay or lack of decisive action; but the scale of the undertaking was enormous.

Within a week, Wren, who had hurriedly clambered over the smouldering ruins, presented the King with a plan, below, in which the old winding streets and narrow alleys were replaced by monumental avenues radiating from circular piazzas. Its virtues were enumerated by the architect's son, Christopher, in a book of filial piety, *Parentalia*, published in 1750. He wrote: 'Dr Wren, immediately after the Fire, took an exact Survey of the whole Area and Confines of the Burning, having traced over, with great Trouble and Hazard, the Plain of Ashes and ruins; and designed a Plan or Model of the new City, in which the Deformity and Inconveniences of the old Town were remedied, by the enlarging the streets and Lanes and carrying them as near parallel to one another as might be; avoiding, if compatible with great Conveniences, all acute Angles; by seating all the parochial Chirches conspicuous and insular; by forming the most publick Places into large Piazzas, the Centers of eight ways; by uniting the Halls of the twelve chief Companies into one regular Square annexed to Guild-hall; by making a commodius Key on the whole Bank of the River from Blackfriars to the Tower. . . .'

Wren's radical idea was rejected (along with equally startling plans by Evelyn and others), and this has given rise to the legend

1

2

that progressive planning was baulked by selfish City merchants. It is said that Wren's plan was 'unhappily defeated by faction' after being approved by Parliament. It was never approved by Parliament: it was considered, and rejected along with others. The equable final arrangement was that, with another brilliant amateur architect, Roger Pratt, Wren was appointed joint head of a group of six Commissioners to work out a more practical solution.

Before actual building could start in the following April, property owners had to clear their house sites of debris so that an accurate ground plan could be made. This was difficult because the rubble was deep and householders scattered. But the City Council knew that haphazard rebuilding would be disastrous. They insisted that sites must first be surveyed and staked out. Then it must be decided who was to rebuild – landlord or tenant – and to what specifications. A Fire Court was set up in Clifford's Inn to settle legal tangles such as the conflict with the Bishop of London who refused to allow booksellers to rebuild their shops in Paternoster Row until they had paid arrears in rent–even though all rents since the Fire had been cancelled.

Whatever their architectural merits, visionary plans like Wren's were impracticable, not only because of the hostility of freeholders loath to make sacrifices, but because there was no money to pay for the changes. A tax on coal raised only limited funds. But the Commissioners saw that this was a golden chance to make what improvements they could. An open quayside was decreed (with warehouses forty feet back from the waterfront) from the Tower to Blackfriars. There was an attempt at a monumental approach from the river to Guildhall by the creation of New Queen Street (just east of Queenhithe: end of modern Southwark Bridge). Most of the important streets were widened and pedestrians were given raised pavements for the first time.

To rebuild a whole street at one time would have required an impossible co-ordination of innumerable independent site owners. Houses had to go up when people could manage it. But to prevent architectural anarchy, they all had to conform to standard measurements, and, to reduce future fire risks, were built in brick or stone. 'In high and principle' streets they had to be four storeys, as is seen in Cheapside houses by St Mary-le-Bow, centre right; three storeys high in secondary streets; and two storeys in side streets. Storeys were of different heights, but on any particular level had to be consistent so that when the houses were joined up, they presented a continuous, roughly uniform facade. Individual mansions like the one

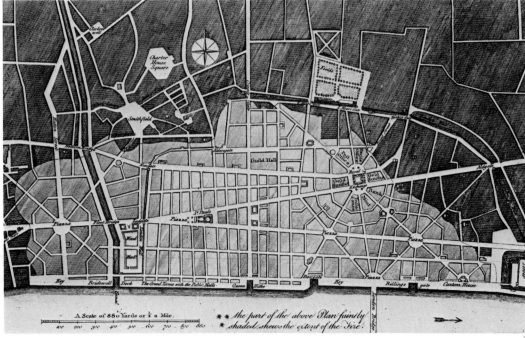

3

built on the Thames, centre left, about 1680 also had to conform to definite rules. This particular house for Sir Thomas Fitch stood at the junction of the river and the Fleet Canal for the creation of which he was responsible.

The building boom threw up its rogues and rebels. A draper named Anthony Selby caused endless trouble by pushing out the frontage of his shop in Mincing Lane by five illegal feet. He defied the Fire Court and everyone else until his premises were forcibly pulled down. But, generally, the task went forward with little corruption and good organization. To cope with the demand, additional timber was imported from as far afield as Norway. Brick kilns were started all round London, and one in Moorfields produced 5,500,000 bricks in four years. To prevent profiteering, the price of materials was fixed, and a great influx of craftsmen and labourers kept building costs competitive.

Many important buildings were finer than before. The new Royal Exchange, bottom right, designed by Edward Jerman, City Surveyor and a Commissioner, was considerably larger and had more shops. The College of Arms, top right, rose again on its pre-Fire site as an impressive building round a quadrangle (now open on to Queen Victoria Street). It was apparently designed by Maurice Emmett, the Master Bricklayer in the Office of Works. Guildhall was given a classical face-lift by Wren with a porch resembling Temple Bar (page 39). Wren also gave the Custom House (page 153) a dignity to match its importance as one of the main sources of the country's income.

Some of the planning went awry. The open quayside was soon encroached on by wharfingers hungry for storage space, and the even more ambitious idea of a wide embankment built out over the river faded away for lack of money. Even sadder was the fate of the Fleet Canal. This was a scheme to improve the whole Fleet valley by straightening and dredging the Ditch into a canal navigable for nearly half a mile to Holborn Bridge. Fitch built this with flanking wharves and uniform three-storey houses in 1675. But it was outdated almost before it was finished, and failed financially because water traffic was declining in proportion to street traffic. Within sixty years it was to be covered in.

Post-Fire London never quite fulfilled the Utopian dreams of the planners – those among the Commissioners who had stood in awe in the Piazza del Popolo in Rome or made notes of the Paris redesigned by Henry IV. But, in place of the medieval maze that had bred the Plague and kindled the Fire, there arose a city of brick and stone where classically proportioned houses in wider, more hygienic streets were ready to serve a new age.

4

5

6

1. In the allegorical bas-relief by Caius Gabriel Cibber on the base of the Monument, the female figure of the City sits in ruins surrounded by well-wishers. Father Time supports her, and a woman with a wand points to two goddesses in a cloud, Plenty with a cornucopia and Peace with a palm branch. The King commands Science with a winged head, Architecture, holding a plan and compass, and Liberty to go to her relief. Behind him is the Duke of York with a garland to crown the risen City. Envy leers from below the pavement.

2. City mansion conforming to the post-Fire regulations – Sir Thomas Fitch's house on the Fleet.

3. Wren's plan for rebuilding the City.

4. The College of Arms showing buildings on three sides of the quadrangle which were completed in stages between 1673 and 1683.

5. These Cheapside houses next to St Mary's are built to the authorized proportions with shop signs set back against the wall, fall pipes, penthouses, balconies and shop-fronts with a general uniformity.

6. The new Royal Exchange was built by 1671.

St Paul's Rebuilt

Although his overall plan for the City was rejected, Wren was still needed. In April 1668, the Dean of St Paul's sent a letter to Oxford imploring his help. A makeshift scheme for patching up part of the ruins for services had proved impracticable, and Dr Sancroft wrote: 'We most earnestly desire your Presence and Assistance with all possible Speed.' Wren still had his pre-Fire plans, and immediately set to work on others. He even had a large model made in oak of the new St Paul's he wanted to build. Half an inch to a foot in scale, it is still preserved in the Cathedral. But to churchmen brought up on Gothic architecture, his dome and classical style were too revolutionary. Pressure was put on the King who rejected the model even though Wren pleaded with him personally.

Next he submitted what has become known as his 'Nightmare' design. This flight of fancy had a spire like a pagoda set on a funnel-shaped dome. Probably he never intended to build anything so hideous; he simply wanted to get a plan, *any* plan, past the King which he could surreptitiously change later. On the drawing Charles noted: 'We found it very artificial, proper and useful', and issued a Royal Warrant for its construction.

All these deliberations took time. It was eight years after the Fire before people on Ludgate Hill were alarmed by what they mistook for an earthquake, but which was the architect – now Surveyor to the King's

Buildings – demolishing the old ruins with gunpowder. The foundation stone was laid without ceremony in 1675. Wren just asked a workman to bring a flat stone from a pile of rubble and drop it where he indicated. It happened to be part of an old gravestone, and on it was the word *Resurgam*.

To pay for the new Cathedral, a nation-wide appeal was launched, a London coal tax imposed, and newly consecrated bishops ordered to contribute. Stone was specially quarried at Portland, and brought round the Nore and up the Thames by boat. To prevent any cheese-paring administration from halting the work after one section was complete, Wren cunningly arranged for the whole building to go up, stage by stage, at the same time. But this meant that it took twenty-one years before the first service could be held there. Even when the Choir was opened in 1697, the dome – the ultimate expression of Wren's sense of the spectacular – had still to be built. Holding that this slowness was unwarranted, a Parliamentary committee halved Wren's annual fee, the hardly generous sum of £200.

Like the false screen which the architect used on the outer wall to disguise that the nave was buttressed, the dome was not strictly structural. As may be seen, right, there were three domes. The one that makes St Paul's such a dramatic landmark is an outer envelope, a metal tureen supported on a timber framework. Beneath it is a conical brick dome, and then a smaller dome low enough for James Thornhill's murals to be appreciated from below. To prevent the stone lantern and cross, which weigh 700 tons, from splaying out the walls, Wren borrowed the device used by Michelangelo at St Peter's, Rome, and secured it by encircling iron chains.

The last stone was placed on the summit on the architect's seventy-sixth birthday. It was thirty-three years after the laying of the prophetic foundation stone. Even in his seventies, Wren had continued his supervision of the work. He visited the site every Saturday, and was hauled up to the lantern in a basket. But in the late October day in 1709 when his masterpiece was finally finished, he seemed reluctant to end his life's work. He deputed the placing of the last stone to his son who had been born in the year new St Paul's was started.

1. Sir Christopher Wren.
2. St Paul's in ruins about 1673 – westerly view, from the rubble-strewn Choir, of the south transept and, on the right, the nave.
3. The Warrant or 'Nightmare' design.
4. The finished Cathedral from the north-west.
5. The model prepared in wood by Wren.
6. Section through St Paul's, showing the three domes.

5

6

3 St Bride**
4 St Andrew, Holborn**
5 St Sepulchre, Holborn***
7 St Martin, Ludgate***
8 St Andrew-by-the-Wardrobe**

9 Christ Church, Newgate**
10 St Benet, Paul's Wharf***
11 St Paul's Cathedral
12 St Mary Magdalen****
13 St Augustine**

14 St Nicholas Cole Abbey**
15 St Mary Somerset****
16 All Hallows, Bread Street****
17 St Mildred, Bread Street*
18 St Michael, Queenhithe****

19 St Mary-le-Bow**
20 St Mary, Aldermary***
21 St James, Garlick Hill**
22 St Lawrence, Jewry**
23 St Anthonin, Watling Street****

24 St Michael Royal**	30 St Clement, Eastcheap***	35 St Magnus**	41 St Dunstan-in-the-East**
25 All Hallows the Great****	31 St Michael, Crooked Lane****	37 St George, Botolph Lane****	* _Bombed 1940–1941, not rebuilt._
26 St Stephen, Walbrook**	32 St Mary, Abchurch***	38 St Mary at Hill***	** _Bombed and now restored._
27 St Margaret, Lothbury***	33 St Michael, Cornhill***	39 St Margaret Pattens***	*** _Undamaged 1940–1941._
28 St Swithin*	34 St Peter, Cornhill***	40 St Dionis Backchurch****	**** _Demolished before 1939._

5

6

Wren's London

The panorama above shows thirty-five of the fifty-one City churches rebuilt by Wren or under his supervision. Breaking the skyline, the forest of steeples indicates the variety and invention he brought to the huge undertaking. St Bride's (3 in panorama, and 6, right) is tiered to look like a pagoda. Four steeples, including St Dunstan-in-the-East (41), are Gothic. The lantern of St Magnus (35) is Flemish. For his greatest achievement, St Mary-le-Bow (19, and 1, far left) Wren built a pilastered tower to house 'Bow Bells' and invented a classic steeple, the columns and consoles of which support an obelisk, a hundred feet above Cheapside.

It was part of Wren's duties as Surveyor General to recommend which of the gutted churches should be saved, and which parishes united. Once a parish had obtained a warrant,

and had sufficient funds, the architect was then approached for a model. Some of his clients, bidding for priority of attention, sent him wine, and among other incentives was the present of money in a silk purse for Lady Wren.

Work on the churches started in 1670. Seven years later about thirty were under construction. And by 1686 their rebuilding was almost over except for certain steeples added later.

By general consent, his finest parish church is St Stephen, Walbrook (26, and 3, left), the small interior with sixteen columns, eight of which support a panelled dome – a study for his _magnum opus_ for St Paul's. For St Mary, Abchurch (32, and 4, left) Wren designed another dome (painted by Thornhill) springing from eight pendentives – curved triangular supports above the arches – in a square interior.

In the fifty-seven years between the Fire and his death, Wren's activity was astonishing. As well as innumerable buildings of which he was the undoubted architect, he also created a 'style' which so influenced his contemporaries, that many attributed to him are suspect. His first authenticated secular building was the Custom House (5, above), probably completed in 1671. It lasted only thirty-seven years before it was destroyed by fire in 1718. His work on the Royal Hospital, Chelsea (2, left) was spread over ten years. Started in 1682, the hospital for 500 military pensioners seems to have been suggested to Charles II by Louis XIV's Hôtel des Invalides which had been built in Paris ten years before.

1. St Mary-le-Bow; 2. Chelsea Hospital; 3. St Stephen, Walbrook; 4. St Mary, Abchurch Lane; 5. The Custom House; 6. St Bride, Fleet Street.

153

The Murder of Sir Edmund Berry Godfrey

In a city as large as seventeenth-century London, it can hardly have been unusual for a man not to be seen for several days. But the disappearance of Sir Edmund Berry Godfrey, coal-merchant of Charing Cross, immediately aroused alarm. Apart from his business, Godfrey was a well-known public figure. He was a respected J.P. for Westminster, vestry-man at St Martin's, and he had been knighted for his services during the Plague. His familiar figure, thin and stooping, was last seen on a Saturday afternoon in the Strand by a fellow-vestryman who asked him to dine. Godfrey had hurried by with a brief apology. He was never seen alive again.

Fears were aroused, and for five days the coffee houses buzzed with speculation because he was known to be in possession of some highly explosive information. A month before, a clergyman, Titus Oates, had come to Godfrey as a J.P. with documents which, he claimed, proved a secret plot to murder the King and replace him with the Catholic Duke of York.

Had Godfrey been done away with in an attempt to protect the Catholics who were implicated? That he was the victim of what was wildly called the Popish Plot seemed confirmed on the following Thursday, the afternoon of 17 October 1678. Two men walking on Primrose Hill saw a body lying in a ditch. The man had a sword through him and his neck was broken. It was the missing Godfrey.

The discovery fanned anti-Catholic prejudice, and sparked off panic. There were rumours of an imminent French invasion. Cannons were set up round Whitehall Palace. Five Catholic peers were sent to the Tower. In fact, there was no Popish plot as the King and the Privy Council well knew after their own examination of the miserable perjurer Oates. But, for political reasons, they had no wish to stem the clamour against the Catholics.

All that was needed was a conspiracy trial, and in December four men were arrested and charged with Godfrey's murder. Under torture, Miles Prance, a Catholic goldsmith living off Drury Lane, confessed to the crime. He named three confederates, an old man named Robert Green, Henry Berry a gate-keeper, and Lawrence Hill, servant of a doctor. All worked at Somerset House, official residence of the Catholic Queen. Extracts from Prance's depositions before a House of Lords committee appear under three of the contemporary prints, far right.

They were found guilty of killing Godfrey, concealing his body for four days in Hill's house, and then dumping him on Primrose Hill. Although he believed them innocent,

Charles signed their death warrants fearing that if he spared them, public opinion would turn against him. History has never solved the mystery of who really murdered Sir Edmund Berry Godfrey, and we are left with a further minor mystery, a curious combination in the names of the accused–Green . . . Berry . . . Hill. If it is not a coincidence, then it was rather a grim jest by whoever rigged the trial to pick as scapegoats those whose names made up Greenbury Hill–as Primrose Hill was then more generally called.

1. Sir Edmund Berry Godfrey.

2. In 1685 Oates's long series of lies and perjured testimony came to roost. He was arrested, and sentenced to stand in the pillory annually. 'I this year saw Dr Oates whipped at the cart's tail the second time. . . . He occasioned a strange turn in the nation . . . yet, after all, he was but a sorry, foul-mouthed wretch . . .'–Edmund Calamy, Nonconformist biographer.

3. Titus Oates informs the Privy Council presided over by Charles II of 'the Horrid Plot' by the Jesuits to depose the king and overthrow the government. 'Mr Oates . . . seemed to be a bold man, and in my thoughts furiously indiscreet; but everybody believed what he said; and it quite changed the genius and motions of Parliament. . . . The discovery turned them all as one man against it [Popery] and nothing was done but to find out the depth of this. Oates was encouraged, and everything he affirmed taken for gospel. . . .' – Evelyn, October 1678.

4. 'Sir Ed. Godfrey did, about nine of the clock at night, pass from towards St Clement's, as far as the Great Water Gate of Somerset House, being watched and followed . . . Hill, making some haste before, stept within the wicket, which was open: and turning soon out again, called to Sir Edmond as he was passing, and said, That there were two men quarrelling within, who might soon be quieted, if once they saw him: Whereupon he entered through the wicket. . . .' – Deposition of Miles Prance, December 1678.

5. 'When Sir Edmundbury Godfrey came down to the bench, Greene, who followed him, put about his neck a large twisted handkerchief: and thereupon all the rest assisted, and dragged him into a corner . . . Greene . . . thumped him on the breast and twisted his neck until he broke it . . . but his body remained warm, and seemed hardly dead. . . . The body lay in Somerset House about six or seven days before it was carried out. . . .' – Prance.

6. 'Hill having got a sedan, and placing it in the long dark entry . . . they put the body thereinto . . . and so carried the sedan and body in it as far as the new Grecian Church in Soho: and there Hill met them with a horse whereupon they took out the body, and forcing open the legs, they set it upon the horse: Hill riding behind to keep the body up . . . and the sedan, which was left in one of the new unfinished houses, they took up, and brought it home, as they came back. . . .' – Prance.

Theft at the Tower

In the same decade as the murder of Godfrey, another crime was committed which though quite different is equally mysterious. It was the attempted theft of the Crown Jewels from the Tower. The main culprit, Colonel Thomas Blood, was arrested in flight, and interrogated by Charles II. Yet he escaped imprisonment and hanging. Instead, he was granted the equivalent of a £500-a-year pension.

The earliest account of this bewildering and sensational exploit appeared in 1680. This was nine years after it took place, and the year in which Blood died. Unsatisfactory, like so much else about the crime, the story tells how Blood, an adventurer and son of an Irish butcher, first saw the royal regalia as an ordinary visitor to the Tower; returned three weeks later disguised as a clergyman, and with a woman posing as his wife; and how this counterfeit couple ingratiated themselves with Talbot Edwards, the elderly custodian of the jewels.

On 9 May 1671, Edwards and his wife invited the couple to dinner. Blood arrived in clerical dress, but accompanied this time by two men secretly armed with swords, sticks and pistols. They asked Edwards to show them the regalia, and the moment they were in the Jewel Room, the door was slammed and a cloak thrown over the old man's head. He was knocked down, clubbed, and stabbed in the stomach. Blood seized the Crown, crushed it, and put it under his cloak. The Orb was taken by a second man who slipped it into his loose breeches. The third was about to file the Sceptre in two, when they were interrupted by the arrival at the Tower of Edwards's son. He had just landed from Flanders, and had come to see his father.

The alarm was raised, Edwards's daughter rushed out into the night crying, 'Treason, the Crown is stolen!' and shots were fired. Blood and his confederates got over the drawbridge and ran to St Catherine's gate where horses were waiting. But they were captured before they could escape. In the struggle a large diamond, pearl, ruby, and other stones were lost, but all were recovered.

Blood took his capture calmly. 'It was a bold attempt,' he said, 'but it was for a Crown.' With what seemed greater audacity, he declined to make a confession to anyone but the King. And the King saw him.

Forty years later, the historian John Strype was to comment that Charles's clemency to Blood 'must for ever be a mystery to the world'. No solution fits the known facts. One suggestion, far-fetched, but just plausible, is that the King was in the plot and had secretly arranged for Blood to steal the regalia on his behalf so he could raise some much-needed money on the jewels.

1. The Martin Tower, the seventeenth-century Jewel House. In earlier times the royal jewellery was generally placed for security in religious houses. The first mention of it being deposited in the Tower is after Henry III's return from France in 1230. Henry built both the Martin Tower (later known as the Jewel Tower) and the Wakefield Tower, to which the jewels were transferred in 1870. The modern exhibition of the jewels dates back to the time of Talbot Edwards, when they were first open to public inspection, and, as custodian, he received money from the public in lieu of salary.

2. A late eighteenth-century picture of the theft.

3. Col. Blood. Evelyn described him as having a 'villainous, unmerciful look; a false countenance, but very well spoken, and dangerously insinuating'.

1

Science in the City and at Greenwich

The foundation of the Royal Society and the Royal Observatory in the mid-seventeenth century was a direct result of the surge of scientific learning encouraged by the King. Charles granted the Society its charter in 1662. Among the members who met twice a week at Gresham College in the City were such great thinkers of the age as Isaac Newton, Edmund Halley, the second Astronomer Royal, Robert Boyle, the chemist, and Isaac Barrow, the mathematician. Evelyn was the Society's prime mover, and others included Wren, Pepys, and John Aubrey, the antiquary and gossip. In the frontispiece, far right, for the *History of the Royal Society* (1667) the King's patronage is symbolized by his bust. It is being crowned by Fame, and pointed to by Lord Brouncker, mathematician and the Society's first president. Francis Bacon represents the scientific inspiration of the previous generation.

The Observatory, the country's oldest scientific institution, was ordered by Charles 'within our Park at Greenwich, upon the highest ground'. It was built by Wren 'for the observator's habitation and with a little pompe' on the site of Duke Humphrey's Tower (page 86). The first 'observator', or Astronomer Royal, was John Flamsteed. He himself laid the foundation stone and noted the precise time – 3.14 p.m., 10 August 1675 – so that he could have the fun of casting the building's horoscope.

The Observatory's main purpose was to build up an accurate catalogue of the stars and so establish lines of longitude and latitude to help ships at sea. With sextants, two clocks, a telescope fifty-two feet long, and a quadrant lent by the Royal Society, Flamsteed 'began to observe ye heavens' a year later.

In 1884, Greenwich Observatory was accepted as lying on the Prime Meridian (Longitude 0°) from which time throughout the world would be reckoned. Fog and smoke drove it to Herstmonceux, Sussex, in 1948.

1. Flamsteed House, the old Royal Observatory, Greenwich, c. 1675.

2. The outside with the Time Ball, erected 1833, which dropped down the mast at precisely 1 p.m. daily to provide seamen on the river with a visual time check.

3. Frontispiece designed by Evelyn.

4. The Octagonal Room at the Observatory showing Tompion clocks and a portrait of Charles II. The room remains much the same today.

2   3

4

The Coming of the Squares

About thirty years after the building of the Piazza in Covent Garden, London's second square – and the first so called – was laid out by the 4th Earl of Southampton on his land in Bloomsbury. Dining with the Earl at Southampton House in 1665, Evelyn noted that 'a noble square or Piazza, a little towne' was being erected. Southampton's scheme was to plot out the land on three sides of the square in front of his house, and then grant leases to individual builders at peppercorn rents of around £6 a year. The plots were uniform, each with a twenty-four-foot frontage, and the initial leases were for forty-two years. When the leases fell in, the houses became the property of the Southamptons. This slow-burning but ultimately highly profitable form of speculation was adopted by other hereditary landlords and half London was to be built in this way. With the increase of costs, however, many leases were lengthened until by the end of the eighteenth century, the present ninety-nine-year term had become general.

When Evelyn speaks of 'a little towne' he is referring to a nearby market, shopping centre, mews, and smaller side streets which served to make the square a self-contained unit. By the time of Sutton Nicholls's engraving, above, Southampton Square was becoming known by its present name of Bloomsbury Square. The dignified, symmetrical prototype of so many later squares, it was a notable feature of London, a sight not to be missed by visiting foreigners.

St James's Square took shape within a few years of the one in Bloomsbury. But Henry Jermyn, Lord St Albans, did not actually own St James's Field which he began to develop in the 1670s. He was granted a 60-year Crown lease on the understanding that he gave the district a character befitting its proximity to St James's Palace and the royal park. A cultivated diplomat who had lived for many years in France, Lord St Albans envisaged a square on a more sumptuous continental scale than Southampton's. He wanted only three or four mansions for noblemen on each side. But the Fire had created a great demand for housing, and St Albans modified his scheme. He leased or sold off twenty-two smaller plots round the square to aristocratic friends or reputable speculators. A certain uniformity in the elevation of the houses was required, but the frontages varied, and a generous 200-foot depth to the site allowed for back gardens. A garden still survives behind No 4 (north-east corner), a house which, though remodelled by Leoni (in 1725), comes nearest to showing the original 1676 design.

A number of secondary streets were built

1. Lord Southampton of Southampton Row. The Earl, ardent Royalist and Lord Treasurer to Charles II, planned the house and square that bore his name in 1652, nearly 30 years after he succeeded to the title and property.

2. Southampton Square and House. By 1754, the date of the view below, the buildings surrounding Southampton Square were completed, and the house had passed into the Russell family through the marriage of Southampton's daughter to the Earl of Bedford. No original houses survive, but Nos 5–6, west side, are mid-eighteenth century. Southampton House was demolished in 1800.

3. The fields in which St James's Square and Leicester Square were built are seen in Faithorne and Newcourt's map (surveyed 1643–1647, published 1658). Because St James's Square would, as the map shows, overlook the royal park, Charles II made stipulations. Leicester House (see page 160) and the Gaming House appear, top right. Bottom left is Berkshire House (built 1627, demolished 1840).

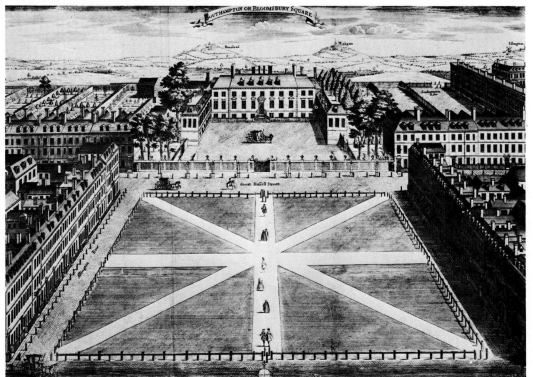

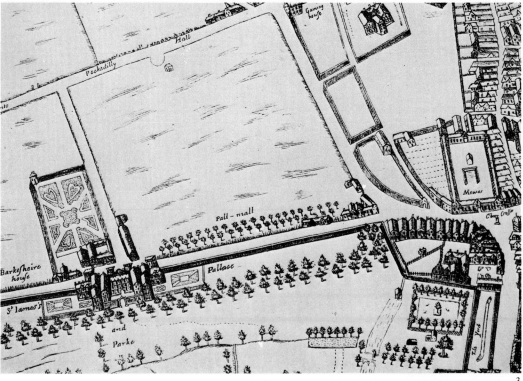

by St Albans as part of his development of the area bounded by St James's Street, Piccadilly, Haymarket, and Pall Mall. And to serve the new residents there was a big poultry and meat market as shown in the 1689 map, right. The new neighbourhood also required a place of worship nearer than the parish church of St Martin-in-the-Fields. In 1676 the foundation stone of St James's, Piccadilly, was laid by St Albans who largely paid for the church. With one side facing Jermyn Street, which took its name from its founder, the church was built by Wren, and provided the square with an architectural feature at the end of a central vista comparable to Southampton House.

Although in its general appearance, Leicester Square with its house on the north side resembles Southampton Square, it did not evolve on hereditary land. Like St Albans, Robert Sidney, 2nd Earl of Leicester, was given a Crown lease. As early as 1631, he had been granted a licence to build a mansion in the meadow that lay to the north of the Royal Mews (now Trafalgar Square). We see it, enclosed by a wall in Faithorne's map, bottom left. The lease required the Earl to pay an annual £3 Lammas rent for the land to the south which he had to lay out with walks for the benefit of the parish.

Leicester Fields, as this soon became known, was slowly encroached on by the Earl until, in 1670, his legal rights were defined. He was then granted a further licence to erect three ranges of houses to the south, east and west of the Fields, and Leicester Square came into being. With Penshurst in Kent as their principal home, however, the Sidneys used Leicester House less and less. Soon they were cutting up the fine garden to create Lisle Street (after the Earl's second title) and by 1721 – the date of the view, left – the house was hemmed in, especially on the west side, by profitably leased buildings. The house itself was occupied for a long time by George III, as Prince of Wales, and was pulled down in 1791.

The financial success of these first squares led to speculation by men who, today, are best remembered by the streets and squares named after them. Colonel Thomas Panton, a noted gamester, built Panton Street (1674) near his *Gaming House*, clearly marked by Faithorne. Richard Frith built Frith Street, Soho (c. 1680), and Gregory King, herald and engraver, King's Square, now Soho Square (1681). Sir Thomas Bond invested unsuccessfully in Bond Street in which buildings went up so slowly that at his death in 1689, the street was described as looking 'like the ruins of Troy'. But Sir Richard Grosvenor was more successful with Grosvenor Square (started c. 1695) as was Lord John Berkeley of Berkeley Square (1698).

4

4. Henry Jermyn of Jermyn Street. Created Earl of St Albans at the Restoration at the wish of Henrietta Maria to whom he had been a close friend and adviser for many years. As Queen-Mother, she leased him 45 acres of what was then called Pall Mall Field, but there were delays of nearly ten years before he was able to develop it as St James's Square. The Earl's house was in the south-east corner of the square (on the site of the present Norfolk House) and is clearly shown on the map below. He died here, aged about 80, in 1684.

5. St James's Square, Market and surrounding streets in Blome's map of 1689. Not until the eighteenth century did Jermyn Street (phonetically rendered as *Ger-man Street*) have access to St James's Street and Haymarket.

6. The one major alteration from the original seventeenth-century St James's Square is the ornamental basin (1728), replaced early in the nineteenth century by the present gardens and equestrian statue of William III.

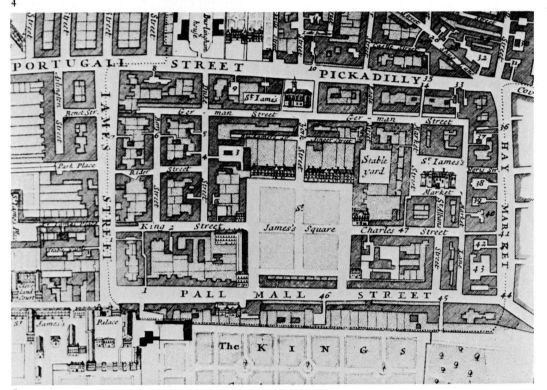

5

6

7

8

9

10

7. Leicester Square in 1727 – the view by Sutton Nicholls. Leicester House, with the coach in the open courtyard, bears no resemblance to the building round a central courtyard and with a gate-house in Faithorne's mid-seventeenth-century map (p. 158). As there are no records that the house was rebuilt in the intervening years, it has to be assumed that the map-maker was using a symbol rather than an actual view. The curious way in which quite illogical streets often survive is to be seen in the diagonal Bear Street which then, as now, branches off the north-east corner of the square.

8. Robert Sidney, 2nd Earl of Leicester.
9. Monmouth House on the south side of Soho Square was built for the Duke of Monmouth, Charles II's illegitimate son. In its early eighteenth-century form, above, it has been attributed to Thomas Archer. Demolish-ed 1773. At the battle of Sedgemoor, Monmouth chose 'So Ho!' as his password but this is not the origin of the word. Rate books refer to 'Soho' as early as 1632 and the derivation is more likely to be from a hunting cry. The fields between the Conduits and St Giles were the scene of an annual hunt attended by the City Mayor and Aldermen.

10. Gregory King, Rouge Dragon pursuivant, in his heraldic tabard. King, who surveyed and created Soho Square, was one of several speculators in the seventeenth-century boom. He was an engraver, and was employed by John Ogilby on his map of London and *Book of Roads*. King's even more successful competitor, Nicholas Barbon, a doctor of medicine, built Red Lion Square (1684), Essex Street off the Strand, and houses in Mincing Lane and St James's Square (he leased the site of No 4). A terrace of Barbon houses – Nos 36–43 – remains in Bedford Row.

Escape by Water

If Charles II was an 'unconscionable time a-dying', his ill-starred brother James, who succeeded him in 1685, was to be an unseemly short time a king. At the very start of his three-year reign, he had to face a Protestant bid for power, a rebellion led by his illegitimate nephew, the Duke of Monmouth. This quixotic disaster ended for Monmouth on Tower Hill, where he was beheaded. He gave John Ketch six guineas 'not to hack me as you did my Lord Russell', but the executioner, right, bungled his job. One account says he was distracted by the anger of the Protestant mob round the scaffold.

After the Bloody Assizes that followed the rebellion, and the repressive sentences of his instrument, Judge Jeffreys, James tried to strengthen the position of his fellow-Catholics. He ordered a declaration of indulgence to Papists to be read from all pulpits. When seven bishops refused, they were taken by water to the Tower. Their acquittal, followed by celebrations throughout London, was the decisive swing of the weather-cock for James. Two years earlier he had ordered an actual weather-cock to be erected on the roof of the Banqueting Hall – it remains there to this day – to serve as an early warning of a Dutch landing. Now the omens, if not the wind, pointed due south-west. When the Whig leaders invited William of Orange to England in 1688, the time had come for flight. Disguised either as a country gentleman or a servant – accounts vary – James slipped out of Whitehall by a secret passage in the early hours of a December morning. A carriage waiting at the door of the Privy Gardens drove him through the darkness and Old Palace Yard to Millbank. At Horse Ferry he took a boat to Vauxhall (depicted with eccentric topography in the Dutch print, bottom right) where horses were waiting. It was an escape route to France already taken by his wife and son. As he crossed the river, he dropped the Great Seal into the water, as a defiant gesture and to prevent orders being issued in his name. It was recovered by chance five months later by Thames fishermen.

Jeffreys, whom James had made Lord Chancellor, planned a similar escape. Disguised as a seaman, he went to Wapping and hid in the Red Cow Tavern, Anchor and Hope Alley, to board a ship for Hamburg. Recognized, he was seized by an angry crowd, top right, and taken to the Tower where he died a few months later and was buried in the chapel of St Peter.

1. Execution of Monmouth.
2. Judge Jeffreys arrested at Wapping.
3. The seven bishops who were brought to the Tower.
4. Flight of James II.

Inburg WILHELM HENRICH Prinz von ORANGE
Zufftügen Römischen England, 18 Dec. 1688.

1

The Arrival of Prince William

The invitation asking William of Orange to take over the country's government was signed at Guildhall by the Privy Council, anxious to restore order to a London seething with unrest. After a march from the West Country at the head of an army of 40,000, and an overnight stay at Syon (a tactful delay to allow James's final departure), the Dutch prince entered London on 18 December 1688. People lined the streets carrying quickly improvised favours–oranges on sticks–but, far from receiving the tumultuous reception

shown above, the Prince insisted on approaching St James's Palace by a back route in a closed carriage.

Determined to convey the sense of occasion, the Dutch artist, Romeyn De Hooge, omits to show that it was a day of pelting rain. His engraving (which, in order to make sense, has had to be reversed) is looking south-east from the palace, in front of which the Protestant peers are paying homage. De Hooge has demolished Horse Guards to give a clear view of the Banqueting Hall where, two months later, William and Mary were formally to be offered the joint

crown. He also seems unaware that by this date the Gothic St Paul's was completely demolished, and Wren's cathedral had reached the cornice of choir and transepts.

When Mary joined her husband in February, she came up the Thames in a procession of barges from Greenwich. She was twenty-six, and Evelyn noted that she was 'laughing and jolly as to a wedding' as she returned to a Whitehall she had not known since childhood. In the palace she found many of her father's personal belongings left behind in his sudden flight. But Whitehall was not to remain the royal palace.

William found it lacked seclusion, and, with the excuse that the river affected his asthma, he bought a house standing on rising ground near the village of Kensington.

The owner, Lord Nottingham, was paid £20,000 for his modest mansion and twenty-six acres of ground, and to give it the dignity of a palace, William called in Wren. A further £60,000 was soon spent in enlargements and adding another floor. In August 1690, Mary wrote to the King in Ireland saying: 'I have been this day to Kensington which looks very well. . . .' and later, impatiently: 'The outside of the house is *fiddling* work which takes up more time than one can imagine.'

The south front, seen right, remains almost exactly as finished by Wren, with the King's Gallery overlooking the ornamental gardens. The long, low range, two storeys high, on the left, is probably part of the original Nottingham House. The impressive but mysterious two-storey wing on the right appears to be a hybrid invention by the artist. Is this meant to be the Orangery which Queen Anne added in 1704 to the designs of Hawksmoor or Vanbrugh? Although the style of the façade is almost identical, it has unaccountably been given two floors, has been brought a hundred yards forward, and joined to the main building. No records or plans of such a wing exist.

Hardly had the palace been completed in 1694, than Mary died there of smallpox at the age of thirty-two, and eight years later William was brought there to die after a fall from a horse. Queen Anne extended the grounds by 100 acres, and it is clear from the 1705 plan, below right, that she had an embryonic idea for the Serpentine. This predates by twenty-five years the actual creation of the lake by Queen Caroline.

In the valley of the Serpentine there existed six marshy ponds through which ran the West Bourne on its course from Hampstead to the Thames. To turn them into a stretch of ornamental water was difficult because there is a fall of twenty-five feet from the head at Bayswater to the Knightsbridge outlet. The plan suggests nine dams which would each permit a controlled fall of about three feet. Then, in 1730, 50,000 tons of earth were excavated and the series of lakes became one open Serpentine on which the Royal Family could sail pleasure yachts.

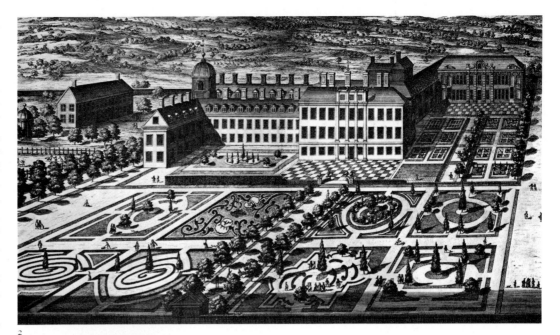

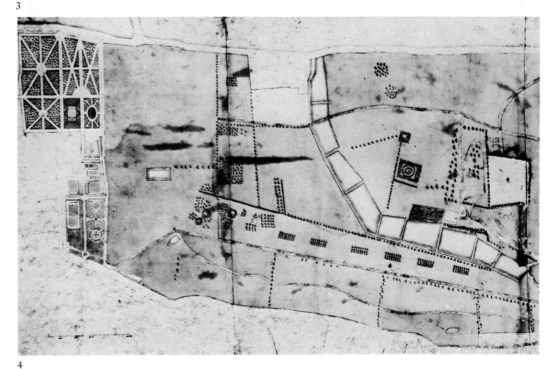

1. In this fanciful impression of William of Orange's arrival, the new king is in the middle distance, his hat doffed, while before him the English peers are collapsing in obsequious welcome.

2. Kensington Palace, about 1720, with the mysterious wing.

3. The free-standing Orangery to the north-east.

4. Plan of Kensington Gardens in 1705 showing the first proposals made by Henry Wise, the Royal Gardener, for the Serpentine.

Peter the Great at Deptford

'The Czar of Muscovy being come to England, and having a mind to see the building of ships, hir'd my house at Sayes Court', wrote Evelyn in his diary in January 1698. Peter the Great, then twenty-five, travelled about London incognito and often on foot. Royal protocol was observed only on such occasions as his visit to Kensington Palace when the King persuaded him to sit for Kneller. The purpose of the Czar's visit was the study of English shipbuilding, and to be near the Deptford yards he and his Russian entourage leased Evelyn's fine riverside house, Sayes Court. A triple-gabled Elizabethan building, it had been acquired over forty years before by Evelyn who had lived there during the Plague and the Fire. He had landscaped the surrounding fields into an elaborate and beautiful garden.

The Czar's days were spent in the docks working with his hands as well as studying methods; but Evelyn's bailiff complained that Sayes Court was 'full of people, and right nasty'. In three months the house and the 'lovely, noble ground', as Pepys called it, were seriously damaged. Three hundred window panes were smashed, and holly hedges, Evelyn's special pride, had to endure the Czar's perverse pleasure of being trundled through them in a wheelbarrow.

1. Sayes Court Manor House.

2. Sayes Court and its garden – part of a sketch plan preserved among Evelyn's papers. The grounds stretched, south to north, 280 yards from the main entrance (122) to the artificially moated island (103) with a drawbridge. A boat and ducks are depicted on the moat. The Thames, beyond the map to the left (East), lay a few yards from the gateway (102) at the bottom (North) end of the garden. The main entrance was approached by 'the new highway' from New Cross. A drive, 100 yards long between lime trees, led to double gates in a high brick wall. This continued between two bowling greens (26) to the house itself (1–15). One feature of the grounds, which set new standards of English garden design, was the small outdoor banqueting house (44) used principally by Evelyn's children for games and picnics, with its long promenade (43) to the island. To the north of the oval garden was one of the assaulted holly hedges (92). The house stood at the extreme east of what is now Sayes Court Recreation Ground. Czar Street and the Royal Victualling Yards have been built over parts of the garden.

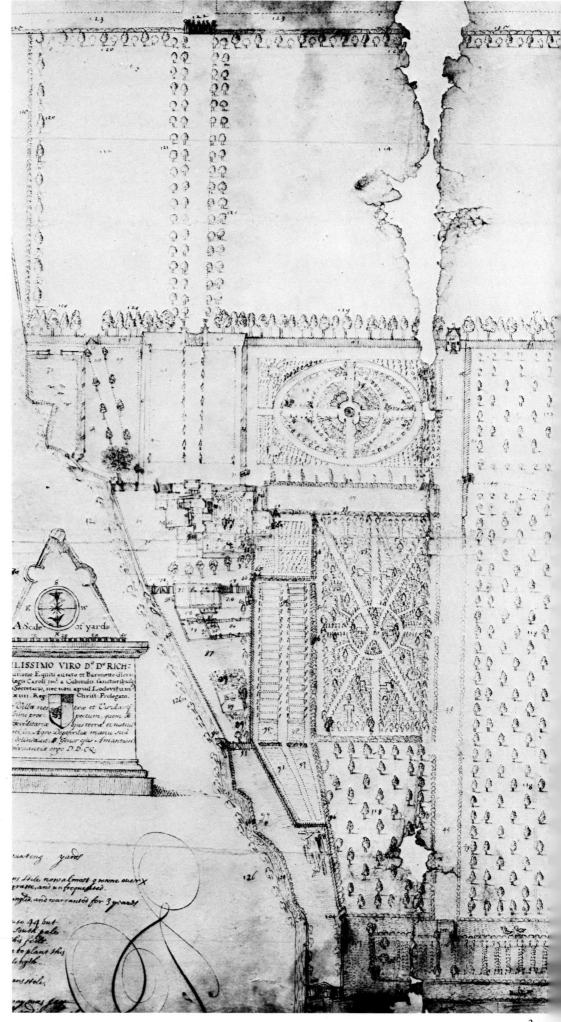

Howland Dock

Half a mile up river from Sayes Court was Howland Great Dock, built at Rotherhithe in 1696, and for more than a century London's largest dock. One of the earliest wet docks, it came into existence after an alliance of two great families. Fifteen years earlier, a marriage was arranged, almost at their births, between two children, the infant grandson of the 1st Duke of Bedford and Elizabeth Howland, only daughter of a Streatham merchant family. The Howlands owned the Rotherhithe land on which the ten-acre dock was constructed. Perhaps the Bedfords contributed the building capital, for exactly a month after the project was given Royal Assent—May 1695—the children were married as if to seal a bargain. The future 2nd Duke was then fourteen and a half, Elizabeth about a year younger.

Howland Great Dock, right, could take 120 merchant ships. It was used for anchorage and repair, not for the unloading of cargo which was the legally guarded privilege of other quays. In an overcrowded river where hundreds of ships were forced to anchor in midstream, the Howland Dock, locked against the tide, provided valuable berths.

At the far end stood 'a noble dwelling house', but to what extent this small mansion was ever a residence of the Bedfords is uncertain. The dock was much used by vessels of the East India Company in which both Bedfords and Howlands had investments, and in 1755 Captain Clive was to sail from here for India. Now part of Surrey Commercial Docks, and greatly enlarged, it was in operation as Greenland Dock until 1970, a reminder that for many years it was an important berth for whaling ships.

1. Kip's 1717 view of Howland Dock, looking due west, shows a ship being winched through the lock at full tide. Trees round the dock's edge were to shield the anchored ships from the wind, a necessary precaution for high-masted sailing vessels.

2. The 2nd Duke of Bedford and his young bride.

3. Deptford Dockyards and storehouse about 1670.

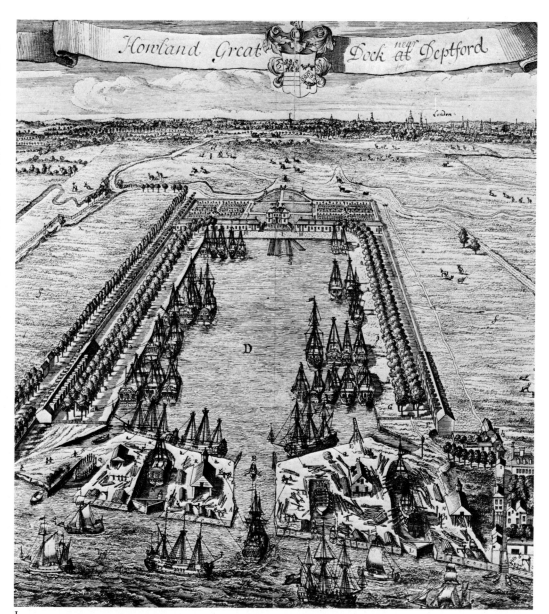

Howland Great Dock near at Deptford

1

2

3

Court of St James's

On her succession in 1702, Queen Anne made St James's Palace–until then the least favoured of all the royal homes–the official residence of the Court. It was to remain so throughout the eighteenth century, and even when the sovereign moved to Buckingham Palace the official phrase, 'At the Court of St James's', still lingered on.

Anne's decision to make the palace her permanent home came six years later, and after the death of her husband, Prince George of Denmark, at Kensington. Still in mourning, she was brought by her close friend, Sarah Churchill, soon to be the Duchess of Marlborough, to the rambling building on the north side of St James's Park. Though always favoured for royal births (Charles II, James II, Mary II, and Anne herself), the palace had been a barracks and prison during the Commonwealth, and had fallen from its mid-seventeenth-century splendour. Now the time was ripe for change and conversion. Wren, Vanbrugh, and Hawksmoor were called in to remodel it. The most important new building was the tall State Room block (to the left and in front of the Tudor gatehouse). It contained a Council Chamber, Throne Room and drawing room; Wren also gave it a crenellated parapet so the classical façade should not be too much at odds with Henry VIII's work.

To the right of the palace is Marlborough House, also Wren's design, built on the site of an old Friary. In granting the Duchess of Marlborough nearly five acres for the house in 1709, the Queen made a serious sacrifice of the royal gardens. Until then, they had stretched along almost the whole north side of the park. But at the time Anne could not do too much for her intimate counsellor and for her counsellor's husband, the victor of Blenheim. The Duke, campaigning in Flanders, was not enthusiastic. 'It is not a proper place for a great home', he wrote. 'I would advise you to think well upon it. . . .' The Duchess was undeterred, but by the time she moved in two years later, she was no longer royal favourite. Tory intrigue had brought about Marlborough's dismissal as Commander-in-Chief of the Army and the Duchess from all her Court appointments. Near neighbours could hardly have felt more constraint.

(The present road dividing the palace from the house is some yards west of the one seen here, guarded by a sentry and leading on to the rear of Marlborough House chapel. After a fire destroyed part of the east wing of the palace in 1809, Marlborough House garden was extended a little to the west, and the previously enclosed Friary Court became the open square it is today.)

Buckingham House   Godolphin House   St James's Palace

From Lord Godolphin's house (second from left, above) to Lord Carlton's house (second from right) and Prince Rupert's L-shaped house (right) there stretches more than half a mile of formal gardens laid out in parterres planted with miniature trees. Like the whole of St James's Park, they owe much to the work of Henry Wise. Wise was the Queen's Master Gardener to whom she entrusted 'the whole care of the park' in 1704. This meant a large programme of tree-planting, the tending of the ponds and islands of the Decoy, and restocking with fish, fowl and animals.

When Wise took over, he found the park badly neglected and its walks 'poachy' from winter flooding by the Thames and Tyburn. His immediate remedies included the repair of more than sixty sluice gates and the widening of Charles II's Canal by twelve

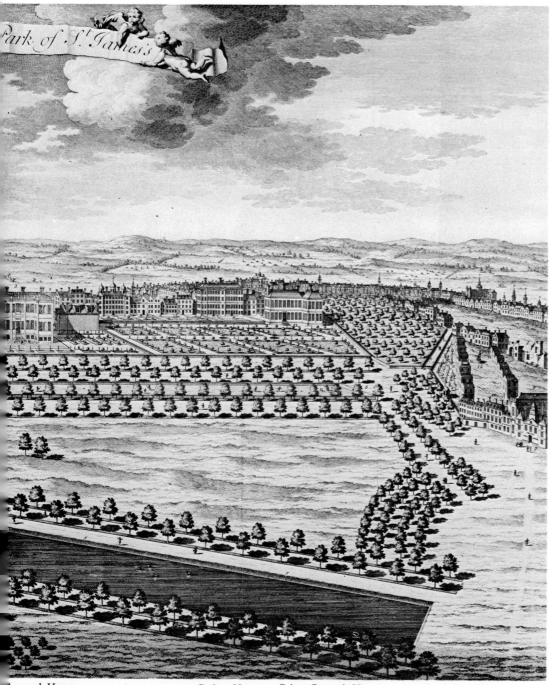

borough House   Carlton House   Prince Rupert's House   I

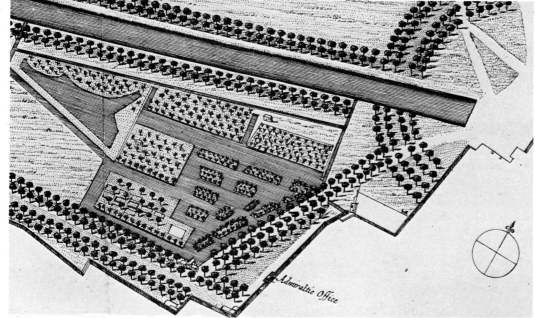

Admiraltie Office

3

feet. He had 350 lime trees planted. Two hundred deer were brought from Hampton Court.

To the south-east of the Canal, and covering about eight acres between the water and Birdcage Walk, lay an area of swampy lakes and reedy channels filled with small artificial islands. Created in 1662 and fenced off from the park, this royal game preserve was stocked with wildfowl. It went under the general name of Duck Island and the Decoy, and Evelyn remarked that it was 'singular and diverting' to see so many species breeding so near the city. He observed storks, swans, pelicans, geese, and a crane with a broken leg which had been fitted with a jointed wooden leg fashioned by a sailor.

To restore St James's Park to the fashionable place it had been in Charles II's time, Wise persuaded the Queen to introduce strict regulations. People were forbidden to walk on the grass or wear clogs. Wildfowl was not to be disturbed and deer left unmolested in their reserve of the Wilderness (the tree-covered area top right). Nothing was to be sold in the park, and no linen dried there. As Deputy Ranger, Wise alone had the right to ride through the park on horseback.

Only coaches bearing the royal arms were permitted to drive in the park, an order which particularly affected the Duke of Buckingham, Lord Privy Seal. In 1703 he rebuilt Arlington House and renamed it Buckingham House. To the Queen's annoyance the fine new mansion was so sited at the end of the Canal that it looked as if the whole park were planned for him. He was also, she believed, encroaching on the park. Reprisal took the form of denying the Duke permission to drive up to his front door through the park. He had to approach obliquely from the north through St James's Mews passage.

1. View of St James's early in the eighteenth century. The exact date and origin of the engraving are unknown.

2. Henry Wise. During four reigns he was part-owner of a 100-acre nursery, Brompton Park, on the gentle southern slope between Hyde Park and Old Brompton Road, and he supplied fruit and forest trees to many great landowners. Following the French tradition of garden style, Wise gave formality to Kensington Palace Gardens as well as to the parks.

3. Duck Island and the Decoy – detail from Knyff's map, c. 1662 – inexplicably not shown in the view above. Part of the swamp was reclaimed and part incorporated in the new informally shaped lake that replaced the Canal in 1826, when the park was redesigned by John Nash. The present Duck Island is on the line of the old Canal.

Greenwich Hospital

The ceiling painted by Rubens for the Banqueting Hall; Kent's murals for the stairway at Kensington Palace; Thornhill's frescoes, emblazoned with gold, in the dome of St Paul's; the bas-relief by Cibber on the base of the Monument; some church carving by Grinling Gibbons. With the Painted Hall at Greenwich—the most sumptuous of all—these are about the sum total of what London can show in the grand baroque manner. Charles I died too soon, and Charles II was too poor to emulate the extravagant fancies of Louis XIV.

But the main dining hall of Wren's Royal Naval College provided a challenge, and it was answered by England's first 'history-painter', James Thornhill. He spent twenty years on the ceiling, right, depicting The Triumph of Peace and Liberty, a vast allegorical painting in which 200 figures, representing Vice and Virtue, Science and the Arts, surround William and Mary.

The King has Tyranny (Louis XIV) under his foot, and is presenting the cap of Liberty to Europe—symbolic view of England's defeat of the French and the 1714 Treaty of Utrecht. Other evils and vices are beaten down by Minerva, and Hercules who wields a huge club. Architecture points to a drawing of the Painted Hall, and around the edge of the oval are the signs of the Zodiac and the seasons. One of the hospital's first pensioners, John Worley, aged ninety-six, posed for the bearded figure of Winter seen, right, warming his hand.

1. Royal Naval Hospital, Greenwich's answer to the Military Hospital at Chelsea. It replaced the old Tudor palace of Placentia—a ruin since the Civil War—when it was demolished in 1694. There was accommodation for more than 2,000 pensioners. One of them, wearing the uniform of blue cocked hat, tail coat, and breeches, is seen smoking a pipe in the gateway, above. Opened in 1705, the Hospital was the combined work of Wren, Vanbrugh and Hawksmoor. Wren, the main architect, wanted to pull down the Queen's House and replace it by a building, centrally placed, on a grand scale and crowned by a dome. When Queen Mary would not permit this, Wren compromised with two smaller domed buildings, twin sentinels to a double colonnade. One of them, the Painted Hall, is seen above (viewed from the Greenwich-Woolwich road looking north towards the Thames).

2. Inside the Painted Hall.

3. Sir James Thornhill, Member of Parliament, Fellow of the Royal Society, and Hogarth's father-in-law, incorporated this self-portrait into his murals. For his work at Greenwich and in St Paul's, Thornhill became, in 1720, the first English artist to be knighted.

4. The Triumph of Peace and Liberty.

1. Interior of the House of Commons, 1710.

170

Queen Anne's Parliament

With the Union of England and Scotland in 1707, room had to be found in an already overcrowded House of Commons for forty-five Scottish members. Wren, the Surveyor General, was ready with a solution. He designed galleries, supported on columns, on either side of the chamber. This was also an apt moment for other alterations. St Stephen's, draughty and uncomfortable, was still more a chapel than a place for debate.

Wren made a characteristic end to the old Gothic building. All the ecclesiastical detail disappeared behind new oak panelling. He filled in the mullioned East window and substituted three small round-headed windows as may be seen in the interior view, left, and on the outside, right. He lowered the roof and destroyed the clerestory windows (visible in Hollar, page 127). He also appears to have lowered the false ceiling of the chamber itself. This allowed room above the chamber for the storing of records and a housekeeper's lodging. It was also a place from which women (not yet admitted to the House) could watch proceedings through an aperture above the chandelier.

Male visitors were accommodated in the new gallery, and some years later a protest was to be made by a member who saw David Garrick sitting there. It was improper, he said, for players to listen to debates. This brought an immediate rebuke from Burke, seconded by Fox, who pointed out that Parliamentary eloquence owed much to the stage and that Garrick was the great master of eloquence.

Even after the conversion, the House remained very small–60 feet by 26 feet–for 558 members. But attendance was spasmodic by members who represented 'interests' rather than parties. Landed gentry held more than half the seats. The City returned four members, and the entire metropolitan area only ten. But there were forty London businessmen in the House, including two Southwark brewers, several West Indies traders, an apothecary, a stationer, and a manufacturer of coins for the Treasury. Seven members were directors of the Bank of England.

The view, left, shows the Commons three years after the completion of Wren's work. At the Bar of the House stands the Serjeant-at-Arms carrying the mace. The Dutch artist, Peter Tillemans, appears to be depicting an actual event and the Speaker, Richard Onslow. The occasion is not known, but the ceremony suggests the presentation of a petition by the Sheriffs of the City. The Speaker asks, 'Mr Sheriff, what have you there?' to which the Sheriff replies by reading out the petition.

2

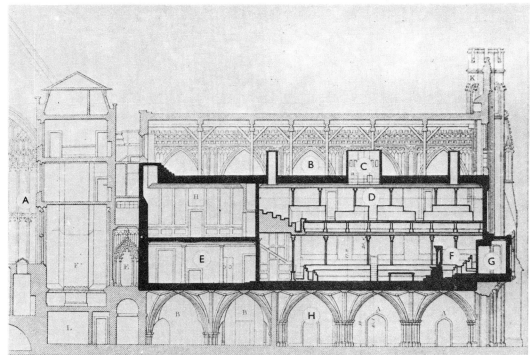

3

2. The semi-classical east end of the House of Commons in the eighteenth century seen from the direction of the river. It shows Wren's three windows. The single window above them gave on to the room over the chamber, and the three pointed Gothic windows on to the crypt which remained a chapel. Behind the Speaker's chair, the old altar steps led up to a doorway cut in the wall in place of the altar.

3. Section showing how the new house was built inside St Stephen's. A. Westminster Hall showing part of great south window. B. Attic above the House with old pointed arches or the original chapel. C. Ventilator over chandelier. D. The House of Commons showing seats and galleries. E. The Lobby. F. The Speaker's chair. G. Retiring room or corridor accessible through door behind chair and lit by three small oblong windows, seen in the exterior view above.

Queen Anne Buildings

Queen Anne gave her name to some of London's most beautiful domestic architecture, but, ironically, the style of well-proportioned simplicity now regarded as typically English was brought over from Holland under the earlier influence of William of Orange and his Court. Many houses were built of bricks actually imported from the Low Countries; pulleys in sash windows were a Dutch invention; and a fashionable designer of lead cisterns in Piccadilly was a Dutchman.

As Kip shows (page 195), Westminster, south of the Park and west of the Abbey was virtually a self-contained town of these houses. The best examples still remain in what is now Queen Anne's Gate (originally Square), one side of which backs on to Birdcage Walk. Some time after it was built in 1704, the residents raised a subscription for a wall dividing the street in half, as shown in the detail from Kip, above right. This was to prevent it becoming a thoroughfare, and also, perhaps, as a protection against the 'noisy nuisance' created by spectators from the Royal Cockpit (the circular building, extreme left in detail). The wall was not removed until 1874 when a statue of Queen Anne, backing on to the wall, was moved to its present position, above.

The Square was immediately fashionable. The Earl of Dartmouth (remembered in the adjoining Dartmouth and Lewisham Streets) was one of the first two residents, and the grotesque heads on the keystones over the windows are also to be found in the houses built by the Earl in Dartmouth Row, Greenwich.

Three storeys high, with hipped roofs and dormers, the houses conformed to a pattern of those going up all over the West End in this period of rapid development. They were built of brown brick, and white bands of stone marked the floors and gave a horizontal continuity to the terraces. They set the London domestic style for two centuries. A peculiarly 'Dutch' feature were the intricately carved wooden canopies, such as the one seen over the front door of No 17, above.

On the instigation of the Queen, an Act of Parliament was passed in 1711 for the building of fifty churches. Only twelve were actually built, but they were of great distinction. The first, St Mary-le-Strand, right, was started three years later and designed in the baroque style which the architect, James Gibbs, had studied in Rome. Gibbs's most famous church, St Martin-in-the-Fields, followed in 1722.

1. Queen Anne's Gate.
2. Kip's view, detail.
3. St Mary-le-Strand.

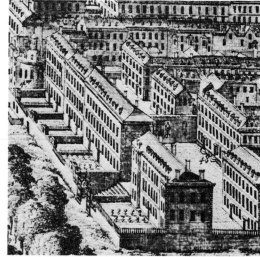

Coffee Houses and Newspapers

A Swiss visitor to London at the end of the seventeenth century found that the City's social life centred in the coffee houses. 'These houses', wrote Misson de Valberg, 'are extremely convenient. You have all Manner of News there: You have a good Fire which you may sit by as long as you please; you have a Dish of Coffee, you meet your friends for the Transaction of Business, and all for a Penny, if you don't care to spend more.'

By the end of Queen Anne's reign there were 497 coffee houses in existence. Offering their varied amenities, they sprang up wherever there was a demand, not only in the crowded City, but in the quiet residential backwaters like Queen Anne's Square. The first coffee house was opened in St Michael's Alley, Cornhill, in 1652 and was known as Pasqua Rosee's. Pasqua was a young Greek brought to London by Daniel Edwards, an English merchant trading in Smyrna. The story goes that the coffee which Pasqua prepared each morning for his master attracted so many visitors that Edwards decided to set his servant up in business.

Forerunners of clubs, coffee houses tended to attract a clientèle of people with the same interests. Fashionable London went to White's in St James's Street; scholars to the Grecian, Covent Garden; the clergy to Truby's or Child's, both near St Paul's; financiers to Jonathan's in Exchange Alley. Merchants who wanted to hear shipping news went more and more to the premises of Edward Lloyd in Lombard Street until, before the end of Queen Anne's reign, ships were being auctioned there and a news sheet of shipping intelligence published.

The Cocoa Tree, Pall Mall, became the meeting place for Tories, and the St James's Coffee House at No 87 St James's Street (referred to by Addison and Steele in *The Spectator*) a rendez-vous for Whigs. Even those less demonstrably political caused official alarm, and Charles II attempted to suppress coffee houses in 1676 as places 'where the disaffected meet and spread scandalous reports'. But this caused such resentment that the order was soon withdrawn, and half a century later the French author, Abbé Prévost, was hailing coffee houses 'where you have the right to read all the papers for and against the government' as 'the seats of English liberty'.

The coffee house was also the breeding ground for both the postal system and newspapers. In 1680 a private Penny Post was devised, in violation of government monopoly, by which letters could be posted there and delivered to individuals who used their coffee house as a *poste restante* address. First, simple news-letters were distributed to patrons, and then printed newspapers. Another Swiss traveller noted, 'What attracts enormously to these coffee houses are the gazettes and other public papers. All Englishmen are great newsmongers.' Among the papers were *The Daily Courant*, the first English newspaper which appeared in 1702 and the first evening (published at 'Six at Night'), *The Evening Post* in 1706.

1. Queen Anne coffee house about 1705.

2. The two foremost literary coffee houses were Will's (patronized by Pepys, Wycherley and Pope) and Button's, both in Covent Garden. Button's, to which Addison and Steele transferred their allegiance in 1713, was virtually the editorial office of the literary and political periodical *The Guardian* and a letter box with a lion's head above, was set up there to receive contributions.

3. Late seventeenth-century coffee boy, from a tiled sign found in a Spitalfields coffee house.

The Bank of England

On 21 June 1694, the doors of Mercers' Hall in Cheapside were opened to admit the first customers of the Bank of England. When the ledgers were closed at noon, eleven days later, the public had deposited a loan-capital of £1,200,000. Their motives were both patriotic and mercenary. They hoped to help in the war against France and to see an eight per cent return on their money.

A national bank had become a necessity. It was impossible to continue with a system whereby the King and Government had to go, cap in hand, to the City merchants and the goldsmith-bankers for loans in every emergency. In their turn, the goldsmiths feared a repetition of the seizure of their money which had been made by Charles II as a desperate remedy against the Dutch.

The idea of such a bank, similar to one already existing in Holland, was put forward by a Scottish financier in London, William Paterson. At first it was viewed with alarm by such private banks as Child's, the oldest, near Temple Bar, founded in 1663, by Hoare's in Fleet Street (1680), and by Snow's in the Strand (1685). Paterson was granted a charter only after much Parliamentary debate and Tory opposition. In time it became the bank where bankers banked; but the Bank of England's main function then, and ever since, was to raise money for the Government. As a profitable sideline, it was also given the privilege of issuing bank notes.

Mercers' Hall served as headquarters only until the end of the first year; then the Bank leased Grocers' Hall off the Poultry for the next thirty-nine years, and until it had built its own premises in Threadneedle Street. The Bank, consisting of a main hall, courtyard, and bullion court, went up on the site of the house and garden of the first Governor, Sir John Houblon. It was next to the church of St Christopher-le-Stocks which was demolished when wings were added to the east and west between 1766 and 1786. The old churchyard forms an inner courtyard of the existing bank.

1. Mercers' Hall, the first home of the Bank of England, as it appeared in 1694.

2. William Paterson, the founder.

3. The 1734 office in Threadneedle Street, looking south-west. The Bank's sign hangs out over the street behind the coach. The church and almost the whole parish of St Christopher-le-Stocks were engulfed by the Bank. After Sir John Soane's late eighteenth-century expansion, it spread over nearly four acres.

GEORGIAN LONDON

A · · · · · · B · · · · · · C

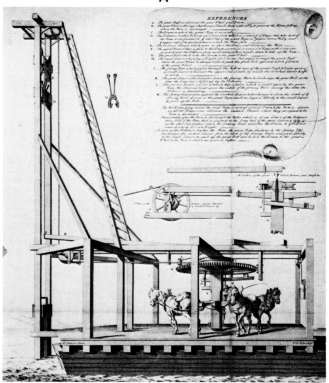

1. The problem of driving piles into the river was solved by James Vauloue, a watchmaker of Panton Street whose invention this is. Part of the inscription reads: 'By the Horses going round, the great Rope is wound about ye Drum & the Ram is drawn up till the Tongs come between the inclin'd Planes: where they are opened & the Ram discharg'd——' This engraving 'humbly inscribed to the Honourable Commissioner for Building' was published on 1 November 1738 and sold 'at the Golden Sugar Loaf in Panton Street near Leicester Fields. Price 2s.'

2. The tree-lined gap in the buildings right of the Banqueting Hall (G in the panorama) is the entrance court of Old Whitehall Palace and the approach to Whitehall Stairs. Though part of the royal precincts, this was always a public right-of-way. Above we see it in 1766 with two watermen hailing customers, two women and a man, who have come through the Tudor gateway from Whitehall Street on their way to the Thames. The wall on the right belongs to the house, just visible, and garden, formerly the home of Sir John Vanbrugh. This access to the river was on the line of the present-day Horse Guards Avenue.

D   E   F   G   H

The Thames in 1749

Two brothers, Samuel and Nathaniel Buck, living in the Temple in the middle of the eighteenth century, spread out before us the whole panorama of Georgian London. Selecting four different points on the Surrey shore between Westminster and the Tower, the artists look across the water to show a city which still regards the river as its main thoroughfare. Every important house has its own steps and watergate. Narrow alleys between warehouses link the Strand, Fleet Street, and Thames Street with piers and stairways where watermen wait for their customers. Wherries, open and sedan, ply up and down, and splendid private barges are rowed by as many as eighteen oarsmen.

The westerly extreme of the view is marked by the trees and market gardens of Tothill Fields. Beyond, round the bend of the river, all is meadowland as far as Chelsea. The first house in what is called Millbank Terrace (A) belongs to the Grosvenor family. Sir Thomas Grosvenor's marriage to Mary Davies, the heiress of Ebury Manor, in 1677 made the family owners of the vast area of London stretching from here to Tyburn Road (modern Oxford Street), and was the foundation of the Westminster fortune.

The four sturdy towers of the Baroque church of St John the Evangelist, Smith Square (B), are said to be the device of the architect, Thomas Archer, to ensure that if his building sank in the swampy ground it would at least sink uniformly. To the right of the church, just before the cluster of trees that screens the Houses of Parliament is the stoneyard of Alfred Jelf. Jelf was the contractor for Westminster Bridge, the new wonder of London. In 1749, and after twelve years of building, London's second bridge is shown as finished; but the artists must be taking prophetic licence, for it is not to be opened until the November of the following year. With central and west London larger than the City, and growing fast, it has become absurd to have to travel all the way to London Bridge to cross into Kent and Surrey. Even so, there was great opposition to Westminster Bridge by the City. The watermen also saw their livelihoods threatened, and it was soon to make obsolete the old horseferry which here is still crossing from Lambeth to Millbank (see also page 187).

However, Parliament passed the Bridge Act, and a lottery was held to raise funds. Various designs, including one by Hawksmoor, were rejected in favour of those by Charles Labelye, a naturalized Swiss. Labelye's bridge in Portland stone has thirteen arches supported on piers which rest on the bed of the river. These piers were floated into the stream in wooden caissons and then sunk. When the first pier was towed out in January 1739, and the sluices opened to sink it, Labelye's men found the watermen had got there first. To delay the work, they had sunk an old barge in the vital spot.

The designer's method of underwater foundation had its critics who said that it was essential for the piers to be driven down into the gravel bed of the river, not lie on top of it. They seem to have been right. As the long-awaited bridge was nearing completion, it was noticed that one of the central piers was subsiding. Under a volley of criticism, Labelye had no alternative but to remove the stonework down to water level and then strengthen the sunken caisson with deeply driven piles.

But these technical problems meant little to a public clamouring to use the fine white bridge which was forty-four feet wide, and, in contrast to London Bridge, unhampered by buildings. Twelve days before the opening, an impatient crowd stormed the barriers, and had to be dispersed by the police. The actual opening in the early hours of Sunday 9 November 1750, was signalled by a salute of guns. After an all-night celebration at the Bear Inn (C, the building seen immediately to the left at the far end of the Bridge), Westminster residents marched in procession to the centre of the bridge where 'God save the King' was sung, and there was a further discharge of twenty-one cannons. So jammed with people was the bridge during the day, that the watermen

I   J   K

3. The slender, octagonal Water Tower, shown by the Bucks (I), and above, in an aquatint of 1795, stood in Villiers Street (on the site of the present Charing Cross Station). It was built towards the end of the previous century. Water, sucked up from the river to the top of the 70-foot tower, had enough pressure to be carried through wooden pipes to a Marylebone reservoir which served the Hanover Square district. Chimneys at the back were for fires which drove a steam engine. As this was unreliable, horse power was often used to pump the water and ensure an adequate supply.

reaped an unexpected harvest. They ferried across people who were in a real hurry.

Between the Bridge and the long building (on previous page) belonging to the Lord Steward's Department (H), lie several houses of the nobility. Among them, from west to east, are the Duke of Richmond's house (D, from which Canaletto painted some of his most notable pictures), and those of the Duke of Montagu (E), and the Duke and Duchess of Portland (F).

To the east of York Buildings Water Tower (I) is the most impressive gateway on the riverside (J). It was built in 1626 with a main gate and side apertures and decorated with two couchant lions and the arms of the Duke of Buckingham. The designer is not positively known. Inigo Jones or his gifted and eccentric subordinate, Balthazar Gerbier, are possibilities. York Watergate survives but is now in Victoria Embankment Gardens, 500 feet from the river. On the west corner of Buckingham Street just behind it is the big house where Pepys lived until 1701 (page 135) and which was the home of Robert Harley, Earl of Oxford, during his time as Queen Anne's principal minister.

The long river wall survived the demolition of the episcopal York House in 1675 of which it was part, and now holds back the high tides from five streets which perpetuate in full the name of the developer of this area – *George* Street, *Villiers* Street, *Duke* Street, *Of* Alley

(now York Place), *Buckingham* Street. From here to the partially ruined Palace of the Savoy (K), private houses are inclined to be modest and there is even a well-stocked timber wharf.

Walls, three feet thick and a deterrent to demolishers, have saved the thirteenth-century castle of the Savoy, but its glory is gone. It is now a barracks, a prison, and the home of the press on which royal proclamations are printed. In the once-magnificent Great Hall a cooper makes barrels. The riverfront rooms of the palace are used as a series of churches for Dutch, High German, and Lutheran residents in London, and for Protestants, Dissenters and Quakers. To the rear of the left-hand tower is the Church of St Mary-le-Savoy which survived early nineteenth-century demolition to remain the 'Savoy Chapel' of modern times.

A little farther east, stands Somerset House (L) which also has only a few more years of existence in the form we see here. The river façade of the Tudor building was altered after the Restoration, and the arcaded gallery and classical front were built probably from the posthumous designs of Inigo Jones who died at Somerset House in 1652. It served as a home for two Stuart dowager queens, Henrietta Maria and Catherine of Braganza, but by 1749 its great days are over. It is divided into grace-and-favour homes for courtiers and the nobility. A last

short flicker of fame came in 1771, four years before its demolition, when rooms were given to the Royal Academy for a School of Drawing.

The next gap is Strand Lane (M), and beyond that a wider gap in the riverfront houses allows a glimpse of the Strand up Norfolk Street (N) which the artists have purposely foreshortened. Between Norfolk Street and Arundel Stairs stood Arundel House until it was demolished in 1678 by the brother and successor of the great art collector (page 114). His idea was to replace it by a new mansion by Wren, and behind it, where the wings and forecourt of the old house stood, he schemed streets lined with profitable houses up to the Strand. Surrey, Norfolk and Arundel Streets appeared and were briefly fashionable, but the new Arundel House was never built. Instead, the property was divided up, and the garden built over with the less ambitious houses and tenements we see here.

The trees on the extreme right (O) belong to Garden Court where the Buck brothers lived. It was from here on 5 October 1749, that they inserted an announcement in the *General Advertiser*: 'This day is published by S. and N. Buck five views of London . . . to be delivered to their subscribers at their chambers No 1 Garden Court, Middle Temple.' The panorama was to continue to sell for the next twenty years.

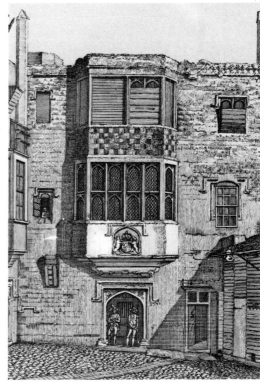

4. A year after the Bucks' drawing, part of the Savoy (K) was converted into a prison. Sentries guard its barred doorway, above. Here men pressed into the Army were held before being shipped to their regiments abroad. It also housed serious offenders like a sergeant and a drummer who deserted to the French in 1749, and were shot at Tyburn. The following year another soldier was imprisoned here. He was a private who, as well as deserting in Flanders, had incited his companions to join the enemy. Early in the nineteenth century the remnants of the old Savoy were demolished to make the northern approach to Waterloo Bridge.

P   Q   R

T   **U**

At the Temple (P), where sweeping lawns and legal chambers form an open quadrangle to the river, we come to the farthermost point reached by the Fire. Many buildings in these Inns of Court were destroyed. Like nearly every building we see between here and the Monument, they have been rebuilt in the previous eighty years.

The artists' angle prevents us seeing clearly the main features of the Temple. Only the roofs of Middle Temple Hall and the round church of the Knights Templars (both of which escaped the Fire) are visible. Inner Temple Hall is obscured by Paper Buildings, and the late Stuart and Georgian beauty of King's Bench Walk is invisible because of the oblique viewpoint. For these we must look at the bird's-eye view of the Temple as it may have looked in 1671.

From the Temple to the Fleet the river-front degenerates into a line of timber and coal wharves which are backed by the notorious district nicknamed 'Alsatia'. This was the refuge of every sort of criminal. For many years it was a sanctuary giving

5. The view, left, is a mid-eighteenth-century engraving, but shows the Temple as it looked in 1671, just about the time rebuilding was completed after the Great Fire. Extreme left is Middle Temple Hall (which escaped the Fire); extreme right, post-Fire King's Bench Walk. As the Bucks show, the curious indentation of the seventeenth-century river wall had been straightened out. Otherwise, the general lay-out of the Temple has changed very little to this day.

immunity from arrest, and although this privilege was abolished in 1697 it remained the home of footpads and murderers, highwaymen, debtors, and prostitutes.

Curiously enough there was a prison on the fringe of this area. This was Bridewell (R) the bell tower of which is visible, given by Edward VI to the City as a workhouse and House of Correction. It was rebuilt after the Fire and is also the home for apprentices, some ninety destitute boys who are taught various trades including weaving and glove-making. They are outnumbered by 'vagrants and strumpets' more than 400 of whom are committed here annually.

The main entrance of the prison faces the Venetian-like bridge over the Fleet. The river, once a foul-smelling, muddy ditch, was dug out and replanned after the Fire to become a canal, forty feet wide with generous quays on either side. With five feet of water at medium tide, boats could unload cargo as far up as Holborn Bridge. It has only ten more years to survive, for in 1760 it was covered over when Blackfriars Bridge was begun. Also Venetian in character is the open piazza on the corner of the Fleet and the Thames. Sir Thomas Fitch's house (S) over-looking it is no longer a private residence; it has become a warehouse with a lean-to roof on pillars to allow loading in wet weather.

From here eastwards the riverfront becomes almost entirely commercial. Swing-

ing wooden cranes unload and stack timber and coal. Warehouses store beer, dyes, and lime. Puddle Dock (named after a Mr Puddle, its owner) was originally used for the landing of corn and adjoins Dung Wharf (T) on which can be seen a great mound. This, like White-friars Stairs (Q) farther west where there is a similar pile, was used as a dump for street refuse which was taken up river by barge to manure the market gardens of Pimlico.

The large recessed harbour – the largest in this whole stretch of the river – is Queenhithe (U), used for landing fish until outstripped by Billingsgate. At this time Queenhithe is the centre of the meal and malt trade. Projecting far out into the river are the stairs of the Steelyard (V, next page), London centre of the ancient German trading company which became rich largely through the importation of steel. Bars of steel are piled in front of the warehouse.

Two impressive buildings – the tall Water-men's Hall (W) and the Fishmongers' Hall (X) with its triangular pediment and classical seventeenth-century façade – lead us to London Bridge. Waterwheels under the northern arches can pump 123,000 gallons an hour into the adjoining watertower.

In 1749 London Bridge is a spectre of its former self. With its double line of flanking houses and shops it recalls Tudor splendour but in the next five years was to change its appearance completely.

181

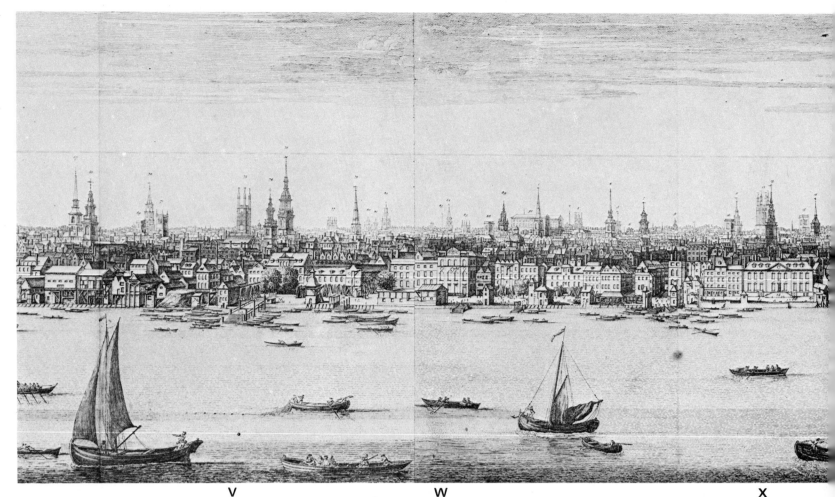

V   W   X

'Narrow, darksome and dangerous', was a traveller's description, and he says the houses 'overhung and leaned in a most terrific manner'. Despite arches of timber tying them together across the street they sometimes collapsed into the water. By now the Elizabethan Nonsuch House (Y, immediately beyond the second gap from the right) is so stripped of its Renaissance features as to be hardly recognizable. The sixteenth-century Chapel House (not visible) is a dilapidated warehouse for storing paper.

To anyone approaching it from Fish Street Hill, the bridge seemed just an extension of the street because the shops continued on both sides, and it was a hundred yards before a gap in the buildings allowed a view of the river. These shops, which sold pins and needles, brushes, gloves, seeds, prints, hats, and wallpaper, were considered good for bargains. But the attractions to shoppers and visitors were outweighed by the crumbling fabric and narrow thoroughfare. The wide, open Westminster Bridge underlined the inconveniences, and the City, foreseeing traffic and trade going west, took action. The unsentimental Common Council reported the houses to be 'a public nuisance' and recommended their demolition. In 1757 the housebreakers went to work, but before they did so, Canaletto who was in London from 1745 to 1755 made the drawing below.

The prospect, stretching as far as the Tower, shows Billingsgate and the Custom House (Z) largely obscured by small wooden sheds in which cargoes could be housed until merchants had cleared them with Excise officials in the main building. In the print right (1757) we see the Custom House designed by Thomas Ripley, which replaced Wren's destroyed by fire in 1718, and was itself burnt down in 1814.

6

Y   Z

6. Canaletto's view of London Bridge.

7. In front of the Custom House, and where they could be viewed from its windows, were twenty quays at which it

was compulsory for ships from abroad to moor. Their owners took advantage of congestion when ships came in heavily laden. Bribes alone secured prompt unloading. The forest of masts is omitted by the Bucks to give a clearer

view of the Custom House. The work of a French artist living in London, Jean Louis Boitard, the picture shows the arrival of a French ship, and is a satirical view of the mass of goods being imported into England.

May and other Fairs

In a London not bursting with diversions for the majority of people, the various annual fairs were thronged with pushing and jostling crowds. A German visitor at the beginning of the century was warned that May Fair, held during the first fortnight in May round Shepherd Market, was 'the chiefest nursery of evil'. Booths, sideshows and temporary theatres offered 'every enticement to low pleasures'. London's two other famous fairs were Bartholomew Fair, started in 1123, and Southwark, which brought music and colour to the street between London Bridge and St George's Church for a fortnight every September.

Bartholomew Fair was lent dignity by being opened each year by the Lord Mayor, and actors from Drury Lane and Covent

Garden did not disdain to go under canvas there. The curiously stylized view of about 1728, above, based on a fan sold at the Fair shows the popularity of sideshows. A rope dancer performs in the booth 'over by the Hospital Gate'; there is Faux, the famous conjuror: and Lee and Harper (from the Little Theatre, Haymarket) present *Judith and Holophernes*, a gory melodrama which brings in the crowds to see the Jewish widow cut off the head of the sleeping Assyrian general. The adventurous ride on the rough wooden predecessor of the Ferris Wheel.

The May Fair, which was to give its name to the whole district, had its centre in the then undeveloped ground, shown in the detail from Rocque's map, right, bounded by Turnpike (Park) Lane, Piccadilly, Curzon Street, and Half Moon Street. Part of it was leased by Edward Shepherd, owner and builder of Shepherd Market. In its booths a wondering public could enjoy fire-eating, prize fights, juggling and wild beast shows. Among its famous characters was a seller of gingerbread called Tiddy Doll who dressed as a dandy in a white shirt trimmed with gold lace. An unusual attraction was the Ducking Pond (possibly the square sheet of water flanked by trees in Rocque) to which people brought their dogs and watched them compete in the capture of ducks let loose on the water.

As the district round the May Fair became more residential, agitation for its suppression increased. The Fair was temporarily closed during Anne's reign, but survived for nearly another hundred years until its final closure in 1809. Southwark Fair was abolished in 1762, and Bartholomew Fair ended its seven centuries' existence in 1855.

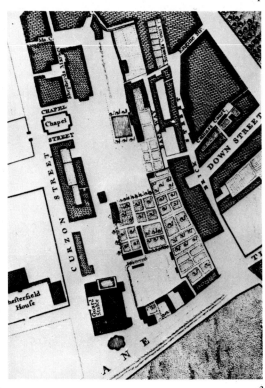

1. Bartholomew Fair in about 1728. It was in this year that Gay's *Beggar's Opera*, first performed at Lincoln's Inn Fields Theatre, was also seen at the fair.

2. Tiddy Doll, the Gingerbread Baker, from a sketch by Hogarth. The artist also introduced him into his picture of the Idle Apprentice's execution at Tyburn.

3. The May Fair area – detail from Rocque's map, with Park Lane at the bottom of the picture. There was room for stalls and booths in the open spaces all round the two-storeyed market house – presumed to be the oblong building labelled *Shepherds Market*. This had butchers shops on the ground floor, and a room above large enough to be used as a theatre at fair time. On the corner of Piccadilly (diagonal road, top right) and Engine Lane (now a continuation of Brick Street) lived the 6th Earl of Coventry. His house backed onto the Fair, and his agitation, combined with increased building in the area, brought about its eventual closure.

...and on Ice

An added excuse for a fair came whenever the Thames was frozen over. This happened about once in a generation. London Bridge reduced the speed at which the tide flowed by about a quarter of what it is today, and this gave the frost a chance to take a grip. On one occasion in the fifteenth century, however, the river froze as far down as Gravesend.

The first real Frost Fair was held six years after Elizabeth came to the throne, and the Queen and her Court are said to have walked on the ice to visit booths and see oxen roasted whole. The next comparable fair came at Christmas 1683, when so many booths selling goods, food and drink were set up that they were arranged in lines like streets. Coaches plied for hire between Westminster and the Temple, and among the attractions were puppets, bull-baiting, horse racing, and football. Evelyn walked across the frozen Thames to dine with the Archbishop of Canterbury at Lambeth, and Charles II took part in the hunt of a fox let loose on the ice.

The 1740 Frost Fair was particularly elaborate. It followed a period of continuous freezing which started on Christmas Day, 1739, and went on until the following 1 February. The intense cold caused tragedy as well as pleasure, as may be judged from *The London Magazine* for 31 January which reads:

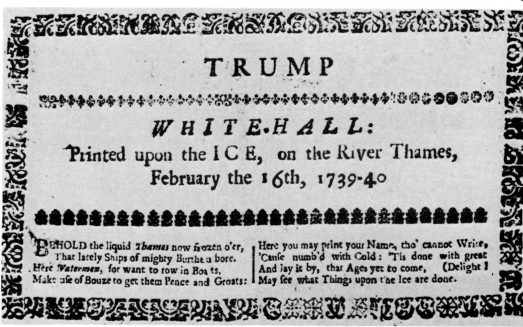

THURSDAY 31.
This Month the Frost, which began the 26th of last, grew more severe than has been known since the memorable Winter of 1715-16; so that many who had lived Years at *Hudson's-Bay*, declar'd they never felt it colder in those Parts. The *Thames* floated with Rocks and Shoals of Ice; and when they fixed, represented a snowy Field, rising every where in Hillocks and huge Rocks of Ice and Snow; of which Scene several Painters took Sketches. Booths, Stalls, and Printing-Presses were erected, and a *Frost-Fair* held on it: Multitudes walk'd over it, and some were lost by their Rashness. Several perished with Cold in the Streets and Fields in and about the City. All Navigation being obstructed, Coals rose to 3 *l.* 10 *s. per Chaldron*; and the Damage among the Shipping between the *Medway* and *London-Bridge* was computed at 100,000 *l.* Flocks of Ducks, Widgeons and Coots were found on the Ice on the *Kent* and *Essex* Shores, perish'd with Cold, or starv'd to Death. Vast Quantities of Fish, especially Eels, were found frozen to Death on the Banks of the *Severn*, near *Thornbury* in *Gloucestershire*, and Flocks of Crows resorted thither to feed on them.

Among the booths was one containing a printing press. The tradition of bringing a press on to the ice, so that a permanent record of a Frost Fair could be made, goes back at least to the late seventeenth century when Charles II and his family all had their names printed on a card. Under a rather crude engraving of the fair a space was left in which a decorative box, like the one above, was added carrying the date and the person's name. At every Frost Fair for 130 years these broadsheets appeared with some doggerel in which the visitor was invited by the printer to have his name recorded for posterity. It ended with the couplet:

And sure, in former ages, ne'er was found
A Press to Print where men so oft were drown'd!

4. One of the attractions of the 1740 Frost Fair was the ascent of the incomplete piers of Westminster Bridge, building of which had started in the previous year. This unique pen-and-wash drawing shows a man blowing a trumpet to attract sightseers. Under a temporary tent money is taken by a cashier behind a table. Having paid, a man with his wife and small boy are walking round to the ladder which will take them up to the top of the pier where two men are already standing. One points with a stick out over the river at a view of London which has never before been possible.

5. When William Hogarth visited the Frost Fair at Whitehall in the middle of February 1740, he had the customary souvenir printed for him on the ice. But instead of his own name, he asked the printer to insert that of his favourite dog – a bull terrier called Trump. The souvenir was given to John Ireland, Hogarth's biographer, by Mrs Mary Lewis, the artist's secretary. He is said to have died in her arms, and she came into possession of many of his manuscripts and drawings.

The South-Sea Bubble

In the autumn of 1720 a disaster hit the City. In Exchange Alley – between Cornhill and Lombard Street – speculators faced bankruptcy. The merry-go-round, satirized, right, by Hogarth, on which life savings had been gambled, and fortunes made during the spring, had come to an abrupt stop. The South-Sea Bubble had burst.

Nine years before, a company had been formed to trade in the South Seas – the Pacific – and was so successful that its directors decided to gamble and challenge the Bank of England. They purchased the management of the National Debt, and offered Government shareholders stock in the South Seas Company in exchange for their five per cent investments. Secretly, and to gain commercial preference, they also issued stock on favourable terms to ministers, royal mistresses, and other people of influence.

The South Seas boom was so big that, in a frenzy of speculation, thousands of gullible investors were ensnared by other fraudulent mushroom companies – one 'for extracting silver from lead'. Promoters used the City coffee houses as their meeting places, much to the delight of the owners. One of the busiest was Jonathan's, in Exchange Alley (from which later grew the Stock Exchange). Fashionably dressed ladies added a new touch to the City. Attracted by the prospect of easy riches, it was the first time that they had ventured into the male preserves of high finance. When the time came for the South Seas Company to pay, there were insufficient funds. Panic set in. There was a rush to sell. In the crash nearly every propertied family in the land was hit, and Kneller, Pope, and Gay were among the thousands who lost money.

There was a howl for revenge. An investigation was held, and the estates of the South Seas' directors confiscated. The Chancellor of the Exchequer went to the Tower. The Postmaster General committed suicide. One of the few to benefit was Robert Walpole who was called to restore order during the crisis, and, as a direct result, became Prime Minister.

1. The harvest of greed, as seen by Hogarth. Symbolically shown, above, are get-rich-quick speculators on the merry-go-round, while below Honour and Honesty are flagellated by Self-interest and Villainy.

2. 'Weekly through the streets of London you may see second-hand coaches, second-hand gold watches, cast-off diamond watches and earrings are to be sold . . . in a word every place is full of the ruin of Exchange Alley. . . .' – *Applebee's Journal*, 22 October 1720. Brokers, like this one, worked in the open passageway, buying and selling stock in the summer before the Bubble burst.

3. Ruined investors bewail their financial losses.

Watermen and the Horseferry

Until Westminster Bridge was built, wheeled traffic that wanted to cross the Thames above London Bridge had to use the horseferry here seen nearing Millbank after a passage from Lambeth. There was a fixed tariff: *Man and Horse – 2d. Horse and Chaise – 1s. Coach and two Horses – 1s. 6d. Ladened Cart – 2s.* The new bridge also meant a serious loss to the ordinary ferries, and the watermen, who numbered about 20,000, protested to Parliament that it was 'pernicious to Navigation, detrimental to Trade, and likely to ruin Thousands of Families'. In compensation, £25,000 was granted them, and invested for the relief of 'the poor watermen of Westminster'. The See of Canterbury, which owned the ferry rights between Lambeth Palace and Horseferry Road, received £2,205. Watermen served a seven-year apprenticeship before they were granted the freedom to row such craft as the eighteen-oar Royal Barge or the small canopied boat seen near it, below. Many were content to ply for casual work in their own boats, like the two sitting outside the White Hart Tavern and looking at the milkmaid in her May Day headdress. The waterman in blue wears a metal shield on an armband which shows that he is a winner of the race from London Bridge to Chelsea for 'Doggett's Coat and Badge'. The award, first given by Tom Doggett, a Drury Lane actor, in 1716, has been competed for annually ever since. The inn is one of a number on Millbank at which travellers waited, sometimes overnight, to take the horseferry across the river.

1. Thames watermen were the first public servants to wear uniform. On their arms were the badges of their employers. This figure is from the Bow porcelain factory.

2. The Horseferry, where Lambeth Bridge is today.

3. Royal Barge and rivercraft – detail from Canaletto.

Hogarth at the Golden Head

Over the doorway of a house at the south-east corner of Leicester Square was a gilded bust of Van Dyck. At the sign of the Golden Head, as he called it, William Hogarth lived and worked from 1733 until his death in 1764. Here he won renown, but also felt anger and hurt pride at an auction which he held in his studio in February 1745. Despite their success as prints, the originals of his two series, 'The Harlot's Progress' and 'The Rake's Progress', remained unsold after ten years. So he put them up for sale with five other canvasses. For a month potential buyers were invited to make their bids in a book. Then, on the day of the sale, a clock striking at five-minute intervals after midday marked the knocking down of each picture to the highest bidder.

As Hogarth hoped, this eccentric sale aroused interest; but it also proved what he feared. Connoisseurs would not accept him

seriously as a painter. Like the rest of the series, *The Arrest*, above, fetched only £22, and others made inconsiderable sums. The art market, influenced by the dealers, was dominated by foreign painters–the 'Black Masters' as Hogarth depicted them, in conflict with his own canvasses, in the satirical invitation he sent out for the sale.

Despite this setback, he was, at forty-eight, at the height of his career. To Leicester Square came sitters as various as the Drury Lane actress, Peg Woffington, and Captain Coram of the Foundling Hospital. Weary of polite 'conversation pieces', Hogarth had become a reformer, castigating the follies of the town. Billingsgate shrimp girls interested him more than duchesses. Covent Garden vice, the degradation of Bedlam and the Fleet, the cruelty of the Westminster Cockpit, East End misery and the affectations of Mayfair were all treated as by a dramatist. 'My picture is my stage,' he said, 'and men and women my players.'

Hogarth had a foot in the world of both poverty and fashion. He had been born in poor lodgings in St Bartholomew's Close, and risen above the craft of engraving to which he was apprenticed. A runaway marriage had won him the daughter of Sir James Thornhill, and by middle age there were servants and comfort at the Golden Head. His circle of friends included Johnson, Boswell, Garrick and Wilkes.

In 1734 he had founded a drawing academy, above, 'to admit thirty or forty persons drawing after a naked figure, in St Martin's Lane', a school which was to lead to the foundation of the Royal Academy thirty-four years later. But, though he believed he could paint as well as Van Dyck, the man over his portal, success as a painter eluded him. Henry Fielding saw him as 'one of the most useful satirists that any age has produced'. But the picture-buying public agreed with Horace Walpole that 'as a painter Hogarth had little merit', unaware that posterity would regard him as the greatest delineator of London and his age.

However bitter his public battles, in private Hogarth enjoyed a happy domestic life, and, after 1749, divided his time between Leicester Square and a small house at Chiswick. The 'villakin', as he called it, was a strange, cramped building with a crooked staircase and a large bow window. In the garden was a shed which he fitted up as a studio. Here the artist had the tranquillity to entertain friends, walk by the river, and take ale at the village inn. He died at the house in Leicester Square, but was buried at Chiswick, in the churchyard by the Thames.

1. St James's Street looking south from Piccadilly – St David's Day, 1735. Tom Rakewell arrested for debt on his way to Court on the Queen's birthday – one of 'The Rake's Progress' series sold for £22.

2. Hogarth at his easel – a self-portrait wearing the Spanish 'montero' cap he affected.

3. The Life School – Hogarth's view of students at his St Martin's Lane academy where many mid-Georgian artists were to train.

4. Hogarth's house in the south-east corner of Leicester Square. By the time of this print it had become Jaquier's Hotel. Behind is the spire of St Martin-in-the-Fields, and in the foreground a statue of George I, now replaced by Shakespeare.

5. The invitation sent out for the sale of paintings with the inscription: 'The Bearer hereof is Entitled (if he thinks proper) to be a Bidder for MR HOGARTH'S PICTURES, which are to be Sold on the Last day of this month.'

189

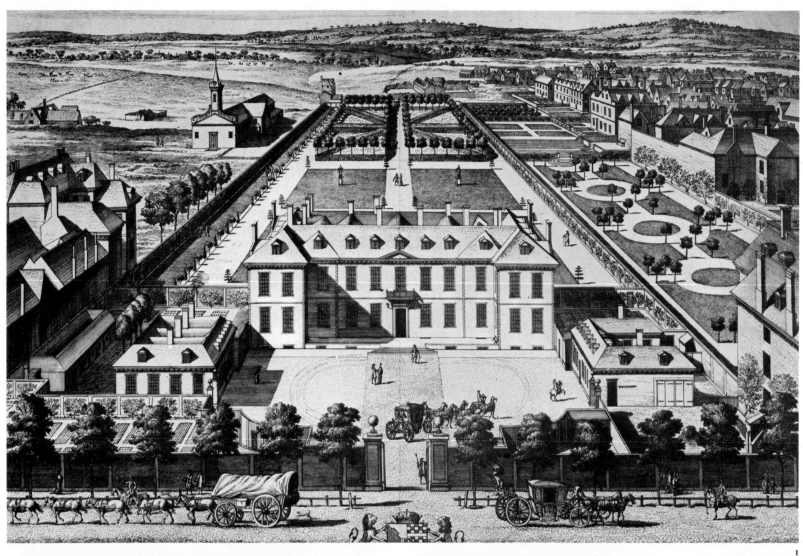

The Palladians

When Lord Burlington returned to London in 1719 after a summer in Italy, he brought with him, like Inigo Jones a century earlier, a tremendous enthusiasm for the work of Palladio which he had seen at Vicenza. That enthusiasm was to radiate, and to have a revolutionary effect on English architectural taste for generations to come.

The engraving (1) shows the pleasant mansion on the north side of Piccadilly which Richard Boyle, 3rd Earl of Burlington, inherited along with his title and considerable wealth at the age of ten. After the palaces of Italy it looked, no doubt, a trifle plain. Straightway he set about 'Palladianizing' it. With the help of Colin Campbell, William Kent, who came back with him from Rome, and Giacomo Leoni, a Venetian whom he also attracted to London, the young Earl – he was only twenty-two – started the conversion.

The view (4) shows the result. The ground floor was 'rusticated'; the windows were given alternatively curved and triangular pediments and set between Ionic columns;

1. Burlington House in 1707 before the conversion.

2. William Kent – Burlington's 'proper priest'.

3. Lord Burlington, with a bust of Inigo Jones emerging from the background in ghostly inspiration. First of the Grand Tourists, patron of architects and the innovator of Palladianism, Burlington was called 'the Apollo of the Arts' by Horace Walpole.

4. Burlington House after the refronting in 1719.

5. Chiswick House, 1729, sarcastically described by Lord Hervey as 'too small to inhabit, and too large to hang to one's watch'. Pen and ink drawing by Kent.

6. Hogarth's lampoon against Kent and the Palladians. Kent (E) stands with his palette on top of Burlington House gate. Below the poet Pope (A) spatters paint on the Duke of Chandos (B), a rival patron of the arts, passing below, while Burlington (F) climbs the ladder in the role of an ordinary labourer.

4

5

6

the old pitched roof was lowered and partly hidden behind a balustrade; two large Venetian windows ennobled the projecting wings. To this was added a double quadrant, a colonnade of Doric columns, and a majestic classical gateway to Piccadilly.

Burlington was a man of taste, a rich dilettante amateur, and though, seemingly, he designed and drew, his main role was that of a patron. The principal architect employed by him was Kent, a Yorkshireman about ten years older than his patron, who was installed in rooms at Burlington House (Handel was another permanent guest) and, one of a charmed circle of architects, prepared designs for houses built on the Earl's lands near and to the north of Burlington House. When Burlington decided to build a house at Chiswick as a gallery for his works of art – a classical villa in the full Palladian manner – Kent was responsible for the interior decorations. The dominating architect for most of George II's reign, Kent was created Portrait Painter to the King in 1739 which brought satirical comment from Hogarth in the form of the cartoon (p.191). As well as satire, 'Palladianism' provoked aesthetic criticism – some held it to be too coldly classical and austere – but this could not stop a movement which was to add so many notable buildings to mid-eighteenth-century London.

Though many have been demolished, sufficient examples of domestic buildings survive in Mayfair to show the brilliance of the Palladians. No 31 Old Bond Street has a magnificent interior which suggests Colin Campbell. Queensborough House, on the corner of Savile Row and Burlington Gardens, is by Leoni who published Palladio's works in England and whose masterpiece is Moor Park, Hertfordshire. Kent's domestic work is seen in the sumptuous interior of No 44 Berkeley Square, though he is chiefly remembered in London for Horse Guards, top right, built posthumously to his designs in 1751. The murals for the staircase of Kensington Palace, bottom right, are among his lesser known pleasantries.

Among other notable Palladians was Isaac Ware, a sickly Cockney chimney sweep whom Burlington is said to have discovered sketching the Banqueting Hall with a piece of chalk on a wall in Whitehall. His benefactor had him educated and sent to Italy. Ware gave London Chesterfield House, South Audley Street (demolished 1937), and to him may be attributed a number of other Mayfair houses illustrated in his *The Complete Body of Architecture*. Henry Flitcroft ('Burlington Harry'), another protégé of Burlington, built what is now Chatham House, St James's Square, and St Giles-in-the-Fields, above right. John Vardy, who executed the Horse Guards to Kent's plans,

7

8

9

was responsible for Spencer House, above right, overlooking Green Park. Vardy's design combined with interior enrichment by James Stuart prompted a mid-century visitor to write ecstatically: 'I do not apprehend there is a house in Europe of its size better worth the view of the curious. . . .' Built for Earl Spencer, great-grandson of the Duchess of Marlborough, this remains one of London's finest examples of domestic Palladian architecture.

7. Horse Guards by William Kent.

8. St Giles-in-the-Fields by Henry Flitcroft.

9. Spencer House, Green Park, by John Vardy.

10. The King's Grand Staircase at Kensington Palace with decorative murals by Kent in which a crowd of courtiers, women with fans, Negro pages and masqueraders appear to be leaning over a balustrade. Kent, two of his pupils, and an actress friend are among them.

10

Buckingham House

'One of the great beauties of London' was the way Buckingham House appeared to a traveller who saw it in 1722. It commanded a magnificent view of St James's Park, and, as Queen Anne had noted with annoyance, gave the presumptuous appearance of owning all it surveyed. Superficially, it seems Palladian. The same classic columns on the façade; the same statues on the flat roof; the same quadrant colonnades and flanking wings. But, built for John Sheffield, Duke of Buckingham in 1703, the house was in the more florid Renaissance style of Wren and Vanbrugh against which Burlington's 'Men of Taste' were in revolt. It was designed by William Winde, an exiled Royalist brought up in Holland, and became the model for many early Georgian mansions. One of its remarkable interior features was a staircase, thirty-five feet high from ground floor to roof, which filled a third of the front of the house.

Immensely rich, the patron of Dryden and the friend of Pope, and also a poet in his own right, Buckingham chose for his town house the site of the demolished Arlington House. This, in its turn, had been built in Mulberry Garden, the fashionable recreation ground at the south-west end of the park. The garden, famous during the Restoration, derived its name from the trees planted there by James I in an abortive attempt to breed silkworms and start an English silk industry.

Another contemporary description of Buckingham House was 'a seat not to be condemned by the greatest monarch'. Royal eyes were enviously turned on it, but it did not become a palace until George III purchased it in 1775 as official residence for the dowager Queen Charlotte. Not until the next century, and after alterations by John Nash (who 'Palladianized' it) was it the residence of a reigning sovereign. To Londoners it has always remained 'Buck House'.

The panorama on the following page shows the fine view commanded by Buckingham House. Some time after 1710, the Dutch artist, John Kip, appears to have made his drawing from the roof. The view was dedicated to the Princess of Wales, which is interesting as the future George II and his wife wanted to buy the house in 1723. Perhaps the Duchess of Buckingham (who asked £60,000, but didn't get it) intended the view as a bait; or Kip may have drawn it in expectation of a sale which never took place.

1 *and* 2. Two views of Buckingham House.

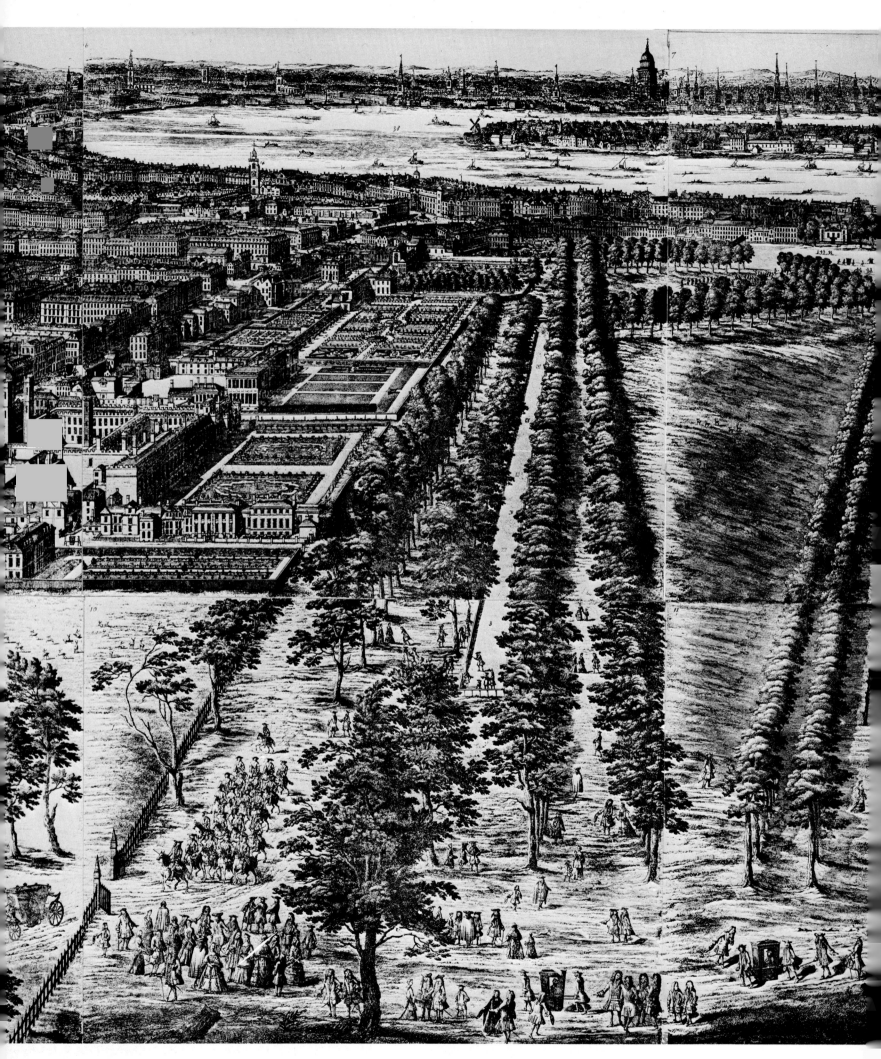

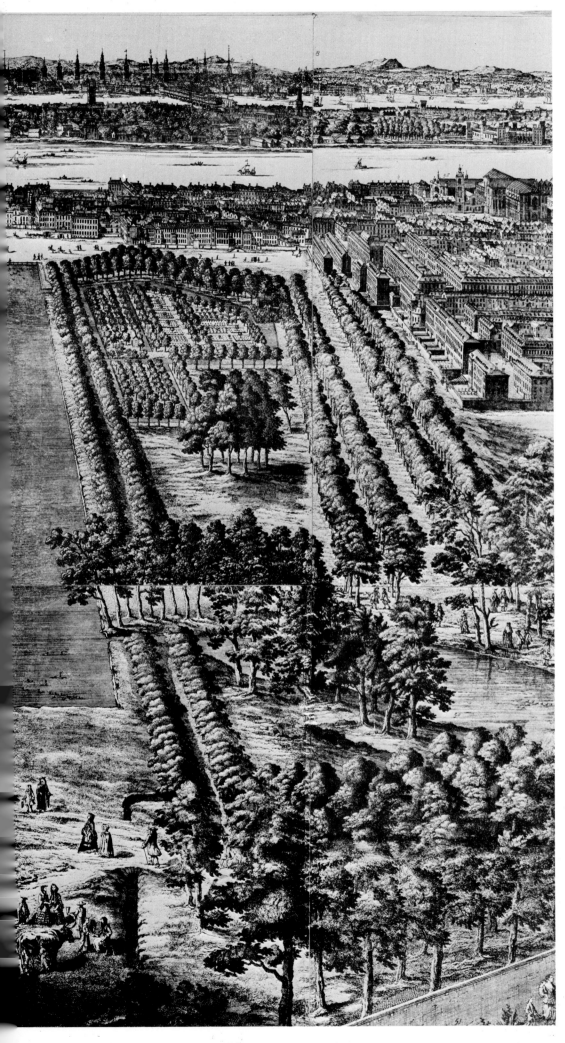

John Kip's View

For the first time we have a really comprehensive view of the West End and Westminster. Expansion outside the City in the fifty years since the Fire has resulted in what are virtually two new towns on either side of St James's Park.

Straight ahead is the tree-lined Mall, flanked on the left by Pelemele Alley, which leads to Spring Gardens and the north end of Whitehall. At the far end of the Canal there are throngs of people, and soldiers parade in front of Horse Guards. The Stuart stairway entrance to Whitehall Palace (page 132) has disappeared, for the direct link with Whitehall Palace is now severed and the palace itself only a memory. Looking down from the roof of Buckingham House, we see in the foreground a milkmaid selling penny mugs of milk. Just behind her is the open conduit which carries water from the Tyburn brook into the Canal, either directly, or through Rosamond's Pond, extreme right.

As far as the Abbey and the river, Westminster is a residential area of quiet squares and streets of impressive terraced houses with fine gardens. Some have direct access to the park through private doors in the surrounding wall. At the far end of the park, a small doorway in the wall on the right leads into Long Ditch, the street in which Kip is to die in 1722, aged about seventy. The Abbey is still without its west towers, designed by Hawksmoor, and completed in 1739 after his death.

Across the river (but out of the true sightline) is Lambeth Palace. Kip has also faked his far perspective. From this viewpoint, the Thames should diminish into the distance, not double back as the artist so conveniently makes it in order to show us the City waterfront, London Bridge, and some distinctly unfamiliar peaks on the Essex skyline.

To the north (left-hand) side of the Park, we see, in the foreground, the road past Lord Godolphin's home to St James's Palace Mews. Then come the formal gardens belonging to the houses facing on to Pall Mall, some of them with small raised terraces from which a view of the Park may be enjoyed. At the top of Whitehall stands Northumberland House with its four turrets, and garden down to the river. We also see the Royal Mews (site of Trafalgar Square) and the tower of St Martin-in-the-Fields before James Gibbs's rebuilding. Then the Strand curves away, following the line of the Thames, to pass the battlemented Savoy and the church of St Mary-le-Strand.

To fit the page, Kip's panorama has had to be trimmed at the sides. For a broader, more comprehensive view to the north, we go over to Rocque's map on the next page.

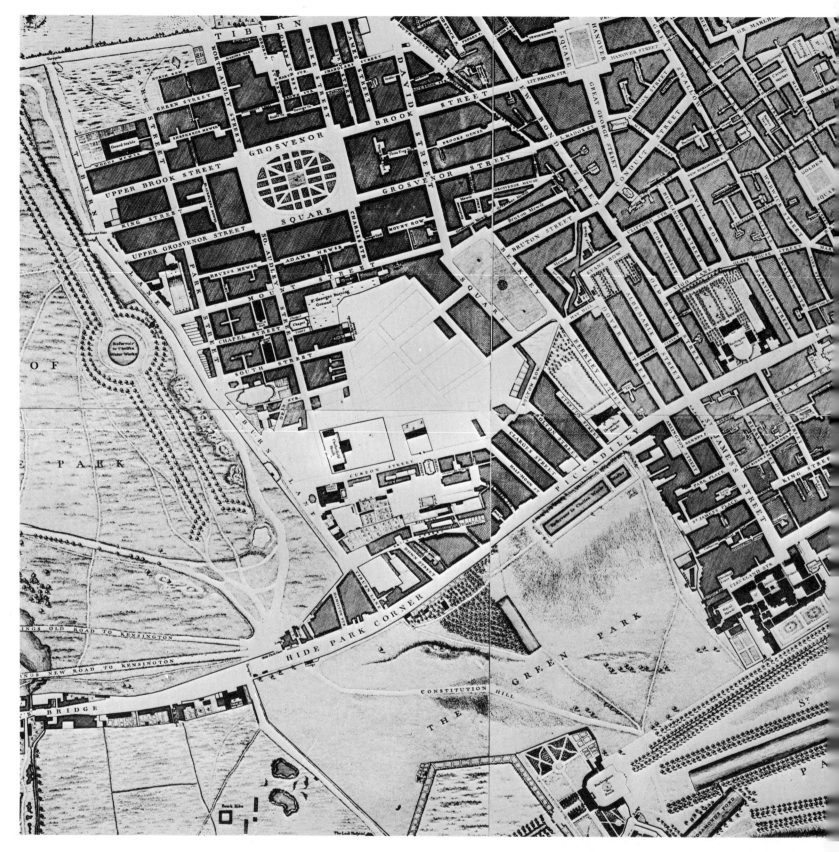

Rocque's Map

This detail from the famous map by John Rocque, chosen to cover much the same area as Kip, shows the West End and Westminster about thirty years later. This 1746 map has a wider angle of view which enables us to see the important residential development farther to the north of St James's Park and Green Park as far as *Tiburn Road*, the western end of modern Oxford Street. This

selective view takes in about one-twelfth of the whole map.

Rocque, who was of Huguenot extraction, and lived for a while in the French quarter of Soho, graduated to this major topographical work from surveying gentlemen's estates. It was a huge task, as every street had to be covered on foot and measured with a waywiser, a perambulator with a wheel 8 feet 3 inches in circumference (1/640th of a mile) as shown on the right.

The mapping of the whole of London's built-up area, and the engraving of the twenty-four sheets, took nine years from 1737. Revisions were made three times during the century to include such additions as the Hill Street area of Mayfair shown as undeveloped (left centre) in this first edition. The original scale was twenty-six inches to the mile, approximately double the size here. Rocque extended his survey to take in the environs of London up to a radius of ten

miles. It was published by his widow in 1763, the year after his death.

This section is particularly valuable in depicting the area between Bond Street and Park Lane which grew up in the twenty-five years before 1750. Just how rural it was north of Piccadilly and west of Sackville Street at the beginning of the century may be judged from the 1707 view of Burlington House (page 190). Now, in 1746, we find the fields covered with streets and squares of imposing

new houses. All had water laid on. Rocque shows the Piccadilly Reservoir in Green Park through which the Chelsea Water Works supplied them with Thames water, steam-pumped from a much larger reservoir situated where Victoria Station is today. Though sanitation was still primitive – there is no record of a water closet before 1764 – Mayfair did not have to rely on cesspools. The smaller oblong pond received and carried away sewage to the river.

'The Late, Great Mr Handel'

In Westminster Abbey, under the bust and monument by Roubiliac, rest the remains of the man whom, on his death in April 1759, the *Whitehall Evening Post* called 'the late, great Mr Handel'. For nearly half a century, Handel had played an outstanding part in English music as composer, conductor, and organist. 'He is the master of us all!' Haydn was to exclaim in the Abbey on another occasion after hearing the *Hallelujah Chorus*.

For the 3,000 people who came to the funeral this was a moment to recall Handel's career, and the nation-wide popularity he had forged out of enmity; his endeavours to make a success with Italian-style operas in London; the *Funeral Anthem* he composed for Queen Caroline; the solemn *Dead March* from his oratorio *Saul* (for the first performance of which he borrowed military kettledrums from the Tower); and remember, too, his devotion to the children of the Foundling Hospital.

German by birth, Handel had taken English nationality in his forties. A Londoner by adoption, he died in the same house where he had lived for thirty-six years, No 57 (now No 25), Brook Street, Mayfair, and where he composed *The Messiah*. Handel had loved London from the time of his arrival in 1710 when, a young man from Saxony, he had been taken up by Lord Burlington and the Duke of Chandos and become Principal Court Composer to George I.

For the King, Handel composed one of his most celebrated instrumental suites. Contrary to legend, it was not the occasion for their reconciliation after a long feud. The King was to dine at the villa of Lord Ranelagh in Chelsea. It was a lovely July evening, and the tide was on the flood so that the Royal Barge could float upstream from Whitehall unaided. Not even the dipping of oars disturbed the purity of sound which carried across the Thames from a following barge on which Handel and an orchestra of fifty were playing the *Water Music*.

To celebrate the Treaty of Aix-la-Chapelle in 1749, George II ordered a display in Green Park and Handel was asked to compose special music for the occasion. An elaborate Temple of Peace was erected, 410 feet long and 114 feet high, to the design of an Italian architect, Servandoni. This rococo edifice with its built-in fireworks and lighting effects provided a stage for a hundred musicians.

1. Handel – his statue in the Abbey.

2. Thomas Britton – as well as small coals man and music lover, he was an amateur chemist, book collector, bibliographer, and dabbler in the occult.

3. Music at Montagu House, Bloomsbury. The Duke of Montagu is immediately to the right of the flautist.

4. The Temple of Peace, scene of celebration and tragedy, from the Piccadilly side of Green Park.

Forty trumpets, twenty French horns and sixteen bassoons were among the instruments needed for Handel's *Music for the Royal Fireworks*. Cannons hidden in alcoves were fired as part of the overture.

Even before the great night, London crowded to see the Temple, below, and 12,000 people paid admission at Vauxhall to hear a rehearsal of the music. For the actual performance on 27 April, the King, Privy Councillors, Peers and M.P.s watched from special stands. Fifty yards of railing in Piccadilly were removed to admit the huge crowds.

At 8.30 p.m. the first of 10,650 rockets went up. The cannons roared. Fireworks exploded in all directions. Finally the building caught fire. Two arches collapsed in flames. Three deaths occurred in the crowd. A burning girl had to be stripped to her stays. A drunken cobbler fell into a pond. An infuriated Servandoni was arrested for drawing his sword. The display went on, and the King retired at midnight. His peace celebration had cost £90,000.

One man who contributed to the musical climate in which Handel flourished was a violinist, John Banister. Towards the end of the previous century he had promoted the first London concerts open to the public with payment at the door. 'He procured a large room in Whitefryars neer the Temple back gate', wrote Roger North in his *Memoires of Music* in 1728, 'and made a large raised box for the musitians whose modesty required curtaines. The room was rounded with seats and small tables, alehouse fashion. One shilling, was the price and call for what you pleased; there was very good musick....'

This was in 1672, and by North's time musicians were very far from playing behind curtains. They were to be seen and heard in raised galleries by crowds strolling under lanterns in Marylebone and Vauxhall Gardens. There was a public concert hall in Covent Garden, and in another – Hickford's Room, Brewer Street – Mozart, aged eight, and his sister, aged thirteen, were to perform in 1765. Concerts were held in all great private houses, and chamber music provided background for conversaziones as seen at Montagu House, Bloomsbury, below left. Amateurs performed at smaller homes, and at Streatham Mrs Thrale played the harpsichord and Dr Johnson contemplated the idea of taking up the violoncello.

At the Haymarket Theatre visiting Italian companies drew the town to formal opera until Gay started a reaction with his satirical *Beggar's Opera*, and taverns rang with singing. The Crown and Anchor in the Strand was the meeting place for the Academy of Vocal Music and the Madrigal Society, while catches and glees were heard at the Thatched House Tavern, St James's, at regular soirées held by the Noblemen and Gentlemen's Catch Club.

In London's increasing enthusiasm for music, an extraordinary role was filled by a man who was a small coals seller by trade. Thomas Britton humped coal on his back for a living, but his heart was in music. He leased a stable on Jerusalem Passage, Clerkenwell, which he divided into two storeys. An outside ladder led up to a long, low room where Britton held choral and instrumental concerts every Thursday for nearly forty years. He made no charge, and served coffee at one penny a cup. Such was Britton's personality that he drew audiences which included the nobility, and musicians as famous as Handel and Dr Pepusch were happy to perform for this unlikely enthusiast. According to a contemporary diarist, Britton's stable was a place to which 'most foreigners of distinction, for the fancy of it, occasionally resort'. Britton was a man of parts. As well as a lover of music, he was an amateur chemist, dabbled in the occult, and, a keen bibliophile, went on book-hunting expeditions with the Earl of Oxford. But until his death, he remained a coal vendor.

The Birth of London's Voluntary Hospitals

The population of London nearly doubled during the eighteenth century, and it was impossible for the old monastic hospitals to deal with disease bred in the filthy over-crowded tenements of the poor. There were epidemics of fever, death-dealing illnesses with imprecise medical terms like putrid fever, spotted fever, relapsing fever. Small-pox, dysentery, typhus and typhoid were scourges, and Londoners' health was insidiously undermined by cheap gin. In some parts of the town, spirits were sold in every fifth house and led to premature death of adults and an ever-increasing mortality among children under five, neglected and starved by fuddled parents. In early Georgian times not only were the poor widely divided from the rich, but the State did not see medicine as its responsibility. It was through the conscience of a privileged and en-lightened few that help was to come.

In 1716, four men met in a Fleet Street coffee house. There was a banker – Henry Hoare – a vintner, a religious writer, and a clergyman; they established between them 'The Charitable Society for relieving the Sick poor and Needy'. Out of this grew the first hospital to be maintained by voluntary subscriptions, the small Westminster Infirm-ary in Petty France which, within twenty years, was to expand into a much larger hospital, St George's at Hyde Park Corner. These philanthropists were only a little ahead of others, and new hospitals followed rapidly – Guy's in 1726, the London, Mile End Road in 1740, the Middlesex in 1745, the Lock Hospital in 1746.

1

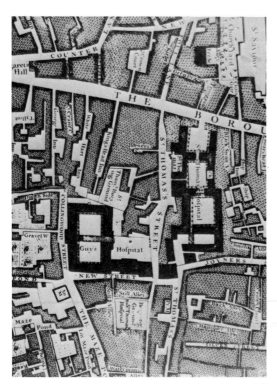

2

3

They came to the rescue of the only two existing hospitals of any consequence, St Bartholomew's in Smithfield, and St Thomas's, Southwark, both refounded medieval institutions, and now inadequate. St Thomas's in the Borough (demolished in 1871, though the old operating theatre still exists by the church tower in the view, far right) grew into its eighteenth-century magnificence round three quadrangles, a design probably influenced by Wren, who was a governor of the hospital. Connected with St Mary Overy, St Thomas's dated back to the twelfth century, and in the 1400s Whittington had endowed a ward for eight unmarried mothers, their names to be 'kept secret . . . for he would not shame no young woman no wise. . . .'

St Thomas's specialized in anatomy and surgery, and from early in the century had an embryonic medical school with three students apprenticed to each surgeon. But it became impossible to accommodate the large number of incurable patients, and one of the governors, Thomas Guy, decided to build an annex. In 1721 he took a lease of land on the opposite side of St Thomas's Street (see Rocque, far left) and, largely with a fortune made out of the South Sea Company, built his hospital to an ingenious plan with a central colonnade that provided all-weather access to the surrounding build-

1. Thomas Guy who, says his epitaph, 'rivalled the Endowment of Kings' by the foundation of his hospital – as seen on his monument in the chapel at Guy's.

2. Rocque's map shows the three quadrangles of St Thomas's (now demolished) that faced onto Borough High Street, and Guy's across St Thomas's Street.

3. The entrance to Guy's with a patient being brought in.

4. Bedlam – St Mary's of Bethlehem, Moorfields. Until the practice was stopped in 1770, fashionable visitors paid a penny admission which gave them the right to taunt the inmates. Bedlam was the only hospital for 'distracted people' before the foundation of St Luke's, Old Street, in 1751.

5. The Queen Anne gateway to St Bartholomew's Hospital with the statue of Henry VIII who, after its surrender, refounded and endowed it in 1554. Bart's is London's oldest hospital.

6. St Thomas's – view from the Borough looking east.

7. Patients in an eighteenth-century hospital.

8. A ward at Guy's as it looked in 1726.

9

10

11

12

ings. Guy, a wealthy publisher and bookseller, died two years before his hospital was completed, but he left it richly endowed. A serving girl with whom he was contemplating marriage is said to have outraged a parsimonious streak by ordering some paving stones outside his house. The wedding never took place, and his fortune went to the hospital.

The first of the 435 poor patients were received in 1726. Under his will admission was restricted to people 'labouring under any distemper, infirmities or disorders thought capable of relief by physic or surgery, but who . . . may be judged to be incurable'. Later, the qualification of 'incurable' had to be modified because so good was the nursing and treatment at Guy's that, of the 1,954 patients admitted during the first eight years, only 256 died.

The hospital had twelve wards with wooden cubicles, and the patients, most of whom paid nothing, were forbidden to swear, smoke or gamble. For the last two offences they could be discharged. The staff at first consisted of two physicians, two surgeons, a chaplain, a matron (at £50 a year with free coal and small beer), eleven nurses, and a man who was paid £20 as a bug catcher. A dental surgeon joined the staff in 1799.

Treatment outside hospitals was in the hands of the Royal College of Physicians at Newgate, the Society of Apothecaries (whose seventeenth-century hall still exists at Blackfriars), and the Barber-Surgeons Company from which the surgeons withdrew in 1745. There were also innumerable quacks advertising every sort of preposterous cure. Among the more flamboyant was Mrs Sarah Mapp, a bone-setter who drove weekly from Epsom to the Grecian Coffee House in Devereux Court off the Strand in a four-horse chariot with splendid equipage to trade in her skill.

One mother in forty-two and one child in fifteen died in childbirth, a mortality rate which led to lying-in wards. Two years after it opened, the Middlesex pioneered with five maternity beds, and when the hospital moved to its present site in Marylebone, set up a separate maternity department. The country's leading obstetrician, Sir Richard Manningham, who was known as a 'man-midwife' opened a house for lying-in patients in 1738, and seventy years later, and after several changes of address, it became the Queen Charlotte Hospital, the first maternity hospital to admit resident male students.

Hospitals worked with the most rudimentary knowledge of infection and without antiseptics. Blood-letting, purges, and sweating were the main cures prescribed by physicians. Without anaesthetics, surgeons were forced to work at great speed, and knowledge of anatomy was handicapped by lack of bodies. The law only permitted those hanged at Tyburn or Newgate to be dissected. Surgeons with pupils to teach sometimes smuggled bodies out of the hospitals into their own homes. Medical schools, like that of the famous William Hunter, bottom left, in Great Windmill Street had to be served, and body snatching from graves was a thriving trade. In 1776 more than a hundred bodies were discovered, ready for disposal, in a shed in Tottenham Court Road. Hunter's even more famous younger brother, John, was also popular with the 'resurrectionists'. Regarded as the founder of scientific surgery, he kept tigers and other beasts for dissection in cages on two acres which he bought at Earl's Court. He also obtained the bodies of animals who died at the menagerie at the Tower of London. On his death in 1793 his museum of specimens went to the Royal College of Surgeons.

The Foundling Hospital, built in 1747 in Lamb's Conduit Fields, north of Red Lion Street, had a special place in the affection of Londoners. On Sundays it was visited by those interested in the welfare of the hundreds of little children cared for by the hospital. They were the illegitimate offspring of mothers unable to look after them. The plight of such children had gone to the heart of a merchant sailor, Captain Thomas Coram, who had seen babies abandoned in the streets near his Rotherhithe home. In the face of the prejudiced who held it an incitement to immorality, Coram devoted his retirement to raising money for the hospital. Hogarth was

13

14

among the artists who gave pictures to be sold on behalf of the foundlings, and Handel conducted benefit concerts as well as donating the manuscript of his *Messiah* to the hospital.

At first no child was refused; but there were so many that this had to be modified. For a while mothers drew lots at the hospital gate to see which could be admitted. Then this cruelly haphazard method gave way to an investigation of the mother's needs and background.

9. St George's as seen from Hyde Park Gate. The wagon heads west down the road to Knightsbridge. In the hospital, which could take 273 in-patients, windows were kept tightly shut, and the doctors carried perfume in the knobs of their canes against the smell. St George's was rebuilt in its present form in 1829.

10. The London Hospital with the, then, Mile End Road in the foreground, built in the fields and with all wards for the 350 patients facing south, that is, looking towards Limehouse. Left is the tower of St George-in-the-East, and, right, the curious artificial hill is the Mount, created from earth excavated from trenches dug for London's defence in the Civil War, and from debris collected after the Great Fire.

11. John Hunter, a governor of St George's and the Royal surgeon.

12. William Hunter, his brother, dissecting at his School of Anatomy, for many years London's main centre for surgical training.

13. Captain Coram with a foundling baby.

14. Foundling children in their special uniforms.

15. The Foundling Hospital, built in fifty-five acres of grounds, as it looked in 1749. In 1926 it moved to Redhill and then Berkhamsted. As Coram Fields, the site is preserved as a children's playground.

15

Sin . . .

As fashionable London moved west into the squares of Mayfair and Soho, Covent Garden changed its character. The houses planned by the Earl of Bedford for the aristocracy were taken over by a very different sort of tenant, and by 1732, when Covent Garden Playhouse was opened in the north-east corner, it was the centre of London night life. As Sir John Fielding, the Bow Street magistrate, observed, 'One would imagine that all the prostitutes in the Kingdom had picked upon that blessed neighbourhood for a general rendez-vous, for here are lewd women enough to fill a mighty colony. . . .'

What Sir John called 'provision for the flesh' was made by 'open houses' or brothels, lodging houses, taverns (with special rooms reserved for assignations), coffee houses, and bagnios—some of which were perfectly respectable Turkish and hot baths, but others simply disorderly houses. There were also twenty-four gaming houses in the area. Tom's Coffee House, a small building in the square opposite St Paul's Church, was the most notorious. It was opened by an Old Etonian, Tom King, and there 'might be found the bucks, bloods, demi-rips and choice spirits of London'. After his death, his wife 'Moll' King took it over, and was fined £200 for keeping a disorderly house.

The arcaded piazza of Covent Garden was the shadowy rendez-vous for ladies of the town and their clients (see right), while the windows of the bagnios were filled from seven at night until four or five in the morning with courtesans of every description who, 'in the most impudent manner invited the passengers from the theatres into the houses. . . .' The description of some 170 of these women was conveniently provided by a 'Who's Who'—*Harris's List of Covent Garden Ladies*. This *Man of Pleasure's Kalendar* gave abbreviated names and addresses and full physical descriptions, and anecdotes about the women. The *List*, revised annually, was sold openly in the piazza to the surprise of a French visitor who was scandalized that 'this trade is publicly cried in the streets'.

At dawn Covent Garden provided a spectacle of spent debauchery for the early morning vegetable sellers who by 1747—the date of the engraving above—had been using the square as a market for 'all manner of fruits, flowers, roots and herbs' for the past seventy years. They are watching the most notorious bagnio owner and noted beauty, Betty Careless, being carried to her premises, the roof of which is seen on the left. Rate books show her there in 1734, but her business was taken over five years later. She died in poverty and was buried in a pauper's grave in St Paul's graveyard.

HARRIS's LIST
OF
Covent-Garden Ladies:
OR
MAN OF PLEASURE's
KALENDAR,
For the YEAR 1773.
CONTAINING
An exact Defcription of the moft celebrated Ladies of Pleasure who frequent COVENT-GARDEN, and other parts of this Metropolis.

THE SECOND EDITION.

LONDON.
Printed for H. RANGER, Temple Exchange Paffage, Fleet-Street.
M DCC LXXIII.

1. Dawn scene in Covent Garden, 1747. Astride the sedan chair of 'charming Betty Careless' sits one of her many lovers, Captain Montague. Pointing at him, and carrying a long-stemmed artichoke on his shoulder is Captain Marcellus Laroon, in more sober moments an artist of delicacy as shown in his Montagu House study (page 198). With Little Casey—in front with a lighted taper—their creature and constant companion, these roisterers caused the Bow Street magistrates constant trouble.

2 *and* 3. Frontispiece and title page of the 1773 edition of the *List*, compiled by Jack Harris, a notorious procurer,

and waiter at the Shakespeare Head, Covent Garden. His List was apparently published annually from 1760 to 1793. A number of the ladies were also on the stage, and the actress, Peg Woffington, Garrick's mistress, is mentioned in some theatrical gossip. Descriptions are not always flattering. One girl is called 'a fine, bouncing, crummy wench', and another with 'scarce a tooth in her head but incomparable fine legs'.

...and Salvation

Vice did not go unchallenged. Converging on London in 1739 were two men who threatened sinners with damnation, and castigated 'the folly and madness of this sensual world'. In the teeth of opposition from the established Church, George Whitefield and John Wesley stormed the citadel of sin. To Anglican clerics preaching to empty or drowsy pews, the dynamism of these evangelists and their 'tumultuous assemblies' were repugnant. As Dissenters, they were denied the right to conduct services in church. They accepted the alternative of the open air.

'Matters go on most bravely in London!' wrote Whitefield a week after he had harangued a congregation of 10,000 on Hackney Marshes on the danger to their immortal souls of the nearby horse-racing. The following day he was at Kensington and Lewisham; the next, crowds on Blackheath heard how Hell-fire threatened those who spent 'their estates . . . on their whores and their earthly sensual and devilish pleasures'. Though only twenty-four, Whitefield swayed 20,000 at Stoke Newington with his sermon, 'The Serpent Beguiling Eve'. A vast assembly of 80,000 came to hear him in Mayfair.

Wesley, slightly older, and less impassioned, set up his Methodist headquarters in London following a mystical experience at a religious meeting in Aldersgate one May evening in 1738. In Moorfields, near modern Finsbury Square, was a disused ordnance foundry. Wesley borrowed £115, bought it, repaired it, and enlarged it to hold 1,500 people. This remained the fountainhead of Wesleyan Methodism for the next forty years. Three years later, Whitefield also came to Moorfields, and set up his pulpit in a large temporary shed called the Tabernacle just 300 yards from the foundry.

The two men differed temperamentally and in points of belief, but they combined to be the most potent force in the eighteenth-century religion. They could not hope to save many souls in Covent Garden, but before Wesley's death there were 134,549 Methodists and more than 350 chapels, including three in London, in West Street, Snow's Fields (Bermondsey) and the City Road. Whitefield's second 'Tabernacle', founded in 1756, was in Tottenham Court Road. The present building is the third on the site.

4. Conventional church worship suffered a decline in Georgian London to the point where Swift, satirically defending Christianity, pointed out how useful churches were as 'rendez-vouses of gallantry'.

5. Whitefield preaching with his wife listening.

6. A penitent prostitute. In her light grey uniform, long black mittens, and with an open prayer book, a reformed lady of the town stands in front of the chapel of Magdalen Hospital, St George's Fields. The hospital was founded in 1758, for reclaimed prostitutes.

7. John Wesley preaching in the open.

4

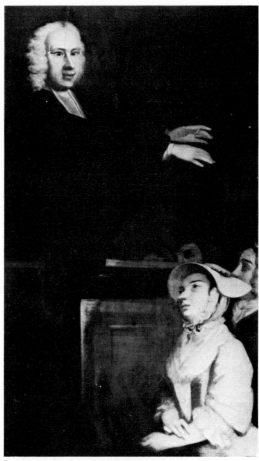

5

6

7

Scare, Hoax and Haunting

Three demonstrations of credulity in the middle years of the eighteenth century throw some doubt on the claim that this was the Age of Reason.

Early in 1750 London was disturbed by two earth tremors severe enough to bring down two old houses and some chimneys. Horace Walpole treated it lightly in a letter to a friend, saying, 'You must not be surprised if by the next post you hear of a burning mountain sprung up in Smithfield'. But there was enough alarm for a quack to do a brisk trade in pills for the warding off of earthquakes, and for a mad trooper (subsequently sent to Bedlam) to get a hearing for a prophecy that on 8 April London would be swallowed up in a fatal eruption. On the evening before, there was a panic flight. Lodgings had been taken as far out as Windsor. But Piccadilly was so choked with traffic that many got no further than Hyde Park where women sat shivering in their specially made 'Earthquake Gowns' and men played cards waiting for the apocalypse that never came.

Only the year before a hoax of classical simplicity had been pulled off by the waggish Duke of Montagu. He advertised a performance at the Haymarket Theatre at which a man would 'get into a tavern quart bottle'. A packed audience who had paid from 2s. to 7s. 6d. for seats sat looking at a closed curtain only slowly realizing that they had been duped. They then broke up the theatre. Everything movable, including curtains, scenery, and benches, was dragged in to the Haymarket and burnt. Added fuel to indignation was supplied by someone who called out that if the ladies and gentlemen would pay double prices the performer would get into a *pint* bottle.

Even so sceptical a person as Johnson spent two nights of vigil in the hope of seeing a supernatural manifestation by the Cock Lane Ghost. The eminent and the curious visited the house off Snow Hill, Smithfield, in 1762 to attend the first séances known of in London. Writers, churchmen, and the Duke of York were among others who crowded into the room of a terrified young girl, Elizabeth Parsons, who was alleged to be 'in touch' with a dead woman. 'To have a proper idea of the scene', wrote Goldsmith, 'the reader must conceive a very small room with a bed in the middle; the girl at the usual hour of going to bed is undressed and put in with proper solemnity: the spectators are next introduced. . . .'

The ghost was then supposed to tap out answers to questions, and these took the form of strange knockings from her bed. But when, under closer scrutiny, some of the manifesta-

tions were seen to be faked, the child's father and his accomplices were tried at the Guildhall for conspiracy, and found guilty. But the public seemed to prefer self-deception to justice. When the father was in the pillory, they pelted him not with rotten vegetables but with money.

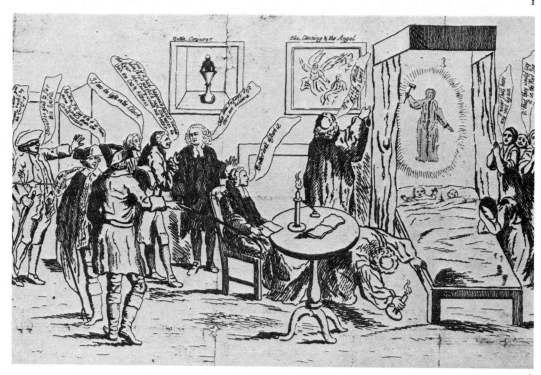

1. The mass exodus along Piccadilly during the earthquake scare of 1750. St James's Street is behind the coaches. On horseback carrying a banner inscribed with 'Prophesy' is the mad soldier who fermented the idea that providence was about to strike down the guilty.

2. In the bedroom in Cock Lane. This satirical view shows a print on the wall illustrating the Haymarket 'bottle hoax'.

The Meeting in Russell Street

When the young man who was to be his biographer arrived in London, Samuel Johnson was fifty-three. Twenty-five years before, he had left Lichfield, just as Boswell had come to seek his fortune from Edinburgh. After more than a decade in Gough Square, Johnson was living in Inner Temple Lane. Aggressive, erudite, scrofulous, and already a legend, he was the formidable centre of the literary world which the ambitious Boswell was determined to join.

Soon after his arrival, Boswell confided to Thomas Davies, a bookseller in Russell Street, Covent Garden, that he 'wanted much to see Johnson'. The meeting when it came six months later was quite accidental.

On that momentous Monday – 16 May 1763 – Boswell started the day by sending his breeches to be mended. He breakfasted with two Scottish friends at his Downing Street lodgings. He tried to recover a debt, but all he could get from the man who owed him money was a guinea. He stayed for a little food. It was after this day of trivialities that he then dropped in on Davies.

He records: 'I drank tea at Davies's in Russell Street, and about seven in came the great Samuel Johnson, whom I have so long wished to see. Mr Davies introduced me to him. As I knew his mortal antipathy to the Scotch, I cried to Davies, "Don't tell him where I come from". However, he said, "From Scotland". "Mr Johnson", said I, "indeed I come from Scotland, but I cannot help it". "Sir," replied he, "that, I find, is what a very great many of your countrymen cannot help".' Boswell noted: 'Mr Johnson is a man of most dreadful appearance. He is a very big man, is troubled with sore eyes, the palsy, and the king's evil. He is very slovenly in his dress and speaks with a most uncouth voice. Yet his great knowledge and strength of expression command vast respect and render him very excellent company. He has great humour and is a worthy man. But his dogmatical roughness of manners is disagreeable. I shall mark what I remember of his conversation. . . .'

How he marked it for the next twenty years, and with what result, we know.

3. Johnson and Boswell in a supper box at Vauxhall Gardens. Boswell is on the right with Mrs Thrale between him and the Doctor. On the left, next to the unidentified woman with a raised glass, is Oliver Goldsmith. Detail from a drawing by Rowlandson.

4. Davies's bookshop on the south side of Russell Street, between Covent Garden and Wellington Street. Perhaps formerly Button's Coffee House. Exact site lost with demolition (after 1857), but possibly two doors from Covent Garden.

5. Johnson's house in Gough Square, off Fleet Street, where he lived from 1748 to 1759.

6. The top-floor garret of the Gough Square house where the *Dictionary*, published in 1755, was compiled. The windows look out on the small square.

1. JAMES MACLEAN, Highwayman. Known as 'The Ladies' Hero', he passed himself off as an Irish squire with lodgings in St James's. Conducted highway robberies with the 'greatest good breeding'. Was apprehended after robbing Lord Eglington on Hounslow Heath. Executed, wearing a silk waistcoat with lace trimmings and yellow Morocco slippers, at Tyburn in 1750.

2. JENNY DIVER, Pickpocket. Her real name was Mary Young. So nicknamed because she had a pair of false arms, and, with hands apparently clasped, dived with her real hands into victims' bags and pockets. From Ireland, joined a gang at St Giles, then worked by herself at fairs, theatres, and even in churches. Executed at Tyburn, 1740; buried in St Pancras churchyard.

3. EARL FERRERS, Murderer. Shot his steward, and tried by his peers in Westminster Hall. Pleaded insanity, but found guilty. The last nobleman in England to suffer a felon's death, he was hanged at Tyburn in 1760. Seen here in his coffin, he is wearing the silver-embroidered coat in which, carried in his own landau, he was taken to Surgeons' Hall, Old Bailey, for dissection.

4. ELIZABETH BROWNRIGG, Murderer. Opened a private lying-in hospital in parish of St Dunstan's, Fleet Street, and employed orphans from the Foundling Hospital whom she sadistically maltreated by whipping, chaining and torturing. One died after violent assault. Tried at Old Bailey. Executed at Tyburn, 1767. Body taken to Surgeons' Hall, under 1752 Act authorizing dissection.

5. JACK SHEPPARD, Robber and prison breaker. Started as pickpocket. Graduated to housebreaking and highway robbery. Escaped twice from Newgate, first from condemned cell using a smuggled file, then from the cell, seen here, when he climbed chimney in fetters. Had a small hidden penknife with which he hoped to cut himself down at his Tyburn execution in 1724.

6. JONATHAN WILD, Thief and thief-taker. Combined large-scale crime, in which he organized gangs in different London districts, with helping the police by informing. Sent over sixty criminals to the gallows, and, as 'Thief-Taker General', purposely lived near Old Bailey. Seen here, passing St Sepulchre's, Newgate, on way to Tyburn in 1725. Pelted by the crowd all the way.

The Newgate Calendar

Lingering over supper one September evening at his house in Arlington Street, Horace Walpole heard shouts of 'Stop thief!' A highwayman had held up a post-chaise in Piccadilly and ridden away after seriously wounding the watch. Walpole, who had himself been held up by James Maclean in Hyde Park, spoke for all London when he said that 'owing to the profusion of house-breakers, highwaymen, and footpads', visiting a friend's house was as dangerous as going to the relief of Gibraltar.

Such a brazen crime was far from extraordinary in mid-eighteenth-century London. The disbanding of soldiers and sailors after the Treaty of Aix had created a new and violent criminal class. As well as highwaymen, pickpockets and robbers roamed the night streets with nothing to hinder them but decrepit and underpaid parish watchmen. More than 6,000 dram shops selling cheap gin increased the menace.

'A general luxury among the lower people' was at the root of all this crime. That, rather than the expected diagnosis of poverty, was the opinion of an expert, Henry Fielding, the magistrate at Bow Street. It was Fielding whom the Government asked to head a committee set up in 1750 to investigate 'the Growing Evil'. Although he had only six unofficial constables–known as 'Mr Fielding's people'–to deal with the crime wave, Fielding did not immediately suggest that the number should be increased and a proper police force started. Any such idea was far too authoritarian for Londoners. It was to be another seven years before John Fielding– Henry's half-brother and successor at Bow Street–announced a scheme whereby, if informed of a crime, he would 'immediately dispatch a Set of Brave Fellows in Pursuit . . . on a quarter of an Hour's Notice'. The Flying Squad was foreshadowed, but the formation of a Metropolitan Police Force was still seventy years away.

Malefactors brought in by inadequate methods faced trial before magistrates like the Fieldings who sat long hours in the lower front room which served as a court in their private house in Bow Street. Those accused of more serious crimes–treason, murder and felony–came up at the Sessions House, Old Bailey. There were eight sessions a year presided over by the Lord Mayor, the Recorder, and judges.

Awaiting trial and before execution, prisoners were kept at Newgate (in part of the original gatehouse), and then, after 1770, in the formidable prison designed by George Dance the Younger. Lesser criminals– quacks, perjurors, and minor frauds–were put in the Old Bailey pillory to be stoned and

7

pelted by the mob. Flogging, branding, the treadmill, and torture by 'pressing' were common, and among fetters and instruments employed at the Fleet and Marshalsea prisons in 1729 was 'The Skull Cap' which constricted the head until blood flowed from nose and ears.

There were 156 capital offences, many of them so trivial that juries often refused to convict even on clear evidence. For the same reason, reprieves were frequent. But there were still enough death sentences to provide ten to fifteen victims a month for London's

7. The inside of the Sessions House in Old Bailey, built in 1773.

8. Outside the Sessions House. Prisoners were brought from Newgate prison to the open courtyard, *The Bail Dock*, to wait the order for their trial. The courtroom is open at one end to reduce the stench and danger of infection from 'gaol fever' carried by prisoners.

9. The blind Sir John Fielding presiding over his magistrate's court in Bow Street.

8

9

grimmest and most popular spectacle, an execution at Tyburn. The three-mile route from Newgate along Holborn to the 'triple tree' was always lined with sightseers, and at Tyburn there were large permanent grand-stands–'Mother Proctor's Pews' for those who could pay for a good view. For a hanging which involved a young girl, a notorious highwayman, or the added refinement of drawing and quartering, a crowd of up to 200,000 could be expected. At Earl Ferrers's execution in 1760, seen below right, the stands earned £500 for their owner, Mother Proctor.

These 'Hanging Matches', as they were called, were given the flavour of a sporting event, stimulating even the victim to bravado so that he went to his death by strangulation in his best clothes and with a well-prepared last-minute quip. This courage amazed visitors from abroad, and for their benefit *The Foreigner's Guide to London* in 1740 provided this detailed description: 'The rope being put about his neck, he is fastened to the fatal tree when a proper time being allowed for prayer and singing a hymn, the cart is withdrawn and the penitent criminal is turned with a cap over his eyes and left hanging about half an hour. . . .' The *Guide* warned: 'These executions are always attended with so great mobbing and impertinences that you ought to be on your guard when curiosity leads you there.'

10. Newgate Prison where the Old Bailey is today.

11. Convicted perjurer in the Mark Lane pillory, 1785.

12. In the Press Yard of the Old Bailey, prisoners were tortured by the piling of weights on their bodies if they refused to plead guilty. If they pleaded, the torture stopped, but then their property was automatically forfeited to the Crown with the result that their dependants were left penniless.

13. Treadmill at Brixton House of Correction. Hard labour in London prisons involved picking oakum (the untwisting of coarse rope), beating hemp, and walking the treadmill.

14. 'The Skull Cap' being applied to a prisoner.

15. A man hanged under the 'triple tree' gallows.

16. Hogarth's 'idle apprentice' is exhorted to repent by the Newgate Chaplain.

17. Detail of 'The Skull Cap' instrument of torture.

18. The approximate position of Tyburn gallows, near the present Marble Arch, is shown on Rocque with the grandstand on the corner. Between about 1170 and 1738, when executions removed to Newgate, at least 50,000 people are estimated to have been hanged at Tyburn.

19. Thomas Tullis, a mid-eighteenth-century hangman. He was known as Jack Ketch, the generic title inherited from Tyburn's most famous executioner.

20. The execution of Earl Ferrers. This is believed to have been the first time that a new form of gallows and drop were used in place of the old triple gibbet and cart. The hearse which is to take his body to Surgeons' Hall waits on the right.

14

15

16

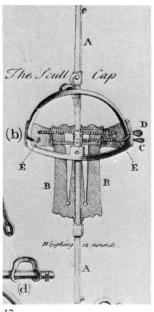

17

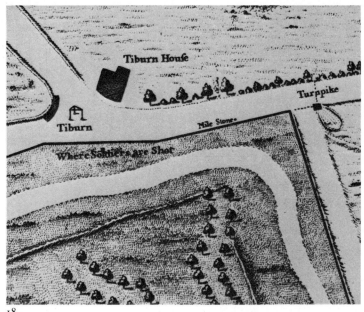

18

19

20

The End of the Fleet

From the heights of Hampstead and Highgate where they rise in the Vale of Health and Kenwood, two streams flow south and join at what is now Camden Town. As one river, they make their way under King's Cross, and down the valley between Saffron Hill and Snow Hill to fall into the Thames at Blackfriars. This is the River Fleet, now almost entirely buried, and already, by the end of the first quarter of the eighteenth century, described by Defoe as 'very much neglected and out of repair'.

Brave plans after the Fire had tried to make the mouth of the Fleet some value to shipping. Wharves and quays, thirty-five feet wide, were built the half-mile up to Holborn. But superb as it looks in the view of 1750, far right, it never caught on. The fine basin fought a losing battle against commercial indifference, irregular flow of water from the upper reaches, and silting by Thames mud, domestic sewage, and all the refuse of Smithfield. It soon merited its Georgian name of the Fleet Ditch.

In 1733 the City decided to cover in the whole length from Holborn Bridge to Fleet Street. Wharves became roads down the side of what is Farringdon Street today, and two lines of one-storey shops with a covered walk between them were built in the middle.

Fleet Market is seen above, and (as the sign '. . . from Stocksmarket' indicates) this was the new site for the old Poultry market which had to make way for the building of the Mansion House. Fleet Street is to the left; to the right is Ludgate Hill. The old man leans on the southern parapet of Fleet Bridge, the point where the ditch dives underground, next to appear in open cuts, like the one on the right, north of Holborn.

For 160 years this area was notorious for 'Fleet Marriages'. Without need of a licence, or any previous formalities, runaway couples came to be married here. Above is a young sailor from Ratcliffe who is planning to marry his landlady's daughter. An obsequious clergyman, who may or may not be genuine, greets them, while a buxom 'matron' who touts for couples climbs hurriedly from a coach. Originally, these ceremonies were carried out by clergymen confined for debt to the Fleet Prison. As many as ten marriages a day were held in the prison chapel. But, after 1710 (when chapel marriages without banns became illegal), Fleet Marriages spread to taverns and rooms throughout the neighbourhood. So-called clergymen split their fees with tavern keepers. This traffic in easy marriages continued until it was stamped out by law in 1774.

As if inspired by Canaletto, a London artist, Samuel Scott, brings a romantic touch

of Venice to his picture of the mouth of the Fleet, above. Even the elegant stone foot-bridge opposite Bridewell (the lantern of which is visible) appears to belong more to Italy than London. In the final decade of its existence, the Fleet seems bathed in the dying sunlight of a Venetian summer. The death of this whole idyllic prospect is near. In 1760 work is to start on Blackfriars Bridge, right, whilst before its completion, the rest of the Fleet must be covered in, and New Bridge Street created to provide an access to it.

1. A Fleet Wedding. Looking north from Ludgate.

2. The Fleet from the mouth to Holborn – detail from Rocque, 1746.

3. An open section of the Fleet Ditch as it appeared near Field Lane, between Holborn Hill and Saffron Hill. This was one of the few open cuts (with timber struts to prevent the collapse of walls) between Holborn and Mount Pleasant, the point where the river emerged into the fields.

4. Mouth of the Fleet, about 1750.

5. London's third bridge, at Blackfriars, took nine years to build, and was opened in 1769. The designer was Robert Mylne, a Scot, who won the competition from nearly seventy other architects while unknown and still in his mid-twenties. Although they do not look it, in Piranesi's engraving, right, the arches were elliptical rather than semi-circular. For no clear aesthetic reason, this was a cause of criticism by Dr Johnson. Originally it was called Pitt Bridge as a memorial to the Earl of Chatham. A halfpenny toll (one penny on Sundays) led to riots, and the tariff was removed after the burning down of the toll house in 1780. Mylne's bridge was replaced by the present one in the 1860s.

5

Canaletto's London

The first important person on whom Canaletto called in London on his arrival in May 1746, was the 2nd Duke of Richmond whose house on the Thames was between Whitehall and Westminster. The artist had letters from his patron, Joseph Smith, the British Consul in Venice, and the Duke's former tutor, Thomas Hill, acted as intermediary. 'I told him the best service I thought you could do him', wrote Hill to the Duke, 'would be to let him draw a view of the river from your dining-room window which in my opinion would give him as much reputation as any of his Venetian prospects'. It was an accurate prophecy. Canaletto's views from Richmond House were to bring him countless commissions during the next nine years.

In his view, above, looking north up Whitehall, people take the sun – the sun always shines with dazzling Venetian clarity for Canaletto – in the open space which was formerly the site of Whitehall Palace. The crescent of posts marks the approach to the Duke of Montagu's house. The artist shows only the corner of Richmond House, on the extreme right, the stables, enclosed by two high walls, and, beyond the further wall, the Duke of Richmond's riverfront garden. This garden shared a common water-gate with Montagu House.

Canaletto was working from an upper window of Lord Loudon's house in Parliament Street, in about 1750. On the left, demolition is starting on the 'middle row', and this cleared away the narrow, congested King Street (consult Rocque, page 197). The Holbein Gate with its Georgian addition is to be demolished within a decade, and Parliament Street obtain the width of modern Whitehall.

In Venice, where his pictures were eagerly sought by travellers as records of the Grand Tour, Canaletto had been accustomed to making a great many copies of his most popular views. To cope with the bulk of work he employed assistants, and as his popularity grew in London, the studio at the back of his house, No 41 Beak Street, off Golden Square, probably served as a factory for elegant duplication. The view, right, of Westminster from Lambeth is one of at least two versions of the same subject. An almost exact replica in Prague has a wider sweep to include Lambeth Palace in the right foreground, and St Paul's in the distance. Shipping, buildings, direction of smoke, and minute detail (down to the dog on the foreshore) are identical. But there is one essential difference. In the Prague version there are wooden supports under the arches of Westminster Bridge. In our view, owned by the Bank of England, all scaffolding has disappeared and the bridge is completed. This dates the painting at 1750 or after.

St John's, Smith Square, is on the left, and on Millbank are factories, wharves, a brewhouse, and stoneyard. The line of trees veil St Stephen's and mark the Speaker's garden. A shaft of brilliant Canaletto light strikes the Bear Inn by the bridge and the cut-off southern end of the Banqueting Hall.

The artist broke his nine years in London with a visit to Venice in 1750 (where he probably worked up a number of English subjects from detailed sketches), and celebrated his return with a painting of the Rotunda at Ranelagh (page 225). Canaletto finally left London for Venice in about 1756.

1. Whitehall and the Privy Garden.

2. Antonio Canaletto – believed to be a self-portrait.

3. View of Westminster from Lambeth.

Covent Garden Market

In his view of Covent Garden in about 1754, Samuel Scott shows the Great Piazza with its architectural splendour bathed in a golden Venetian light. The artist, living there at the time, is earning his title of 'the English Canaletto'.

By the middle of the eighteenth century, Covent Garden had been deserted by nearly all its earlier titled ratepayers. Most of the houses had become taverns, coffee houses, and dubious hotels. It was under the portico on the right that Boswell sauntered up and down waiting for a new mistress 'in a sort of trembling suspense'.

The square was also growing into a considerable market. A trade in fruit and vegetables had started here in a haphazard way in 1654 with a few market gardeners who had come to town to sell their produce from carts, trestles and baskets. This had been encouraged as a source of revenue by the landlord of the square, the 5th Earl of Bedford. He had built and leased shops against the wall of his garden, and in 1670 was granted a royal charter 'for the buying and selling of all manner of fruits, flowers, roots and herbs'. Covent Garden Market was established.

By the time of Scott's painting, Bedford House had been demolished, and the shops moved further into the square. There were 106 of them in two rows of permanent, single-storey buildings which may be seen on the left. With a considerable area filled with trees and shrubs for sale in tubs, the market occupies nearly half the square. On the north side trading appears less organized. In the right foreground an upset handcart has led to blows. Dealers sell from baskets. These, presumably, are the 229 'stands' for which the Bedford Estate also charges small rents.

Twice the size of any other London market except Smithfield, Covent Garden was selling produce from 15,000 acres of market gardens by the beginning of the next century. All were within ten miles radius, and arriving by cart and waggon through the night, growers were ready for traders who started to buy as early as 3 a.m. The time was approaching for a large, comprehensive building to house all the shops. This was built in 1830.

1. Covent Garden Market in the mid-eighteenth century.

2. The market building designed by Charles Fowler in 1830 and in use ever since. It is due to disappear with the market's removal to Battersea scheduled for 1974.

Foundation of the British Museum

When he died in 1753 at the age of ninety-three, Sir Hans Sloane, royal physician and antiquary, bequeathed a very large private collection to the nation in return for a nominal £20,000. His 'cabinet of curiosities' included 50,000 books, 3,500 manuscripts, gems, prints, paintings, Greek and Roman marbles, and a remarkable miscellany of natural history specimens. Probably it did not contain (as Horace Walpole ironically suggested) sharks with one ear and spiders big as geese.

To this was added 6,000 volumes of manuscripts collected by Robert Harley, Earl of Oxford, the smaller, but extremely important, collection of manuscripts of Sir Robert Cotton, and 9,000 printed books from the Royal Library presented by George II. These collections formed the nucleus of the British Museum, opened to the public in Bloomsbury in January 1759.

Sloane, whose museum had been laid out in his home – the Manor House on Chelsea Embankment – had hoped it would stay there. But a bigger building was needed, and Montagu House was bought by the Government. The main building, designed 'somewhat after the French', as Evelyn put it, stood in seven acres of ground. To raise about £83,000 needed to buy and adapt the house, pay for the collections, and endow the museum, a lottery was held at the Guildhall, right, where a Blue Coat boy (A) is seen drawing winning tickets from the wheel (E) in which they are churned. In its early years, the admission of 'studious and curious persons' to the new Museum in Great Russell Street was limited to three days a week.

1. Sir Hans Sloane.

2. Lottery at the Guildhall.

3. Montagu House from the south looking west down Great Russell Street.

4. View of Montagu House from the fields to the north with St George's Church in the background.

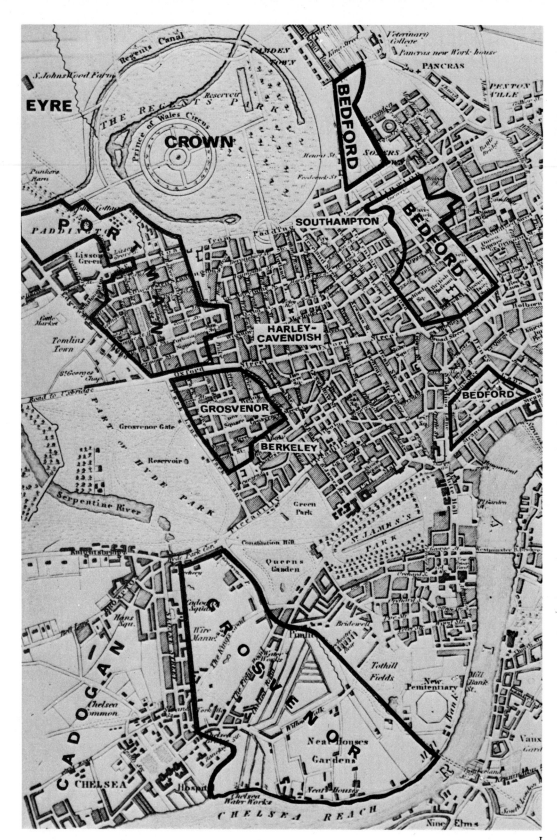

1. Detail of George Jones's 1815 map, on which are overprinted the main estates and the families with interests in various areas.

2. Mary Davies, founder of the Grosvenor Estate.

3. Richard Grosvenor of Grosvenor Square.

4. Edward Harley, Earl of Oxford, who gave his name to Harley and Oxford streets.

5. Earl Cadogan of Cadogan Square.

6. Grosvenor Square in 1731 – the North side with Duke Street, right, and North Audley Street, left, leading up to Tyburn Road, later Oxford Street. Beyond are the fields of Marylebone.

7. An attempt was made to turn Grosvenor Square into not only the largest, but architecturally the most

impressive London square. This came to grief through a conflict of interests. The north side, seen here, was described in 1734 as 'little better than a collection of whims and frolics'. The main house with its six-columned façade was off-centre, and also (by 1800) appears to have lost its pediment.

8. Chesterfield House, built in 1749 by Isaac Ware, for the 4th Earl of Chesterfield at the bottom of South Audley Street, was one of the great mansions on the Grosvenor Estate. This is the view looking east from Hyde Park before Stanhope Gate was built. Curzon Street is on the right. Demolished 1934.

9. Entrance to Upper Grosvenor Street from Park Lane seen over the wall from Hyde Park. St George's, Hanover Square is the church in the distance.

Estates, Squares and Landlords

In George Jones's map, opposite, we see the pattern of residential London as it was set by the end of the eighteenth century, and as it has remained with little change ever since. Overprinted are the boundaries of the main, privately owned estates, and, where these are not precise, the areas of influence of the landlords are indicated. All over Westminster, Marylebone, and Chelsea, families like the Grosvenors, the Portmans, the Bedfords, Cadogans, Cavendishes and Portlands gave their names to squares and streets. Their titles, the families with whom they intermarried, and their country properties are similarly commemorated. But, as sheep and cattle were driven off the meadows, and little farms demolished to make way for the large estates, the ground landlords imposed more than just their names. They set a permanent stamp on the layout and influenced the architecture. While the City, and much of the West End as far as Regent Street, was an unruly tangle of twisting streets, many of medieval origin, these new estates consisted mainly of squares from which streets run in a grid-pattern of Georgian formality.

Grosvenor Estate

By far the largest estate is that of the Grosvenor family which came into existence as a result of the marriage in 1677 of Sir Thomas Grosvenor, a great Cheshire landowner, and Mary Davies, a girl of twelve. To the marriage, this young heiress brought two areas of land, the largest of 608 acres between Piccadilly and Oxford Street, the other of 482 acres between Hyde Park and the Thames. They themselves never saw much development of the estate. Sir Thomas died in his mid-forties, and his wife became deranged. It was left to their three sons, and principally Richard, the eldest, to start the work. Following prevailing custom, he laid out a square as the nucleus of his scheme and endowed it with the family name. Six acres in extent, Grosvenor Square was the largest residential square in London. It was completed in 1725 when Oxford Street was still the rural Tyburn Road, and the area west of North Audley Street still fields.

Around the square were marked out a network of uniform streets lined with large houses which at once attracted rich, fashionable owners. The Duchess of Kendal, mistress of George I, was among the earliest residents, and from her windows looked out on the equestrian statue of her royal lover in the centre of the square. Petronella Melusina, her daughter by the King, married Lord Chesterfield, and he built a magnificent house, upper right, in South Audley Street, one of the square's main arteries.

6

7

8

9

The wonder aroused by all this development is reflected in an article that appeared in *Applebee's Weekly Journal* in 1725. 'I went towards Hyde Park,' the writer reports. 'In the tour I passed an amazing scene of new foundations, not of houses only, but as I might say of new cities, new towns, new squares and fine buildings. . . .' It was impossible to judge, he concluded, 'where or when they will make an end or stop of building'.

Portman Estate

A stop, however, did come; or anyway a slowing-down after 1730. It lasted about thirty years. Then, with the Peace of Paris in 1763, came another boom. London began to spill north across Oxford Street, as we see above. This happened when Henry William Portman decided to develop 200 acres of farmland in Marylebone. They had come down to him from Sir William Portman, a Lord Chief Justice who had bought the freehold in Tudor times. He, too, started with a square (in 1764), and offered frontages to speculative builders. Even so, it took twenty years to complete, and probably owed its ultimate popularity to Adam, Wyatt, and 'Athenian' Stewart, the architect responsible for Montagu House. Built for Mrs Montagu, the notable hostess, in the north-west corner of Portman Square, the house was a setting for salons, meetings of the Blue Stocking Club, and a curious annual party (possibly depicted in the middle picture, right) for all the chimney-sweeps in London.

Like Grosvenor, Portman imposed a rigid ground design on his streets, and this is emphasized by the contrast of Marylebone Lane. Following the line of an ancient footpath, this winding road defied the strict planning on each side of it.

Berkeley Estate

Smaller, but in a most valuable area, the Berkeley Estate covered most of south-east Mayfair between Bolton Street and Bond Street. It marches with the Grosvenors', and might well have been part of it, for the much sought-after Mary Davies was first betrothed at the age of seven to the second Lord Berkeley of Stratton, then a boy of twelve. But the marriage never took place, and when Berkeley Square was created in 1745 it was carved out of the fields that lay beyond the garden of Berkeley (later Devonshire) House, Piccadilly. The Grosvenor Estate line cuts just across the square's northern side.

Near, but not part of a large private estate, Hanover Square was laid out in 1713 and its houses leased by a group of Whig generals. These veterans of Marlborough's campaigns struck a loyal note with their choice of name, and followed it up with Great George Street to the south. The Whigs and Tories faced each other as if from opposing camps (with Oxford Street as a no-man's-land), for Cavendish Square, conceived seven years later, was the enterprise of Tory peers.

Harley-Cavendish Estate

Cavendish Square was the central feature of the Harley-Cavendish Estate, yet another result of a shrewd marriage alliance. The 2nd Earl of Oxford (of Oxford Street) married Henrietta Cavendish (of the square), and in this estate are to be found Portland Place (after the 2nd Duke of Portland who married their daughter), Holles Street (after Henrietta's father), Harley Street (family name of the Oxfords), Welbeck Street (after Welbeck Abbey, the Portland family home) and Wimpole Street (after the Cambridgeshire home of the Harleys).

Cavendish Square was the grandiose scheme of the future Duke of Chandos and five peers whose idea it was to lay it out with noblemen's palaces designed by James Gibbs, architect of St Martin-in-the-Fields. On a plan, top, far right, by the architect John Prince, we see that Chandos had arranged for his house to stand at the end of a magnificent vista up Holles Street from Hanover Square. But the square was also caught in the lull between the building booms. In 1731, when the recession began, only fifteen of the proposed twenty-eight houses were finished, and the most important – Chandos House – not even started. All that existed on the north side of the square were two flanking houses on the corners of Chandos Street and Harley Street. Between them the Duke had built a high wall and handsome gates but those gates were never to open on to a great house. As poor compensation for the expected Chandos House, the Duke filled up the empty space with two buildings. These twin mansions, far right, had stone porticoes and Corinthian columns, and are all that survive of the abortive scheme.

Cadogan Estate

Yet another marriage gave birth to the Cadogan Estate in Chelsea. On his wedding to Elizabeth Sloane in 1771, the 2nd Earl Cadogan received two-thirds of the extensive property left by his father-in-law, Sir Hans Sloane. The names of these two families have dominated the eastern part of Chelsea from the time they leased 100 acres to Henry Holland. He laid them out as Cadogan Place in 1770 with Sloane Street running through it and culminating in Sloane Square. Holland proposed that this new district created out of meadows and market gardens should be called Hans Town, and the Sloane family name is commemorated in nine streets, two squares and a crescent; the Cadogans in four streets, two squares, and a Thames pier.

Later Estates

By the end of the century three more big private estates were being prepared. The 5th Duke of Bedford was about to develop his Bloomsbury estate with Russell Square as its main feature. In St John's Wood, immediately north of the Portman Estate, lay the Eyre Estate for which Col. W. S. Eyre had plans for comprehensive suburban building. With Fitzroy Square, Grafton Street and Euston Square, Augustus Henry Fitzroy, 3rd Duke of Grafton (of Euston Hall, Suffolk) was enriching the so-called 'Southampton' Estate. But the full development of these estates belong, like the southern part of the Grosvenor Estate (Belgrave Square and Eaton Square), to the late Regency period.

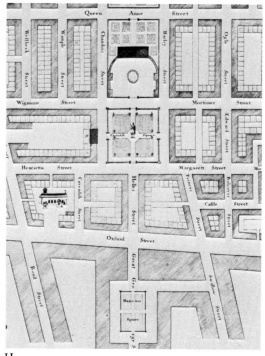

11

10. North-east corner of Hyde Park during a military parade in 1799 shows Bayswater and Edgware roads coming into Oxford Street at the Tyburn turnpike, the park gate (where Marble Arch now stands), and Park Lane down as far as Upper Grosvenor Street.

11. John Prince's 1719 Plan. The names of Harley Street and Chandos Street were subsequently reversed. The plan shows how Chandos House, on the north side of Cavendish Square, would have been the focal point of a vista. The house was never built, but this did not deter Prince, speculator and self-styled 'Prince of Builders', from naming nearby Princes Street after himself.

12. West side of Berkeley Square looking south towards Lansdowne House.

13. Montagu House, Portman Square, showing what appears to be the sweeps arriving for the annual party.

14. Statue of William, Duke of Cumberland, in Cavendish Square as seen by an ironical artist in *The Town and Country Magazine*, 1771. Beyond are the twin houses built by the Duke of Chandos.

15. Cavendish Square – north side, 1800. The twin porticoed houses survive, and are now joined by a bridged passageway.

16. Hanover Square – looking north, 1751. Cavendish Square, then largely unbuilt, does not appear, as Prince envisaged, at the end of the vista.

12

13

14

15

16

1

Adam and the Adelphi

Following the Palladians, who dominated London architecture for the first half of the century, Robert Adam and his brothers held sway in the thirty years after 1760. By then, Kent, Leoni and Lord Burlington were dead. The way was clear for new ideas, and they arrived from Scotland with John, Robert, James, and William Adam, whose father was an eminent Edinburgh architect.

Like so many leaders of new movements, the brothers were critical of their immediate predecessors. On a visit to Vicenza, James Adam condemned Palladio's private houses as 'ill-adjusted to their plans and elevations'. Robert wrote that he wanted to 'explode' the Roman temple style and replace it with 'a beautiful variety of light mouldings, gracefully formed, delicately enriched. . . .'

A journey made by Robert down the Dalmatian coast in 1757 was destined to bring about a major change on London's riverfront. He visited the palace of Diocletian at Spalato, and published his drawings and reconstruction of the palace in 1764. Four years later, the Adam brothers took a 99-year lease on the site of Durham House between the Strand and the water. Their plan was 'to

2

raise a great building of a semi-public nature in the monumental manner'. The Adelphi was the result. Supported on massive arches and vaults, the terrace of eleven houses owed its inspiration to Diocletian. It commanded a view of the Thames in much the same way that the palace of the Roman emperor overlooked the Adriatic.

Building of the Adelphi took four years from 1768 to 1772, a grandiose undertaking which ran the Adam brothers into difficulties. A special Act of Parliament had to be passed to reclaim part of the river and build the straight wharf. The wharf proved too low and flooded at high tide. The Ordnance Department failed to rent all the vaults as had been expected. Worse, the houses did not sell, even though Garrick set what should have been the fashion by moving into the terrace. Faced with bankruptcy, the brothers had to dispose of the entire property by means of a lottery.

Garrick's house, right, was in the centre of the terrace, and he lived here for seven years. He died in a first floor room in 1779. Leaning on the rails looking out over the river, Johnson and Boswell sadly recalled his death and that of their friend Topham Beauclerk, another resident.

The terrace was demolished in 1936 (page 367), but a small part of the pilastered façade of the flanking building on the left is still to be seen.

Its genesis is now recalled by three streets—John Street, Robert Street and Adam Street—consisting of dignified, classical houses. Of the original houses only No 7 Adam Street survives. The one important remaining feature of the great, now almost totally obliterated Adelphi scheme is the Royal Society of Arts designed by Robert Adam in 1772.

Three London houses—No 20 Portman Square, No 20 St James's Square and Chandos House, off Cavendish Square—typify Adam's elegant planning for the leaders of eighteenth-century society. He not only built, but furnished the house in Portman Square for Lady Home. It possesses a splendid staircase, top right, a beautiful music room, an Etruscan bedroom, and a number of those fireplaces for which Adam is a household word.

In the same square James Wyatt was working on Portman House and 'Athenian' Stuart on Montagu House. Probably spurred by this competition, Adam brought all his decorative skill to make No 20 a setting for a great hostess and a glittering array of guests. In the same way, he made the dining and drawing-rooms of Northumberland House in the Strand an elegant background for social gatherings. The walls were covered in his characteristic designs of wreath and ribbon, urn and medallion.

Like Lansdowne House (mutilated 1936), most of the houses for Portland Place, and a number of other fine town houses, Northumberland House with its gilt stucco ceilings and marble mantelpieces disappeared when the building was demolished (1874). But, of Adam's surviving work, there is the screen with columns he designed for the Admiralty in Whitehall, the south and east sides of Fitzroy Square, and No 20 St James's Square which preserves part of his original façade and rooms with delicate Adam mouldings on ceilings and walls.

1. The Adelphi, showing the wharf which was to have provided an income.

2. Adelphi Terrace looking south. On the left is the Water Tower (p. 178) with smoke pouring from the chimney of the pumping house.

3. Garrick's house.

4. Staircase of No 20, Portman Square.

5. Curved ceiling and half-domed apse at the end of the library built for the Earl of Mansfield at Kenwood, Hampstead, in 1767. This is one of the finest rooms Adam ever designed. The ceiling is coloured, and the frieze of lions, urns, and deer-heads on the screen is in white and gold. The architect was not too modest to describe his curved ceiling, an innovation in England, as 'extremely beautiful'. The painted panels are by Antonio Zucchi.

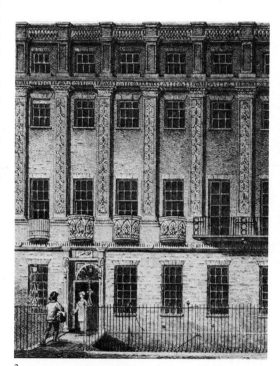

3

4

5

223

Vauxhall and Ranelagh

The Age of Elegance deserved gracious entertainment, and found it in the pleasure gardens which were London's principal places of diversion. For more than a hundred years the most famous gardens were at Vauxhall. Twelve acres on the river were laid out by an amusement caterer, Jonathan Tyers, and on summer evenings royalty, nobility and the general public came to stroll through woodland avenues and take supper in romantic alcoves under coloured lanterns.

As New Spring Gardens, this fashionable rendez-vous had existed since Charles II's times, but Tyers enlarged it and added fresh attractions in 1732. The usual approach was by boat to Vauxhall Stairs (near the south end of the present bridge), and through an unimposing entrance (admission 1s.). But, once past the austere brick wall, the visitor found himself in a Baroque wonderland. Promenades were spanned by triumphal arches; Mr Handel's music floated down from a raised bandstand; cold suppers were served in a crescent-shaped Chinese pavilion; there was a classic ruin and the painted vista of an Italian landscape.

Fireworks, dancing, and flirtation under trees festooned with lights – these delights inspired one foreign resident in London to describe Vauxhall Gardens as having 'no equal that I know, or ever heard, in Europe'.

They remained fashionable until the end of George III's reign, then became a favourite place for ballooning, and enjoyed fluctuating popularity until they closed in 1859.

The success of Vauxhall in its heyday tempted a syndicate to promote a rival pleasure garden on the opposite side of the river in the grounds of a house once owned by Lord Ranelagh. The main attraction was an assembly room housed in the large Rotunda. Built in the style of the Pantheon in Rome, and opened in 1742, the Rotunda was described by a character of Smollett as an 'enchanted palace'. Tea was served in boxes round the perimeter, and an orchestra provided the background to polite conversation.

There were concerts and here Mozart as an eight-year-old prodigy performed on the harpsichord. It was the occasional setting for masquerades. But, more than anything else, the Rotunda was for promenading. Round and round the ornate central fireplace and under the chandeliers moved the *beau monde* simply for the pleasure of looking at each other. It was all very elegant, vain, and perhaps grew a trifle tame. Canaletto makes it look sumptuous, but a Frenchman decided it was 'the most insipid place of amusement you could imagine'. Others seem to have agreed, and the verdict appears to be an epitaph, for Ranelagh died and the Rotunda was demolished in 1805.

3

4

1. Vauxhall Gardens and entrance gates. 'Afterwards I was taken for a drive, and so saw the gardens at Vauxhall myself. They are fine and large, as is necessary for the inhabitants of London, numerous and wealthy as they are. Half this excellent area is occupied by boxes where people can . . . eat and drink during the evening. The rest of the garden is divided into attractive walks. . . . In the evening there are 3,000 lamps alight. . . . Sixty thousand guineas' profit are reckoned during the summer contributed by the Londoners and surrounding population.' – From the diary of Sophie v. la Roche on a visit to London from Germany in 1786.

2. The Grand Walk, Vauxhall Gardens, 1751.

3. Canaletto's interior view of the Rotunda at Ranelagh.

4. The Rotunda looking away from the river with Chelsea Hospital on the left.

1

Art and The Royal Academy

Faced with large blank walls in their imposing new homes, the people coming to live in the fashionable parts of late Georgian London required pictures. Angelica Kauffmann or Zucchi might fill decorative panels; but where could they find the family portraits, the historical scenes, and delicate 'fancy pictures' they needed? The ever-increasing demand could no longer be supplied by émigré artists in Soho or by raids on Italy

during the Grand Tour. A cultivated taste for the foreign and the antique had to give way to modern English work.

Art patrons turned their steps towards Reynolds's studio in Leicester Square, to Gainsborough's in Pall Mall or travelled up to Hampstead to see what Romney had to show them in the studio he had built on Holly Bush Hill. Four drawing schools were opened to train young artists, and a popular painter, like Gainsborough, was inundated with commissions.

Historical pictures in the grand manner were in vogue, and so were 'conversation pieces' of the kind painted by Zoffany, above, which shows a well-known art patron, Charles Townley. A book open on his lap, he sits in the library of his house in Queen Anne's Gate surrounded by his collection of classical statuary. This includes a Venus with arms restored by Joseph Nollekens, who was the most prolific sculptor of the day.

By the 1770s, the artist, who forty years earlier was regarded as a tradesman, had

acquired standing. Sir Joshua Reynolds, first President of the Royal Academy, led a new generation of artists into fashionable drawing rooms. About the same time, a revolution took place in the way pictures were sold. The old system of personal patronage and visits to artists' studios began to be supplanted by public exhibitions.

The Academy had its genesis in the exhibition held at the Foundling Hospital in Hogarth's time. Gradually the most important artists of the day came together, and, after a vagrant existence, found a home in Somerset House. This was nearly a hundred years before the move to Burlington House. Somerset House was designed by Sir William Chambers, the Academy's first treasurer, and also housed learned societies and government departments. The centre of its annual exhibition was the Great Room, below, and, from the start, more than 500 pictures had to be hung. Gainsborough was only one of many artists–then, as now–to object to being 'sky-ed'. If his painting of the Royal Family were above the line, the hanging committee were warned in 1783, he would 'never more, whilst he breathes . . . send another picture to the Exhibition'. The committee ignored the threat, and, although he remained interested, and offered to paint a picture for the Council Room four years later, Gainsborough never exhibited again at the Academy.

1. Charles Townley in his Westminster library with the statues and antiques which he had collected in Italy. On his death in 1805, they were bought by the British Museum for £20,000. He was a member of the Society of Dilettanti, which consisted of like-enthusiasts who, at their weekly dinners in Cavendish Square, raised their glasses to 'Grecian Taste and Roman Spirit'.

2. Royal Academicians gathered round a model in the Life School at Somerset House, 1770. Painting by Zoffany whose self-portrait is bottom left. Next to William Hunter with hand on chin is Reynolds, his ear trumpet turned towards Chambers. To the left of them, with legs straddled, is Francis Hayman.

3. In the Great Room of the Academy in Somerset House, Reynolds, carrying an ear trumpet, shows the Prince Regent round the 1787 Exhibition. Reynolds saw a warning in these exhibitions–the wish to please everyone being a dangerous temptation to the serious artist.

Garrick's 'New Order'

Every box was crammed; the whole theatre was packed from pit to gallery; and, openly crying, his fellow-players crowded into the wings on the night that David Garrick gave his farewell performance at Drury Lane. Admirers had come from Dublin, Edinburgh, and even Paris to see him as Don Felix in *The Wonder*. At the end of a short speech on an empty stage applause and tears mingled with cries of 'Farewell, farewell!' Their 'humble servant' bowed and left the stage for ever.

This was London's good-bye in June 1776, to the actor, manager, and part-owner of Drury Lane who, in thirty-five years, had not only made himself the stage's jewel, but influenced the whole course of the English theatre. As the playwright Richard Cumberland had written (after seeing him at Covent Garden many years before): 'Heavens, what a transition! It seemed as if a whole century had been step't over in the changing of a single scene – old things were done away and a new order brought forward.'

This new order had initiated a revolution in acting, production, and the behaviour of audiences. Garrick's 'natural, simple, affecting' style discarded all barn-storming. For more than a century, flagrant liberties had been taken with Shakespeare's plays. Even if he did not completely restore them to the original, Garrick treated the texts with far more respect. By insisting on strict rehearsals, he also saw that his company – a brilliant one – really knew their lines and did not improvise.

As manager of Drury Lane, Garrick employed a designer to replace formal backdrops and wings with realistic settings. From France he imported stronger, more effective lighting. Auditorium lights were still on throughout a performance, but by using lamps behind the proscenium and 'floats' – wicks floating in tallow – for footlights, more light was concentrated on the stage.

Privileged spectators had long enjoyed the right of sitting on the stage which hardly increased realism or helped the actors. Stage boxes, set well behind the footlights, made the audience almost part of the play. In one early eighteenth-century performance of *Macbeth* a privileged person sitting at the side had interrupted the play by walking across the stage in front of the actors to chat to a friend in the opposite box. Garrick firmly put the audience into the auditorium, and the change may be seen by contrasting the boxes at Drury Lane in 1777, right, with those in the rebuilt theatre, far right, seventeen years later.

In a Prologue, spoken when he took over

Drury Lane in 1747, Garrick said, 'We that live to please, must please to live.' But he would take this only so far. As well as removing spectators from the stage, he stopped the practice of 'tasting' a play – of refunding money, if people didn't want to stay after the first interval. But when he, and John Beard, the manager of Covent Garden, tried to stop another old custom – admission at half price after the third act – they were beaten by outbreaks of rioting. 'Half price at nine o'clock' was not to disappear from the London theatre for another century.

At the time of Garrick's farewell, and when Sheridan bought half his shares in Drury Lane, only two theatres, Drury Lane and Covent Garden (built in 1732 with entrances in Bow Street and the Piazza round the square) were protected by patent – that is legally entitled to present spoken drama. But this was only nominal. There were, in fact, six unlicensed theatres in London, the most important of which were: Goodman's Fields Theatre, Leman Street (opened 1729, burnt down 1802), where Garrick made his London debut; Sadler's Wells (built about 1740), famous for pantomimes and musical pieces; the Opera House in the Haymarket (1705) on the site of the present-day Her Majesty's; and the Theatre Royal, Haymarket (opened 1766 by Samuel Foote).

1. Drury Lane Theatre in 1775, the year of Sarah Siddons's debut, as it looked from Bridges Street (now Catherine Street) after Garrick had commissioned its redecoration by the Adam brothers. This was the second Drury Lane and held 2,000. The first Theatre Royal (capacity about 700) was opened in 1663, and burnt down in 1672. No pictures survive. Wren rebuilt it in 1674 and, with various alterations, the above building existed until 1791 when it was demolished.

2. The screen scene from *The School for Scandal*, produced at Drury Lane during Sheridan's management in 1777. This shows the boxes and the interior as rebuilt and decorated by the Adam brothers.

3. David Garrick as Macbeth.

4. Sheridan became manager of Drury Lane after paying Garrick £10,000 for a part share in the theatre. This political cartoon of 1789 shows him peering through the curtains and telling the orchestra not to play *God Save the King*. George III was ill at the time, and the implication is that Sheridan, as a Whig ally of Fox, did not want him to recover. The drawing is valuable in showing the use of 'floats' – wicks floating in tallow – in the footlights.

5. Riot at Covent Garden. During Arne's opera *Artaxerxes* in 1763 the stage was stormed by young bloods. Led by a man named Fitzpatrick, they had already forced Garrick to admit the public at half price after Act III. At first John Beard stood out against them, but damage and nightly barracking made him concede.

6. The third Theatre Royal, Drury Lane, in 1794 as rebuilt by Henry Holland. Described by Mrs Siddons as 'a wilderness of a place' it held 3,600 people, 800 more than the present Drury Lane (built 1812, interior reconstructed 1922). Though overhanging the forestage, the boxes are now behind the proscenium arch, and their distraction reduced. In 1800 George III was shot at while sitting in the Royal Box, on the opposite side of the stage from that shown here. The bullet, fired by an insane ex-soldier from the right-hand side of the pit, missed the King by about a foot.

1. The house of a Roman Catholic in New Broad Street is looted and his furniture burnt while soldiers block the advance of the rioters.

2. Attack on Newgate Prison – 'You have no idea of the frenzy of the multitude', was the description of the poet, John Crabbe, in his diary.

3. Lord George Gordon.

4. The 1784 Westminster Election scene at Covent Garden depicted by Robert Dighton.

The Gordon Riots . . .

In the decade before the Commune set up the guillotine in Paris, London had its own outbreaks of mob violence. Too mild, comparatively, to be called a reign of terror, they were numerous and varied. They reflected a growing social unrest, dissatisfaction with the monarchy and government, and a lively determination by Londoners not to sit down under things they disliked. In a city still unpoliced, it was fairly easy to make unruly demonstrations against anything from the employment of cheap Irish labour to the repressive Gin Act. Only once, for a week in June 1780, however, did hysteria really threaten London's safety.

On a Friday afternoon a crowd of over 30,000, which had come across London, Blackfriars and Westminster bridges after a meeting in St George's Fields, Southwark, converged on the House of Parliament. On their banners was the slogan 'No Popery!' and they shouted 'Repeal, repeal!' as their leader, the fanatic Protestant nobleman, Lord George Gordon, presented their petition demanding the repeal of the Catholic Relief Act. Among other things, this Act restored to Papists the right to buy and inherit land.

The Commons received the deputation in the Lobby with a fair assumption of composure, and voted against considering the petition until after the week-end. It was a fatal decision. When the rioters dispersed from New Palace Yard they plundered and fired a Catholic chapel off St James's and another off Lincoln's Inn Fields. On the Sunday they attacked the Catholic district of Moorfields. The next day rioting spread to Smithfield and Wapping, and on the Tuesday the mob broke into a London equivalent of the Bastille, the seemingly impregnable new gaol built by Dance at Newgate. They set fire to it, and released five of their number who had been arrested. Then they stormed the Clerkenwell prison and the Bloomsbury Square house of the Lord Chief Justice.

On 'Black Wednesday', as Walpole called it, the Gordon Riots reached their climax. Catholic homes, shops and chapels were attacked from Westminster to Bethnal Green. That night a terrible fire was started when 120,000 gallons of unrefined spirits were set alight in a Holborn distillery. More prisons were attacked and Catholic houses, like the one in New Broad Street, top left, were looted. With London's night sky red from the flames of thirty-six individual fires, action was imperative.

The authorities, reluctant to read the Riot Act, at last bestirred themselves. In Westminster the King called out his Guards with orders to shoot, and in the City, Alderman John Wilkes – in his day a stout

4

defender of liberty – bullied the terrified Lord Mayor into mustering the volunteer militia to protect the threatened Bank of England.

The riots were quelled, but before order was restored 458 Londoners had been killed or wounded by the militia. A dozen public buildings and over a hundred private ones had been destroyed or damaged. One hundred and sixty people came up for trial. Four women and a boy of sixteen (but not Lord George Gordon who ended up in a madhouse) were among twenty-five hanged.

Assessing the real causes of the Gordon Riots, Edmund Burke described religious convictions as the 'pretenses' for violence. A fear of Papists that went back to Elizabethan times probably combined with mass hysteria and the first stirrings of resentment against wealth and privilege. Told that the house he was attacking belonged to a Protestant not a Catholic, a rioter in Bermondsey made a significant comment. 'Protestant or not,' he replied hotly, 'no gentleman need be possessed of more than £1,000 a year; that's enough for any gentleman to live on.'

. . . and Election Riots

The passions aroused by politics stimulate rioting, and the Westminster Elections turned Covent Garden into what a contemporary writer called 'a scene of outrage and even of blood'. An eyewitness from Switzerland, Carl Moritz, saw 'the rampant spirit of Liberty and wild impatience of the English mob' manifested when, after the results, a delirious crowd smashed up the hustings, benches, chairs, and carpeting.

Westminster was one of the few democratic constituencies. Nearly every householder had a vote, and for three weeks in 1784 Covent Garden was a battleground in an epic struggle by the Tories to exclude Charles James Fox from election.

Through the milling crowds, above, passes the coach of Georgiana, Duchess of Devonshire, Fox's ardent supporter. Aged twenty-seven, and a great beauty, the Duchess is said to have kissed a butcher in Long Acre to secure his vote. Fox carried the day with a majority of 236, and was chaired through the streets.

Shops: 'The most striking thing in London'

In her diary during September 1786, a German traveller, Sophie v. la Roche, wrote enthusiastically of an evening spent strolling up and down 'lovely Oxford Street'. She noted, 'First one passes a watchmaker's, then a silk or fan store, now a silversmith, a china or glass shop. . . .' Wide pavements and handsome glass windows allowed her 'to gaze at the splendidly lit shopfronts in comfort'.

Her enthusiasm seems general. Two years later a visitor from Prussia wrote, 'The magnificence of the shops is the most striking thing in London', while another traveller decided they outshone even the finest in the Rue St Honoré in Paris. 'The greatest series of shops in the world', was Johnson's dogmatic assertion to Goldsmith as he proposed a walk eastwards from Charing Cross. This meant starting down the Strand which, since the seventeenth century, had become a major shopping thoroughfare.

In the Strand, like Oxford Street, shops of all kinds stood side by side. But there is a forerunner of the large general store in the Exeter 'Change, right, opposite the Savoy, where various merchandise was sold in small stalls under one roof. Some goods could be found in particular streets – textiles and lace in Paternoster Row, hosiery in Cordwainer Street, fine books in Pall Mall, and luxuries of all sorts in New Bond Street. A 'Cranbourne Alley article' was synonymous with cheap millinery or straw bonnets.

Shopkeepers generally lived over their premises, and their apprentices, who 'unbuttoned' the shutters at 6 a.m., might well have slept under the counter. As larger window panes replaced those of 'bottle' glass, window displays were possible. Considerable capital was spent on counters and interiors. Shops had come a long way from the stalls and wooden sheds with penthouse roofs which were common a hundred years before.

Competition was fierce, and, until banned in 1762, elaborate signs, like those in Cornhill, far right, vied for trade. Beautifully designed trade cards provided additional advertisement. Opening hours were long (8 a.m. to 10 p.m. was not uncommon); customers were given endless credit; and even the smallest purchase would be delivered. In smart Cheapside shops, wives of the owners, if attractive, stood at the doorways to entice customers in with flirtatious small talk.

Early in the century, Defoe said that a retailer must have the patience 'to bear all sorts of impertinence. A tradesman behind the counter must have no flesh and blood about him; no passions; no resentments.' But by now the fashionable shopkeeper,

1

3

1. Exeter 'Change by Burleigh Street on the north side of the Strand, 1772. Laid out with small shops – mostly milliners, seamstresses, hosiers and booksellers – on either side of a long gallery. As this was in a direct line with the pavement it provided pedestrians with a covered shopping area. Much favoured for assignations. Demolished 1829.

2. Snuff and tobacco shop in the Haymarket. Late eighteenth century with large window panes. Still in existence.

3. Trade card of a Seven Dials stationer and printer.

2

4

especially in the West End, was losing his servility. In wig, silk waistcoat and with modulated familiarity, he was doing his best to turn shopping into a social pleasure.

Josiah Wedgwood helped to set a new trend when he insisted: 'We must have an Elegant, Extensive and Convenient show-room' for his china in Grosvenor Square. And, for his vast bookshop in Finsbury Square—it had a 140-foot frontage—James Lackington supplied rooms for lounging and browsing. But he also marked all the 30,000 volumes in his shop with the lowest price he would take. This was a radical departure from the bargaining over all goods that was general up to then. Also putting a firm price ticket on all his goods, and requiring cash on the nail, was a Mr Palmer, in whose general store by London Bridge the assistants were instructed not to waste time on hesitating customers. Instead of alienating shoppers by these more business-like methods, Palmer and Lackington made a fortune.

4. Lackington's 'Temple of the Muses' bookshop, Finsbury Square.

5. In 1782 a linen draper named Gedge opened a shop on the north side of Leicester Square at the corner of Cranbourne Street (or Alley) with what was virtually the first London shop-front. Set on iron columns and with steel frames for the windows, it allowed an unobstructed view of the displayed goods.

6. Shops, each with its individual overhanging sign, in Cornhill. View looking east, with the Royal Exchange on the left, and the churches of St Michael and St Peter in the distance. These elaborate signs and symbols were abolished by the authorities in 1762 as dangerous to the public if they collapsed.

5

6

London's First Aerial Voyage

Nearly 200,000 people, excited and intensely curious, crowded into the grounds of the Honourable Artillery Company, Moorfields. Among them were the Prince Regent, Fox, and Edmund Burke. At St James's Palace, the King interrupted a Council of State to watch the flight through a telescope. Only Dr Johnson seems to have been bored by the flying fever that gripped London. 'I have had three letters this day all about the balloon,' he wrote testily to Reynolds. 'I could have been content with one.'

The event stimulating so much interest was England's first balloon ascent on 15 September 1784. The flyer was a handsome Italian of twenty-five, Vincenzo Lunardi, an attaché at the Neapolitan Embassy. Until his ascent, London had had to be content with a toy balloon sent up from Cheapside, a matter of some concern as France was nearly a year ahead in the air race, and there was vague talk of a danger to England's safety. There had even been a successful flight in Scotland. But now, at last, a man was to go up into the English sky.

Red and blue striped, made of oiled silk, and 32 feet in diameter, Lunardi's balloon was filled with hydrogen under the direction of Dr George Fordyce, lecturer in chemistry at St Thomas's. The containers are seen under the raised platform on the right of the view below.

After flying at such a great height that his balloon looked 'like a tennis ball', Lunardi came down near Ware in Hertfordshire. His precaution of making a will had been unnecessary. He was quite unharmed. Back in town he was received by cheering crowds in Essex Street, and taken to the Prince Regent to describe his flight. Later Lunardi was presented at Court, and became the lion of the season. He made considerable sums by exhibiting his balloon and giving talks at the Pantheon, Oxford Street.

1

1. Nine months after his initial flight, Lunardi, waving his tricorn, is seen with his assistant, George Biggin, and Mrs Sage – the 'First English Female Aerial Traveller' – in a balloon at St George's Fields, June 1785. On this occasion weight prevented Lunardi from flying. Biggin and Mrs Sage landed at Harrow where they were entertained by the boys at the school.

2. 'At five minutes after two the last gun was fired, the cords divided, and the Balloon rose, the company returning the signal of adieu with the most unfeigned acclamations and applauses. . . . When the thermometer was at fifty, the effect of the atmosphere, and the combination of circumstances around, produced a calm delight, which is inexpressible. . . . At twenty minutes past four, I descended in a spacious meadow at Standon, near Ware, in Hertfordshire. Some labourers were at work in it. I requested their assistance; they exclaimed they would have nothing to do with one who came in the Devil's house. . . .'–from Lunardi's letter to his guardian, later published as *An Account of the First Aerial Voyage in London*, 1784.

2

REGENCY LONDON

John Nash's Regent Street

Regent Street owes far more than its name to the Prince Regent. Without his vision and personal interest, this important feature of London's development would never have been built. In 1811–the year he formally assumed full powers of regency–the private leases of Marylebone Park fell in, and, with its reversion to the Crown, a scheme was suggested for turning the park into a garden city for the nobility. What better for its central feature than a summer villa for the Regent? But any such scheme required a link with Westminster–a main artery cutting through the West End. The Prince envisaged a 'Royal Mile' to challenge the magnificent boulevards of Napoleon's Paris. Carlton House, his official residence, would stand at one end; at the other, his summer retreat.

To fulfil this dream, there could hardly have been a better choice than the Regent's favourite architect–the Surveyor General. John Nash was then sixty-one. From a humble boyhood in Lambeth, Nash had become wealthy and influential by way of

1

2

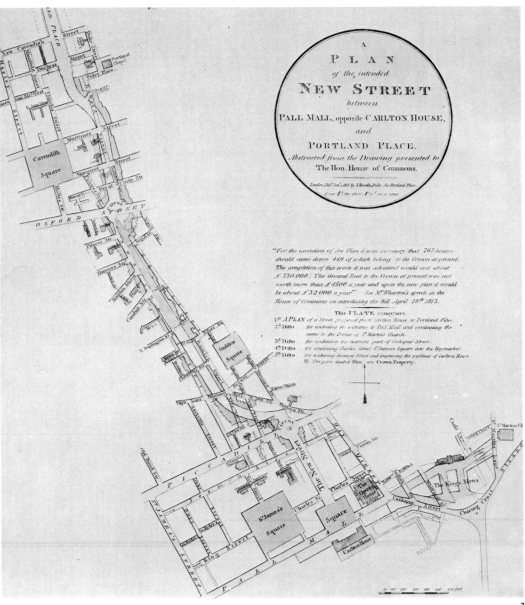

3

236

some country-house architecture, and after marriage in middle-age to a beautiful young woman popularly believed to be the Regent's mistress. He was a planner of imagination. He had great determination. His architecture, if insufficiently pure for the fastidious classicist, was peculiarly suited to the various practical and aesthetic problems involved in 'metropolitan improvements' and the building of Regent Street.

He started by sweeping away the small streets and dingy alleys in front of Carlton House (site of the present Duke of York's Steps) and creating a monumental, symmetrical square–Waterloo Place. Northwards from here ran the wide roadway flanked with classical buildings. The Regent insisted that something must be done to prevent 'the sensation of crossing Piccadilly'. Nash's solution was a Circus. Instead of an abrupt crossroads, he put curved buildings at each corner. As seen, top right, this gave enough of an illusion of a complete circle to justify the name of Regent Circus, as it was called until it became 'Piccadilly Circus' in 1880. To the north of the Circus, and terminating the vista from Carlton House, was built the County Fire Office, clearly based on Inigo Jones's façade for old Somerset House.

Nash's next problem was to find a pleasing way to change the axis of his street after the Circus. The answer was a quarter circle or Quadrant. With its sweeping colonnade of Doric columns in front of two continuous rows of shops, the Quadrant curved round into the main stretch of Regent Street. Because he did not want speculators tampering with his concept, Nash financed this himself. But within fifteen years of his death it was to be demolished, its beauty sacrificed to the moral stricture that street-walkers were using the arcade for rendez-vous.

The straight quarter of a mile up to Oxford Circus 'hugged' (as Nash put it) the coast of the West End. This involved the demolition of over 700 poor shops and houses in Soho which could be bought cheaply. Forming as it did a boundary between 'the streets of the Nobility and Gentry on the west' and 'the narrow streets and mean Homes occupied by mechanics and the trading part of the community to the east', this new street separated Soho from Mayfair for ever.

Between Oxford Circus and Portland Place there was an unavoidable kink in the road, and here again Nash made a virtue out of a difficulty. Disregarding orientation, he built All Souls, Langham Place, so that its circular vestibule would provide a climax to the vista looking north. Its uncomfortable architectural combination of Gothic spire and classical colonnade was satirized in the cartoon, far left, of Nash, over the caption, '*Nashi*onal Taste!!!!'

4

5

6

1. The Quadrant, Nash's happiest invention for Regent Street, with its colonnade of cast-iron columns, demolished in 1848.

2. Nash impaled on his own spire for All Souls', Langham Place.

3. Contemporary plan of the Regency development.

4. Regent (now Piccadilly) Circus in 1820 looking south down to Carlton House.

5. Waterloo Place and Regent Street, as seen from Carlton House.

6. Carlton House, demolished 1826. The portico was transferred to the National Gallery, built nine years later.

Abused, ridiculed, financed only with difficulty, most of Regent Street was built between 1817 and 1823. There was a constant struggle between architect and speculator because of Nash's determination to preserve some sort of architectural unity. People prepared to lay out money for sites in the new street wanted them for various kinds of buildings. They might be planning a private house or hotel, a church or a bank. One speculator had a scheme for blocks of residential chambers and shops. But they were not happy to lose their individuality and sacrifice their particular requirements behind an anonymous façade, however elegant. It was Nash's triumph that he still produced a Regent Street of distinction.

Regent's Park itself never became the garden city planned by Nash. The forty or more villas among woody groves were never built, nor was the Regent's villa. Its glory was restricted to the perimeter where rows of terraced houses were given the unity and pretensions of palaces with their white stuccoed columns, pediments and sculpture. Posterity was to regard them as architectural shams, but (like Carlton House Terrace overlooking St James's Park) their romantic splendour has guaranteed their preservation.

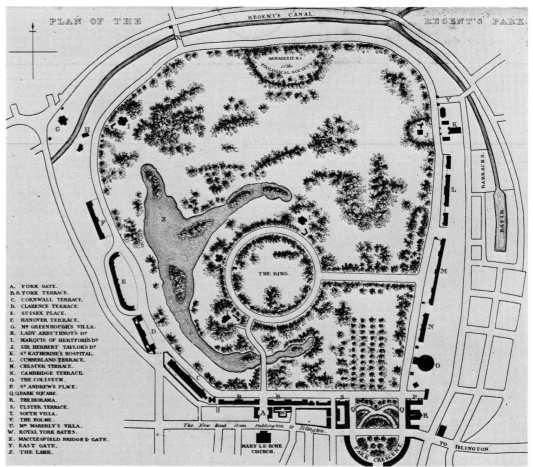

7

9

10

7. Regent's Park in 1826. The Prince's proposed villa was to have faced Cumberland Terrace (L) which Nash gave a special splendour to make it worthy of a royal vista.

8. Chester Terrace with 'triumphal arch' entrance.

9. Cumberland Terrace showing its most magnificent portico.

10. Idyllic scene on a first floor balcony of Hanover Terrace.

Gas in Pall Mall

'The Mall continued crowded with spectators until near twelve o'clock, and they seemed much amused and delighted by this novel exhibition.' So reported *The Monthly Magazine* following a demonstration of gas lighting outside Carlton House in 1807. By the end of the year, thirteen lamp-posts with three gas jets on each had been erected on the south side of Pall Mall for occasional displays.

Until seventy years before, London by night had remained almost as dark as in medieval times. The streets relied on a provision of 1416 which obliged a householder to burn a candle in a lantern outside his house from dusk to 11 p.m. on dark nights. People venturing out after dark did so with link-boys carrying burning torches, and link-extinguishers, like the one right, were a regular feature by Georgian front doors.

Night crime and suspicion of debauchery in the dark led to the erection of oil lamps, 15,000 of which were burning from sunset to sunrise by 1738. In Oxford Street there were more lamps than in the whole of Paris and foreigners found the effect 'exceedingly grand'.

But oil lamps consisting of cotton twist floating in tins of crude oil (tended by lamplighters and assistants, like those far right) were dim beside gas lighting, first demonstrated in Soho in 1802 to celebrate the Treaty of Amiens. Its development in Pall Mall was due to the enthusiastic pioneer work of the German-born Frederick Albert Winsor, who took over two houses where he installed carbonizing iron furnaces to generate gas and from which iron pipes were laid to the lamps. As the cartoon below suggests, the idea met with much fatuous opposition and it was not until 1814, seven years later, that gaslighting was really established by its permanent installation in Piccadilly, Coventry Street, and part of Princes Street.

1. Link extinguisher outside a house in Curzon Street, Mayfair.

2. Regency lamplighter at work.

3. 'A Peep at the Gas Lights in Pall Mall' – a contemporary cartoon lampooning early opposition.

1

2

3

The Regent's Canal

In the same year – 1811 – that he drew up his romantically conceived plans for Regent's Park, John Nash became an enthusiastic promoter of London's first and only really important canal. The Grand Junction Canal, completed six years earlier, came only as far as Paddington. But if this were extended another nine miles to Limehouse, there would be a direct link between the midlands and the commercial port of the Thames. It would serve Camden Town, Islington and Hackney.

In the original plan, right, the canal cuts right through the *centre* of the proposed park. Nash wanted this as 'a grand and novel feature', but, faced with opposition, settled for the Regent's Canal to run round the northern periphery (see map, page 238).

At a time when one canal boat could carry as much as four big wagons each requiring eight horses, and railways were still undreamt of, canals appeared a fine speculation. There was no difficulty in raising £234,000 capital for the north London scheme, and digging started in 1812. But it was to be eight years before the canal opened. Twelve locks were needed to cope with the 84-feet fall between Paddington Basin and the Thames. Forty bridges had to be built and two tunnels, one 372 yards long under Maida Hill, the other stretching half a mile under Islington.

Landlords fought the development, and, to protect the Agar Estate in St Pancras, William Agar led his gardeners and servants into a pitched battle against the canal diggers. Thomas Lord, who had already moved his cricket ground once because of the New Road development, had reopened it in the line of the proposed cutting. It cost the canal company £4,000 to move the ground to the present site, a few hundred yards farther north.

The company's secretary embezzled. Costs rose to £500,000, and by the time the canal was opened in 1820, railways were only a few years away, and it never repaid its investors.

The Lost Croydon Canal

The short-lived Croydon Canal was another victim of railway competition. Opened in 1809, it ran from the Thames at Rotherhithe (as an offshoot of the Grand Surrey Canal at New Cross) to the Croydon Basin (site of the present West Croydon Station). The view, right, looking towards London from Brockley, shows one of the twenty-six locks needed in a two and a half mile stretch to lift boats over the heights of Sydenham. Their main cargoes were stone, lime, and coal. A commercial failure, the canal was filled in and much of its length replaced by the Croydon Railway thirty years later. The railway paid £40,250

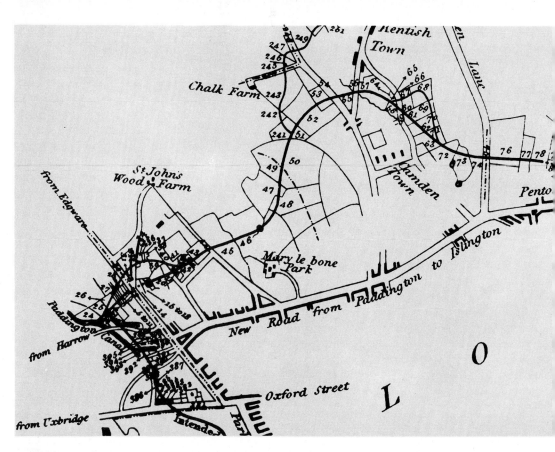

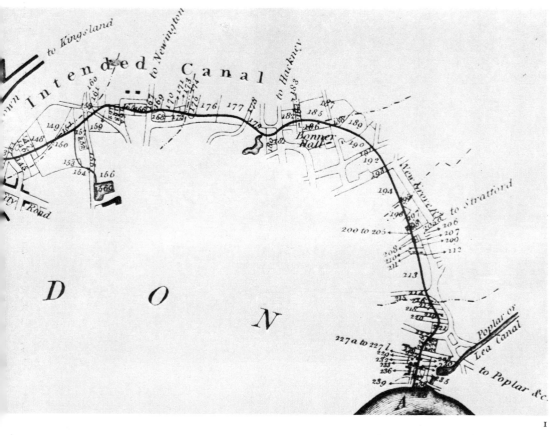

for the canal; it followed the general line pioneered by the waterway. Some of the irregular course was intersected by the rails, but for the last few miles into Croydon, they were laid on the actual bed of the canal. The deep cutting needed for trains is shown, bottom right, from almost the same viewpoint looking towards the present New Cross Gate Station. A stretch of the canal was preserved for some years at Anerley for boating, fishing and bathing, with excursions from London Bridge. The towpath provided a walk through the unspoilt woods of Norwood.

1. The 'Intended Navigable Canal' plan, submitted to Parliament in September 1811 in support of the scheme. It was followed except for the alternative upper loop (25–43) in Paddington; the feeder from Chelsea to the south; the course at Regent's Park (45–51) which now follows a more northerly arc; the feeder (241) from Hampstead; and the awkward alternative northern loop (63–56) at Camden Town.

2. Paddington Basin – now the residential 'Little Venice'.

3. Islington Tunnel, east entrance.

4. Limehouse entrance.

5. The Croydon Canal from Brockley heights, 1815.

6. The canal replaced by the Croydon Railway, 1839.

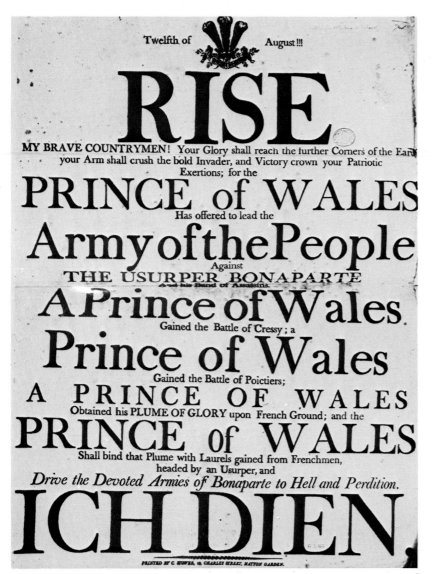

Twelfth of August!!!

RISE,

MY BRAVE COUNTRYMEN! Your Glory shall reach the further Corners of the Earth; your Arm shall crush the bold Invader, and Victory crown your Patriotic Exertions; for the

PRINCE of WALES

Has offered to lead the

Army of the People

Against

THE USURPER BONAPARTE

And his Band of Assassins.

A Prince of Wales

Gained the Battle of Cressy; a

Prince of Wales

Gained the Battle of Poictiers;

A PRINCE OF WALES

Obtained his PLUME OF GLORY upon French Ground; and the

PRINCE of WALES

Shall bind that Plume with Laurels gained from Frenchmen, headed by an Usurper, and

Drive the Devoted Armies of Bonaparte to Hell and Perdition.

ICH DIEN.

PRINTED BY C. HOWES, 13, CHARLES STREET, HATTON GARDEN.

'Boney is Coming!'

Nearly half a million men were under arms. In the City, sites were chosen for 'barricadoes', and suspicious foreigners smoked out of cellars. Pitt called for reports on how Elizabeth had prepared London's defences against the Spanish, and locks were built on the River Lea so that the Essex approaches to the capital could be flooded. Fleet Street print shops sold engravings of the French Grand Army crossing the Channel by balloon and a huge raft powered by windmills. But this fantasy was backed by alarming reality. Bonaparte was known to have 150,000 men poised for invasion at Boulogne. Not without reason, generations of children grew up frightened by the night whisper, 'Boney is coming!'

Although Napoleon never came, he kept the country in a spasmodic frenzy of preparation for two decades. Nelson and a highly efficient Navy prevented landings, while a largely amateur Army drilled, often with pitchforks instead of muskets. Volunteer units paraded in fine uniforms, were reviewed in Hyde Park by the King, and received their Colours from Regency beauties whose flowing white dresses were suitably topped with regimental coatees.

The first serious invasion scare, in 1798, ended with the Battle of the Nile–a triumph dramatically re-enacted at Sadler's Wells 'on real water'. The next threat came three years later when Nelson sent the Admiralty a much underlined memorandum about the defence of the Thames. Fears, briefly dispelled by the Treaty of Amiens, were again revived in the summer of 1804. Danger was then so grave that arrangements were made for Exchequer, Treasury, and Bank of England records to be evacuated to Worcester Cathedral. The Cabinet was informed that, if the French succeeded in landing, the fall of London was inevitable. In Paris a confident Bonaparte cast a victory medal prematurely inscribed, '*Frappée à Londres*'.

Trafalgar, the next year, brought relief; but not until the news of Napoleon's abdication in 1814 did people feel easy. As part of the subsequent revelry (and also to mark the centenary of the Hanoverian accession), a great spectacle took place on the Serpentine. A 'Naumachia', or mimic sea engagement, with miniature ships re-staged the Battle of the Nile. Three-decker men-o'-war, built from ships' timbers at Greenwich, were just big enough to carry three sailors who navigated and fired blank ammunition. As an after-dark climax, the French ships were set ablaze, and, said one spectator, at this grand climax 'the water seemed on fire'. The Serpentine swans, it was observed, did not enjoy these celebrations.

Waterloo, the following year, ultimately ended the twenty-one years of national unease. Time so quickly banished fears, that, when told of Napoleon's death in 1821, the story has it that the King completely misinterpreted the dramatic announcement, 'Sire, your greatest enemy is dead!' His mind on his unloved Queen, he is said to have exclaimed, 'No, by God! Is she?'

1. Satirical poster printed in Hatton Garden during the Napoleonic scare.

2. Houses in Edwardes Square, Kensington, built in 1812 by a Frenchman named Changier. He is said to have planned them on modest lines as quarters for Napoleon's lower ranked officers after the occupation of London. Leigh Hunt, who later lived there, said the square offered 'cheap lodgings and *fête champêtre* combined; here economy in-doors and Watteau without; here repose after victory . . . a French Arcadia. So runs tradition. . . .'

3. Battle of the Nile fought on the Serpentine.

4

5

6

4. In scarlet and gold, with bands playing and fair ladies to applaud their patriotism, volunteers flocked to the colours to repel the French. Among these Fencibles or Home Guards was the Bank of England Volunteer Corps, seen above parading on Lord's Cricket Ground in September 1799. They are receiving their Colours from Mrs Samuel Thornton, wife of the Bank's Governor.

5. A fashion plate shows what the well-dressed woman should wear on such patriotic occasions.

6. On a sombre January day in 1806 – a day heavy with hail clouds – an 'innumerable multitude' lined the Thames, and stood silently in bitter wind to watch Nelson's body carried by funeral barge from Greenwich to Whitehall. For three days the man who had done more than any other to save England from Napoleon had lain in state in the Painted Hall of the Hospital. Thousands, including the crew of the *Victory*, had paid their respects. Now, to the thud of minute guns, the coffin, draped in black velvet, was rowed upstream by forty-six seamen, while the flags of all ships in the river were lowered to half-mast. In the water entourage, nearly a mile long, were the barges of the Lord Mayor and City Companies. After a night at the Admiralty, watched over by his chaplain, Nelson was then carried by a Funeral Car, fashioned at front and stern like the *Victory*, to St Paul's. There he was buried in the crypt.

In 1820 . . . Cato Street, 23 February

Under the heading, 'DREADFUL RIOT AND MURDER', the *Morning Chronicle* of 24 February 1820, reported: 'Yesterday evening the west-end of the town was thrown into the utmost confusion, the streets were lined with soldiers and spectators, and the greatest alarm prevailed in consequence of the following circumstances. . . .'

The newspaper went on to describe how a 'formidable body' of Bow Street officers had raided the upper room of a stable in Cato Street, an alley just off the Edgware Road. There they surprised a meeting of about twenty men who were armed with guns, swords, and daggers. With the words, 'We are officers! Seize their arms!' Constable George Ruthven burst into the small room which also contained home-made grenades and bags of gunpowder. Their ringleader, Arthur Thistlewood, a known political extremist and malcontent, picked up a long sword and ran it through another officer, Richard Smithers, who fell back dead with the cry, 'Oh my God, I am done!' After a stiff fight, nine men were captured by the police and a detachment of Guards, and taken to Bow Street.

So ended, almost before it had begun, the Cato Street Conspiracy (for which eleven were tried and five hanged at Newgate) a preposterous plot in which, it was alleged, Thistlewood and his group of fanatics planned to assassinate the whole British Cabinet at one stroke while they were dining in Grosvenor Square. Thistlewood was to have gone to the front door with a note. When it was opened, the conspirators would have rushed in and seized the servants. Then they would have murdered and decapitated the fourteen ministers, who included Wellington and Castlereagh. Their arrest was made on the very night chosen for the dinner. This last-minute intervention was so fortuitous (and oddly reminiscent of the Gunpowder Plot) that it has not escaped suspicion of Government double-dealing.

. . . Hammersmith, 3 October

Not even at the funeral of Lord Nelson, said *The Times*, was such a prodigious concourse ever witnessed on the Thames. From Southwark to Hammersmith 'every creek and landing place sent out fresh numbers to swell the augmenting procession'.

With flags flying and bands playing aboard steam yachts and civic barges, the Company of Lightermen and Watermen and the loyal parishioners of St Saviour's, Southwark, sailed up river to Brandenburgh House. Here they presented addresses to Queen Caroline, estranged wife of George IV, expressing 'detestation of the vile persecution your Majesty has suffered'.

The demonstration coincided with the speech in the House of Lords made by Lord Brougham in defence of the Queen, who was charged with adultery. Anxious to dissolve his marriage and prevent her taking the royal title, the King claimed that she had conducted a liaison with the Italian courier with whom she had travelled abroad.

There was evidence that she had been indiscreet, but popular sympathy was behind her to an extraordinary, almost hysterical degree. Scenes like that, lower left, were frequent. Dressed in silver-embroidered muslin, and with a diamond aigrette in her hair, the Queen appeared several times on the balcony of the centre window. From all over the country loyal addresses poured in from sources as varied as the Females of Bath and the weavers of Spitalfields, which considered she was being victimized by a profligate monarch.

A month after these scenes, the King's case was abandoned. Caroline was voted £50,000 a year and allowed to assume her title. But she was denied admission to Westminster Hall at the Coronation in July 1821. Three weeks after this insult she died at Brandenburgh House, which the King promptly demolished.

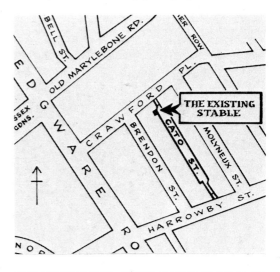

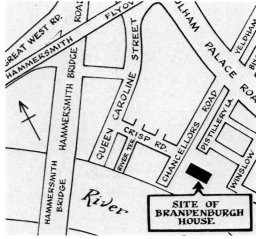

1. Smithers is stabbed by Thistlewood – as seen by Cruikshank whose drawing carries the caption: 'The Scene faithfully represented from the Description of Mr Ruthven. The View of the Interior correctly Sketched on the Spot.' The stable, almost unaltered, still exists in Cato Street.

2. 'The lawns before the ground in the vicinity of Brandenburgh House were thronged beyond expression. . . . Her Majesty showed herself several times in the balcony of the principal window. . . .' – from *The Times*'s description of the deputation to Queen Caroline's residence in Hammersmith (then Fulham).

3. Arthur Thistlewood at his trial, by Richard Dighton.

4. Queen Caroline at her trial, also by Dighton.

The New Road and the Spread of London

When the first census was taken in 1801, it revealed London's population to be just under a million. (There were 958,865 people living in the 117 square miles of the County of London: that is, the area covered by the City and the twenty-eight old L.C.C. boroughs.) The City (pop. 64,615) still remained the most crowded area, as it had been since Roman times. But only just. This was only a few hundred more than Marylebone (63,982), the flourishing district to which so many new residents were attracted by the Portman and other estates. The third largest district was Whitechapel (57,202) which had absorbed the overflow of the City's poor.

The growth of population was interrelated with the development of roads. An ever-increasing network was linking up the outlying districts, and the volume of horse-drawn traffic was already demanding diversions. The most foresighted of these was the New Road (present-day Marylebone, Euston and Pentonville Roads) created as early as 1756 as a circular by-pass of north-western London into the City. Cutting through hedges, spanning ditches and crossing open fields, as we see below, this brave new road, forty feet wide, linked the villages of Paddington Green and Islington.

Until the end of the eighteenth century the New Road was virtually London's northern boundary; then building spilled across it. Somers Town was built in 1786 and absorbed most of the 40,000 refugees from the French Revolution. Next came Penton-

ville (1790) which, like Camden Town and Kentish Town (both 1791), attracted a large middle-class population. In 1820 Lord's cricket ground, just north of the New Road, had to be removed to make way for Dorset Square. The later Regency also saw a new development–detached and semi-detached villas–a special feature of the Eyre Estate which enticed the rich merchant to live out at St John's Wood. These villas set a pattern of Greater London development that has continued ever since.

South of the Thames, residential growth was slower. The river was a natural barrier to expansion. But with the building of Waterloo Bridge (1817) and Southwark Bridge (1819) there came a change helped by the creation of an important southern artery in 1770 from Blackfriars Bridge to St George's Circus. Robert Mylne, architect of the bridge, designed the road (now Blackfriars Road) and the obelisk for the Circus. Four main roads radiated south from the Circus, and their value was enhanced in 1817 by London's first 'macadamizing'–the surfacing process invented by the Scottish engineer, John McAdam. London Road leading into Greenwich Road (now New Kent Road) became a main thoroughfare to the south-east lined with houses and with graceful features like the Paragon Crescent.

Elaborate plans were prepared in 1807 by George Dance for the development of the wet and muddy hundred acres of St George's Fields. With the Circus at its centre, it was to be laid out with crescents, polygons, and circuses of houses. These never materialized, but elsewhere in Southwark squares of terraced houses were built–Surrey Square, West Square, Trinity Church Square–comparable to those in north London.

6

7

8

5

1. A pair of semi-detached villas (by Nash about 1824) in Park Village East, a type of house pioneered on the Eyre Estate, St John's Wood, thirty years earlier.

2. Devonshire Place leading into Wimpole Street, looking south from the New Road during the Regency.

3. The New Road in 1806.

4. Houses bordering the New Road about 1794. Possibly Primrose Hill in the distance.

5. Part of Southwark in 1806 showing the road from Blackfriars Bridge to St George's Circus and to the junction with the Old Kent Road where the Paragon was built.

6. St George's Circus, Southwark, in 1810 looking north towards Blackfriars Road and turnpike. Behind the obelisk is the Royal Circus and Equestrian Philharmonic Academy, later the Surrey Theatre (demolished 1934). Beyond it is the Magdalen Hospital for penitent prostitutes (demolished 1865). The obelisk was moved to the junction of Lambeth and St George's Roads in 1905.

7. The Paragon, consisting of fifteen houses, was designed by Michael Searles for the Rolls family, prominent landowners in this area. Demolished 1898.

8. Searles's other Paragon on Blackheath, of about the same date, still survives.

The Berners Street Hoax

Among the wits and dandies who gave the Regency its flavour of cultivated high spirits, Theodore Hook had an unusual distinction. Beau Brummell and Count d'Orsay dazzled with the cut of their coats; Sydney Smith and Henry Luttrell with the cut of their tongues; but Hook won immortality for himself and for a London street with a practical joke.

Until the day in 1809 that he sauntered up it with his friend, Sam Beazeley, Berners Street was sedate and nondescript. At one end was Oxford Street; at the other the Middlesex Hospital. Two rows of modest houses faced each other down the 400 yards of its length. Hook, then twenty-one, knew how to deflate pomposity ('Pray, Sir,' he once enquired of a swaggering stranger in the Strand, 'may I ask if you are *anyone in particular?*'); on this occasion he seems to have wanted to detonate respectability. Pausing at No 54, he said suddenly to Beazeley, 'I will lay you a guinea that in a week that nice quiet dwelling shall be the most famous in all London'.

What followed has been improved by a thousand tellings. But the essence is the same. In the next few days Hook wrote several hundred letters to tradesmen all over London asking them to deliver goods to No 54–the house of a well-to-do widow–at a particular time on a particular day. Coalmerchants, greengrocers, dairymen, bakers, and undertakers were all summoned. Among the varied goods sent for were china, glass, books and harpsichords. Beer was ordered by the dray, wine by the dozen bottles.

Members of Parliament, lawyers and preachers, were among those invited on various ingenious pretexts. So was the Lord Mayor, the Governor of the Bank of England (promised an exposé of fraud by a clerk) and the Duke of Gloucester (his curiosity whetted by the news that a former royal servant wished to make a death-bed confession).

The response was overwhelming. The confusion and damage to goods catastrophic. The street ran with wine and was littered with smashed articles. Horses fell, coach panels were smashed in, vegetables rolled into the gutter, and pickpockets enjoyed a field-day. Latter-day artists depict an appalling mêlée of snarled traffic and fighting people, while Hook watches from behind the curtain of a window opposite. The picture showing the scene, above (believed to be unique and contemporary), is less spectacular, but probably far nearer what really happened.

1. The bewildered owner, Mrs Tottingham, comes to the door of No 54. The house is now demolished, and is the site of Sanderson's.

2. Theodore Hook – portrait by Daniel Maclise, R.A.

248

The Colosseum, Regent's Park

For more than forty years, the Colosseum, a specially built rotunda in Regent's Park, was the most popular attraction listed by the guide books under 'Panoramas and Elegant Places of Amusement'. In 1829, the year it opened, a million visitors came to admire the vast aerial panorama of the city displayed there.

The panorama was the work of an artist and land surveyor, Thomas Hornor. Seven years earlier, he had obtained permission to do some drawings from the lantern on the dome of St Paul's. Scaffolding was being put up at the time for the replacement of the ball and cross, and on the highest point Hornor was given a little cabin. Starting at 3 a.m. to catch the first light, and before smoke obscured clarity, he worked daily through one summer. At the end he had prepared 300 detailed sketches of London stretching to the horizon 130 miles away.

Hornor's original project was modest. Simply the preparation of four engravings. But, perhaps inspired by panoramas on show in Leicester Square and the Strand, he developed a far more ambitious scheme. For the huge panorama which he envisaged, he needed a special setting, and he raised £23,000 for the so-called Colosseum. Designed by Decimus Burton on the model of the Pantheon, it was built on the east side of Regent's Park just south of Cambridge Terrace.

Suspended in cradles, and working from 2,000 scaled drawings, one principal artist and a handful of assistants went to work. On more than an acre of canvas stretched round the inside of the rotunda, they recreated the bird's-eye view of London. The combination of minute detail and realism, said one guide book, 'amounted to deception'. To add to this deception, there were sound effects like chiming clocks and peals of church bells.

Over the years, the Colosseum was to house other panoramas such as London by Night (with moonlight reflected on the rippling Thames), Paris, and the Lake of Thun. There were alternative attractions like the Hall of Mirrors, the Gothic Aviary, and the Stalactite Caverns. Forty years ahead of other places, roller skating was pioneered here in 1844. But its popularity declined in the 1850s, and, after an abortive plan to convert it into a grand hotel, the Colosseum was demolished in 1875.

1. The Colosseum, Regent's Park.

2. Hornor's cabin above the dome of St Paul's. 'On one occasion the night was passed in the observatory,' he wrote, 'but the cold was so intense, as to preclude any wish to repeat the experiment.'

3. After coming through the main entrance with its Doric portico, visitors walked down the closed passageway, left, into the salon, the tent-like roof of which prevented them seeing the panorama. A spiral staircase or a lift carried them up to the promenade which simulated the dome of St Paul's and gave them a 360-degree view of London. Workmen and painters are seen here in the final stages of preparation.

Diversions for the Curious

In a city with a million people, and with a constant influx of visitors, there arose a demand for new, more varied forms of entertainment. Showmen were quick to supply unusual diversions to satisfy wide-eyed curiosity and semi-scientific interest. They ranged from Toby 'The Sapient Pig' in Spring Gardens to Miss Linwood's prim display of needlework pictures ('Jephthah's Rash Vow' and 'Litter of Foxes at Play') in Leicester Square. A wondering public could choose between the Heaviest Man that Ever Lived and the Human Skeleton. In Fleet Street Mrs Salmon's Waxworks offered pastoral scenes of shepherds and shepherdesses 'making violent love'. There was Burford's Panorama in Leicester Square (views of Pompeii, Niagara Falls and George IV's Coronation); the Regent Park Diorama (Canterbury Cathedral on a screen 80 feet by 40 feet); the Cormorama in Regent Street (showing the overland route from Southampton to Calcutta); and the St Martin's Lane Appollonicon ('performing by mechanical powers' overtures, songs and duets, four times daily, admission 1s.).

There were two places where the public could be sure of finding something of particular interest. The Egyptian Hall on the south side of Piccadilly, almost opposite Bond Street, was opened as a museum in 1812 by a Liverpool collector, William Bullock, and four years later drew the town to see Napoleon's carriage captured at Waterloo. When the museum exhibits were sold in 1819, the shows at the Egyptian Hall became more varied. The other was Exeter 'Change in the Strand which housed a menagerie, visited by Byron to see 'the tigers sup', and the roar of whose animals were said to have frightened horses in the street.

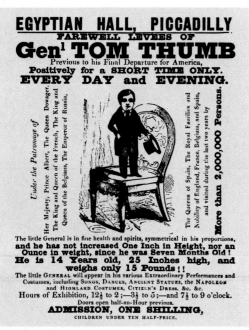

A herd of reindeer and a family of Laplanders were attractions at the Egyptian Hall in 1821. Rowlandson, right, shows the crowds who came to see them against an Arctic backcloth. Bullock always liked appropriate backgrounds. He converted one gallery into a medieval hall for a display of armour, and the Egyptian décor provided a natural setting for the model of a tomb which the explorer Belzoni had discovered near Thebes. Freaks were always popular. A mermaid (manufactured in Japan from the tail of a fish and the head and shoulders of a monkey) drew 400 people a day. Among a wide variety of exhibits were an artificial chicken hatchery, prehistoric skeletons, and speaking automatons. The Siamese Twins (4) were a great attraction in 1829, but were topped by the American midget, 'General Tom Thumb', some years later.

Before the Zoo in Regent's Park (page 286), the main place for seeing wild animals was the Royal menagerie above the shops in Exeter 'Change. Chunee, a five-ton elephant brought from India at a cost of 900 guineas, was the greatest attraction. Byron thought him so well behaved that he wished he were his butler. But he was subject to short annual fits of ferocity. To keep these fits in check, he was doped. But this did not always reduce his violence and his worst outbreak came in March 1826, when he had been captive in the Strand for twelve years. He hurled his great weight against the reinforced wooden bars of his cage, and when he broke through, the alarmed owner of the menagerie, Edward Cross, ordered him to be shot. But this was not easy. No one knew how to shoot an elephant and his hide was so tough that it needed more than a hundred shots (including those from soldiers rushed over from Somerset House) before Chunee was killed.

6

7

8

9

1. The Egyptian Hall, Piccadilly, opened 1812, demolished 1905.

2. Exeter 'Change, Strand. Opened 1676, demolished 1829. Site of the Strand Palace Hotel.

3. Tom Thumb – Charles S. Stratton of Bridgeport, Connecticut – was brought to England and exhibited in 1844 by the American showman P. T. Barnum.

4. The Siamese Twins at the Egyptian Hall, 1829 – advertised as 'two youths of eighteen, natives of Siam, united by a short band at the pit of the stomach – two perfect bodies bound together by an inseparable link.'

5. Daniel Lambert – 'Of Surprising Corpulency' – born in Leicester, 1770. Had to have a specially built carriage to bring him to London. Maximum weight: 52 stone 11 lb.

6. The Laplanders who were on show for six weeks.

7. Death of the furious Chunee.

8. Toby, 'The Sapient Pig', exhibited in 1817.

9. The Horned Woman exhibited at Weeks's Museum, Piccadilly, early nineteenth century.

Shillibeer's 'Parisian' Omnibus

The coaching era was at its height. From one tavern alone eighty coaches left every twenty-four hours for the north; from another, fifty-three rolled away to the West Country. Altogether, 1,500 coaches started and ended their journeys in London. More than a thousand hackney carriages plied the streets. Short distances between the City and the inner suburbs were covered by 418 short-stage coaches. London's first railway was still seven years away.

This was the position in July 1829, when George Shillibeer, a Bloomsbury coach-builder, revolutionized London's transport by starting the first regular bus service. His inspiration was Paris which already had bus services, and he was careful to stress the French name of 'omnibus' in his advertising. Crowds gathered in Paddington Green to cheer the first omnibus ('running upon the Parisian mode') as it set out from 'The Yorkshire Stingo' along the New Road. Three horses pulled the twenty-two passengers who, for a fare of 1s. 6d., were taken to the Bank via 'The Angel', Islington.

Attended by a conductor ('a person of great respectability') each of Shillibeer's two omnibuses left Paddington and the City at three-hourly intervals. The fares were less than for the short-stage coaches, no advance booking was needed, and passengers were picked up anywhere en route. Three years later, ninety buses were running on the Paddington-Bank route, and there was another regular service between Hammersmith and Somerset House.

Most omnibuses were licensed to carry twelve passengers inside, while three others sat on the roof by the driver. On an outside step at the back stood the conductor who collected the fares and kept the bus as full as possible. The buses had straw on the floor, and people sat on forms along each side.

To stop the bus, you banged on the roof or prodded the conductor. This simple method was replaced by a bell, and one company used a device of two leather straps attached to the driver's arms. The passenger pulled either the right or left 'rein' to indicate which side of the road he wanted to be put down.

By 1835 there were 600 buses operating in London, and nearly half a million people—the first commuters—were being carried in and out of central London every day. So fierce was the competition that the man who had pioneered it went under. Faced with ruin by rivals like the London Conveyance Company, which had a fleet of sixty-five buses, and stables for 500 horses off the Edgware Road, Shillibeer sadly turned his buses into hearses. 'Shillibeer's Original Omnibuses' became 'Shillibeer Funeral Coaches'.

1. Archway Road in 1823 looking north. A mile long, and built by Thomas Telford, this road cut through the hill to provide coaches travelling between Holloway and East Finchley with a route less steep than Highgate Hill to the left. In 1812 an attempt had been made to tunnel through the brow of the hill, but the tunnel collapsed. In its place, Highgate Archway, designed by Nash, was built the following year to span the new road and carry Hornsey Lane which had been severed. The brick and stone bridge was replaced by the present iron one in 1900. The tollgate (which made a heavy levy of 6d. per horse and 1d. for foot passengers) existed for fifty years. More than eighty London tollgates, or turnpikes, which provided revenue for the upkeep of roads, ceased to exist after 1864. This gave an added incentive to the bus services.

2. Shillibeer's omnibus. Larger than those in Paris and the majority in later use in London, they could seat 20 passengers inside. His short-stage buses had only two horses.

3. George Shillibeer. The promoter of the London omnibus was born in Tottenham Court Road, and, while working as a coachbuilder in Paris, decided to bring buses to London. He died in 1866, aged 69, and was buried at Chigwell.

4

5

4. Thronging with passengers, luggage, porters, ostlers and drivers, the coaching inn was as full of activity as a latter-day railway terminus. From the courtyard of 'The Swan with Two Necks', off Cheapside, seen above in 1831, coaches carrying passengers and mail started on their journeys to the West of England. The Bristol Mail is going through the archway into Lad Lane (now Gresham Street), so narrow that it required the most skilled coachmanship. More passengers and mail were picked up in Piccadilly at the Gloucester Coffee House (site of the old Berkeley Hotel). Though one of the most important, this was only one of a hundred taverns in the City and the Borough which were arrival and departure centres for coaches and wagons. The coaching operations here were run by William Chaplin who owned, or part-owned, sixty-eight coaching lines and kept over 1,800 horses.

5. Attempts to supplant horse buses by buses run on steam were tried for twenty years after 1821, but never overcame the hostility of horse interests, the authorities, and bad roads. 'The Enterprise Steam Omnibus', seen, left, on the New Road in 1833, was made by Walter Hancock at his Stratford East factory. This was the third steam vehicle built by Hancock who, after apprenticeship to a London watchmaker and jeweller, became interested in engineering. It took him seven years of trial and error before his first steam carriage, the 'Infanta', was ready to run regularly between Stratford and London. Altogether he built ten steam omnibuses. But though he perfected a light and efficient boiler, Hancock's buses, carrying only about ninety passengers a day, even in summer, were never much more than a novelty.

'Life, Fashion and Frolic'

Sporting life and social diversions in Regency London were captured in a series of drawings which George Cruikshank made for a book published in 1821. *Life in London; or The Day and Night Scenes of Jerry Hawthorn, Esq., and his elegant friend Corinthian Tom . . . in their Rambles and Sprees through the Metropolis* was not only a best-seller running into innumerable editions. It was a guide book which, using the thread of fictitious characters, provided a unique record of what was called at the time, 'life, fashion and frolic'.

The author was Pierce Egan, a sporting journalist, who conducted the lively young blades, Tom and Jerry, through the London of the day–dancing at Almack's, ambling in Rotten Row, watching a Newgate hanging, pushing over the box of a Charley at Temple Bar. The couple personified the popular idea of Regency men about town, and Thackeray was to recall that, when the book first came out during his schooldays, he and his friends regarded Tom and Jerry as the ultimate in elegance and fashion.

Mr Egan (a spendthrift with italics, and reluctant to let his heroes just 'go' somewhere) makes them take 'a *stroll* through Piccadilly, a *look in* at Tattersalls, a *ramble* through Pall Mall. . . .' When they 'take *a turn* in Bond Street', it involves a visit to Gentleman Jackson's Rooms where the Art of Self-Defence is taught, and 'no person can be admitted without an introduction'. Tom puts on the gloves with Jackson who was said to earn over £1,000 a year coaching young aristocrats, among whom was Lord Byron.

At an unspecified house near St James's Park, the two friends are invited by '*swell* BROAD coves' to play 'a *friendly* game at whist', but soon find themselves '*had*'. Jerry's cards are spied on by a confederate at the mirror. They reckon the *swell* dinner they enjoyed first cost them *five guineas* a mouthful at the card table afterwards.

On another evening they '*toddle*' to the Westminster Dog Pit, Tothill Fields. Here an Italian monkey, 'JACCO MACCACCO', is fighting a dog, twice his weight, and 'the property of a Nobleman', for a hundred-guinea purse. The monkey is tethered by an iron chain two yards long and brings saw-sharp teeth to the throat of this and several other dogs. 'I would not,' Jerry tells Tom equivocally, 'have missed this curious scene for a trifle.'

The tremendous popularity of Tom and Jerry led to a musical version of their adventures being staged at the Adelphi, and at one time plays about them were being performed simultaneously in ten theatres in London and the suburbs.

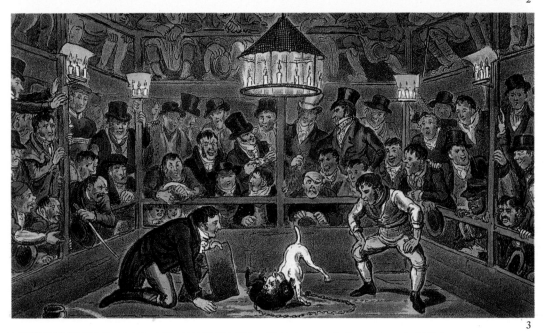

1. Among swell broad coves at St James's.
2. The Art of Self Defence in Bond Street.
3. Sporting their blunt at the Westminster Pit.

1. Opening of the St Katharine's Dock, 1828.

2. Congestion in the Thames. Ships lying off the Legal Quays in 1804. Many were forced to wait for weeks, midstream in the Pool, for lighters to unload them. Three and four abreast, they queued all the way up the river from Woolwich. The addition of 'sufferance' wharves on the south shore only helped slightly.

The Docks

For nearly 250 years, and under regulations dating from Elizabethan times, every ship coming up the Thames to London had to unload all dutiable cargo on what were called the Legal Quays. These twenty quays were all crowded together side by side on the north shore of the river between London Bridge and the Tower. By the beginning of the nineteenth century, as William Daniell shows, left, they were already hopelessly inadequate. Apart from delays leading to increased costs, there was mass pilfering by riverside gangs. One in every five Indiamen was said to be marked down for plunder. Dutiable merchandise were surreptitiously ferried ashore to elude Customs officers. Food was stored under appalling conditions.

The establishment of the River Police in 1801 was an attempt to halt the crime. But the only real solution was to build large wet docks farther down river. Unaffected by tides, ships could moor and unload on their quays. They would be lined with adequate, well-protected warehouses. There was opposition from the City and the Legal Quay wharf-owners, but the necessity was too pressing. Starting with the West India Docks in 1802, and culminating in the opening of St Katharine's Dock, in 1828, the start of the

The City Canal (later South Dock)　　　Export Dock　E　　　Blackwall Basin　Import Dock　　3

new century saw a tremendous development of docks from the Tower to Blackwall.

The West India Docks, created by the enterprising merchants of the West India Company, were the largest. With two extensive basins–the Import and Export Docks–and surrounded by high walls to prevent theft and to safeguard customs inspection, they covered 295 acres on the Isle of Dogs. They were ideally placed. The Blackwall Basin received incoming ships, and then lighters from the Limehouse end carried their cargoes into the City.

Daniell's view, above, looking due west towards London, and with St Paul's in the far distance, shows the West India Docks soon after their completion in 1802. It embraces most of the Isle of Dogs, and the artist's view-point was from Blackwall Point which is marked on the map, top right. To the south of the main docks was the City Canal through which ships were dragged by hauliers singing dirges as they pulled on the ropes. Although this cut out the loop of the Thames down to Greenwich, the canal was not a success, and by 1834–the date of the map–it had been turned into South Dock with the Timber Dock built alongside it.

The idea of providing a short cut was not new. For sailing vessels the great loop of the river round the Isle of Dogs and two smaller ones at Blackwall and Ratcliff added hours or even days to the voyage if the winds were wrong. To shorten the journey, and also provide three huge docks, an ingenious scheme was proposed in 1796. Willey Reveley, an architect and engineer, suggested cutting a channel, three-quarters of a mile

long, to join up Blackwall and Limehouse reaches.

As his plan, upper right, indicates, this channel would have become the main course of the river, and would have left the great horseshoe and the two other loops for conversion into docks. But it was too difficult an engineering feat for that time, and only a vestige of Reveley's idea took shape in the far less ambitious City Canal.

Seeing the threat of the West India Docks, the City raised £4,000,000 to build the London Docks opened at Wapping in 1805.

They were far smaller, but they had vast warehouse space and acres of underground cellars to take all the tobacco, rice, wine and brandy. They were granted a monopoly on all these goods unless they came from the East or West Indies. Further large storage space was created when St Katharine's Dock was opened twenty-three years later only a few hundred yards to the west. The tall warehouses designed by Thomas Telford, were built almost on the water's edge so that cargoes could be unloaded straight into them.

The building of St Katharine's, so near to

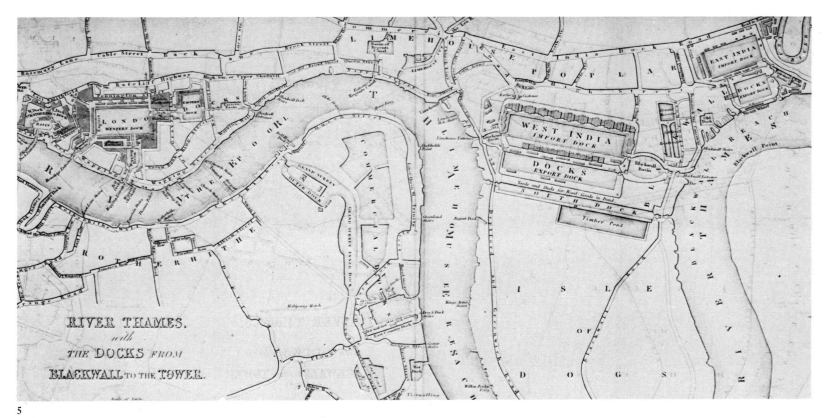

RIVER THAMES.
with
THE DOCKS FROM
BLACKWALL TO THE TOWER.

5

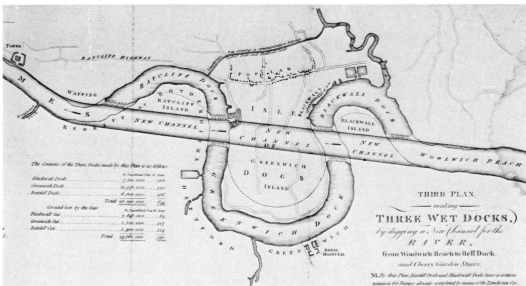

6

7

the City, involved far greater devastation than the other docks farther down river. Created out of a Stepney slum and an ancient church foundation, it involved the demolition of 1,200 houses, and made 11,300 people homeless. It was built in seventeen months, and involved the enormous activity, seen bottom left.

Meanwhile across the river in 1804 there appeared the Surrey and Commercial Docks, a sprawling, irregular system of basins built by conflicting interests. Its nucleus was Howland Great Dock (page 165), most southerly of the Commercial Docks on the map, top right. Unlike those north of the Thames, the Rotherhithe docks did not handle exotic, highly dutiable goods. Timber from the Baltic, grain and other bulky articles were the chief cargoes landed there. It was planned to disperse these goods as far as Epsom on the Grand Surrey Canal, but it never reached beyond Camberwell. The Croydon Canal (page 240) was to have been another link with the southern counties, but never extended, as planned, to Portsmouth.

3. West India Docks soon after their completion in 1802. As their name suggests they were planned for colonial cargoes.

4. Unloading in West India Docks in 1830.

5. The docks from Blackwall to the Tower in 1834. Not shown in this map, or in Daniell's view, because it was not opened until 1868, is the L-shaped Millwall Dock with entrances in Limehouse Reach and South Dock.

6. Reveley's plan for shortening the Thames journey.

7. Excavation of St Katharine's Dock in 1827. Among the buildings demolished was the ancient collegiate church of St Katharine-by-the-Tower (founded by King Stephen's queen in 1148). This was rebuilt in Regent's Park. No longer used commercially, St Katharine's is being developed as a residential and recreational area with the basin as a 'Marina' for private craft.

I Houses in Thames Street

St Michael's, Crooked Lane (demolished 1831)

The 1831 London Bridge

For over 500 years, the bridge built across the Thames by Peter de Colechurch stood proudly and seemingly immutable. But from the beginning of the nineteenth century affection for a romantic landmark was tinged with practical worries. Its foundations had become unsound. The old bridge was a danger to shipping, and every year about fifty watermen lost their lives shooting the rapids created by the small arches. In 1821 Parliament decided it must be replaced.

The new London Bridge, wider, and set on five arches instead of twenty, was sited 100 feet west of the old one. In June 1830, a year before it was opened, and six years after the first pile was sunk in the river, it had reached the stage shown by George Scharf, above (1) and from the other direction, bottom right (4). The above view is of the northern end of the bridge, just across the water, where it crosses Thames Street. To complete the approach to Gracechurch Street, workmen are seen pulling down one of the 182 houses in its path, and are nearing Wren's church of St Michael's, Crooked Lane, which will be demolished in the following March. On the

right can be seen the balustrades and watch-house of the old bridge. A coach is passing the West front of St Magnus and heading up Fish Street Hill.

The old bridge remained in use until the opening of its successor in 1831, and did not finally disappear for a year after that. By then only someone in his eighties would have any clear memory of the bridge lined with houses as it was in 1758, right (2). Condemned as a 'public' nuisance, this was two years after the Act of Parliament that authorized the removal of all the houses and the remains of the Becket Chapel, Nonsuch House, and Southwark Gate. During the demolition of the houses a wooden footbridge was put up for the use of pedestrians. This caught fire, and as the 1758 view shows, the drawbridge was destroyed, and half-burnt timbers collapsed into the water.

The last of the houses was pulled down in 1762. The old starlings and Gothic arches remained but, in an attempt to help shipping, one of the central piers was removed, as may be seen, far right (3), and replaced by a wide, curved arch. This arch was the bridge's undoing. The current was drawn to the widest opening and this eroded the founda-

tions of the adjoining piers. A Select Committee called for a new bridge, and designs were submitted by Mylne, Telford and George Dance the Younger; but in 1821 the choice went to John Rennie, the Scottish engineer who had built Waterloo Bridge.

The old bridge had twenty arches; the new one, only five. This meant a more even flow of water and no build-up like a weir. Built of Scottish and Devon granite, the new bridge was finally 64 feet wide. The cost of about £2 millions was met by £150,000 Government grant and from the reserves of the Bridge House Estate which derived a huge income from London property bequeathed from medieval times onwards when all trade to and from the City passed over the bridge. Grateful citizens remembered it in their wills. They left money or property 'For God and the Bridge' which had increased enormously in value over the centuries. Rennie died in the same year that his plans were accepted, but was posthumously honoured by a knighthood for his son. An unnamed grave believed to be that of Peter de Colechurch was discovered during the demolition of the bridge.

The Monument   Fish Street Hill   St Magnus   End of old London Bridge

1758 (2)

1762–1831 (3)

August 1830 (4)

1831–1967 (5)

Sir Robert's Peelers go on the Beat

It had taken seventy-two years for John Fielding's proposals (page 209) to be adopted. Until 1829, fears for the freedom of the individual were a constant brake on the formation of a police force. Then the Home Secretary swept these misgivings aside with a single sentence. 'I want to teach [people],' said Sir Robert Peel, 'that liberty does not consist of having your house robbed by organized gangs of thieves.' With this he introduced the Police Bill, and on Saturday, 26 September, the new police force paraded for the first time in the grounds of the Foundling Hospital, Bloomsbury.

A thousand strong, and mostly ex-soldiers, they had to face derisive shouts of 'Lobsters!' 'Coppers!' and 'Crushers!' as they made their nightly patrols. Organized in six divisions, the police operated in a seven-mile radius of Charing Cross. They could not go into the City which, with its usual display of independence, set up its own Night Watch three years later, and was not fully organized until 1839.

To minimize fears, the new police were dressed in civilian-style dress of top hats and blue frock coats, for which each man paid 2s. out of his 21s. weekly wage. They carried no weapons except a tactfully concealed truncheon, lantern, and emergency rattle, although cutlasses and pistols were kept in reserve at the police stations. Their manual insisted, 'The constable . . . must be civil and obliging to all people of every rank and class. He must be particularly cautious not to interfere idly or unnecessarily . . . He must remember that there is no qualification so indispensible to a police officer as a perfect command of temper.' But for all this, it was to take years to break down prejudice, before 'Peel's Bloody Gang' won the kindlier nicknames of 'Bobbies' and 'Peelers' after their founder.

1. The policeman – detested figure of authority.

2. No 4, Whitehall Place, first headquarters of the Metropolitan Police Force. The Police Office remained here from 1829 to 1890 when it moved to New Scotland Yard on the Embankment. Though in Whitehall Place, this house backed on to Great Scotland Yard, and this may have brought about the general reference to 'Scotland Yard'. It may, however, date only from 1842 when the detective branch was established in a separate building which was actually in Scotland Yard. The building, right, is now demolished.

3. Sir Robert Peel – satirical cartoon showing him kicking out the 'Charleys' (the old night-watchmen) in favour of his 'New Police'.

4. The earliest large-scale duty of the newly formed police was to keep order during the Chartist riots. When a crowd of 25,000 marched on Parliament to deliver the vast Chartist petition in 1848, they kept the peace. Later 'acting on information received' they arrested fourteen leaders in a Blackfriars inn, and on Whit Monday of that year went to Bonner's Fields, Bethnal Green where, right, armed with swords they awaited an unruly meeting which never took place.

NEW POLICE A-LA-MILITAIRE!!

1

2

3

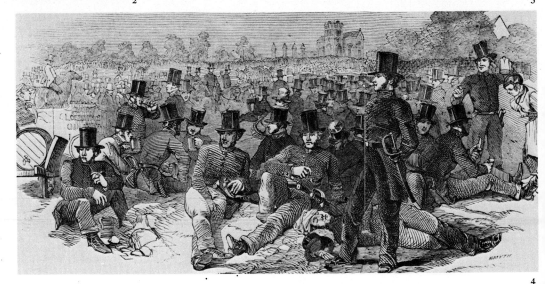

4

VICTORIAN LONDON

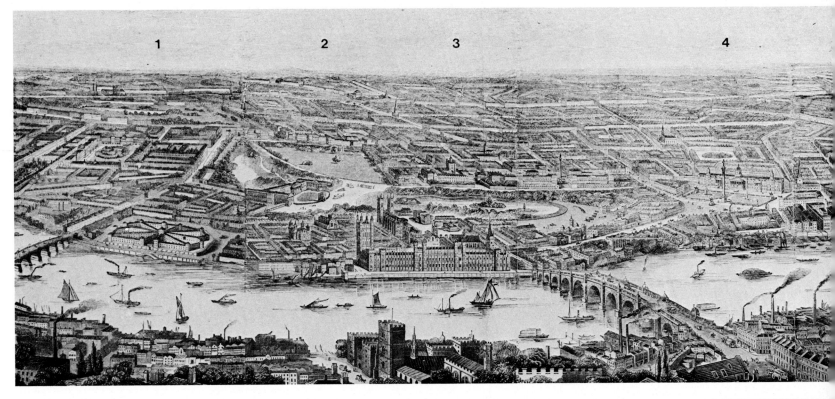

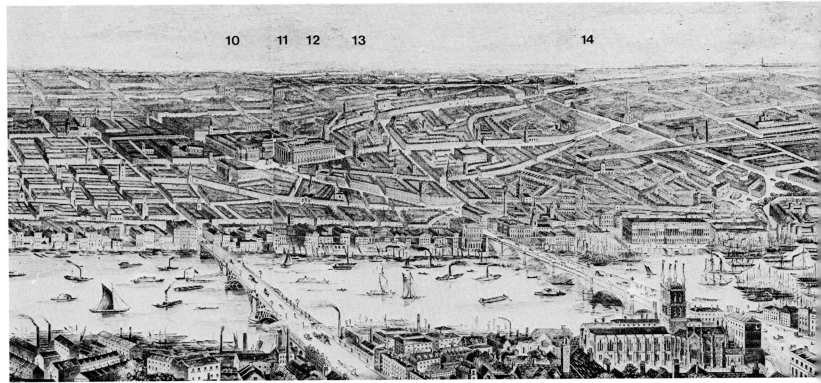

London in 1844

Seven years after the accession of Queen Victoria, this crude, yet oddly evocative woodcut shows us a London under the oppressive shadow of industrial development. The gracious Georgian city of Kip and Buck seems to have become a place of drab, barrack-like buildings and grimy rooftops. Smoke pours from factory chimneys, the funnels of paddle steamers, and from trains on the viaducts which stretch tentacles across the last remaining green fields. Stern walls surround the new docks. But an eighteenth-century spaciousness is retained by streets and squares, for their scale has not yet been destroyed by gross mid-Victorian buildings. Proportions have not been ruined by the attic storeys which the landlords of mid-Georgian houses will impose at the end of 99-year leases.

In this period of change and extensive, varied building, we note some features which appeared about this time, and others that have been demolished or radically altered. Gone now, and replaced by the Tate Gallery, is Millbank Prison (1), built 1816, demolished 1903, designed on the reforming principles of Jeremy Bentham for 1,200 convicts. In front of Buckingham Palace stands the Marble Arch (2), designed by Nash in 1827, and due to be moved to its Hyde Park site in 1851. Barry's Houses of Parliament (3), started 1840, are being built, and at this date the Big Ben Tower (1857) and Victoria Tower (1860) are prophetic. Erected in 1842, Nelson's Column (4) is still without Landseer's 1867 lions. Brunel's graceful Hungerford Bridge, a suspension footbridge (5) leading to Charles Fowler's Hungerford Market, is under construction.

With the coming of the railway, and

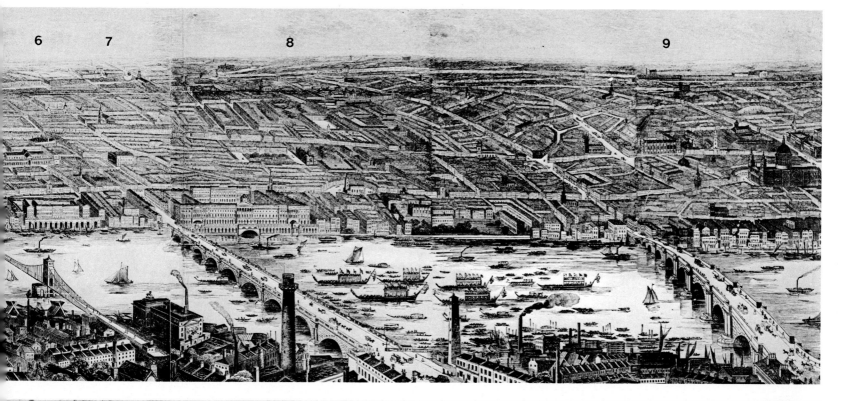

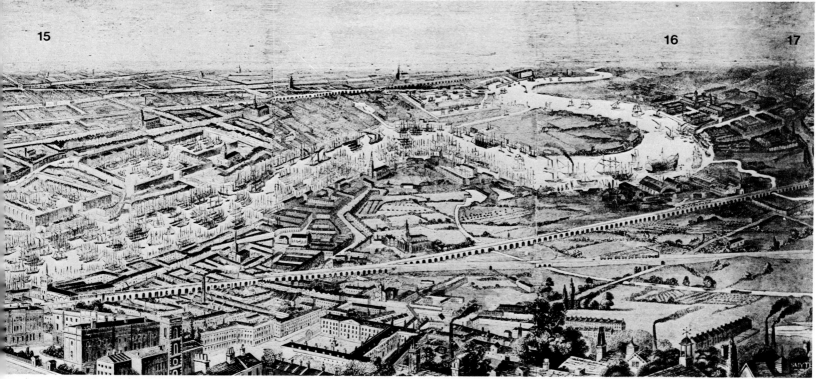

Charing Cross Station in 1860, the market is to be demolished, and the bridge sold for incorporation with the Clifton Suspension Bridge. Also by Fowler is the 1830 quasi-classical market with Tuscan columns in the centre of Covent Garden (6). Almost on the horizon is the Doric portico (1839–1961) of Euston Station (7). In the foreground is the Shot Tower (8), built 1826, pulled down 1962. Molten lead is poured through a sieve on the top floor and falls 200 feet into a water tank to solidify into a myriad of round balls of shot. Conspicuous in Newgate Street stands the 1829 Gothic Revival front of Christ's

Hospital (9), demolished in 1902 with the school's removal to Horsham. The City's one major circus–the residential Finsbury Circus (10) built 1814–has the London Institution Library, demolished 1936, on the north side. On Rennie's 1819 Southwark Bridge (11) is the tollgate, abolished when the City buys the bridge in 1866. The Royal Exchange (12) by Sir William Tait is being built at this time after the 1838 burning of the previous seventeenth-century Exchange. To its right, the oblong building with fore-court in Threadneedle Street is the Hall of Commerce (13), opened 1842, now de-

molished, as a mercantile centre pending the Exchange's completion. Fenchurch Street Station (14), opened 1841, is a cable railway link with the docks $3\frac{1}{2}$ miles and 8 minutes' journey away. The cable railway, to be abandoned 1849, is remembered by Cable Street. London Bridge Station (15) is being built at this date in Italian style with a campanile. Passing a Trafalgar relic, the Dreadnought Hospital Ship (16) for seamen of all nations, London's first railway goes on an arched viaduct to Greenwich terminus (17). The branch line to Croydon, Dover and Brighton also crosses the Surrey Canal.

Fire Fighting

Three disastrous fires in seven years, starting with the Houses of Parliament in 1834, showed how ineffective were London's methods of dealing with outbreaks. With the destruction of the Royal Exchange, left, and the burning of the Armoury at the Tower, lower left, the need for a centrally organized fire brigade became even more obvious. Yet the Government still maintained that this would stifle free enterprise. It was not until the Tooley Street fire in 1861 (page 297) that the Metropolitan Fire Brigade was started. So, for nearly 200 years after the Great Fire, London's outbreaks were fought by insurance companies and volunteers. With a vested interest in preserving property, insurance companies like the Sun and the Phoenix organized their own brigades and issued their particular metal badges to policy holders. For some years a brigade would only come to the rescue of a building showing the 'fire mark' of its own company. But this absurd situation came to an end and the fixing of marks faded out at the beginning of the nineteenth century. When a fire broke out, brigades from all companies would race to the scene, anxious for the advertisement which their speed and efficiency would provide. Enthusiastic amateurs also organized mobile pumps. One of them, Frederick Hodges, a Lambeth distiller, formed a brigade to protect his own distillery which had twice been burnt out. Then he built a 120-feet tall tower as a look-out for fires so that he could rush his two forty-men manual pumps in an emergency to any part of London.

1. Royal Exchange – 1838. Crowds in Cornhill watch flames lick up round the grasshopper, symbol of Sir Thomas Gresham, as the Royal Exchange – the second Exchange, built after the Great Fire – burns through the January night. Eight engines and sixty-three men were powerless because fire plugs supplying water and even the manual pumps froze up. Gresham's statue escaped, but the entire building was destroyed. It was replaced by the present Royal Exchange in 1844.

2. The Armoury of the Tower – 1841. Some 280,000 objects, including historically priceless arms and armour and the wheel of Nelson's *Victory*, were destroyed in this outbreak. It started in the Bowyer Tower, and, fearing for the Crown Jewels and Regalia, warders rescued them from the adjoining Martin Tower. Hopelessly inadequate buckets, hand pumps and dilapidated small engines could not cope with the fire, seen here from Tower Hill looking east across the moat with the Mint in the distance.

3. A fireman in the uniform and badge of the Sun Insurance Company.

4. Three engines of different insurance companies race to a fire. The firemen of each wear distinctive uniforms. Fights between them were not uncommon as rivalry was intense. Each engine tried to get the best source of water and so display the most powerful jet. Drivers were paid a 5s. bonus by their companies if they were first at a fire.

5. The Houses of Parliament – 1834. While three regiments of Guards and an attachment of Cavalry vainly help fight the fire, the public cheer and clap as the roofs fall in. Flames swept from the House of Lords, right, and on to the House of Commons. Westminster Hall was saved by taking fire-engines into it and playing water on to the hammer beam roof. The flames lit up the sky in a red glow which was seen by an architect travelling on a coach from Brighton. He was Charles Barry who was to be responsible for the rebuilding.

4

5

265

The Young Queen in Society

In the early years of Queen Victoria's reign, a ball or reception at Stafford House was among the great occasions of the London season. The Queen was a close personal friend of Harriet, Duchess of Sutherland, who was her Mistress of the Robes. The balls could be glittering and lavish and the receptions seriously intentioned, for the Duchess, who came of a reforming Whig family attracted not only society to Stafford House. She made her home a rallying ground for political and social causes, and for distinguished foreigners like Garibaldi. Lord Greville described one of her assemblies as the most magnificent he had ever seen. 'Such prodigious space, so cool, so blazing with light!' he exclaimed. 'Everyone was *comfortable even*.'

Like Spencer House, Bridgewater House and several others behind St James's, Stafford (now Lancaster) House was one of the great homes of the nineteenth-century aristocracy. Overlooking the Mall and Green Park, the house made the Sutherlands the Queen's nearest neighbours. A frequent visitor, Victoria looked around the vast rooms with their magnificent pictures, and on one occasion told the Duchess: 'I have come from my home to your palace.' Lami in 1849 catches the moment, left, when, attended by the Prince Consort, and with her hostess and husband, the 2nd Duke of Sutherland, she is receiving guests on the stairs of the Great Hall.

At Buckingham Palace, Victoria herself was doing her best to give Court life some decorous gaiety. As Queen, she felt it her prerogative to become the sort of leader in society that in the reigns of her uncles had been left to hostesses like Princess Esterhazy, Countess Lieven and the notorious Lady Blessington at Gore House. As a girl she noted, with underlining and two exclamation

1. 'WELL SIR! AND PRAY WHAT ARE YOU LOOKING AT?' is the caption to this print of a mid-Victorian under-housemaid, who, working a sixteen-hour day, kept the steps of houses shining, and oiled the wheels of society, for a wage of £9 a year.

2. Going to the ball. A scene in Eaton Square about 1850. It is by Eugene Lami, the French artist, who also painted the Stafford House scene, opposite. Lami, who was born in Paris, first came to London in 1827 tempted by all he had heard about the city from Bonington, with whom he had studied water-colours. He was enchanted by English

marks, that her first Royal Ball had gone on until ten minutes to *four*!! She gave regular dinner parties with an orchestra playing. There was a small weekly dance at the Palace at which she would take part in the quadrille but insisted on chaperones for all unmarried girls and forbade the waltz. Balls were held in the Throne Room often for charity and in fancy dress like the Plantagenet Ball (to help the Spitalfields weavers) in which Albert appeared as Edward III and the Queen as Queen Philippa. There was a *bal poudré* with Georgian costumes in 1845, and in the year of the Great Exhibition a Restoration Ball when, in view of the moral tone insisted upon at Court, a number of ladies deemed it wiser not to specify their historical counterparts.

life, and returned after the Revolution of 1848 in the wake of the deposed Louis Philippe. Victoria greatly admired his work, and commissioned a number of paintings of royal occasions. Acclaimed and fêted by London society, Lami lived and worked here for a further four years.

3. A promenade in Hyde Park in 1842. This part of Park Lane, looking north at Grosvenor Gate, was the rendezvous for society on Sunday mornings when the Dowager Duchess of Richmond, the Countess of Jersey, and the Queen herself were frequently to be seen in their fine open carriages.

London's First Railway ...

The first railway in London was a suburban enterprise. Carried on arches, and straight as a Roman aqueduct which it greatly resembled, the line ran from Southwark to Greenwich. Less than four miles long, its whole concept seems one of romantic novelty if compared with the sterner railways to come. The 878 arches spanned lanes, the Surrey Canal and the Ravensbourne, and passengers, twenty feet above the fields, enjoyed a fine view on the short, exciting journey.

Could a railway be entirely serious that is said to have had one carriage shaped like a Roman galley? There were bridges supported on Doric columns–they still survive–and at Deptford station the staircase (demolished 1927) was modelled on a monument on the Acropolis. Bands played the trains in and out of the terminals at holiday times; there were flanking tree-lined boulevards said to outdo Paris; and little bijou villas were designed to go under the arches. Someone even had the idea that rich Londoners might wish to bring their horses and private carriages down from London for a turn in Greenwich Park, and a long, gently inclined, and now decaying, ramp at Deptford is a reminder of this vain hope. It does not seem entirely a coincidence that George Walter, the promoter and first secretary of the London and Greenwich Railway Company, was a keen antiquary.

But there was nothing frivolous about the prospectus issued by the company in 1832. It needed to raise £400,000, a capital sum later to be increased to a million pounds. The new railway, it said, would reduce the bus and steamer time of an hour to twelve minutes. Businessmen travelling to and from the City would save eight hours a week. The prospect of thirty per cent dividends was dangled before the shareholders.

A man with local interests was brought in to design the railway. Lieut.-Col. G. T. Landmann had been born in Woolwich and spent his boyhood on Blackheath. Now retired, he was a Royal Engineer who had served under Wellington in the Peninsular War. His heroic, imaginative concept of elevating the railway, and his use of spanning bridges to cross canal, river and roads has survived all modern changes.

The first brick of the Greenwich railway was laid in April 1834, opposed, it was said, chiefly by cads and coachmen. Two years later the service began, but initially only between Spa Road in Bermondsey, and Deptford. This was extended to the London Bridge terminus within a few months, and in 1838 the last of the arches was completed. A swing bridge across Deptford Creek then carried the railway on to Greenwich.

Fares had to be high, by the standards of the time. A single First Class journey in an 'Imperial' carriage cost a shilling, and it was sixpence to stand in the open, seatless Third Class. But the trains ran every quarter of an hour, and the fast service drew the public. By 1844 the Greenwich Railway was carrying two million passengers a year. This provided a working profit. But a reasonable return on the capital depended on the houses under the arches, and this scheme failed. The arches leaked and people disliked the noise. For years the shares yielded little or nothing, and Walter declared himself and his family ruined. Finances were not stabilized until the line was carrying some of the Croydon and Brighton traffic (which joined it obliquely at Corbett's Lane), and not until after 1845 were shareholders assured of a 4½ per cent dividend.

... and Mainline Terminus

While the last section of the Greenwich Railway was being laid, a far more important line was under construction. Euston was the London terminus; Birmingham–England's second largest city–its objective. 'The Premier Line', boasted the London and Birmingham Railway Company (later the L.M.S.), 'is noted for Punctuality, Speed, Smooth Riding, Dustless Tracks and Comfort....'

The original plan was to make the terminus in Camden Town with provision for a later branch line which would loop round north-east London. This would give Birmingham and the Midlands a direct link with the docks at Blackwall. The Camden Town station was at the point where Chalk Farm Road crosses the Regent Canal. But almost at once the line was extended south to Euston Grove so that passengers would be taken farther into London. This extension crossed over the canal and passed under street level. The gradient was so steep that for six years trains

out of Euston had to be worked up the 1 in 70 Camden Incline by an endless rope from an engine-house with tall chimneys, far right. Coming in from the north, engines were simply uncoupled at the Camden Town depot and the carriages completed the last mile by their own volition, at 10 miles an hour, controlled by 'bankriders', men who worked the brakes.

Euston Station, enthusiastically acclaimed as 'the Eighth Wonder of the World', was opened in 1837. Its classical splendour was partly propaganda. The pioneers of the dawning railway age wanted to impress the public. They were determined to silence those critics who regarded trains as noisy and dangerous, and tracks as desecration of the countryside. So they spent £35,000 on the Doric portico alone, and Philip Hardwick brought all the inappropriate glory of the Greek Revival to this and the flanking pavilions. The regal Great Hall, sixty feet high, used as a waiting room, was decorated with statuary. A hotel was built, the first of the great railway hotels built at all the main termini.

All these splendours threatened to eclipse the actual railway. Behind so grand an entrance and so lofty an entrance hall, the train sheds were something of an anti-climax even though one platform was dignified by the title of the Departure Parade–on the site of the present platform 6. But as many features as possible were designed to give the passenger the impression of opulence when, after buying his numbered and reserved seat, he was ready to start on the great adventure of a train journey.

1. Boarding point at Spa Road, Bermondsey.

2. The line crossing Southwark Park Road, with a train heading for Deptford.

3. Houses were planned to sit snugly under the arches at Deptford.

4. The cable descent from Camden Town.

5. Entrance to Euston, 1838.

2

3

4

5

Free 'Seasons' and the First Commuters

At first the main trunk lines ignored the suburbs. But the railways soon saw that there was money to be made from the daily traveller. In the great railway boom which transformed the whole country in the 1840s, hundreds of suburban stations sprang up along the main lines. When the London and Birmingham opened, the first stop was Harrow eleven miles out, but in 1841 Willesden was opened, and Sudbury (now Wembley Central) the following year. Trains linked villages like Blackheath, Ealing, and Hornsey with the City. Within twenty years, Greater London was to be covered in a maze of criss-crossed lines.

As well as serving existing places, the railways created new communities. A Parliamentary Committee was asked to approve the North Kent Line in 1846 because of the large number of houses it would encourage. Beyond Wimbledon and Raynes Park a station was opened called Kingston-on-Railway within easy reach of which were built eight hundred 'desirable villa residences' called Railway Town. Today this is Surbiton.

Taking the long-term view that where there were houses there would be future passengers, the London and North Western even offered free season tickets for a span of years to anyone building well-to-do houses at Pinner and Harrow. The South Western gave a ten per cent reduction to residents on Kingston Hill. There were also cheap fares for workmen, as at Victoria, right, but these were imposed on the railways by Parliament. Thousands of labourers and artisans lost their homes through demolition in the path of the railway builders and, driven farther out, some compensation was needed for what it cost them to travel to their work. On the Great Eastern an early morning 'workman's train' had to be run from Edmonton and Walthamstow into Liverpool Street and back again at night, charging only 1d. for the journey.

In the Railway Mania of 1845, when speculation was on the scale of the South-Sea Bubble, hundreds of new companies were floated. New termini sprang up (Waterloo for the Southampton line in 1848; King's Cross, 1852). Lines radiated farther and farther out year by year. From Nine Elms (the inconvenient Battersea predecessor of Waterloo) the South Western reached Richmond in 1846; pushed on to Twickenham; was at Datchet by 1848; and made a loop round to Hampton Court a year later.

Lines with fanciful names, long-since swallowed up in regional anonymity, came into existence, among them the West End

and Crystal Palace Railway in 1853. Even though Sydenham was already well served by two lines, speculators thought it worthwhile to create yet another with the northern terminus at a steamboat pier to the west of Battersea Park. From there it ran across Wandsworth Common, via Norwood and Gipsy Hill, to its southern terminus, the Crystal Palace High Level Station (demolished 1961), a vast enclosed building of ornate windows and chateau-like turrets. To match the aristocratic architecture, an exclusive platform was reserved for First Class passengers.

1. By 1844, the London & Birmingham Railway, here coming out of Primrose Hill Tunnel, was serving Willesden and Sudbury.

2. Plebeian travel. The arrival of the Workmen's Penny Train at Victoria at 6 a.m. in March 1865.

3. Patrician travel. A First Class passenger of the same period sits in well-upholstered comfort.

Until the railways started running to the West Country, every town happily set its clocks to suit its own meridian. There was about ten minutes' difference between London and Bristol, even a variation of nearly a minute between the extreme East and West of London. This posed a problem which the makers of railway timetables could solve in only one way. They imposed London Time. Whatever it might say on the church clock or private watch chain, the station clock showed London Time which, after 1852, was kept right by an hourly telegraph signal. This was resented, especially by passengers who arrived at the station at what they held to be the correct time only to see their London Time train disappearing.

With the opening of the London to Bridgwater line in 1841, the G.W.R. tried to help with the announcement:

LONDON TIME is kept at all stations on the Railway which is about 4 minutes earlier than READING time; $5\frac{1}{2}$ minutes before STEVENTON time; $7\frac{1}{2}$ minutes before CIRENCESTER time; 11 minutes before BATH and BRISTOL time; and 14 minutes before BRIDGWATER time.

As a further precaution public clocks in some towns were fitted with two separate minute hands to show both railway and local reckoning. But there was always local prejudice against this, and Railway Time caused nationwide confusion which was not effectually ended until the invention of Standard Time. With the world divided into twenty-four meridian zones, each with its own uniform time, the whole of Britain came into the Greenwich meridian. In 1880 'British Time' (the name which tactfully embraced both London and Railway Time) was made compulsory throughout the country, and the discrepancies finally disappeared.

4. The Battersea Pier-end of the West End and Crystal Palace Railway. On the south side of the river a train, leaving the so-called Pimlico Station, runs alongside Queenstown Road and Battersea Park. A paddle-steamer is bringing passengers from Charing Cross and Westminster to join the train whose destination is the Crystal Palace at Sydenham. In 1859 piles are being sunk this side of Chelsea Bridge for the London, Brighton and South Coast railway which is to run into the new Victoria Station the following year. The building of Victoria meant an end to the plan for a south bank terminus, for which twenty-two acres had been purchased. It is now South Lambeth Goods Depot.

4

Northern & Eastern Railway 1840   Great Northern Railway 1850

London & Birmingham Railway 1837

Great Western Railway 1838

London & South Western Railway 1846

Eastern Counties Railway 1839

London & Blackwall Railway 1840

London & Greenwich Railway 1836

EUSTON 1837

KING'S CROSS 1852

PADDINGTON 1854

BISHOPSGATE 1847

WATERLOO 1848

FENCHURCH ST. 1841

LONDON BRIDGE 1836

BRICKLAYERS ARMS 1844

London & Southampton Railway 1838   London & Croydon Railway 1839

1. The nightly scene at the General Post Office in St Martin's-le-Grand. The year: 1830. The time: a few minutes after eight o'clock. Exactly on the hour porters dragged out the bags of letters, handed them over to scarlet-liveried guards, and loaded them on to the mail coaches. Of the twenty-seven coaches leaving London each night with letters for all over Britain, twenty started from here. Committed to an inflexible timetable and a speed of 9 miles per hour, the mail coaches permitted no delays. Passengers were already aboard. Many had taken their seats at the Bull and Mouth, the coaching inn immediately opposite, which had underground stabling for 400 horses. Pollard's view shows Robert Smirke's vast new classical building a few months after its completion. Coaches held a virtual monopoly on mail for nearly half a century, but the railways completely superseded them by 1848.

2. The inland Sorting Office where, with the coming of the Penny Post in 1840, 1,360,000 letters were handled a week. Smirke's building was demolished in 1913 and a new Post Office built across the street.

3. London's first letter box, 1855, had ten collections daily.

4. Its successor, 1857, festooned with cast-iron flowers. Rowland Hill also envisaged letter boxes in front doors, to save waiting, 'into which the letter-carrier could drop the letter, and, having knocked could pass on as fast as he could walk'.

The Penny Post and the First Letter Box

'Rose at 8h. 20m. PENNY POST extended to the whole Kingdom this day!' Rowland Hill wrote in his diary on 10 January 1840. 'The Tory Papers for the most part sulky . . . I have abstained from going to the P.O. tonight lest I should embarrass their proceedings.' Had he done so, Hill would have seen the extraordinary climax of his four-year campaign. All day crowds surged up the steps, under the Ionic portico, and into the hall of the General Post Office in St Martin's-le-Grand. Clerks opened extra windows to deal with those eager to send letters by the new method. By six o'clock when they closed 112,000 letters – three times the normal number – had been despatched. The crowd sent up a cheer for the Post Office and another for the man who had made it possible.

Until then, the receiver not the sender of letters had paid the postage. Postmen had to find the person to whom a letter was addressed and collect the fee. They also went around the streets to receive letters which were posted in the locked bag which they carried. Irritated by this untidy, time-consuming system, Hill, a schoolmaster's son, advocated a penny rate for a ½oz. letter for any distance throughout the country, all to be prepaid.

'Fallacious and preposterous' was the Post Office's first reaction, but within a year the number of letters trebled, and increased so fast that in London the 436 Post Receiving Houses for sending them were inadequate. Adopting a Parisian idea, the letter box was introduced. The first one appeared in 1855 on the corner of Fleet Street and Farringdon Street. There were ten collections a day (9 a.m. to 10 p.m.) and ten deliveries (8 a.m. to 8 p.m.) were promised within 1½ hours of collection for central London and within three hours up to a 12-mile radius. Cast in iron by a Hoxton firm, these squat, square boxes, much ridiculed as resembling stoves, were replaced two years later by 'pillar' boxes, hexagonal, and with the four points of the compass on top.

5. A walking pillar box. Long before boxes were built in the streets, postmen, like this one in 1827, not only delivered letters but collected them as well. After suburban receiving offices closed, they toured the streets ringing their bells. Customers posted their letters through the slit of the locked bag and paid a penny fee – but this was for the added service, not the postal fee. This system ended in 1846.

6. A pneumatic tube railway was invented to carry mail as quickly as possible from sorting offices to trains. In 1838 post-office officials saw the first transmission by permanent tube from the North-Western District Post Office in Eversholt Street, St Pancras, to Euston Station. The train, driven by compressed air, was loaded with mail bags in two minutes. The journey of three-quarters of a mile took one minute. This early idea was developed in 1927 into the six-and-a-half-mile postal tube which carries 40,000 mailbags a day between Whitechapel and Paddington, picking them up at Liverpool Street, Mount Pleasant, Oxford Street and other sorting offices.

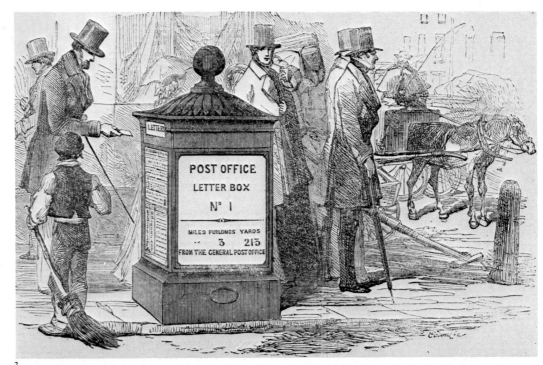

3

4

5

6

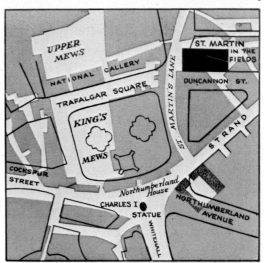

1. Nelson's Column and Trafalgar Square under construction. This photograph, one of the earliest of London, was taken in the summer of 1844.

2. Old Charing Cross (1740) showing the Royal Mews which were displaced by Trafalgar Square. Northumberland House is in the background.

3. The creation of Trafalgar Square. The black outline indicates the modern plan superimposed on the eighteenth-century map which is shown in grey.

4. On the week-end before it was erected, the statue of Nelson, hidden behind hoardings at the base of the column, was on show to the public.

5. Landseer modelling one of the lions in the studio of Baron Marochetti, who was responsible for the casting. Sir Edwin was paid £6,000 for his work.

Nelson comes to Trafalgar Square

Almost forty years passed between Nelson's funeral at St Paul's and the raising of his statue in Trafalgar Square. Even in 1843 when the statue – 17 feet high and weighing 16 tons – was hauled with difficulty to the top of the column, the 'Nelson testimonial' was still incomplete. The lions for the base were not commissioned from Sir Edwin Landseer until sixteen years later, and not put into position until 1867.

But had it not been for what a contemporary guidebook called the 'beggarly subscription' and 'tardy decision of a supine Government', London might never have acquired its most famous landmark. Delay, a chance suggestion, and the development of the perfect site just happened to coincide.

In 1818 when Parliament first debated the idea of a monument to Nelson, the open space which was to become Trafalgar Square was occupied by the Royal Mews. It had been used for stabling and keeping of the King's falcons since medieval times. The mews (bottom left) were demolished along with the flanking 'vile houses' in Lower St Martin's Lane in 1826 as part of a plan by Nash. The new National Gallery was thus given a proud position at the end of a vista up Whitehall. About four years later the square was prophetically – but with no idea of a Nelson monument – named Trafalgar Square. Another seven years passed. Then, in 1837, an initialled letter in *The Times* threw up the chance suggestion that here would be the ideal spot to honour Nelson.

This apparently sparked off action, and within a few months subscriptions had been raised, official sanction given, and a competition opened. The winner was William Railton, an ecclesiastical architect, then little known. His massive Corinthian column and pedestal, 170 feet tall, took three years to build, and like the statue by E. H. Bailey and Landseer's lions, came in for much criticism.

Purists held that the column was disproportionately high and spoilt the Whitehall vista. Though visited by 100,000 over the week-end before it was hoisted up (top right), the statue was held by the *Spectator* to be in the style of a ship's figurehead and have 'a daring disregard of personal resemblance'. The sculptor's broad technique was mistaken for coarseness. The seeming crudity was essential in a statue which would always be seen from a distance. As Augustus Hare pointed out, the flaws would only be noticeable by those viewing Nelson from the top of the Duke of York's Column.

As for the lions, it was a standing joke that the lion on Northumberland House (far left) would not acknowledge them as brothers.

4

5

1. The tunnel being built – from the southern end on the Rotherhithe shore.

2. Section view of the vertical shaft sunk at Rotherhithe. Brunel's approach was typically unorthodox. Instead of digging a vertical shaft, and lining it down to the depth at which the tunnel proper would branch out horizontally under the river bed, he built upwards. A tower of bricks, forty-two feet high was erected on a circular metal hoop, fifty feet in diameter. Digging then began inside the tower, and, as the wooden under-pinning of the hoop was removed, the hoop and the whole tower sank into the ground a few inches at a time under its own weight. The sixty-four-foot shaft was thus sleeved against subsidence all the way down.

3. The Wapping entrance as it looked shortly after it was opened as a pedestrian thoroughfare under the Thames in 1843.

4. Brunel waves to the crowds at the opening.

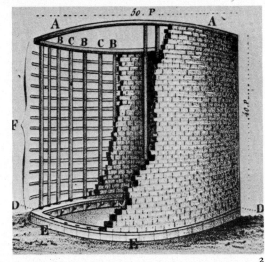

2

The Tunnel

The Thames watermen hung out black flags. Who now would need to be ferried between Wapping and the Surrey shore? On the March day in 1843 when the first tunnel under the river was opened, they saw it as the end of their livelihood.

But to the crowds lining the streets of Rotherhithe this was an historic occasion. A practical necessity was at last answered. The tunnel was a link with the docks across the water and would cut down by nearly a day the time it took goods to reach south London in a detour over London Bridge. It was an engineering miracle – the first tunnel ever built under a navigable river. After twenty years of waiting, they were seeing yet another achievement in a century of great mechanical progress.

So there was a special cheer for the little old man in gaiters who, waving his top-hat, was part of the procession to the entrance. In honour of Sir Marc Brunel the military band played 'See the Conquering Hero Come!' Brunel had succeeded where all other engineers had failed. He had overcome dangers, flooding, lack of money, and a scoffing press.

At seventy, Brunel had got up from his sick bed to see the opening of the tunnel on which he had laboured since 1825 when 300 navvies had started work at Rotherhithe. With the originality that marked everything he touched, the French-born engineer had devised a special tunnelling shield. This enabled miners, each in separate alcoves on a large iron frame, to concentrate on a small area at a time. Every few inches they burrowed

3

forward were secured against inundation before they went on. Breakthroughs of water could be isolated and, he hoped, contained.

In these alcoves, the miners worked thirty at a time–side by side, ten men on three levels. Progress was slow on the tunnel-face which was 15 feet high and 36 feet wide, to allow two carriages and a footpath. The rate of progress was only eight to twelve feet a week, and every foot was barrel vaulted with 5,500 bricks. Even with this cautious method, water came through. Working by the light of candle lanterns, the miners were in constant terror of a sudden inundation. Several times a warning shout of 'The Thames is in!' sent them rushing from the tunnel face to the entrance shaft.

At some points the tunnel passed less than six feet below the river bed, and at high tide when the water pressure was at its greatest, the shield had to withstand a weight of 600 tons. One night, when the tunnel was a little more than half-way under the Thames, water burst through with the force of a mill race. The whole tunnel flooded, and by morning the water level was within three feet of the top of the vertical shaft. 'A just judgment on the presumptuous aspirations of mortal man,' was how a Rotherhithe clergyman described the setback. 'Poor man!' was all Brunel said when he heard the comment, and he promptly went out into midstream and was lowered to the river bed in a diving-bell to investigate the damage. He plugged the hole with tons of clay and rubble, pumped out the tunnel, and work was resumed. After this, the weak part of the river bed was strengthened by a tarpaulin ninety feet long which was lowered and chained down over

the area threatened with the greatest pressure. But there were to be two more serious inundations and seven drownings before the tunnel under the river was completed.

In 1840, Brunel, over seventy and fighting ill-health, was knighted by the Queen. On a November day two years later, Sir Marc with his son and chief assistant, Isambard Kingdom Brunel, were down in the shaft on the Wapping side when contact was made with tunnellers from the opposite shore. With them was Isambard's son and Marc's grandson. The child was the first to walk through the hole into the arms of a Rotherhithe miner.

5. The tunnel (precursor of Blackwall, 1897, and Rotherhithe road tunnel, 1909) was never used as planned, or fulfilled its grand conception, largely because of insufficient money to build approach ramps for carriages. Thanks to Wellington, a Government grant of £250,000 was advanced to finish it; but there was no more money to build the ramps which were so essential. It became a tunnel for foot passengers (toll 1d.), one of the 'sights' of London visited by about a million people a year to attend bazaars and illuminated anniversary fêtes, like the one above in 1858. 'An admirable prison', thought Nathaniel Hawthorne, who saw it neglected and gloomily lit with gas jets. In 1864 the East London Railway Company bought it to link north London with Brighton, as seen below (6). Then it was absorbed by the Underground, and now serves the Whitechapel-New Cross line.

1

2

Cholera and 'The Great Stink'

In the age of engineering marvels like the Thames Tunnel and the spread of the railways, there remained extraordinary deficiencies in sanitation and domestic water supplies. Water closets had replaced cesspits in only a few houses of the rich. The vast majority still relied on the street pump, and even in big houses water was supplied for only two or three hours a day, three times a week. In the midst of ever-increasing prosperity, there was terrible poverty and disease. The average age of mortality among the London working classes was twenty-two.

Typhus and smallpox killed thousands each year in overcrowded tenements and slums from Soho to Whitechapel, and when cholera broke out in 1848 there were no real means of combating it. As news came that the plague was spreading across Europe to this country some preparations were made. But they were half-hearted. The newly created Board of Health had no powers to enforce precautions in London which was a mass of conflicting interests, by-laws, and governing bodies.

Most of London's 270,000 houses had cesspits under them which were infrequently cleared by 'nightmen' or had the waste carried by porous drains into the river. All the sewage of two million people emptied into the Thames to move, black and foul-smelling, up and down the river as far as Teddington Lock on every tide. From this same 'open sewer' independent water companies pumped

3

1. Plague spot near the London Gas Works, Lambeth . . .

2. . . . and the nearby burial ground for cholera victims.

3. Lodging House in Fish Lane, Holborn, about 1840, showing an open sewer running under the floor.

4. Despite its deceptively dignified look, the Infant Pauper Establishment at Tooting, right, was a grossly overcrowded 'baby farm' housing 1,400 children. In January 1848, 300 contracted cholera, and 150 died. Chadwick's inspector found the boys' dormitory was directly over a stagnant sewer. The manager, Peter Drouet (who received 4s. 6d. a week per child), starved and ill-clothed the children. He was charged with manslaughter, but acquitted.

4

drinking water straight into domestic cisterns often without filtering. As Sydney Smith put it, there were 'a million insects in every drop'.

Fears about the plague were expressed by slum-dwellers in a 'rookery' of St Giles, fifty-four of whom signed a letter which the militantly reforming *Times* printed as written: 'Sur, May we beg and beseech your proteckshion and power. . . . We live in muck and filthe. We aint got no privez, no dust bins, no drains, no water splies, and no drain or suer in the whole place . . . if the Colera comes Lord help us. . . .'

The cholera did come. From 54 deaths in the first week of November 1848, the mortality roll rose to 2,026 in a week eleven months later. In the last three months of 1849 the cholera deaths in London totalled 12,847. Significantly, districts by the river were worst hit, and an early outbreak was in Fore Street, Lambeth, where victims were described as 'more like ghouls and maniacs than human beings' and where doorways had to be blocked at high tide to prevent the river getting in.

Edwin Chadwick, an indomitable and dogmatic sanitary reformer, and architect of the Public Health Act, fought against conditions and upper-class apathy. A former journalist, Chadwick took nothing at second-hand. He explored the sewers. He interrogated people in the slums. He poured out reports and pamphlets, and these were reinforced by 'the Great Stink' of 1858 when the stench from the Thames was so bad that the windows of Parliament were draped with curtains soaked in chloride of lime, and there was talk of moving the Law Courts to Oxford.

Chadwick's plans for pure water from reservoirs had to wait another half century, but at least a system for preventing the pollution of the Thames was devised. Joseph Bazalgette, engineer of the Metropolitan Commissioners of Sewers (founded 1855), devised a scheme in which five main sewers – three north of the Thames, two south, all running west to east – intercepted the sewers that were previously fed into the river. They carried the sewage over ten miles to Barking and Plumstead where it was at first allowed to go into the river, but, after 1887, was taken out to the North Sea and dumped by sludge vessels.

5   6

7

8

5. Edwin Chadwick. 'Had he killed in battle as many as he saved by sanitation, he would have had equestrian statues by the dozen put up to his memory' – obituary in *The Daily News* at his death, aged ninety, in 1890.

6. An open stretch of the Fleet at Clerkenwell in 1844 showing chutes discharging directly from houses into the polluted river. Other Thames tributaries like the Tyburn, Effra, and the Neckinger (which flowed through a part of Bermondsey described by *The Morning Chronicle* as 'the very capital of Cholera') also carried sewage into the river.

7. Fleet Street, looking towards Temple Bar, in 1844 during the deepening of a sewer which fed into the Thames through Whitefriars Dock (site of the present Carmelite Street). After 1889 it became part of one of the five main intercepting sewers and now runs across London from Hammersmith to West Ham.

8. With the aid of a candle, a social worker discovers an ill-clad child sleeping on a bed of straw in the sort of conditions that lead to the spread of cholera and other diseases – from a wood engraving.

The Great Exhibition of 1851

Its official title was the Great Exhibition of the Works of Industry of All Nations. But right from the start, everyone preferred the more romantic name of the Crystal Palace. Covering nineteen acres in Hyde Park, this revolutionary building was made of delicate cast iron ribbing and nearly 300,000 panes of glass. 'One of the wonders of the world which we English may be proud of' was how Queen Victoria described it in February 1851, just after its completion and three months before the opening. 'The sun shining in through the Transept gave a fairy-like appearance,' she wrote in her journal. 'The building is so light and graceful in spite of its immense size.'

The Great Exhibition was a development of a series of smaller industrial displays promoted by the Society of Arts. The Society's president was the Prince Consort, and its most dynamic member, Henry Cole. Cole was the prime mover and suggested Hyde Park; it was the Prince Consort's decision to extend its scope to all countries and make it the first international exhibition ever held.

The Queen supported them, but enthusiasm was not universal. The critics said that Hyde Park would be ruined and become a 'bivouac of all the vagabonds of London'. Visiting foreigners would assassinate the Queen; infiltrating Papists would spread idolatory; and rats start a bubonic plague. 'It is the greatest trash, the greatest fraud, and the greatest imposition ever attempted to be palmed off upon the people of this country,' declared that arch-protester, Col. Sibthorpe, in the House of Commons.

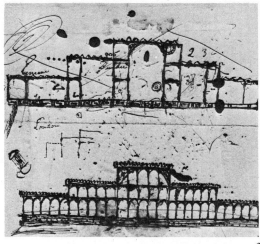

1. An 'aeronautic view' of the great expanse of the Crystal Palace looking south–east towards Hyde Park Corner. St Paul's and the Thames in the distance.

2. Paxton's sketch. It shows the end elevation with three tiers almost exactly as it was finally built.

I

The building, destined to be regarded as one of the architectural marvels of the age, evolved from two rough sketches doodled on a sheet of blotting paper, left, by Joseph Paxton. He was presiding at a railway board meeting in Derby at the time – June 1850 – but his mind wandered to the problem facing the Commissioners in London who were planning the Exhibition. A competition for a pavilion had produced 245 designs, none of which they liked.

Paxton, friend and rather superior gardener of the Duke of Devonshire, provided a gardener's solution. He conceived the pavilion as a huge glasshouse on the lines of the lily house he had just designed for Chatsworth. Nine days after making the doodle, he had produced full drawings. Five days after that he took them to Buckingham Palace. The Prince and the Commissioners

thought the conception daring, but, pressed for time, they took a gamble. Within seven weeks, concrete foundations were laid in the park.

Using mass-produced prefabricated girders and columns, a labour force of about 2,000 men completed the building in four months. Covering nineteen acres, it stood between Rotten Row and Knightsbridge, with its main entrance opposite Ennismore Gardens. It was 1,848 feet long (more than three times the length of St Paul's), and at its highest – the great arched transept – was 108 feet tall and so able to house three large elm trees. There were 1¾ miles of exhibition galleries, and 900,000 square feet of glass was used, in panes 4 feet long by 1 foot wide.

The Times might prophesy the collapse of this 'monstrous greenhouse', but elaborate precautions were taken to test the strength of

the building. Carts filled with cannon balls and weighing 8 tons were pulled up and down the galleries. Soldiers from the Royal Sappers and Miners spent hours marching round the Palace in close formation and marking time on selected spots.

In fact, one of the few difficulties were sparrows which nested in the enclosed trees. How to get rid of a nuisance that threatened to damage the exhibits and might even embarrass royal dignity? Shooting them was out of the question as the glass would be shattered. Legend insists that the Queen consulted Wellington. The old campaigner, then eighty-two, and a man of few words, gave his solution: 'Sparrow-hawks, Ma'am.'

By the end of April London had become a cosmopolitan city, full of foreigners. The South-Eastern Railway was running a special daily two-way cross-Channel service, and the

3

4

Morning Chronicle was printing articles, in parallel columns, in English, French and German. On the morning of 1 May, when the Exhibition was opened, the critics and Cassandras were finally silenced. Col. Sibthorpe (still warning wildly 'Beware of mantraps and spring-guns') was unheard. No one believed now that the building would crash in a high wind; that the sun's rays, magnified by the glass, would start a huge fire; or that 'the finger of the Almighty' would infallibly descend on 'so presumptuous an enterprise'.

London converged on the Park on that fine May morning when the Queen, dressed in pink and silver, and wearing a crown, arrived in a procession of nine State carriages. There were 25,000 people in the building as the *Hallelujah Chorus* soared up to the curved glass roof. 'This day,' wrote Victoria in her journal, 'is one of the greatest and most glorious days of our lives. . . .'

From all over the country, and from Europe, Russia, and America, 100,000 exhibits had poured in. They demonstrated the height of mid-century ingenuity and ornamentation. Wonderful were the things to be seen – the Koh-i-Noor diamond (protected by a sort of bird cage specially designed by Chubb); the model of a floating church for seamen in Philadelphia (a Gothic edifice with a spire built on a raft); a fountain running eau-de-Cologne; a Sportsman's Knife with 80 blades; a mechanical harvester pulled by a 'Puffing Billy' engine.

There were a 'silent alarum bedstead' which at a given hour could push the sleeper out of bed into a cold bath; a collection of stuffed animals which included a frog shaving his companion; and a group of cats seated on chairs and drinking tea, which the Queen described as 'really marvellous'. The French, of course, went too far. Wives and daughters

5

had to be hurried past a piece of sculpture of a nude, ecstatically drunk Bacchante rolling voluptuously on a bed of vine leaves.

Special juries awarded medals for the best exhibits. Prizes went to manufacturers who showed the most novelty, ingenuity, economy in cost and maintenance, durability, excellence of finish, and fitness for purpose. The Great Exhibition set a standard of workmanship which was to be the British hallmark for a century. But the Fine Arts section, especially the British contribution, came in for a good deal of criticism. One paper noted a 'prodigious amount of ugliness', and William Morris, then seventeen, attacked 'the heaviness, taste-lessness, and rococo banality of the entire display'.

Prince Albert's derided brainchild attracted six million people – one third of the population – to the Crystal Palace in the five months it was open and before it was demolished. It was purchased (for £70,000) by the Brighton Railway Company, and re-erected at Sydenham, where it remained for exhibitions and entertainments until it was burnt to the ground in 1936. Its original concrete foundations still remain beneath the grass in Hyde Park.

By the end, even *The Times* relented and talked in a farewell leader of the splendours of its 'wonderful career'. Impetus was given to the soaring graph of Victorian prosperity, and the Great Exhibition ended with a nice solid profit of £186,000.

3. The men who planned the exhibition. Round the Prince Consort, studying the plans, are the Commissioners. Paxton leans forward next to him, his finger on the table. Henry Cole is standing third from the left.

4. A Five Shilling Day. This entrance fee (against the usual 1s.) ensured an uncrowded, leisurely visit.

5. The raising of the first of the sixteen main rib sections over the transept. The arch helped to span three large elm trees which harboured the offending sparrows.

6. The official painting of the opening ceremony, right, shows the Queen, the Prince Consort and the Prince of Wales in Highland dress in the central group. On the left are British Commissioners and officials, and at the back, next to the Archbishop of Canterbury, is the Duke of Wellington. Foreign diplomats are on the right, and from their ranks the Chinese in blue satin robes was a notably dignified figure as he came forward and made deep obeisance to the Queen. Only later did it leak out that far from being accredited to the Court of St James, he was a sea captain named Hee Sing who had sailed his junk up the Thames for exhibition.

7. Each country had its own section, and Belgium was particularly well represented as the country had a tradition of national exhibitions held in Brussels, Antwerp and Ghent. Sculpture, dominated by the huge equestrian figure of the Crusader King, was a feature of the fine arts, and examples of art and manufacture were sent by 500 Belgian exhibitors.

8. At the closing ceremony in October the Commissioners gathered at a round table for a meeting presided over by Prince Albert who sat on a raised chair presented by an Indian rajah. About 50,000 people watched from the surrounding galleries. The Queen was not to be able to be present, as she was not one of the Commissioners, and – as Albert had told her – she 'could hardly have been there as a spectator'.

6

7

8

1. SCENE IN CREMORNE GARDENS.

2. SCENE IN REGENT STREET. Philanthropic Divine: 'May I beg you to accept this good little book. Take it home and read it attentively. I am sure it will benefit you.'

Lady: 'Bless me, Sir, you're mistaken, I am not a social evil. I am only waiting for a bus.'

3. SCENE IN HYDE PARK.
'*The pretty horse-breakers ride in the Row
And cause crowds to assemble wherever they go.
But the one who is easily Queen of them all
Is dainty Miss Skittles, who holds us in thrall.*'
– popular song about Catherine Walters ('Skittles'), darling of the aristocracy, sung by the *lion comique*, The Great Mackney.

Cremorne and 'The Seclusives'

'Cremorne Gardens! Can it be a garden from some fairy tale to which those dark arboured ways lead? . . . wide lawns, colourful flower beds shimmering . . . kiosks in Moorish style, Turkish minarets, Arabian columned ways . . . artificial caves, rushing water, crumbling ruins and shell grottos . . . a magic garden lighted by a thousand sparkling gas lamps held by garlanded statues–that is Cremorne Gardens.'

In his ecstatic description, Julius Rodenberg goes on to exclaim: 'How lovely the dancers are, their light beautiful feet moving on the shining parquet floor to the rhythm of a Strauss waltz!' This visitor from Germany clearly found the Chelsea successor to Vauxhall and Ranelagh very heady. His excitement becomes intense when his eye catches sight of 'a lovely full bosom heaving from the exertions of the dance', and he wonders if its owner is a duchess.

On the Thames, between the river and the King's Road just west of Battersea Bridge, Cremorne Gardens flourished for thirty years after 1846. Steamers brought visitors from the City for 3d. The centre of attraction in its twelve acres was the pagoda-shaped bandstand in the middle of a circular, open-air dance floor. Off it were amorous alcoves and private rooms from one of which a couple lean out in the view, left. These gave Cremorne a bad name. 'The nursery of every kind of vice,' thundered a Chelsea minister, and at closing time the impressionable Herr Rodenberg learns that his 'duchess' is not quite what she seems. She is catching a solitary cab back to the West End and indicates that he may accompany her. As she gets into the carriage a Biblical tract is thrust into her hand by a man whom he discovers is 'a member of an organization which for years has been trying to save the beautiful sinners who dance at Cremorne and after midnight crowd the pavements of the Haymarket and Regent Street. . . .'

Compared to many other places that the town had to show, Cremorne was comparatively innocent. At least vice was not organized there as in the low-class brothels in Shoreditch, the dubious bagnios of Panton Street, and the dozen or so Night Houses that flourished round Piccadilly. The most exclusive Night House was Mott's, rendez-vous of men-about-town like the spendthrift Marquess of Hastings (who once lost £103,000 on a single race) and *demi-mondaines* such as 'Sweet' Nelly Fowler whose perfume was so intoxicating that love-sick suitors are said to have paid just to have their handkerchiefs impregnated under her pillow. The most notorious was Kate Hamilton's in Coventry Street where the proprietress, a massive, dissolute woman, presided over her girls from a raised platform, and is shown, backed by a mirror, in the picture below, from Henry Mayhew's encyclopaedic *London Labour and the London Poor*.

Mayhew's report, published in 1862, is a complete exposure of vice in mid-Victorian London. Remarkably fully documented, it contains a wealth of statistics and dozens of detailed interviews with courtesans and street-walkers, of whom he reckoned there were 80,000 in London. He gives accounts of what he calls 'seclusives', women living 'under lordly protection' in St John's Wood. Though he does not name them, he is thinking of Cora Pearl, Mabel Gray, and Catherine Walters ('Skittles'), who regularly caused a sensation when she rode in Hyde Park. A fine horsewoman, she would appear in Rotten Row on an almost unmanageable racehorse.

At the other end of the scale, Mayhew wrote of 'troops of elegantly dressed courtesans, rustling in silks and satins' on the pavements. It was to save these girls that the Society for the Suppression of Vice was founded, one of whose members may well have been handing out the tracts at Cremorne. In the fight against prostitution, the London-by-Moonlight Mission held street meetings in notorious areas, and in the early sixties the Rev. Baptist Noel conducted Midnight Meetings at which sermons and hymns were helped down by tea and cakes. But it was an unequal battle. After twenty meetings, the distribution of 23,000 scripture cards and preaching to 4,000 girls, the Mission could claim the reform of only about thirty.

4. Kate Hamilton's Night House off Leicester Square–illustration from Mayhew's report.

5. Depravity at the Victoria Saloon in Catherine Street off the Strand as illustrated in *Paul Pry*, a salacious 1d. magazine masquerading as an organ of reform, which appeared in 1848. It was closed down and its publisher imprisoned for obscenity after a few months.

6. The Rev. Baptist Noel at a Midnight Meeting of prostitutes–also from Mayhew.

Around the Town

For the London visitor in the summer of the Great Exhibition, the town held many delights outside Hyde Park. A family could arrange several days of sightseeing. The weather was generally wet and cold, but a fine morning would be chosen for the Zoological Gardens. Established twenty-three years before on the north side of Regent's Park, the Zoo consisted of the largest and most complete collection of animals in the world. Decimus Burton planned the lay-out, and the animals had been augmented by those of the Tower Menagerie, London's earliest zoo, started in medieval times when Frederick II of Sicily presented three leopards to Henry III.

In August alone, 145,000 visitors went to the Zoo. Chief attraction among the new acquisitions was a four-ton hippopotamus brought from the Nile which, asleep or awake, Macaulay decided was 'the ugliest of the works of God'. An orang-utan arrived from Borneo in 1851; there was a new reptile house; and a favourite pastime, seen below (1), was to tempt the bears to climb the 'ragged staff' in their pit with buns on sticks.

From the Zoo it was only a short walk across the park to Madame Tussaud's (2). The old lady who founded and gave her name to the waxworks had died the previous year, but her collection of 190 figures was firmly established in Baker Street. An extra 6d. was charged for the Chamber of Horrors with wax heads of the decapitated Louis XVI and Marie Antoinette, part of the original guillotine, and—rushed on show for the Exhibition crowds—effigies of two recent murderers, Frederick and Marie Manning who two years before had killed Mrs Manning's lover in Bermondsey. For another 6d., visitors could

1

2

3

enter the Napoleonic 'shrine' and see the actual coach in which the Emperor tried to escape from Waterloo. This, one of Tussaud's greatest finds, was to be destroyed in the 1925 fire.

For a shopping interlude, Burlington Arcade (3) had a particular fascination with its covered promenade of small shops between Piccadilly and Cork Street. Visitors were always beguiled by the story that it had been created in 1818, by the angry Lord George Cavendish, owner of Burlington House, to thwart tradesmen in Old Bond Street who would throw oyster shells and litter over the wall into his garden.

In Leicester Square was what a guide book called 'one of the most pleasantly instructive sights in the metropolis'. This was 'The Great Globe' (4) built by James Wylde. Working by gas flares and moonlight, he completed it in May to coincide with the Exhibition's opening. Wylde, an M.P., geographer, and publisher of atlases, filled the whole of the centre of the square with his Great Globe. It was 60 feet in diameter and surrounded by exhibition rooms. The world was modelled in relief (scale: 10 miles to one inch) on the inside and viewed from four landings, right (5). This concave projection enabled the spectator to get a sense of the whole world's surface at one view, while the size prevented the concavity from being unduly apparent.

Also in the square on a more modest scale were sideshows at Saville House like the Young Italian Giant (6), while, if it can be believed, and if it survived from 1847 (the date of the advertisement), The Singing Mouse (7 and 8), gave a free recital for all who went down the Strand for a haircut.

4

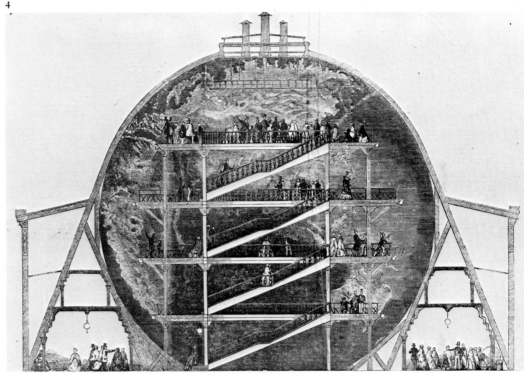

5

6

7

287

Almost directly across the road from the Exhibition, and calculated to catch weary and hungry people coming out, was the Gastronomic Symposium (9). Alexis Soyer, a noted chef, opened it in the Countess of Blessington's Gore House (present site of the Albert Hall) with a dining saloon which could seat 1,500. The gardens were laid out with statues and grottoes and there was an open-air 'American' bar which served Victorian equivalents of the cocktail such as Brandy Smash and Sherry Cobblers. Soyer, who gave his name to a sauce, and whose book of recipes, *The Modern Housewife*, had sold 21,000 copies by 1851, made his reputation in the Reform Club kitchens, where he is seen (10) with his wife. He lost money on the Symposium because he was refused a licence after the Exhibition closed.

Attracted by his trade card (11), people flocked to Richard Beard's studio in

9

11

10

12

Westminster (12), or his other premises in Regent Street and the City. A daguerreotype portrait or family group was a permanent record of the London visit. Beard had opened Europe's first professional photographic studio ten years before. The photographs–direct positive images on silver-plated copper–required a two-minute exposure.

Five minutes from the Exhibition, off Victoria Road, Kensington, William Batty, who was connected with Astley's circus in Lambeth, opened the Hippodrome in May. In the large amphitheatre on the Roman plan, he staged tournaments, pageants ('The Field of the Cloth of Gold'), ostrich races, steeplechases with well-known jockeys, and chariot races, seen on the right (13), for which he brought over a troupe from Paris. Batty's did not continue after the Exhibition, but for a number of years afterwards was used as a riding school.

With the children in bed, and his wife writing up her journal, a man might seek a little night adventure. Among the possibilities were the Coal Hole off the Strand, and the rather more notorious Cider Cellars in Maiden Lane. Among the varied entertainments were Poses Plastiques–immobile ladies in statuesque, classical roles of near-nudity–and ribald trials conducted by a man who styled himself 'Baron' Nicholson. At the Coal Hole, and later at the Cellars, as advertised on the broadsheet below (14), he presided in wig and gown at these mock trials in which actors, M.P.s, and other prominent personalities appeared as barristers and witnesses.

The cases heard were all concerned with divorce or rape, and were described by the journalist, Edmund Yates, as 'clever, but so full of grossness and indecency, expressed and implied, as to render it wholly disgusting'.

Another night haunt for the man with Bohemian leanings who considered himself a cut above the rowdy taverns, was the exclusively Male Song and Supper Room.

The first and most famous was Evans's in Covent Garden. In the basement grill (15), chops, devilled kidneys, and baked potatoes were on the menu. With his back to the stage, the chairman presided at entertainments from which the music hall was soon to evolve. He welcomed guests, offered snuff to celebrities and habitués like Thackeray, John Leech, the *Punch* artist, and Augustus Sala. Then he called order for Sam Cowell who would burlesque *Hamlet* or give a rasping rendering of *The Ratcatcher's Daughter*.

13

14

15

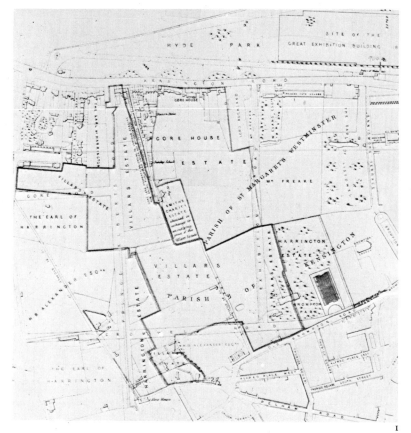

Results of the Exhibition

The Great Exhibition was the first—and last—international exhibition to make a profit, and with a surplus of £186,000 the Commissioners decided to create a permanent centre for industrial education. The idea was the Prince Consort's; and, as with the Crystal Palace, it was carried out by that tireless administrator, Henry Cole. British design and scientific research were not equal to our craftsmanship. They lagged behind other European countries. Albert saw the need for institutes and training colleges where art and science would be applied to manufacture.

Ideally they needed to be concentrated in an area with museums and learned societies, and two estates were purchased just south of Kensington Road. Thus they were near enough to the site of the dismantled Crystal Palace to serve as a reminder of the source of money and inspiration. With the addition of two more estates, eighty-seven acres 'safe for future years amidst the growth of the metropolis' were ready for a unique piece of civic planning.

Three roads were built across the meadows bought from Baron Villars and the gardens of the demolished Gore House. With Kensington Road to the north, they formed a rectangle and were virtually the boundaries of this university city. The southern limit was the new Cromwell Road, a westward extension of Brompton Road. The parallel east and west boundaries were Exhibition Road and Prince Albert Road (now Queen's Gate). Here, during the next fifty years, was to be created a district of museums, colleges, and institutes.

The first building to go up was just outside the rectangle. This was the South Kensington Museum (now the Victoria and Albert), a girder and glass building, bottom left, which echoed the style of the Crystal Palace. In this embryo of the great art museum of the future was housed £5,000-worth of monumental art which had been purchased from the Exhibition. Among its most prized possessions were the seven Raphael Cartoons which came from Hampton Court in 1865 and are seen, right, arriving in special cases. This first light and graceful museum was dismantled and re-erected as the Bethnal Green Museum in 1872. This allowed for the spread of the Victoria and Albert up the Exhibition Road in various stages until 1909.

6

7

1. By 1856 four estates with a total of eighty-seven acres had been bought at a cost of just over £280,000, new roads planned, and the South Kensington Museum was being built.

2. View of the area looking north and slightly west from the Cromwell Road which is under construction in the foreground. The back of Kensington Road terraces in far distance. Prince Albert and Exhibition Roads are to run north at the extreme left and right of the picture.

3. 'The Model Dwelling House' removed after the Exhibition to its present site in Kennington Park. Designed by Prince Albert, who was President of the Society for Improving the Dwellings of the Working Classes, it consisted of four labour-saving flats which could be let at 4s. 6d. a week. Nothing materialized from this example.

4. Building the South Kensington Museum in 1856 . . . and (5) the public entrance facing Brompton Road.

6. The Albert Memorial in Hyde Park built in marble, granite, bronze and mosaics at a cost of £120,000. It is 175 feet tall, and decorated with more than the same number of life-size or larger than life-size figures. Twenty-four steps lead up to the canopy and statue of Prince Albert. Completed to ecstatic praise in 1872, it was grudgingly being called 'an uncomfortable feat of engineering' twenty-five years later.

7. The arrival of the Raphael cartoons at the Museum.

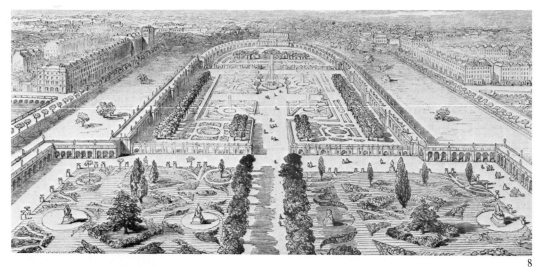

8

9

10

At the start, development of the main site was so slow that the Prince Consort never saw his ideas realized before his death in 1861. The Commissioners were frustrated by political opposition, apathy from learned societies, and even Church attacks on what were called 'Godless institutions'. So, for thirty years, twenty-two acres stretching from Kensington Road nearly to Cromwell Road were leased to the Royal Horticultural Society for a garden where it could hold exhibitions and admit the public. The Commissioners undertook to lay out the ground in three terraces and surround it in Italian arcades at a cost of £50,000. The Society agreed to spend a similar sum on planting the gardens and building a glass Winter Garden, left. The Gardens look impressive, top left, but by English standards are unduly formal. Statuary, fountains, bandstands, and rigidly symmetrical parterres were not to the taste of members concerned with experiments in horticulture.

When the Society's lease ended in the 1880s, the time was ripe for the development for which the Prince Consort and Cole had worked so hard. But even before this, a great Romanesque building heavy with gargoyles—the Natural History Museum—was built in the sixteen acres between the gardens and the Cromwell Road frontage. From the start this site had been reserved for a second international exhibition which was held there in 1862, but was over-shadowed by the death of Albert. Though even larger than the 1851 Exhibition, it did not capture the public

8. The Royal Horticultural Gardens opened in 1861. They stretched in rising terraces north to Kensington Road and were flanked by Exhibition Road and modern Queen's Gate. The semi-circular arcades at the end were inspired by those of the Villa Albani in Rome. In the centre is the conservatory or Winter Garden.

9. The conservatory seen in 1871 when the Albert Hall had been built behind it. A combined memorial to Albert and the Great Exhibition was erected in front of the conservatory, and is all that remains of this part of the garden now that it has been built over by Albert Court flats and part of Imperial College.

10. The 1862 Exhibition building. View from the west shows the side facing on to Queen's Gate at the corner of Cromwell Road. Though Fowke, the designer, was the logical man to plan the Natural History Museum for the

same site, his competition-winning designs were set aside in favour of those by Alfred Waterhouse.

11. The Byzantine style of Fowke's design is reflected in Waterhouse's museum as is shown by the main entrance of the present building.

12. Royal College of Organists, near the Albert Hall, 1875. By Lieut. H. H. Cole, R.E. Vertical emphasis gives impression of organ pipes.

13. Royal College of Science, Exhibition Road, 1873. By Capt. Fowke. Italian Renaissance style. Arcaded, overhanging loggia, suggesting troubadours, designed to give chemists fresh air.

14. Imperial Institute, 1893. By T. E. Colcutt. Outcome of 1886 Colonial Exhibition. Tennyson apostrophized: 'Raise a stately memorial . . . which may speak to the centuries.' All but tower now demolished.

11

imagination in the same way. The building with its two huge domes–the largest ever constructed–was intended as a permanent home for exhibitions held at ten-year intervals. But it was pulled down two years later, and the Natural History Museum built to house exhibits badly cramped at the parent British Museum in Bloomsbury.

The Exhibition building was designed by Capt. Francis Fowke, a Royal Engineer officer who left his mark all over the area. He was the designer of the Albert Hall (1871) inspired by the arenas at Nîmes and Arles which he had visited on a holiday with Cole; the Huxley Building (1872); and the quadrangle of the Victoria and Albert (1868). He was also winner of the competition for the Natural History Museum (1881) but his plans were superseded by those of Alfred Waterhouse.

With the end of the Horticultural Society gardens, two crossroads–Prince Consort Road and Imperial Institute Road–were built in the late 1880s to provide access to the vast Imperial Institute (1893. By T. E. Colcutt. Subscriptions by Indian princes. Chambord style with 280-foot tower) and the Royal College of Music (1884. By A. Blomfield. French baronial style). Varied institutions– the colleges of Art, Organists, Science and Technology, the museums of Natural History, Science, and Geology, the schools of Mines and Needlework–finally fulfilled the Prince Consort's mid-century dream in a bewildering variety of archaic architectural styles. But the most remarkable structure of all is Gilbert Scott's Albert Memorial (1872), under the Gothic canopy of which sits the bronze statue of 'our Blameless Prince' looking out over the area he conceived.

12

13

14

Site of Crystal Palace

Albert Memorial (under Scaffold)

Kensington Road

Albert Hall

Prince Albert Road (now Queen's Gate)
Prince Consort Road

Imperial Institute (with tower)

Royal College of Science (facing Imperial Institute)

Natural History Museum
(with semi-circular forecourt)

Brompton Road (with Victoria and
Albert Museum far right)

Mid-Century Development

In the fifty years leading to the middle of the century, London's population had more than doubled. In 1801 London was still a leafy city of under a million people: by 1851 two million were living and working in a metropolis whose rooftops were blackened by smoke from factory chimneys. Fine new terraces and overcrowded tenements were both the outcome of mid-Victorian commercial prosperity. Cruikshank, below, shows regiments of New Streets marching ruthlessly out into the surrounding country under the leadership of 'Mr Goth'.

The City was no longer the most populated area. Sixteen other districts now had more residents. First among them was St Pancras which, with buildings in Bloomsbury through Holloway almost to Highgate, had a population of 167,000 – five times the numbers in 1801. Marylebone remained second with 157,000, more than double the figure of fifty years before. But it was Lambeth, which leapt from fifteenth place to third, that showed the most remarkable change. In 1801: 27,000, in 1851: 139,000. The increase

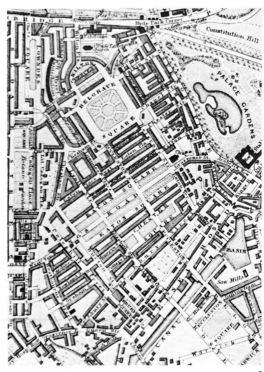

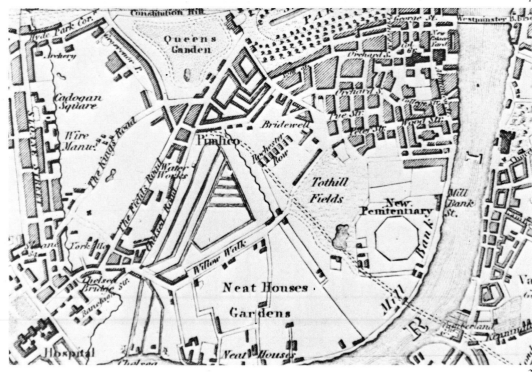

was largely due to the bridges, Vauxhall, Waterloo and Lambeth. To be 'transpontine' was no longer to be inaccessible.

The most outstanding residential development was the laying out of Belgravia. This was the work of Thomas Cubitt, the first building contractor in the modern sense. He employed permanent teams of craftsmen and labourers whom he sent out from workshops in Gray's Inn Road. The need to keep these men continually busy spurred Cubitt on in his enormously successful career as a speculative builder.

When Buckingham House became the royal palace in 1821, the area immediately to the west became ripe for fashionable development. But most of the 140 acres between Knightsbridge and the Thames were marshy and unsuitable for anything but market gardens. Cubitt leased five fields from Lord Grosvenor (whose other title, Viscount Belgrave, gave the district its name), and raised the low-lying ground, through which flowed the Westbourne river, with earth excavated from St Katharine's Dock.

Cubitt was also responsible for large parts of Belgrave Square, Eaton Square and Chester Square with their inter-connecting streets of fine houses and well laid-out gardens. Following the style of Nash, he gave the whole area a simple, classical beauty especially with terraces with long, unified fronts like the one on the north side of Eaton Square built in 1827. In Bayswater, developed a little later, but not by Cubitt, this attractive simplicity became submerged under Italian decorative detail as is seen, below, at Lancaster Gate started in 1857.

To link Belgravia with Westminster, Victoria Street, right, was opened in 1851. It was to be another thirty-six years before this street was fully lined with those tall blocks of business and residential chambers which were such a novelty in late Victorian London. With the filling in of the Chelsea Waterworks reservoir (the Basin in the map, far left), and the building of Victoria Station on the site in 1860, the fashionable northern part of Belgravia was permanently separated from Cubitt's Pimlico development of Eccleston and Warwick Squares.

1. London going out of Town or The March of Bricks and Mortar By George Cruikshank.

2. Belgravia in 1843 . . .

3. . . . and as it was in 1815. The transformation of the low-lying marshy ground between Knightsbridge and the Thames was largely achieved in the thirty years between 1825 and 1855. In the eighteenth century the one transversing road was the King's Way – now the King's Road section of Eaton Square – and the whole area was a place of fens, osier beds and market gardens. Cubitt raised the ground along the banks of the little Westbourne River with earth excavated from St Katharine's Dock and built Belgravia and Pimlico.

4. Thomas Cubitt. He revolutionized his trade by starting the first firm to offer clients all branches of building work.

5. Albert Gate, Hyde Park, and the twin houses built by Cubitt at the northern limit of Belgravia for George Hudson, the railway king.

6. Victoria Street, 1851.

7. Lancaster Gate, Bayswater, in 1866.

4

5

6

7

295

8

9

10   11

The spread of industry, congestion, and the rising cost of living in central London forced people outwards. Lining the roads to Clapham, Camberwell, Norwood, and Brixton there appeared rows of small terraced houses for the ever-expanding commercial class of small shopkeepers, clerks and artisans. And, for the more prosperous middle-class Londoner, there were larger houses like those built between 1855 and 1868 in Angell Terrace, Brixton Road, left.

Built by Benedict John Angell, who belonged to a notable family of Brixton landowners, the terrace displays classical niceties unexpected in a mid-Victorian main road, and reflects Angell's late-Georgian upbringing. Three centre houses, set slightly forward, are symmetrically flanked by two end ones. There are Doric porticoes, skilfully varied window pediments, ornamental friezes, and a bold, attractively festooned cornice.

For the even more well-to-do merchant who chose to live south of the Thames, Denmark Hill, Tulse Hill, and Herne Hill provided the south's answer to Campden Hill, Primrose Hill and Haverstock Hill. From the solid impressive house he built for himself, he travelled to the City daily in his own carriage or a first-class railway compartment.

Changes of address made by John Ruskin's family over the years are an example of the move out of central London. The writer's father was a City wine merchant, and until 1823 the Ruskins lived in a terraced house near Brunswick Square, St Pancras. When Ruskin was four, they moved to a three-storey semi-detached house at Herne Hill from which his father went each day to his office. Then in 1842, they bought the larger, detached house on Denmark Hill, left, which remained Ruskin's home until he gave it up in 1871.

Two houses on Tulse Hill, built nine years and four hundred yards apart, show the final phase of the change in suburban taste from Georgian to Victorian Gothic. No 155, Berry House, below far left, was built with a white, stucco façade in 1856. Corinthian columns and pilasters are in the style of a grand Georgian house, but the effect is Italianate rather than classical. A little farther up the hill, No 107, below left, built for a Gray's Inn solicitor in 1865, received the full Gothic treatment with florid embellishments, ponderous balconies, cast ironwork, and pointed arches over first floor windows picked out in red and yellow brickwork.

8. Angell Terrace, Brixton.

9. John Ruskin's house on Denmark Hill. The pattern of existence for this typical nineteenth-century middle-class home was completed by the last stages in its career. It was converted into a residential hotel, and then demolished to make way for council flats.

10. No 155 and (11) No 107 Tulse Hill.

A Fire Brigade at Last

As Chadwick had found with the Public Health Act, reform often had to wait on disaster and personal tragedy. Alone among the capital cities of Europe and America, London was still without a Government-financed fire service in the 1860s. Despite a series of great fires (page 264), Parliament continually refused to help. The excuse was that it would stifle the spirit of private enterprise. James Braidwood, chief of the totally inadequate force of thirty-seven lumbering horse-drawn engines financed by the insurance companies, was hamstrung. Too few men and engines, too few stations with no linking telegraph service, too few stopcocks and erratic water pressure. Often he had to rely on help from amateur brigades run by sporting aristocrats.

In June 1861, London paid for this apathy. Three acres of warehouses, crammed with valuable food and silks, caught fire in Tooley Street near London Bridge. Fourteen fire engines galloped to the scene, but most of them had to stand by helpless and unable to find the mains as eight six-storey buildings were destroyed. Braidwood was killed when a wall collapsed. Crowds lined the route of his funeral procession to pay tribute to the civil engineer who had given his life for their protection. The Tooley Street fire, with its devastation, its huge loss of property, and the death of Braidwood, brought an abrupt end to the era of haphazard fire-fighting. Claims for £2,000,000 so crippled the insurance companies that they threatened to disband their fire service.

Only then – after the worst disaster since the Great Fire – was a Select Committee set up to investigate. Even so, it took a further three years before its recommendations (whittled down financially) were adopted. Finally, in 1866, the Metropolitan Fire Brigade which we know today, organized by the Board of Works, came into existence.

1. With bell clanging, one of the early horse-drawn 'steamers' races to a fire. The leather helmets of Braidwood's men were replaced by brass ones by the Metropolitan Fire Brigade.

2. Capt. James Braidwood, formerly an Edinburgh fire chief. He ran the insurance companies' force for twenty-eight years.

3. The memorial plaque to Braidwood in Tooley Street. His funeral procession was one and a half miles long. Shops were closed, and City church bells tolled all day. Queen Victoria sent a message of condolence to his widow.

4. Disaster in Tooley Street, Southwark – the scene at 2 a.m. – nine hours after the outbreak.

ERECTED BY THE M. OR SOUTHWARK DIVISION OF THE METROPOLITAN POLICE.

The New Parliament House . . .

Among the crowds who had watched the old Houses of Parliament going up in flames (page 265) was a man in his late thirties. As any architect would, Charles Barry visualized the chances rebuilding would bring; but he had no idea that they were to be part of his own destiny. Yet sixteen months later in 1836 he was announced winner of the competition for the new Palace of Westminster. When his designs were selected from those of nearly a hundred rival architects, Barry was committed to a tremendous undertaking that was to take him twenty-four years and was still not complete at his death.

His preference was for the Italian style – something after Inigo Jones's grand conception (page 115) – but Parliament demanded Gothic. So he visited Brussels and Louvain for inspiration, and collaborated with Pugin, a dedicated medievalist, on decorative detail.

Barry's task was to give unity to the jumble of remaining buildings, preserve the dignity of Westminster Hall, and double the size of the previous Parliament. He achieved this partly by building out 100 feet over the river for the Members' terrace, committee rooms and libraries. Because the site was flat and unimpressive, he gave the long, low river façade a dramatic importance with flanking towers.

The work was beset with difficulties. Apart from criticism of his design ('Sham Gothic', 'meretricious', 'dangerously artistic') Barry had to face continual interference, conflicting demands from divided authority, and financial skimping. He estimated six years and £80,000 for the work. Because so many changes were demanded, it took over twenty-five and cost £2,000,000. When he designed a small Commons (for intimacy of debate), he was asked to make it larger. His acoustics were baselessly criticized. Important points of design were decided by a Fine Arts Commission on which he was not even invited to sit.

But Barry never gave up, even when the Treasury arbitrarily cut his fees and refused to answer his protests. From six in the morning until midnight, he was on the site or at his drawing board in the house which he took in George Street nearby. His son, who completed the work, held that the strain shortened his father's life.

On the day of Barry's funeral at Westminster Abbey in 1860 a flag was flown at half mast on the Victoria Tower. He had been recognized by a knighthood, but had just failed to see the completion of his masterpiece. Driven into a madhouse through excessive work, Pugin, his collaborator and the underlying genius, had died, scarcely acknowledged, eight years earlier.

1

2

3

4

. . . and Big Ben

Of all the many contretemps in which Barry was involved, the most futile, and longest drawn out, concerned Big Ben. It straggled over fifteen years.

A huge clock was needed for the tower which the architect was building at the north end of the palace. It was to replace the old clock tower of 1288, demolished in 1707. The Queen's Clockmaker was asked to prepare designs in 1844, but did nothing about it.

After two years a competition was opened, but the dilatory royal clockmaker then furiously asserted that there was bias in favour of another contender, E. J. Dent, because the referee for the competition, the Astronomer Royal, had given Dent a testimonial supporting his tender.

Perhaps to show his disinterested integrity, the Astronomer Royal set down fifteen stringent conditions. He insisted that the first stroke of each hour must be right to within a second–almost impossible for a clock with a two-cwt. minute hand exposed to heat and weather. A six-year deadlock followed before the contract went to Dent's.

On the day in 1852 when the Queen opened the new Parliament, bottom left, the tower was still just a stump of 150 feet (against a final 316 feet). Not for a further seven years would the clock tell London the time and the bell strike the hours.

Big Ben–the bell itself which has given a generic name to clock and tower–was also a source of trouble. Even its name sets problems. It is uncertain if it was named after 'Big Ben' Caunt, a popular seventeen-stone prizefighter, or Sir Benjamin Hall, the Commissioner of Works. During a sluggish debate on a name for the bell the latter, a corpulent Welshman, is said to have drawn from a back-bencher the derisive shout of, 'Let's call it Big Ben!'

1. Building the Houses of Parliament. At this stage of construction in June 1842, completion was predicted for 1845. But it was not until after 1860 that Parliament appeared as seen top right.

2 and 3. Controversy raged after the death of Charles Barry (2), and August Welby Pugin (3) about the division of credit. Technically Barry's assistant, Pugin always acknowledged that he was a subordinate but as he was responsible for all the decorative work, inside and out, he has a claim for fuller recognition.

4. Opening of the new Parliament, 1852. Big Ben Tower, on the right, is still incomplete.

5. The completed Houses of Parliament.

6. The first Big Ben, cast near Stockton-on-Tees, is brought from London Docks across Westminster Bridge. Sixteen white horses draw the sixteen-ton hour bell. It cracked during tests.

7. Union Jack at half-mast, and black flags hanging from the turrets of the Victoria Tower for Barry's funeral.

8 and 9. The second Big Ben, cast in Whitechapel, is brought on rollers to the base of the clock tower (8) and then raised 190 feet on its side (9). That also cracked, but was never replaced.

5

6

7

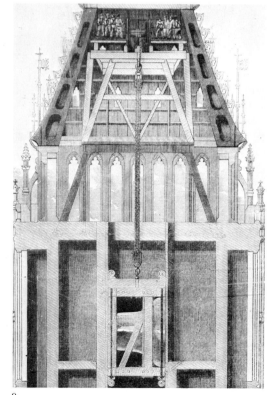

8

9

The River Highway

In the 1870s twenty million people a year were using the Thames, not just for pleasure, but as the most practical east-west highway of London. From the day when the first paddle-boat on the river–George Dodd's *Thames*–drew jeers from the sailing ships as she churned up the waters of the Pool, the importance of the steamers had steadily increased. That was in 1815, and regular services started a year later. By 1840 the river was alive with tall-funnelled boats plying up to Richmond and down to the Estuary. There was a quarter-hour service to Greenwich, and between Westminster and London Bridge. Woolwich alone received 250,000 passengers from London annually. There were also longer trips. *Lloyd's Guide* advertised 'fast and splendid' services to Ramsgate, Margate, and to Herne Bay where, 'immediately on arrival', the packets were met by coaches for Canterbury and Dover.

The connection with coaches (and later with the railways) was an important factor in the steamboat's popularity. Land and water services supplemented each other. Before the railways from the south crossed the river, passengers arriving at London Bridge, Pimlico Station, by Battersea Park, Nine Elms, Vauxhall, and, later, Waterloo, needed the steamboats to complete their journey to the West End and City. The 'penny steamers'–they charged one penny from pier to pier–carried 120 people at a time. They were fast and ran regularly. Piers at all the bridges were bustling termini in the morning and evening rush hours. The scene, left, shows a landing at London Bridge at 9 a.m. in 1859. Every Saturday afternoon *The Eagle*, nicknamed 'The Husbands' Boat', far left, took men who had been working in town all week to join their families at Margate and Ramsgate. The confusion on the river, especially under the arches of the bridges, as is seen, above left, could be considerable, but the public learnt to choose the right vessel at a glance by the colour of the ring round the funnel.

Competition from the Underground forced the five main steamboat companies to merge in 1876. For many years the combined company provided a half-hourly, all-the-year-round service linking all the piers between Chelsea and Greenwich. But in 1878 the pleasure trips received a blow from which they never fully recovered. At Galleon's Reach, Erith, the *Princess Alice* came into collision with a collier one summer's evening. More than 600 holidaymakers were drowned. The disaster, so graphically depicted, right, led to such a decline in trade that when fifty-seven paddle steamers had to be sold six years later there were no bidders.

1. Illustration from *Lloyd's Guide*.

2. Confusion at London Bridge.

3. *The Eagle*–one of London's first steamboats.

4. River commuters–1859.

5. 1846. So congested was the river with steamboats that in 1845 it was decided that it was too hazardous for the Oxford and Cambridge boat race to be held over the previous Westminster to Putney course. So in that year the race was rowed from Putney to Mortlake Church. In the following year, the race, seen here, was won by Cambridge by two lengths. The same course was rowed – but in the opposite direction. Outriggers were used for the first time. In the background: Putney Church and typical Thames steamboats.

6. 1856. Up to this year, when they were finally abandoned, the prison hulks at Woolwich were an object of morbid curiosity to steamboat passengers going down river. They recalled Pip's description from *Great Expectations:* 'By the light of torches, we saw the black Hulk lying a little way from the mud of the shore, like a wicked Noah's Ark. Cribbed and barred and moored by massive rusty chains, the prison ship seemed to my young eyes to be ironed like the prisoners.' This is the leaking, decaying *Warrior* which housed up to 500 shackled convicts.

7. 1857. Noon, 3 November. After three years' building on the Thames at Millwall, the *Great Eastern* was ready for launching. Designed to carry 4,000 passengers, she was five times the size of the largest vessel afloat. Watched by 100,000 people, her designer, I. K. Brunel, stepped on to the platform (under the paddle wheel) to direct launching which, because of her vast size, had to be done sideways. Tugs pulled, hydraulic rams pounded, chains snapped, two workmen were killed. She moved only inches. Three months later, with no visitors present, she was finally launched.

8. 1861. Crowds saw Selina Young–'The Female Blondin'–attempt to cross the river from Battersea to Cremorne Gardens, Chelsea, on a tightrope. She failed because a thief stole the lead weights of the securing guys and the rope went slack. She slid down into the water and was rescued.

9. 1878. Recovering bodies from the Thames after the *Princess Alice* disaster. As there was no passenger list, the exact mortality is unknown. It has been estimated as high as 700.

5

6

7

8

9

The New British Museum

By the middle of the century the old British Museum in Montagu House, Bloomsbury (page 217), was bursting at the seams. A converted private house which had been adequate for Soane's 'cabinet of curiosities' could no longer accommodate the treasures that were being acquired. From Egypt after the Napoleonic campaign had come not only the Rosetta Stone but colossal monuments like the four-ton head of King Thothmes which were far too heavy for the old floors. When the Elgin Marbles, the museum's great showpiece, arrived from Athens in 1816 they had to be displayed in a wooden shed. For over two years the 20,000 volumes of the magnificent Grenville Library lay in piles on the floor or stacked three deep on the shelves. With the presentation of the royal library by George IV in 1821 something radical had to be done, as a new building for the housing of the 120,000 books was a condition of the gift.

During the next quarter of a century the garden of Montagu House was transformed. Apart from acquisitions, the growth of public interest forced the hand of a reluctant Treasury. Criticisms of the Museum voiced in Parliament by William Cobbett in the 1830s were no longer valid. 'If the aristocracy wants a lounging place, let them pay for it,' he had said, and asked why farmers and tradesmen should pay for it through taxes. But by 1847 there were around 900,000 visitors annually, a figure which was to increase to over 2,000,000 in Exhibition Year.

The last vestiges of what Charles Lamb called 'poor condemned old Montagu House' disappeared in 1845. The new museum with its monumental Ionic front reached completion two years later. The change-over had been accomplished piecemeal but under a master plan of Robert Smirke, the architect whose other classical buildings include the Mint and the General Post Office. With Montagu House still open to visitors, he built a gallery to the north-west for the Egyptian treasures. It was followed by the present east wing containing the King's Library. Stage by stage, the north side of the house was surrounded on three sides, the new galleries forming a hollow square. When, finally, the house came down to be replaced by the colonnaded façade, entrance hall, and Grenville Library, the square was complete with galleries all round an open central quadrangle.

The new British Museum was ready to receive the trophies of what was to become known as the era of 'battleship archaeology'. Shrewd diplomats and museum officials with roving commissions in the Aegean were to co-opt the Navy's help to bring back monu-

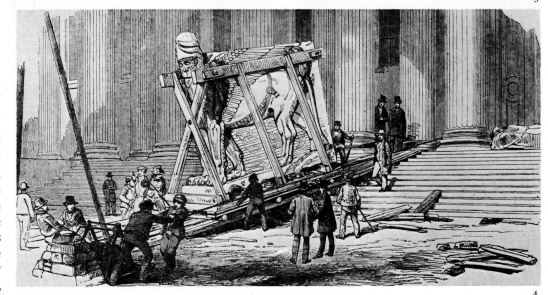

1. The front of the new Museum as it looked after 1852. The view is looking west down Great Russell Street.

2. The exact opposite of the view above, showing the old entrance gateway of Montagu House demolished seven years earlier.

3. Top of the main staircase at the entrance of Montagu House as it looked up to the time of demolition. The stuffed giraffes and the Natural History Department removed from Bloomsbury to Kensington in 1880.

4. Arrival of the winged lion from Nineveh in 1852.

5. The gallery for Egyptian sculpture. The granite lions from Nubia of 1400 B.C. were presented to the museum in 1835. The twin obelisks, 350 B.C., were gifts of George III. In the distance is the colossal head of King Thothmes, 1500 B.C., discovered at Karnak by Belzoni.

6. The Reading Room under the dome (140 feet in diameter, 1 foot wider than St Peter's) as it appeared within twenty years of its opening. Two rows reserved for 'Ladies Only', largely unoccupied, existed until 1907.

7. The previous Reading Room at the north end of the King's Library.

8. Panizzi – 'This cursed fellow who came to England with a rope round his neck' was the jealous description of a subordinate. He became Sir Anthony Panizzi in 1869.

ments from Asia and the Middle East. At the height of the Crimea, C. T. Newton obtained shipping space for 384 crates which brought to Bloomsbury the sculpture from Halicarnassus and Cnidus. Sir Charles Fellows sent home the Nereid Monument from Turkey, and the frieze of the Temple of Apollo from Bassae was bought by the British Government. To the Museum came Sir Henry Layard's Assyrian antiquities, including the colossal winged lion from Nineveh.

In the east wing the librarians, struggling to catalogue and store the vast accumulation of books, looked enviously at the spacious exhibition galleries. Their difficulties were increased by the Copyright Act of 1851 which required a copy of every published book to be deposited at the museum. The Reading Room was congested, and loudly criticized by Carlyle who, unlike Thackeray, unsuccessfully demanded the privilege of a private room. The unconventional solution of the problem was provided by an unconventional man. Antonio Panizzi, an Italian lawyer and revolutionary, had come to England almost penniless. From a junior position in the library, he rose to become Keeper of Printed Books, by brilliant administration, minute regard for detail, and knowledge of foreign libraries. His charm and enthusiasm overcame prejudice against him as a foreigner with a quick temper.

'I want the poor student to have the same means of indulging his learned curiosity ... as the richest man in the kingdom,' he said as if answering Cobbett, and made a rough sketch of a vast circular reading room which would fill the museum quadrangle. Around it would be cast iron shelving which so saved space that it could take nearly a million books.

For some years various ideas for a new reading room and storing space for books had been proposed, and Panizzi's plan undoubtedly owed its inspiration to these earlier ideas. The domed reading room of the Radcliffe Library at Oxford must also have been an influence, while Paxton's Crystal Palace would have suggested iron construction. His scheme combined the advantages of many foreign libraries, and iron shelving, substituting metal for brick, was economical and reduced fire risks. When Smirke came to draw up the detailed plans, he found he could not improve on it.

Panizzi, whose bust stands over the entrance to this day, created order out of chaos and instituted methodical cataloguing. In the radial seating of the new Reading Room, space was provided for over 300 readers. After the domed rotunda was opened in 1857 it was to be used by researchers as varied as Marx (who sat in Row G), Lenin, Ruskin, Samuel Butler, and Swinburne who once complained that it was stuffy, and fainted.

5

6

7

8

Demonstration

In the year when Disraeli was framing the second Reform Bill (and Marx was putting the final touches to *Das Kapital* in the British Museum), political agitation took a militant turn in London. Hyde Park was the scene of demonstrations during the summer of 1866, and when the authorities tried to prevent an evening meeting of the Reform League by closing the park gates, the crowd took the law into their own hands.

They tore down the railings in Park Lane and fought a pitched battle with the police (seen, right, in helmets which had just replaced top-hats) who were armed with truncheons. With the aid of the Life Guards, the police forced them back, but the battle of the railings had a symbolic consequence. 'Speakers Corner' by Marble Arch became privileged as an open forum for free speech where anyone may say anything short of blasphemy, obscenity and incitement to violence.

In December the following year London was rocked by an explosion. The wall of Clerkenwell prison, twenty-five feet high and two feet thick, was blown up by gunpowder in an attempt to release two prisoners. Both were 'Fenians', Irish republicans resolved to end the union with England.

The escape failed, but twelve people living near the prison were killed, and the police came under serious criticism. Seemingly, they had ignored advance warning of the attempt and had taken no decisive action against the plotters who were actually seen arriving with the gunpowder. This incident also had a significant consequence. It led to the formation of the Special Branch, the semi-secret intelligence force responsible for state security.

Disaster

'. . . For many minutes after the breaking of the ice, a multitude of people, amongst whom were several women and children, were struggling in the water, and trying to save themselves by holding onto pieces of ice, and most of them screaming in despair,' runs a description of the disaster in Regent's Park in January 1867.

There were about 500 skaters and people sliding on the ice, watched from the banks by several thousand spectators, some of whom tried to give help, but many 'were struck with horror and could do nothing but utter cries of lamentation'.

The number drowned was forty-one, and, following as it did a long series of ice disasters, rigid regulations were introduced. Even though a number of the lakes have been made very shallow to reduce risk, there is a ruling which forbids skating in all London parks unless the ice is five inches thick.

1. The battle of the railings in Hyde Park.

2. Searching in the prison ruins after the Clerkenwell explosion.

3. The Regent's Park ice disaster – looking towards Sussex Terrace. Boats are being rushed down to help in the rescue.

Demolition

The south-western end of the Strand, once the village of Charing, saw two major acts of development between 1862 and 1876. Both involved the demolition of historic landmarks.

The first was the extension of the South Eastern Railway from London Bridge across the river and into the West End. After the rejection of Battersea, Pimlico, and Waterloo, Charing Cross was chosen as the new terminus. This meant the end of a market that had existed since Restoration times between Villiers Street and Craven Street. It was named after Sir Edward Hungerford, a wildly extravagant courtier on the site of whose house it was built.

In 1831 Hungerford Market had been rebuilt on a larger scale in Italian style with two quadrangles surrounded with shops, the lower one on the river for the sale of fish, the upper for fruit, vegetables and meat. On the Strand side, horse-buses started from here for Paddington and Camden Town.

To make way for the railway, the second market—only moderately successful—had to be pulled down. The suspension bridge linking it with Lambeth was replaced by the present Hungerford Railway Bridge, and the station and hotel in French *château* style built on the site.

As an antiquarian gesture, and to give visible meaning to the station's name, a copy of the Queen Eleanor Cross was built in the forecourt in 1855. The original, erected by Edward I, had been demolished by the Puritans in 1647. The new one, seventy feet tall, and carrying eight statues of the Queen, was based on three very imprecise prints. It is about a hundred yards north-east of the original which stood where Charles I's statue is today.

A far more serious loss to London was Northumberland House (page 274) next to Charing Cross. A new and sinister hand—authority using powers of compulsory purchase—swept aside public protest and the wishes of the owners to bring about the demolition of the great early Jacobean town house of the Dukes of Northumberland in 1874. An access road was needed to link the new Embankment (page 314) and Trafalgar Square, and, to make way for the wide, austere Northumberland Avenue, the last of the old private palaces of London was sacrificed. With it went gardens to the river, Inigo Jones's river façade, Mylne's pavilion, Adam's interior decoration, and the Percy lion (to Syon). The price was £500,000.

4. Demolition of Hungerford Market from Villiers Street.
5. Charing Cross Station and Hotel.
6. The restored Eleanor Cross.
7. The end of Northumberland House.
8. Northumberland Avenue in 1876.

4

5

6

7

8

The First Underground

Traffic congestion on roads leading into the City was relieved in the south by the river boats. But another solution was needed for the north side of London. It came in the revolutionary idea of an underground railway put forward in the 1830s by a City solicitor, Charles Pearson. He was concerned not so much with traffic as with the difficulties faced by people who were forced to move out of central London when their homes were converted into business premises. Pearson argued that by building an underground railway between the City and Paddington, these people could travel in and out of London daily for a nominal fare. His proposal included a specially planned estate of 10,000 cottages seven miles out.

The estate was never built, but thirty years later he saw his scheme materialize as the Metropolitan Railway. Just under four miles long, it linked Paddington, Euston, and King's Cross stations with the City Terminus near Smithfield. It was the world's first underground railway.

To prevent costly demolition, the line followed the New Road, and at King's Cross turned south-east along and under Farringdon Road. For once, Parliament raised no objections, and New Road residents agreed, influenced by the plausible argument that it would reduce surface traffic past their doors. Costs were further kept down by 'cut and cover' construction. Instead of tunnelling (as for the Tube later), a trench between 25 and 59 feet deep was cut, the sides revetted with bricks, arched over, and the road replaced.

Work, which started in 1860, took three years. West of King's Cross, the work was easier as the tunnel ran through gravel, and there was only one main sewer, the Tyburn, to be negotiated. But to the east, it ran through clay, and the Fleet Sewer had to be crossed three times. During building the sewer burst, and serious flooding delayed completion. But all was ready for the opening in January 1862.

From the start, the Metropolitan was an immediate success. In the first six months 26,500 people used it daily. With a threepenny fare for the 18-minute Paddington-City journey, the horse-bus was outrivalled. And there were cheap fares for workmen, too. The visionary Pearson died three months before the opening.

The way was now open for the whole complex network of lines—the District, Inner Circle, City and South London, and Central—which was to burrow under London in the next fifty years.

1. Work in progress on the Metropolitan Railway – view from Pentonville Road looking west towards King's Cross.

2. Plan for the Metropolitan Railway, 1860.

3. After this trial trip – immediate success.

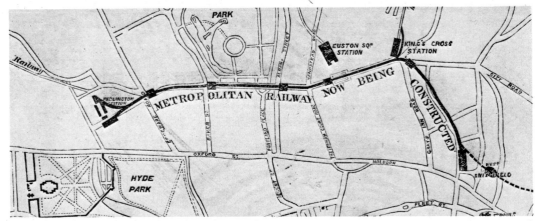

Holborn Viaduct

In the same year as the Metropolitan Railway opened, a road scheme was begun close to Farringdon Station. It was designed to ease the flow of traffic in and out of the City. From earliest times, the Fleet valley at Holborn had been a hazard to travellers, and Henry V had ordered it to be paved. For horses pulling heavy loads and passengers, the steep inclines of Snow Hill and Holborn Hill were an agonizing ordeal. With its 1:18 gradient, Holborn Hill was long known as 'Heavy Hill' either because of its physical difficulties, or because of the feelings of all the prisoners who travelled that way from Newgate to Tyburn. Pearson, the Underground pioneer, suggested a plan for filling the valley with earth and raising it seventeen feet. But this gave way to a monumental solution—the building of a viaduct, quarter of a mile long, right across the valley from Newgate to Hatton Garden.

All that is now visible of the viaduct, which cost over £2,000,000 to build in 1863, is the short span of 120 feet, the ornate, cast-iron bridge that crosses, thirty-one feet high, over Farringdon Street. Buildings on both sides of the viaduct hide the extent of the work, a feat of engineering which involved tiers of arches. These arches were converted into vaulted cellars on several storeys, and were leased as warehouses. Virtually invisible, too, is the railway which it spans. This northern extension of the London, Chatham and Dover line is the one rail link from the south of England to the north through central London. After Holborn Viaduct Station, it passed (and still exists for freight) under the viaduct, Snow Hill, and Smithfield Market, to emerge at Farringdon Station and continue on, partly underground, to King's Cross.

1. 'The Omnibus Brutes – which are they?' was Cruikshank's caption to his cartoon which shows an early bus going up Holborn Hill.

2. The viaduct under construction in 1860, looking east. Newgate Prison (on the site of the present Old Bailey) in the far distance, centre. Left, behind houses, the tower of St Sepulchre. Temporary fence, left, appears to bar the way to Snow Hill. Under scaffolding, right, is one of four Italian Gothic style buildings at the approaches to the bridge which carried statues of London worthies in niches. Behind the fence, right, was built Holborn Viaduct Station. The Viaduct was opened by Queen Victoria in 1866 on the same day as the second Blackfriars Bridge.

3. The viaduct over Farringdon Street.

The Cry of 'No Popery!'

Although they were only a small minority in mid-Victorian London, Roman Catholics aroused illogical suspicion. Three centuries after the Marian executions in Smithfield, they still provoked fear and prejudice in Protestants for many of whom Foxe's *Book of Martyrs* was the only permitted Sunday reading after the Bible.

London's Catholic population was 27,000, about one in every sixty people. Mass was held in only twenty-six churches. Yet in 1850 when the Pope decided to make Bishop Wiseman a cardinal and Archbishop of Westminster there was an immediate outcry. The restoration of the Catholic Hierarchy – Wiseman's administration of twelve English dioceses – was described by the Prime Minister, Lord Russell, as 'a pretension of supremacy over the realm of England'.

A frenzy of anti-Catholic feeling was whipped up by the newspapers, and on 5 November when the Cardinal was on his way home from Rome, his effigy was paraded through the streets and burnt at Bethnal Green. 'No popery!' was chalked up on walls, priests were pelted, and windows of Catholic churches smashed. Peckham staged a mock arrest in which two men dressed as Wiseman and his chaplain were dragged from a house by armed men. Solemn resolutions were taken after heated demonstrations like the one, above, held at the Guildhall by the Lord Mayor.

Back in London, jeered at in the streets and his carriage stoned, Wiseman wrote and had printed in record time an *Appeal to the English People*. In this he defined the purely spiritual scope of the Hierarchy, and appealed for justice. Sanity was sufficiently restored for Wiseman's enthronement to take place without riots, but popular fears remained. Popery was still a dirty word, and Protestant nostrils recoiled at even the hint of incense. A few years later the Protestant vicar of St George-in-the-East, Wapping, had bread and pudding thrown at him for daring to put the choir in surplices, burn candles on the altar, and wear a chasuble while celebrating Holy Communion.

1. Anti-Catholic demonstration at the Guildhall.

2. In the pulpit of St George's, Southwark, Cardinal Wiseman gives the blessing after his enthronement as Archbishop of Westminster in December 1850. The ceremony in the cathedral church restored the Catholic Hierarchy in England, abolished by Queen Elizabeth nearly 300 years before.

3. 'The Guy Fawkes of 1850' was the caption to this cartoon in *Punch*'s anti-Catholic campaign.

4. Brompton Oratory. Wiseman's successor, Cardinal Manning, bought a prison site off Victoria Street in 1867 where Westminster Cathedral with its towering Byzantine campanile was completed thirty-six years later. In the interim, London's most fashionable Catholic church was Brompton Oratory, built in 1878 in baroque style under the influence of Catholic converts anxious to create an atmosphere of Italian devotion.

1

2

3

4

Wrath of God

To those Victorians who feared Popery yet found the gentle message of the Church of England too undemanding, Nonconformity offered a welcome alternative. Pounding their pulpits, and raising an arm, admonitory and unencumbered by vestments, the evangelists offered vast congregations the simple alternative of heaven or hellfire. Most potent of them all was Charles Haddon Spurgeon who burst on London at the age of nineteen.

Three years after Wiseman's enthronement, Spurgeon was 'called' to a Baptist chapel in New Park Street near London Bridge. His rhetoric, appeals to personal conscience, and touches of humour drew such huge crowds that he was forced to move to Surrey Gardens, Walworth. There in the Surrey Music Hall he preached to at least 10,000 people every Thursday and Sunday.

Within four years his fame had so spread that at a Crystal Palace meeting, top right, he was heard by 23,654. He told them that the Indian Mutiny, then raging, was God's visitation on the British for permitting 'the vile religion of Hindooism'. On the day before this meeting (according to a legend of the kind Spurgeon inspired) he had brought about a conversion. A carpenter working high up in the roof of the Crystal Palace suddenly heard a voice crying, 'Behold the Lamb of God which taketh away the sins of the world!' The sinner was at once reformed, little knowing that what he took to be a private exhortation from heaven was Spurgeon trying out the acoustics.

In 1859 work started on the building which was to be the centre of Spurgeon's ministry for the next thirty years. The Metropolitan Tabernacle, right, held 6,000 people. Here were to be delivered the sermons which drew all London to the Elephant and Castle.

Spurgeon inspired many followers. Among them was the American evangelist, D. L. Moody who, with his partner I. D. Sankey, crossed the Atlantic a few years later and packed the new Agricultural Hall, Islington. It was claimed they 'reduced the population of hell by a million souls'.

1. Spurgeon preaches to the largest indoor audience of his life at the Crystal Palace in October 1857.

2. 'Carnality and pride are at the root of the world's evils' – Spurgeon preaching with evangelical fervour.

3. Evangelism came right to the people in 1865 when William Booth, founder of the Salvation Army, started preaching on street corners in Whitechapel. In his fight against drink, he often held meetings outside public houses like the Vine.

4. The Metropolitan Tabernacle at the Elephant and Castle, built by Spurgeon, and his headquarters until his death in 1892. Burnt out six years later. Reopened 1900. The portico alone survived German bombs in World War II. It has now been rebuilt.

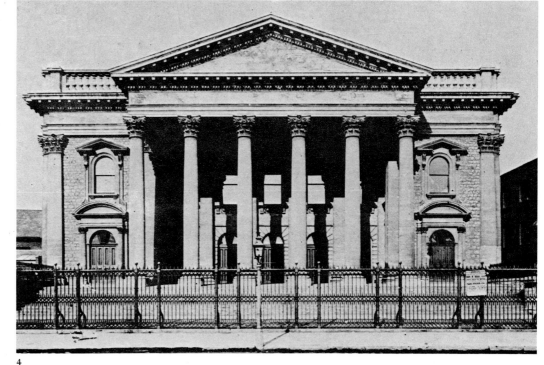

'The Bitter Cry of Outcast London'

Opening the *Illustrated Times* in February 1857, the reader was confronted with the dismal picture, right. It showed how London treated the homeless poor. Overnight shelter for paupers in this casual ward was simply a stable without either straw or bedding. Arrivals to the workhouse annexe in Battle Lane, St Pancras, were given some bread. In the morning they were turned out without food unless they first broke stones in the yard.

Stonebreaking, seen lower right in Bethnal Green, was one of two 'tests' by which the Poor Law official decided if applicants for help were genuinely destitute. The other was a willingness to pick oakum. Poverty in mid-Victorian London was so widespread, and the cost of relief considered so heavy by the ratepayer, that officials were expected to prevent malingering.

Exact figures of poverty do not exist before 1881, but for forty years previously it had been steadily rising. The worst district was Bethnal Green, where nearly half the population applied for relief at least once during the year. In Kensington only five per cent were paupers. The average for London: between a third and a quarter of the population. Conditions were worst in the East End due to Irish immigration and the influx of Poles and Jews from Middle Europe after the Russian pogroms of the 1860s.

Radical journalists were combining with authors, artists and social reformers to prick the public conscience. There was no excuse for ignorant apathy. Edwin Chadwick, John Simon (who carried on Chadwick's sanitary reforms) and Lord Shaftesbury bombarded the complacent with reports. Dickens painted a grim picture in *Bleak House* and *Oliver Twist*, Charles Kingsley in *The Water Babies*. The most primitive Polynesian native, asserted T. H. Huxley, was 'not half so savage, so unclean, so irreclaimable as the tenant of a tenement of an East End slum'. Arthur Mearns summed up matters in the title of his book – *The Bitter Cry of Outcast London*.

Propaganda for reform was made even more vivid by illustration. Tragic figures like those opposite were photographed and engraved to accompany Mayhew's descriptions in *London Labour and the London Poor*. Alarming pictures of conditions in the pages of the *Illustrated London News* now disturbed comfortable homes. But change came slowly, though not because 'the rich man in his carriage' was necessarily inhumane. It was simply that he saw the answer for 'the submerged tenth' in charity like the Spital-fields free soup kitchen, right. He believed in the Victorian precept about 'helping the

poor to help themselves'. The needy must constantly be reminded of Him whom they must thank for help. When a model Casual Ward, top far right, was opened in Marylebone in 1867, the beams and walls were covered with exhortations and Scriptural texts. In another refuge, (see 8), Doré shows the Bible being read. Those who found themselves in penury must reflect that this was God's will, not society's fault. It took the fire out of revolutionary ideas. Not for many years did the inbred belief in *laissez-faire* and charitable palliatives give way to Government-backed reforms in housing, education and properly organized social welfare.

1. Overnight shelter in St Pancras.
2. Stonebreaking in Bethnal Green.
3. Spitalfields free soup kitchen.

4. A 'crock' – one of about 250 street-sellers of crockery and glassware. Earnings: around 10s. a week.

5. Girl seller of 'lucifers', or matches. Profits as little as 2s. 6d. a week. Often used matches as a cover for begging.

6. 'Old Tom' aged seventy-three, street-seller of dog-collars. Profits: An average of 4s. a week.

7. Crippled seller of nutmeg graters. Legs and arms withered. Crawled two miles a day. Weekly earnings: 6s. to 7s.

8. Bible reading to the poor.

9. Casual Ward in Marylebone.

10. Crossing-sweeper begging a coin – from Mayhew.

Relief of the Poor...

An immigrant who might have been expected to find conditions here better than in his native Russia described London's mid-century slums as 'this dreadful ant-heap'. 'Every night a hundred thousand men know not where they will lay their heads,' wrote Alexander Herzen, 'and the police often find women and children dead of a hunger....' Building could not keep pace with population. Tenements and 'rookeries' were appallingly overcrowded. In Spitalfields, the worst district in the East End, a single house held sixty people, seven to a room, and with only nine beds between them.

After describing the notorious Seven Dials area of Holborn, the historian, Charles Knight, commented that 'far too rarely do we make any provisions' for the homeless. One person who did make provision was George Peabody. In 1864 this rich American philanthropist built the first Peabody Building, right, in Commercial Street, Spitalfields. An austere, red-brick building, five storeys high, it provided three-room flats for 5s. a week with water, decent sanitation and laundry facilities. Thanks to £500,000 given by Peabody, it was followed by model dwellings in Shadwell, Islington, Chelsea and twenty-six other districts in London. Of these dwellings designed for working people, twenty-nine blocks are still in existence.

There was no equivalent generosity from English sources, but efforts were made on a smaller scale by the Society for Improving the Conditions of the Labouring Classes. A woman reformer, Octavia Hill, also set an example. With financial help from Ruskin, she bought three run-down houses in Marylebone, put them in order, and installed poor tenants at small (but economically feasible) rents. Then she bought six more, and her success encouraged people to put up money for similar work. But she was sadly to record that in the thirty years up to 1875 private benevolence housed only 26,000 Londoners – a fraction more than the population increase every six months.

1

2

1. The desolation of London slum conditions – rows of poor terraces, back-to-back under railway arches – was caught by the French artist, Doré, in the 1870s. The growth of the railways destroyed houses and forced overcrowding. With the building of Marylebone Station, 1,750 homeless families had to be absorbed in the Lisson Grove area.

2. The first Peabody Building.

3. George Peabody – statue behind the Royal Exchange.

4. The first 'Model Dwellings' for families built by the Society for Improving the Conditions of the Labouring Classes off King's Cross Road, in 1844. Demolished.

5. Ragged School in Bedfordbury.

6. Bootblacks and their hero, Lord Shaftesbury.

7. Vagrant children under Charing Cross arches.

8. Typical London 'Board School' in the Caledonian Road.

3

4

... and the Children

Slum poverty turned children into beggars and street arabs, artful dodgers and young criminals. To scratch up 3d. a day, 280 'mud larks' scavenged along the river at low tide. As late as 1864 at least 2,000 sweeps between the ages of five and ten were still climbing chimneys. In East End sweat shops, pickle and match factories young girls led lives of drudgery.

Their greatest champion was the Earl of Shaftesbury who personally explored the slums and organized a brigade of bootblacks. Two of them, bottom left, are affectionately looking at his portrait in a shop window. But his most important work for the young in London was the Ragged School Union of which he was president for forty years.

By 1852 there were 110 Ragged Schools in London attended by 13,000 children, about half of them under ten. Any destitute child was admitted to schools like the one in Bedfordbury near Charing Cross, below.

Emphasis was on Scripture and the Three Rs; food was given where necessary; young criminals were taught even though they sometimes drove their teachers from the classroom in search of police protection.

When the 1870 Education Act made schooling compulsory to the age of thirteen, the London School Board employed an ex-policeman who with a constable searched cellars, sheds and alleys for vagrant boys. In the early hours, bottom centre, he is capturing boys under Charing Cross arches.

5

6

7

8

Somerset   Surrey   Norfolk   Arundel   Temple Station   Electra House   Milford Lane   Essex   Middle
House   Street   Street   Street   to be built here   to be built here   behind Gwynne & Co.   Street   Temple

Building the Embankment

A familiar stretch of the Thames is almost unrecognizable in the above view of the riverfront. This desolate expanse of no-man's-land is the Embankment between Somerset House, extreme left, and the Middle Temple, right, as it looked in the spring of 1869. After five years' work, the most revolutionary scheme in London planning had come almost to a halt. The new river wall was completed and a footpath, fenced off from the rough ground, open to the public. But the land between fence and houses could not be laid out with a carriageway and gardens until the underground railway had been dug. The extension of the Metropolitan Railway was an integral part of the Embankment, and the company had run out of money. But fresh capital was raised to complete the southern part of the 'Inner Circle', work was resumed, and fifteen months later the Embankment was formally opened.

Stretching for one and one-third miles from Blackfriars to Westminster, the Victoria Embankment transformed the north side of the river, and its new carriageway, sixty-four feet wide, relieved congestion in the Strand. As may be judged from the view of the same area seen from Somerset House, top right, it gave London one of its finest views looking towards St Paul's and the new public gardens. But there was a more mundane, practical reason for the whole project. A sanitary one.

By building out between 100 and 400 feet into the Thames, and reducing the river's width, it disposed of the mudflats, largely composed of sewage which contributed to 'The Great Stink' and which, at low tide, had to be treated with quantities of chalk, chloride of lime and carbolic acid. The Embankment also carried a conduit, eight feet in diameter, one of three west-to-east sewers. This was part of Sir Joseph Bazal-gette's system for intercepting sewage that previously would have gone into the river, and piping it to Barking.

Bazalgette was not just a great sanitary reformer. As chief engineer of the Metropolitan Board of Works, he was the designer and guiding genius of the Victoria Embankment. The first idea of a river wall had come from Wren after the Fire, and other schemes had been put forward in Parliament since

3

George IV's time. The line of the Embankment–the one adopted by Bazalgette–had been suggested nearly thirty years before, but had been blocked by wharf owners and those with a vested interest in keeping their river frontage. It was opposed by firms such as the City Gas Company which demanded that a covered way should be built under the road. This was to enable coal, landed by barge, to be carried up to the twin gasholders without interference from traffic. The Duke of Norfolk stipulated that Temple Station must have a flat roof so as not to impede his view.

Thirty-seven acres were reclaimed from the river. The ragged riverfront of projecting wharfs, docks and inlets was transformed, and one famous London landmark, Whitehall Stairs, sacrificed. In their place was built a massive brick and granite wall stretching for over a mile in a gentle, even curve. This retaining wall was sunk into the river bed thirty-two feet below high-water mark. Great watergates and steps were constructed, and there were two particularly happy pieces of decoration–lamp standards with dolphins round their bases, and seats supported by camels and sphinxes. Thousands of tons of earth were brought from Haverstock Hill for the public gardens.

The Embankment quickly attracted High Victorian architecture, notably the baronial New Scotland Yard; Whitehall Court with roof pinnacles to rival Chambord; the Accountants' Hall, lavishly Elizabethan; and

4

Sion College whose clerical Gothic façade defied the pagan classicism of the City of London School next door.

By projecting his Houses of Parliament out into the river, Barry had created an obstruction which made it impossible for the Embankment to carry through, as logically it should, to join up with the mile-long Chelsea Embankment (opened 1874). But continuity of a sort was achieved by the Albert Embankment (1869) on the other side of the river though only half of it was open to traffic.

1. The Embankment in 1869.

2. Section of the Embankment south of Charing Cross Station (here seen with the curved roof which collapsed in 1905). 1. Conduit carrying water, gas mains and telegraph lines. 2. Main sewer. 3. Underground railway. 4. Tube for a pneumatic railway under the river, abandoned 1866 before it was finished.

3. Victoria Embankment soon after its completion. The gasholders were demolished, 1873.

4. Northern stretch of the one-and-three-quarter-mile Albert Embankment during construction in 1866. St Thomas's Hospital was built on the ground sloping down to the riverside walk in 1871. The Albert Embankment cost £909,000 and was financed out of his own pocket by the builder Thomas Cubitt.

The Wheels of Mid-Victorian London

The great railway-building boom of the early 1860s was not just something created by businessmen; it found an excited response in the London public. They ate, drank, and slept railways. When Frith decided to devote more than a year to painting a single picture–his view of Paddington Station (7)–he did so with the shrewd knowledge that it would attract enormous topical interest. He was right. It sold for £4,500, and a dealer paid him an additional £750 for the privilege of having it exhibited at his gallery instead of the Royal Academy.

Crowding round the canvas in 1862, railway enthusiasts spotted that the engine looked like the famous G.W.R. express, *Hirondelle*, designed for the broad gauge by Daniel Gooch in 1848. The more aesthetically inclined noted that Brunel's station with its curved roof, its arches and pillars, its nave, transepts, and ornamental ironwork had almost the right to be regarded as a cathedral.

Not only railways, above ground, under ground, and crossing the Thames, were coping with travel mania and the necessity of the public to get to work from the expanding suburbs. London was at last getting a properly organized service of horse-buses. In 1856, nearly thirty years after their start, hundreds of independently run buses were bought up by the London General Omnibus Company and formed into a fleet with regular services, timetables and fixed fares. Until London Transport secured a monopoly in 1933, more than half London's buses were 'Generals'. A critic might object that inside passengers were 'packed like trussed fowls', but Egley has a romantic eye for travel in the glimpse he gives us, right, of the crowded interior of a horse-bus in 1859.

1

2

4

3

5

1. Horse trams did not really start until 1870, but an American, G. F. Train, pioneered three experimental routes in 1861 – a mile stretch down Bayswater Road from Marble Arch; along Victoria Street from Westminster Abbey to the station (shown in the earliest surviving photograph of a London tram, left); and from Westminster Bridge to Kennington. Two horses could pull up to fifty passengers – double the bus load. But trams caused obstruction in busy streets and often jumped the rails which, though only half an inch above the road surface, were objected to by other traffic. Train's trams did not catch on, and disappeared the next year.

2. The invention of Joseph Aloysius Hansom, who sold the patent for £10,000 in 1834, the hansom cab was faster, and cut more of a dash than the four-wheeled 'growler'. By 1886 there were 7,000 in London; 11,000 in 1900. Virtually all disappeared after the First World War. Convention forbade respectable young women to use them unchaperoned.

3. In 1856 there were 810 independently run buses, 600 of which were taken over by the London General Omnibus Company by the end of that year. One of the first private services taken over by the 'General' was the 'Favourite', one of whose dark green fleet is seen below, left. Route: Hornsey to London Bridge Station, via Holloway and Islington. Normal complement: twenty-two passengers – ten sitting outside, back to back, on a central 'knifeboard' (gradually replaced by 'garden seats' facing front in the 1880s). Speed: 5 m.p.h. Fare: 1d. a mile.

4 and 5. With the completion of the Inner Circle (page 306), excavation involved demolition of valuable City and residential property. In the stretch between Paddington and Notting Hill Gate, dug in 1866 (4), the line cut at right angles through fashionable Leinster Gardens. Two dummy, false-fronted houses (5) with the central sixteen windows blank were erected to disguise the gap in the terrace. They are still there.

6. Omnibus Life in London, by William Maw Egley.

7. Paddington Station – the bustle at departure time with a schoolboy being kissed good-bye, a bearded man (a self-portrait by Frith) arguing a fare with a cabby, and, right, a criminal being arrested.

6

7

I

Work and Cockney Impudence

July was very wet in the year that Ford Madox Brown started the painting called *Work*, above. Excavations were going on in the road leading up to Hampstead Heath and, with a Pre-Raphaelite passion for realism, he preferred to draw from life. So, on rainy days, he set up his canvas, six and a half feet long, in an unhorsed four-wheel cab. He was not an artist to hurry. It was eleven years later–1862–before he finished his picture which exalts the virtue of industry and carries the inscription: 'In the sweat of thy face shalt thou eat bread.'

Actual people modelled for nearly every figure. The two apparently indolent men on the right–'the brain workers'–are the bearded Carlyle and the Rev. F. D. Maurice, organizer of the Working Men's College. The painting had 'a message' of the kind in which visitors to the Royal Academy revelled. Each figure was symbolic. There was the central one, whom Brown described as 'the young navvy in the pride of manly health and beauty'. The rich passersby and the ragged child show the contrast of capital and labour.

This painstaking style of painting, to be seen in the 'conversation pieces' and 'problem pictures' of mid-Victorian artists (with titles like *The Last Day in the Old Home* and *A Hopeless Dawn*), was to be radically challenged in the 1870s. The method and subjects chosen by J. McNeill Whistler were very different. Whistler would step out of his house on Chelsea Embankment–No 2, Lindsey Row–see the lights reflected in the river and the rising evening mist. He stored the impression in his mind, and then–in the phrase of a denigrator–he would 'knock off' a painting in a couple of days. This was how he came to create his famous *Nocturne in Black and Gold: The Falling Rocket* which he said was not intended to be a literal picture of fireworks at Cremorne, but 'an artistic arrangement'.

The impressionism of the new Aesthetic Movement, drawing its inspiration from Japan, was not calculated to please older pundits. To John Ruskin, the prophet of the Pre-Raphaelites, it was abstract, foreign and–even worse–immoral. Outraged by the 'nocturne' which was exhibited at the Grosvenor Gallery in New Bond Street,

Ruskin stormed out and wrote: 'I have seen and heard much of Cockney impudence before now, but never expected to hear a coxcomb ask two hundred guineas for flinging a pot of paint in the public's face.'

In the famous libel action which Whistler brought against the critic, the picture was brought into court upside down (laughter). Ruskin's counsel wanted to know if the artist was asking two hundred guineas for 'the labour of two days'. Looking, we may surmise, very much as Max Beerbohm depicted him on another occasion, Whistler made his immortal reply. 'No,' he said, 'I ask it for the knowledge of a lifetime.' Ruskin lost the case, but the damages were only a farthing, and Whistler's costs crippling.

Frith was one of the witnesses against Whistler, and his *Private View of the Royal Academy*, right, exhibited four years later, contains reminders of the *cause célèbre*. His aim was to 'hit at the folly of listening to self-elected critics in the matters of taste'. So he shows Oscar Wilde (W. S. Gilbert's 'greenery-yallery, Grosvenor Gallery' young man) surrounded by 'a herd of eager worshippers'. The women and child on the

left Frith called 'a family of pure aesthetes absorbed in the affected study of the pictures'. Among others depicted were Du Maurier, who regularly ridiculed the new aesthetes in *Punch*, Baron Huddlestone, who presided at the trial, and Sir Frederick Leighton, President of the Royal Academy, who, called as an expert witness, escaped the hearing because he went to Windsor to be knighted.

1. Hampstead – seen by Ford Madox Brown.

2. Whistler in the witness box – seen by Max Beerbohm.

3. The New Bond Street entrance to the Grosvenor Gallery opened in 1877, the year when Whistler's picture was exhibited. The owner was the art patron, Sir Coutts Lindsay. The portico designed by Palladio came from the Church of Santa Lucia in Venice. Now the Aeolian Hall.

4. Burlington House – seen by W. P. Frith. From left to right: Anthony Trollope, bearded, in a top hat and marking his catalogue, looks at the 'aesthetes', one of whom wears a green dress, amber beads and a sunflower; behind them Mr Gladstone, bareheaded, and George Du Maurier in top hat; Browning, bearded and white-haired, talks to another aesthetic lady; T. H. Huxley with side-whiskers; Frith, in the background, leans forward; Countess of Lonsdale, seated, talks to Sir Frederick Leighton, bearded and standing on her left; Archbishop of York; Lily Langtry; Wilde instructs his satellites; behind him Ellen Terry and Irving; Augustus Sala in white waistcoat; Millais in top hat, far right. Frith obtained private sittings from many of the people he portrayed.

Two Monuments

Within a few days in January 1878, London lost a famous monument, and gained an alien one that was even older. While workmen with a steam crane were demolishing Temple Bar, Cleopatra's Needle was towed up the Thames and brought alongside Adelphi Steps on the Embankment.

Cleopatra's Needle was deviously acquired, grudgingly received, and curiously delivered. After Napoleon's defeat in Egypt, the British forces had subscribed to bring home the monolith, lying prostrate in the sand of Alexandria, as a victorious trophy. But its 193 tons proved too heavy to move. Then, in 1819, the Turkish ruler of Egypt formally presented it to the British Government. Though the offer was renewed a number of times over the years, the gift was constantly declined. An idea to bring it over for the Great Exhibition was turned down as too costly.

Only when the land on which it lay was sold in 1867, and the purchaser, a Greek merchant, threatened to break it up, was £10,000 privately raised for its transport. No naval help was offered; it was ridiculed as 'fatally suggestive of a factory chimney'; a site in Parliament Square (where a trial model was erected) was rejected; and the Board of Works only found a place for it on the Embankment after District Railway officials had protested that, if put in Embankment Gardens, it might crash through on to the trains.

A special submarine-shaped cylinder was designed in which the obelisk was towed by

a small steamer from Alexandria. This had to be cut adrift during a storm in the Bay of Biscay. A lifeboat was lowered to rescue the crew of eight clinging to the superstructure of the cylinder. The lifeboat was sunk and the six sailors manning it drowned. The crew were rescued, and the cylinder picked up by another ship and taken into a Spanish port.

Three months later it was brought safely to England, raised horizontally on a wooden scaffold by hydraulic jacks, and then tipped to the vertical. On the day it was lowered into place, two earthenware jars were placed inside the pedestal. Their contents included Queen Victoria's portrait, Bradshaw's Railway Guide, and that day's copy of *The Times*. A rare photograph, extreme left, shows Cleopatra's Needle with the guarding sphinxes facing *outwards*. By a later contractor's mistake, they were turned inwards as they are today. With an equally irreverent disregard for the dignity of foreign treasures, a contemporary doggerel ran:

This monument, as some supposes,
Was looked upon of old by Moses.
It passed in time from Greeks to Turks,
And was stuck up here by the Board of Works!

Temple Bar, the historic boundary between the City and Westminster, had existed in various forms since the thirteenth century. In its final design by Wren, it had stood for 200 years when a general outcry that it was a traffic bottleneck–'the bone in the throat of Fleet Street'–brought about its demolition.

Wren's Temple Bar (1672) replaced a wooden gateway (built in or before 1502) which was repaired (1554) before the newly married Queen Mary and Philip of Spain were received there. In earlier centuries the boundary was marked with posts and chains–a bar set up by the Knights Templars as the City's western limits outside the walls. By tradition, every sovereign is met at the bar by the Lord Mayor who hands and takes back a ceremonial sword, a gesture symbolizing the City's loyalty and independence.

After the City Council conceded the long battle to retain the gateway, it was knocked down and lay in a thousand stone blocks for nearly ten years in a yard off Farringdon Street. It was then given to Sir Henry Meux, the brewer, and still stands at his country house, Theobald Park, Cheshunt.

In the view, top left, looking west from Fleet Street into the Strand, trees round St Clement Danes and Wych Street (demolished 1899) are seen in the distance. Behind hoardings on the right the Law Courts are being built. Over the gateway and lit by the central window, is a room leased by Child's Bank (on which Temple Bar abuts) for the storage of ledgers and cash books. Two years after the demolition, a memorial to Temple Bar, left, was erected in its place.

1. The sixty-eight-foot granite obelisk on the Embankment known as Cleopatra's Needle is about 3,400 years old, and by far the oldest outdoor monument in London. It is one of a pair originally erected by Thothmes III in front of the temple of the sun god at Heliopolis, c. 1450 B.C. Augustus Caesar ordered their removal to Alexandria in 23 B.C. where they were placed in front of the palace where Cleopatra had died seven years before. This is the excuse for the popular name.

2. Launching the obelisk at Alexandria where it had collapsed in the sand during the sixteenth century. The second of the pair – presumably the one seen still standing – was given to New York, and is now in Central Park.

3. The voyage.

4. Its erection on the Embankment.

5 and 6. Temple Bar shortly before and during its demolition in 1878.

7. The memorial designed by Sir Horace Jones with the City dragon on the top.

Turrets, Pinnacles, and Gothic Follies

When Gilbert Scott settled at his drawing-board to design St Pancras Station, James Penthorne to prepare his plans for the Record Office in Chancery Lane, and G. E. Street the nearby Law Courts, their instinctive choice of style was Gothic. They chose it in preference to such lively alternatives as Greek Revival (Royal Exchange), Byzantine (Westminster Cathedral), Scottish Medieval (New Scotland Yard), French Renaissance (Grosvenor Hotel), Italian Cinquecento (Foreign Office).

But in pirating just about every alien and historical style under the sun, the mid-Victorian architect acted deliberately. If 'a distinctive style of our own' existed, said Gilbert Scott, he would have used it. But, he went on, 'Are we to invent a spick-and-span new style?' Already he was anticipating those critics who were to query if fourteenth-century Gothic was suitable for a nineteenth-century railway station.

With the Houses of Parliament, Pugin and Barry set the predominating High Victorian style. In the 1860s Gothic reared its pinnacles and pointed windows in every district of London. Its ecclesiastic flavour suited a pious age, and architects happily adapted it from religious to secular use.

Classical Revival and Italian Renaissance fought a losing battle despite the championship of Lord Palmerston who, as Prime Minister, rejected Scott's designs for the Foreign Office because they were Gothic. Scott promptly changed them to an Early Venetian palazzo style ('a regular mongrel affair', growled Palmerston), and then made a full compromise. Much of his Gothic detail for Whitehall (but not the whole plan, as legend has it) went into St Pancras.

Though eccentric detail and exotic flamboyance have been so concealed by soot as to be almost invisible to later generations, the eclectic, inventive, historically obsessed, Victorian builder was to leave London with a weird and wonderful inheritance.

2

1

3

This is to be seen at its strangest in the Tower House, a capricious folly in Melbury Road, Kensington, far left. It was the home of its designer, William Burges, who gave full rein to his love for medieval turrets, pointed roofs, and mullioned windows.

The late-Victorian architect did not reserve ecclesiastical detail for churches. In the Venetian and Lombardy Gothic St Pancras can be seen ornamentation lifted from English and French cathedrals. And when it came to an actual church, of course, no excuse was needed. At All Saints, Marylebone, right, William Butterfield, a devout Anglican, spared the congregation nothing. Butterfield's apologists claim that his cult of ugliness was deliberate–that simple, good taste might smack of too-sensuous pleasure!

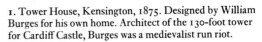

4

5

6

7

1. Tower House, Kensington, 1875. Designed by William Burges for his own home. Architect of the 130-foot tower for Cardiff Castle, Burges was a medievalist run riot.

2. The library at Tower House was lined with bookcases (after the style of the armoire at Noyon Cathedral in France), each painted by different artists ranging from Poynter to Burne-Jones. The mantelpiece was the chief feature of every room. Here, crenellated, machicolated, and with arrow-loops, it is sculptured as a Tower of Babel with parts of speech, emerging, as human figures, from the central portal.

3. Harrington Gardens, Kensington, 1881. After a visit to Holland, Ernest George brought back sketchbooks of Flemish early Renaissance detail which, with his partner Harold Peto, he adapted to a whole colony of houses for very rich clients. This elaborate façade is of No 39, built for W. S. Gilbert, the playwright.

4. All Saints, Margaret Street, Marylebone, 1859. Principal London church of William Butterfield, Anglican and designer of nearly 100 emphatically Gothic churches. His ruthless restorations put their dread 'Victorian' mark on dozens of innocent parish churches. For All Saints, where an awkward site prevented Gothic proportions, he used a welter of fourteenth-century detail with red brick mixed with black stone zig-zag bands in the style of Siena. The interior was smothered in geometric designs in a wild variety of colours.

5. Prudential Assurance Company, Holborn, 1879 and 1899. In medieval fortress style, this office started a vogue in terracotta which blazed its fiery trail through late Victorian London. Alfred Waterhouse used terracotta again in St Paul's School, Hammersmith, and University College Hospital, and its employment by other architects led to an industry. Highly regarded in his day, Waterhouse grew to be derided after his death (1905), but his qualities as a designer have become reluctantly acknowledged.

6. Columbia Market, Bethnal Green, 1869. Appalled by the dishonesty of East End street traders, the Baroness Burdett-Coutts built the market at a cost of £200,000. Fish and meat were to be made available at fair prices to the poor. The architect, H. A. Darbishire, used ecclesiastical Gothic to emphasize godly purpose. A quadrangle was entered by a gatehouse. There were cloistered walks, a central tower like a Flemish guildhall, and a great hall carrying such carved inscriptions as: 'Speak everyman truth with his neighbour'. Resented by the traders, the market was a failure, and handed back to the Baroness within five years. It was let as workshops, and demolished in 1958. Darbishire also designed the nearby Peabody Trust flats for the poor, with vaguely Gothic windows.

7. St Pancras Station, 1874. View from the back, showing how the glass and iron roofed train shed (with an unprecedented unsupported span of 240 feet) was hidden behind Gilbert Scott's façade. Scott used cathedral detail for the luxurious hotel accommodating 600 guests (turned into railway offices 1935) that went across the front of the terminus. This turreted castle, fairy tale from a distance (page 335), even had linenfold panelling on the ticket-office.

Three Violent Years

It began with the tinkle of glass as stones smashed the windows of clubs in Pall Mall; it ended with a hoarse roar of victory by East End dockers when they were granted a basic rate of 6d. an hour. In the three years that separated these events, London became a violent battleground.

Until the 1880s, London workers had very few trade unions. At the first Trades Union Congress, held twenty years earlier, skilled crafts had been well represented; but unskilled labourers were unorganized to face the threat of foreign competition and seasonal unemployment. In this, London was far behind the provinces. So it was not surprising that strikes, street fighting, and mass demonstrations flared up in the great depression of the eighties.

To the rich, and to the prosperous middle classes, these eruptions were more ominous than the roll of tumbrils. The supercilious smiles on the faces of clubmen watching the surge of unemployed quickly changed as their windows were shattered. In well-ordered, comfortable lives this violent demonstration in 1886 was a disquieting phenomenon. The behaviour of 'the ruffianly mob' was roundly denounced as 'brutal violence and infamous rapine'.

The men's leader John Burns (arrested for incitement, but acquitted) had to be reckoned as something more serious than a rabble-rousing orator. H. M. Hyndman, Marxist founder of the Social Democratic Federation, also arrested that day, could no longer be dismissed simply as a crank from a rich family who had turned his back on Cambridge and the City. The wealthy had to get used to the idea that not all Socialists wore cloth caps, and that conventional remedies like contributions to the Lord Mayor's unemployment fund would no longer quell the rising tide of discontent.

The most highly organized rally came in the November of the following year when 100,000 marched on Trafalgar Square. Three Fabians – the artist and poet William Morris, Annie Besant, freethinker and brilliant woman orator, and the then-unknown Bernard Shaw – were among those who marched together from Clerkenwell. They were met by 4,000 police, and dispersed by mounted Life Guards and Grenadiers with fixed bayonets.

'I have never seen anything like the brutality of the police,' wrote Eleanor Marx, daughter of a famous father, to the *Pall Mall Gazette*. 'I was in the thick of the fight at Parliament Street, and afterwards in Northumberland Avenue. I got pretty roughly used myself.' This was 'Bloody Sunday', a rather overdramatic description of a day with only

one fatality, but still a landmark in the development of British Socialism.

That Socialism had teeth as well as a noisy voice showed itself seven months later when Annie Besant stirred the exploited girls working at Bryant and May's match factory to revolt. The firm in Bow was paying a twenty-three per cent dividend to share-holders, but as little as 4s. a week to girls working in bad conditions, with arbitrary fines, and in danger of disease from the phosphorus. The 1,400 girls came out on strike, won the day, and formed their own union. In the spring of the next year– 1889–another union was organized by gasworkers in Canning Town who quickly achieved their first objective–an eight-hour day. Will Thorne was its leader, with Eleanor Marx as his assistant.

All this served as a preparation for the first really big test of trade unionism. This was the dock strike which paralysed Thames shipping in August 1889. To get more reasonable wages and conditions, 60,000 dock workers came out, and won a great deal of popular sympathy through the carefully organized propaganda of John Burns. There were huge marches through the City with bands and tableaux. Daily on Tower Hill, and with fiery oratory, Burns exhorted thousands of near-starving men to stand out for a basic 6d. an hour. The bitter battle was won by two strange interventions. Australian dockers sent £30,000 to the strike fund at a critical moment; then the Church, in the conciliatory figure of Cardinal Manning, negotiated with the dock companies and they agreed to pay 'the dockers' tanner'.

1. Whipped up by speeches in Trafalgar Square, 2,000 unemployed march through the West End in February 1886, carrying red flags, cudgels, and stones. At the bottom of St James's Street on their way to Hyde Park, they smash the windows of the Conservative Club, seen in the background, and go on to loot shops.

2. In the struggle between police and Clerkenwell demonstrators in St Martin's Lane, Helen Taylor – Socialist woman leader and stepdaughter of John Stuart Mill – fights for her flag on 'Bloody Sunday' – 13 November 1887.

3 Another clash on 'Bloody Sunday'. In Parliament Square by Westminster Hall, the police are caught between two converging contingents. In the foreground are South London demonstrators who have come over Westminster Bridge. Those from Vauxhall and Battersea surge from the Victoria Tower direction.

4. Annie Besant and Herbert Burrows, her assistant, with some of the matchgirls whose strike they organized. 'White Slavery in London' was the title of Mrs Besant's explosive articles exposing their working conditions and the risk of a disease called 'phossy-jaw'.

5. 'Courage! . . . Relief is at hand . . . I see on the horizon a silver gleam . . . the silver sheen of the full round orb of the dockers' tanner.' – John Burns speaking on Tower Hill, September 1889.

6. From the edge of a fountain in Trafalgar Square, an officer instructs special constables issued with truncheons to deal with demonstrators.

7. In the critical last days before their victory, strikers mass outside West India Dock gates to vote for the Manifesto demanding 6d. an hour.

New Scotland Yard and 'The Ripper'

After sixty years, the police were in urgent need of new quarters. A force of nearly 15,000 was administered in conditions of confusion. In Whitehall Place (page 260) staircases were piled with books, and the Commissioner and his hard-pressed men were spread over several buildings. So it was with relief that in 1890 the staff of Scotland Yard, carrying the old name with them, moved to the Embankment. Norman Shaw's building, sombre as a Highland keep, was designed to suit its name and function, and– gentle hint to the criminal underworld–it was partly constructed in granite quarried by Dartmoor convicts.

While New Scotland Yard was still only half-built, and as if urging the necessity for its completion, five murders were committed in the East End within ten weeks. All the victims were prostitutes, or near-prostitutes. All had their throats cut, and were dismembered or sexually mutilated. The body of the last, and only attractive victim, Mary Kelly, a blue-eyed girl of twenty-five, was stripped, carved up, and her parts–breasts, heart, and kidneys–laid out in a symmetrical pattern on a table by her bedside.

These were the 'Jack the Ripper' murders which created hysterical terror in Whitechapel in the autumn of 1888. More than 600 plainclothes policemen infiltrated a quarter of a square mile of sordid streets near Spitalfields. Their failure to catch the murderer prompted testy advice from the Queen at Windsor, and led to the resignation of Sir Charles Warren, the ineffectual Police Commissioner who at one point was pursued on Tooting Common by bloodhounds whom he was training to track the Ripper.

The first definite Ripper murder took place in the early hours of 31 August in Buck's Row (now Durward Street), Whitechapel. Polly Nicholls, aged forty-two, a gin-soaked doss-house inmate was found with her throat cut. The second (Annie Chapman, aged forty-seven) followed a week later in Hanbury Street just over half a mile away. Then one night, 30 September, two more unfortunates (Elizabeth Stride, forty-five, and Catherine Eddowes, forty-three) were killed and carved up with a sharp knife within forty-five minutes of each other. Finally, Mary Kelly met the most violent end of them all after taking a man back to her dingy 4s. 6d.-a-week room in Miller's Court. This courtyard was off Dorset (now Duval) Street, the haunt of beggars, petty thieves and prostitutes.

Three days before the double murder, a letter was received by a Fleet Street news-agency asserting, 'My knife's so nice and sharp, I want to get to work right away. . . .'

1

It was signed 'Jack the Ripper'–the first use of the name. That this was not just one of hundreds of hoaxes seemed proved by the threat to cut off the ears of the next victims –an attempt started, but interrupted, on both Stride and Eddowes.

Despite Warren's bloodhounds, night patrols by amateur vigilantes, and the concentrated police hunt, the Ripper was never found. Then, and ever since, theories have raged about his identity. He was a butcher run amok called Leather Apron, a homicidal Polish Jew, a mad Russian spy and–the most widely held view because of his supposed surgical skill–a doctor with a sexual abhorrence of immoral women.

Because Mary Kelly's inquest was summarily closed, and investigations called off very soon after this fifth murder, it has to be supposed that the police received some private, but never disclosed, information. This was possibly told them by the family of a man, allegedly sexually insane, who drowned himself in the Thames soon after the Miller's Court murder. Improbably–yet most likely of all in a welter of improbability–he was a bachelor of forty-one, M. J. Druitt, Wykehamist, Middle Temple barrister, and at the time of the Ripper murders, a schoolmaster in Eliot Place, Blackheath.

1. New Scotland Yard was built on the site of the proposed National Opera House, a third larger than Covent Garden, started in 1875. After £97,000 had been spent, the opera house was abandoned for lack of funds. It remained derelict for nearly ten years. Then it was demolished, and Norman Shaw's police headquarters built on the foundations. Some of the basement dressing-rooms were incorporated in the new building, and a tunnel from Westminster Underground Station (planned for opera-goers) was retained for secret concentrations of police in emergencies. Already too small when occupied, two annexes followed. The present Scotland Yard opened in Broadway in 1967.

2. The first victim–Polly Nicholls–lying on her back with her throat cut, eyes open, bonnet knocked off, and, as the constable noted, 'warm as a toasted crumpet'.

3. During the building of New Scotland Yard in 1888, a woman's torso, headless and without limbs, was discovered hidden in the foundations. Inevitably it was associated with the 'Ripper' murders that started ten days later. But as 'The Whitehall Mystery' was never cleared up, the new police headquarters were, ironically, built on the site of an unsolved crime.

4. The two bloodhounds, Burgho and Barnaby, who so signally failed to find the Ripper, but successfully pursued the Police Commissioner.

5. *Illustrated Police News* picture of how Catherine Eddowes's kidney was sent through the post to the Whitechapel Vigilance Committee with a note in 'The Ripper's' writing.

6. Dorset Street, off which was Miller's Court where Mary Kelly, the last victim, went with her murderer.

7. Mary Kelly invites the Ripper into the building where she has a cheap room in Miller's Court. The drawing is based on an eyewitness description that he was well-dressed and had a curling moustache. The doctor's bag is an artist's touch.

2

3

4

6

7

327

Electric Light and the Telephone

About two years after Paris, and using the French system invented by a Russian engineer, Paul Jablochkoff, London saw the first large-scale experiment in street lighting. This was on the Embankment in 1878, and followed closely on smaller displays at Billingsgate and outside the Gaiety in the Strand. Further installations were tried out on Holborn Viaduct, and, among other places, at the Reform Club and the Langham Hotel. But this system which relied on erratic carbon rods was almost immediately overtaken by Edison's and Swan's far more efficient incandescent lamps. Enclosed filament bulbs were used for the first electric lighting of a theatre–the Savoy in 1881–and their use spread rapidly. A pioneer power station opened at the Grosvenor Gallery, Bond Street, two years later, and in 1888 this was boosted by the first really massive station–at Deptford–which carried high voltage current into central London by cable laid alongside the railways.

The telephone, an American invention, reached London in the same year as street lighting. In the following year, 1879, the first exchange opened in Coleman Street in the City. Seven or eight original subscribers increased to 914 in less than two years. Individual lines came in overhead to the roof of exchanges, and joined up by multi-line cables with other exchanges. By the end of 1882 subscribers had the use of fifteen exchanges including Westminster, Chancery Lane, Bermondsey and Southwark. Link-ups with other cities followed more slowly–with Brighton (1884), Birmingham (1890) and, by submarine cable, with Paris (1891). Several rival companies were gradually absorbed by the National Telephone Company which was to have a virtual monopoly until the Post Office took over in 1911. Though acclaimed, the telephone caused one newspaper, concerned with privacy, to ask: 'What will become of the sanctity of the domestic hearth?'

1. Wonder on the Embankment. Between Westminster and Waterloo Bridges, twenty lamps were lit by the Jablochkoff system of carbon 'candles' in glass globes.

2. The lamps were powered from a 60 h.p. semi-portable steam engine in a wooden shed at Charing Cross.

3. Within ten years the system required power stations on the scale of Deptford, which had two 10,000 h.p. generators for distribution of electricity all over London.

4. Overhead wires at Coleman Street, 1883.

5. Girls at the Eastcheap Exchange.

Start of the London County Council

To reform and co-ordinate the government of London, a new administration began work early in 1889. The London County Council assumed powers over parts of Surrey, Kent and Middlesex. It was ultimately to extend over twenty-eight boroughs and a total of 117 square miles. The boundaries of County of London–the area shaded on the map– have been taken, in general, as the limits of London in this book. Previous to the Local Government Act, by which the L.C.C. was created, street maintenance, fire-fighting, housing, help for the poor and all the other varied services of a great city had been carried out by overlapping, sometimes conflicting, bodies. There was jobbery, and officials of the Metropolitan Board of Works were accused of corruption. But though an overall government was obviously needed, the City fought the idea for twenty-five years. Determined to keep its power and traditional privileges, the City financed widespread propaganda, and even hired people to break up meetings where municipal reform was demanded. When the change came, it succeeded in retaining its autonomy–a small, independent county within the County of London.

1. Lord Rosebery, the Chairman, addressing the first official meeting of the L.C.C. in 1889 in the council chamber of the old Metropolitan Board of Works. Two women members are seated, just out of view on the right, and a third is trying to enter through the door on the left. They were later disqualified, and it was not until 1907 that women had the right to sit on the Council. The Council inherited the Board's premises in Spring Gardens, off Trafalgar Square, which it used until the formal opening of County Hall in 1922.

2. The L.C.C. area (shaded) was extended (to perimeter line) with the inauguration of the Greater London Council in 1965. Many old boroughs disappeared with the change. In the 616 square miles of Greater London live eight million people–more than one sixth of the total population of Britain.

3. County Hall–Ralph Knott's winning design. Whitehall, the Adelphi and Aldwych were suggested sites for the new building before a wharf called Pedlar's Acre was chosen in 1905. World War I interrupted building.

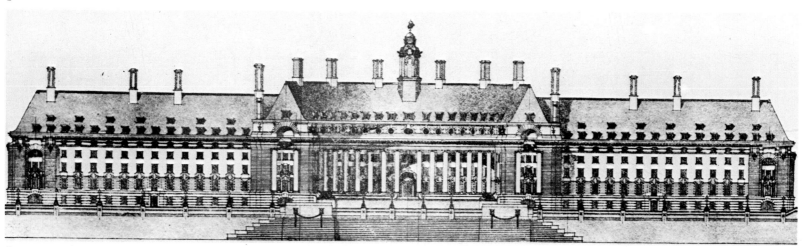

The Squaring of Piccadilly Circus

Two important thoroughfares were opened in the 1880s: Charing Cross Road and Shaftesbury Avenue. They were created by the Board of Works which was concerned about providing a north-south route between Bloomsbury and the West End to cope with the increased traffic to and from the northern railway stations. Shaftesbury Avenue, over a mile long, was driven through some of the worst slums in London, and this took nearly ten years because 3,000 displaced people had to be rehoused. Many of them were given new homes in artisan dwellings built in the Newport Market area on either side of Charing Cross Road.

The most radical change took place at the southern end of Shaftesbury Avenue where it was obviously necessary for traffic to have free access into Piccadilly Circus, then called Regent Circus South. This meant the demolition of a triangular block of buildings (as shown in the unique sketch, bottom right, drawn on 29 July 1885) and the disappearance of Titchborne Street. (The pediment of the new London Pavilion–two months from completion–is just visible on the right.) It was also the beginning of the end of Nash's small, delightful circus. With the opening of Shaftesbury Avenue in 1886, the Circus, made up of four concave segments and concealed crossroad (page 237), was transformed into an irregular square or rhomboid. It became a vortex of bustling, converging streets–a 'horrible shape', thought the sculptor Alfred Gilbert, only suitable for a public lavatory. One idea which might have prevented architectural disaster was to extend the Regent Street Quadrant to form a complete crescent that would lead in a natural curve into Shaftesbury Avenue. But this never happened. Instead, the other segments were demolished and the Circus lost all its original character in a bizarre blaze of illuminated signs, the first of which appeared in the 1890s.

Though he shuddered, Gilbert provided a central feature–Eros. Then thirty-two, and rigidly opposed to 'coat-and-trousers' statuary, he accepted the commission to design the Shaftesbury Memorial Fountain on one condition. It must *symbolize* the work of Lord Shaftesbury, much of whose work for the poor had been done in the area through which was built the Avenue named after him. Instead of a formal statue, he proposed a figure of 'Love sending forth indiscriminately, yet with purpose, his missiles of kindness. . . .' Whether he also intended a pun–the arrow *shaft* being *buried* in the ground–is uncertain.

His inspired creation aroused hostility. A naked boy to commemorate an august Victorian philanthropist was thought undignified, if not immoral. Soured by the reception, and his financial ruin precipitated by the cost, Gilbert later took refuge abroad. On one of his rare returns–to receive a knighthood in 1932–he was to be ironically amused that his despised Eros had become almost a national emblem.

1. Piccadilly Circus before 1885. View looking north-east with Lower Regent Street to the right, and Coventry Street straight ahead. The columned fronts of the auctioneer's and railway offices form two concave segments of Nash's original Circus. Already debased by hoardings, this was destroyed when the triangular block of buildings backing on Titchborne Street was demolished.

2. Piccadilly Circus after 1894. This photograph is taken from an almost identical viewpoint. The auctioneer's segment and the triangular block have disappeared. Titchborne Street is now part of the so-called Circus. The rebuilt London Pavilion and Shaftesbury Avenue stand revealed. The Oyster Supper Rooms have been replaced by Scott's Restaurant (1894-1968).

3. Alfred Gilbert in his Fulham Road Studio at work on his statue of Eros.

4. The finished statue which first shocked London.

5. Before 1885, showing Nash's Circus.

6. After 1894, when it became an irregular square.

7. The 1885 demolition which destroyed the symmetry of the Circus so cunningly contrived by Nash. Ever since then plans for giving the Circus some architectural form have been bedevilled by conflicting private interests, Crown leases which have fallen in at irregular intervals, and uncertainty about what the 'Hub of Empire' should look like.

3

4

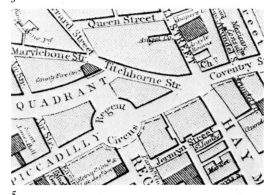

5

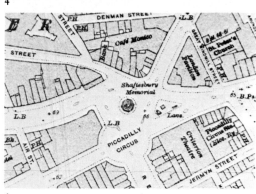

6

7

United Service   Athenaeum   Travellers'   Reform   Carlton

Sherry and Leather Armchairs

'Very handsome and admirably fitted up, affording every possible comfort,' acknowledged Baedeker in his description of West End clubs towards the end of the century. Some, like White's and Boodle's, owed their origins to the coffee houses and the gamesters of the eighteenth century; but it was in the long prosperous peace after Waterloo, in the high summer and mellow autumn of Victoria's reign, that clubs grew into institutions. Built on the scale of palaces, and often in the same style, they gave a young man the assurance of a Renaissance prince as he climbed the staircase at the Travellers' in the footsteps of Talleyrand, or sat down to a sumptuous meal prepared in Soyer's kitchens at the Reform. At the Athenaeum, scholars had the best club library in London. At the Garrick, actors could gain inspiration from walls hung with pictures of Macklin and Rich. An officer lunching in a window table at the United Service's might be in Wellington's favourite seat, and recall that here the Iron Duke once queried a 3d. overcharge on the meat course.

Every interest was served. The Turf, Arts, Royal Thames Yacht Club, Farmers, Guards – their names were self-explanatory. All offered the ultimate in unthinking comfort. Here a gentleman could sip sherry and snooze away his life in a deep leather armchair until, as the apocryphal story has it, a club servant was summoned and told sternly: 'Kindly remove the General. He's been dead for three days.'

1. From his country exile a nineteenth-century clubman cried in anguished verse: 'Oh, give me the sweet shady side of Pall Mall!' This is the shady south side looking, in 1839, as it was to remain, almost unchanged, for a century. We see: the United Service (by Nash, 1826); the Athenaeum (Decimus Burton, 1830) with a frieze copied from the Parthenon; The Travellers' (Charles Barry, 1832); the Reform (Barry, 1839), the great Liberal stronghold in the style of the Farnese Palace, Rome; and the corner of the Carlton (Robert Smirke, 1836), the famous Conservative club (rebuilt by his brother, Sydney, 1856, bombed 1940), now in St James's. Out of view, and also in Pall Mall, is the Oxford and Cambridge (Robert Smirke, 1838). The artist has his back to what will be the Junior Carlton (1869) and the Army and Navy (1851).

2. A great clubman when Prince of Wales, the future Edward VII leaves his club possibly with Lord Rothschild. His fire-fighting companion, Capt. Sir Eyre Massey Shaw, watches their late night departure.

3. In the hall of the Athenaeum in the nineties are four judges, a bishop, and the organist of Westminster Abbey.

4. Window table, looking out on Duke of York's column, in the dining-room of the Athenaeum where Longfellow was once entertained, Theodore Hook ordered brandies in what his fellow members ironically called 'Temperance Corner', Dickens preferred sandwiches at lunchtime, and Darwin proclaimed that he dined 'like a lord'.

5. The Athenaeum library of 70,000 books.

6. Reading room at the Garrick where the order to the servant has evidently been carried out.

7. The Card Room at the United Service. Gambling has always been a major club pastime, and, at Brooks's, Fox is said to have staked £5,000 on a single card at faro.

3

4

5

6

7

Sport at the Oval

Thirty-six years after ten acres of market garden at Kennington had been converted into a cricket ground with turf from Tooting Common, the first Test Match in England was played at the Oval. This was in 1880. The ground's shape was determined by a building plan for the site, never fulfilled, with houses laid out in a double crescent forming an oval. Captained by Lord Harris, and with W. G. Grace and his two brothers in the side, England only narrowly beat Australia. A crowd of 20,000 saw 'W.G.' score 152.

At the Oval two years later England was to lose. This match was 'the death of English cricket', and the *Sporting Times* minted an immortal expression with the sentence: 'The body will be cremated and the Ashes taken to Australia.'

The Oval was used for various sports, and was the scene of the first Cup Final in 1871 when fifteen clubs, thirteen of them London sides, competed. The Cup was won by the Wanderers composed of former public-school boys. A year later the first international Rugby match in England was played there. The game, left, in which leg-hacking and fierce charging were permitted, 'excited more interest than any previous match in the metropolis', according to *The Times*.

Fairy-tale St Pancras

In John O'Connor's romantic view, top right, down the Pentonville Road, St Pancras Station, wrapped in a golden mist, looks like a fairy-tale castle. The date must be 1883 or after, for that was the year the London Street Tramways opened their route from King's Cross to the Angel. A third horse is seen attached to the tram to get it up the hill. This route was one of a whole network established by tramway companies in the twenty years after 1870. The City and the West End kept free of trams, regarding them as obstructions.

Tower Bridge Opening

Tower Bridge, right, which took nine years to build, was needed to relieve congestion on the other City bridges, but could not be a barrier to large vessels wanting to enter the Upper Pool. The designers hit on the idea of a double-drawbridge. Two bascules, each weighing over a thousand tons, are lifted by hydraulic machinery housed in the flanking towers. It was hoped that the Gothic design would blend in with the nearby Tower.

1. Lord Harris saving a four.
2. International – England beat Scotland.
3. St Pancras from the Pentonville Road.
4. Opening of Tower Bridge, 1894, and (5) photograph, taken soon afterwards, showing traffic waiting for lowering of bascules.

5

3

4

I

Birth of 'The New Journalism'

Through the wet streets of the City on a dismal November day, a gilded coach arrives at the Mansion House. Baroque, ponderous, and looking as if it has come out of a pantomime, the coach weighs nearly four tons, and needs six horses. In the background are the Bank of England and the Royal Exchange. The crowds, braving the weather, have come to see the great annual pageant of the Lord Mayor's Show.

Until 1856 the spectacle was provided by a procession on the Thames, but when the City's sole powers over the river were taken over by the Thames Conservancy Board, it was decided to hold the show 'entirely by land'. For many years the traditional day was 9 November, and on this particular occasion–1888–the new Lord Mayor, Sir James Whitehead, had some of his thunder stolen by Jack the Ripper. Newsboys shouting, 'Murder! Horrible murder in Whitechapel!'

had a ready-made sale among the spectators lining the streets. The midday editions told of the death of Mary Kelly, the Ripper's last victim.

At this time, the public had the choice of a dozen London evening papers. For lurid details they would not buy the 'literary' evenings like the *Pall Mall Gazette*, small-circulation journals kept going as a hobby by wealthy proprietors. For all the gore that was fit to print, they would prefer the new energetic competitors–the *Evening News*, the *Star*, and the *Evening Standard*. The former two both started in this decade. With the purchase of the *Evening News* by the Harmsworths in 1894, the headlines were to reflect a new spirit–'Servant's Baby in Box', 'Was it Suicide or Apoplexy?' The battle for mass circulation was on.

At the birth of the New Journalism, 'the Street' was startled by W. T. Stead's exposé of child prostitution, and greeting new crusaders like Labouchère, founder of *Truth*,

and 'Tay Pay' O'Connor, first editor of the *Star*. J. A. Spender was editing *The Westminster Gazette*, Bernard Shaw writing dramatic criticism, and Chesterton soon to join the *Daily News*. The Linotype machine was just replacing hand setting, but newspaper offices still had no telephones.

On the tide of increased literacy fostered by the 1870 Education Act, there was a demand for magazines with a wider appeal than *Cornhill* or the *Contemporary Review*. One of them, *Tit-Bits*, published by George Newnes in 1881, was a rag-bag of trivial but diverting news items. Its immediate success was to be matched seven years later by the Harmsworths' *Answers* — basically 'Answers to Correspondents' — published from a small office near St Paul's. The way was now open to a flood of magazines varying from boys' weeklies to women's papers and 'comics'.

One of the most famous had a London name and a London street scene on its cover. The *Strand Magazine* with its view looking

336

east towards St Mary-le-Strand was to be familiar on the bookstalls for more than half a century. Its popularity was assured from the day that two stories were submitted, hand-written on foolscap paper, from a Dr A. C. Doyle, 2 Devonshire Place, W. Based on the *Adventures of Sherlock Holmes* (for each of which Conan Doyle was paid thirty guineas), and stories by W. W. Jacobs, A. E. W. Mason and H. G. Wells, the fortunes of *Strand* were secure. Like *Wide World* (covers of intrepid explorers fighting boa-constrictors), *Cassell's Illustrated Family Paper*, and *Pearson's*, the readership was partly a railway one, catered for at every terminus by W. H. Smith.

1. The Lord Mayor's Show in 1888.

2. Journalists at work in 1882. Each night about 150,000 words of debate must be condensed in the Reporters' Room of the House of Commons.

3. Fleet Street towards the end of the century.

4. The old Queen Victoria Street office of *The Times*, with its famous clock pediment. Demolished in 1962.

5. 'Help! Again I feel the demons of Sensationalism rising in me. Hold me fast! Curb me, if you love me!' – Northcliffe's reaction (as visualized by Max Beerbohm) after taking control of *The Times* in 1908. He raised circulation from 38,000 to 318,000.

2

3

4

5

Our Theatres in the Nineties

In the last two decades of the century, London assumed a position it was never to lose as the leading theatrical capital of the world. A dozen new theatres were built in the West End. In Shaftesbury Avenue alone, the Lyric, Shaftesbury, Palace and Apollo went up between 1888 and 1901. By the nineties audiences had a choice of thirty-eight central London theatres, and another twenty-three in the suburbs.

The raw era of the Penny Gaffe, Drury Lane spectacle, and blood and thunder on the Surrey side of the river gave way to realism, to a new kind of play, and acting which did not rely on empty bombast. The change began in 1880 when Squire Bancroft took the Theatre Royal, Haymarket, and made play-going fashionable with the works of Tom Robertson and the 'cup and saucer' dramatists. Pinero, Henry Arthur Jones, and Wilde created a public for 'society' drama and the comedy of manners. Shaw was waiting in the wings, and as a critic was already heralding Ibsen whose first London play, *A Doll's House*, was produced in 1889.

Riotous, cat-calling audiences were replaced by more intelligent ones. Theatres began to be made more comfortable. At the Haymarket, Bancroft made a big change by abolishing the pit and replacing it with stalls. He also introduced the first 'picture frame' stage with the proscenium in the form of a large golden frame completely surrounding the stage on all four sides.

Bancroft was just one in a distinguished hierarchy of actor-managers who put their individual mark on the theatres where they reigned for long periods, and whose knighthoods conferred respectability on a previously suspect profession. With money he gained from his success in *Trilby* at the Haymarket, where he followed Bancroft, Herbert Beerbohm Tree was able to build his own theatre opposite. Tree made Her Majesty's famous for Shakespeare, spectacular and so realistic that in *A Midsummer Night's Dream* he had live rabbits hopping about the Athenian woods.

For more than twenty years the Lyceum meant Irving. When he took over the management of the theatre in 1879, he was in the vanguard of London's theatrical renaissance. With Ellen Terry as his leading lady, he remained there until 1903, playing in Shakespeare and melodramas like *The Bells*. Certain in his effects, resisting electric stage lighting and the 'New Drama', Irving was the dominating figure of his period, and the first theatrical knight. The St James's in the nineties meant George Alexander and social comedies like *The Importance of Being Earnest* (playing there when the Wilde scandal broke); the Garrick meant John Hare; the Savoy meant Gilbert and Sullivan; at the Criterion, Charles Wyndham held sway for twenty years, and when he moved to the Charing Cross Road in 1899, the theatre he had built there and the actor-manager became indivisible: he called it simply Wyndham's.

1

2

3

1. Queue at the Haymarket for the first night of *Trilby* in 1895. It ran for 260 performances. Tree called the play 'hogwash', but it enabled him to build Her Majesty's (5).

2. The Haymarket in Bancroft's time showing the 'picture frame' stage and new stalls. To meet the costs of his expensive productions, Bancroft moved the pit audience to the Upper Circle, and faced a first night storm of protest by going on stage to explain his reasons. In other theatres the pit – unreserved seats at the back of the stalls – was jealously guarded by the 'pittites' for another seventy years.

3. At Her Majesty's, in 1898, Tree staged Julius Caesar with characteristic opulence.

4. On the stage of the Savoy, W. S. Gilbert reads the libretto of 'Utopia Limited' to the cast, the bearded Richard D'Oyly Carte and to Arthur Sullivan who sits on his left. Temperament caused a rift in the partnership, and this picture of 1893 is believed to be the only contemporary one of them together.

5. The building of Her Majesty's, 1897.

6 *and* 7. While the audience besieged the pit entrance of the Lyceum (6), Sir Henry Irving (7) made his way into the theatre through his private door. Bricked up, the doorway still exists at the back of the rebuilt theatre.

8. The pillars of the Lyceum, the theatre Irving made famous, were draped in black to mark his death in 1905.

End of an Era

'A never-to-be-forgotten day. No one ever, I believe, has met with such an ovation as was given to me, passing through those six miles of streets . . . every face seemed filled with real joy. I was much moved and gratified. We went up Constitution Hill and Piccadilly . . . St James's Street was beautifully decorated . . . Trafalgar Square was very striking. . . . The streets in the Strand are now quite wide, but one misses Temple Bar. Here the Lord Mayor received me and presented the sword which I touched. . . . As we neared St Paul's the procession was often stopped, and the crowds broke out into singing *God Save The Queen*. . . .

'In front of the Cathedral the scene was most impressive. All the Colonial troops, on foot, were drawn up round the Square. My carriage, surrounded by all the Royal Princes, was drawn up close to the steps, where the Clergy were assembled, the Bishops in rich copes. . . . A *Te Deum* was sung. . . .'

—Extract from the journal of Queen Victoria, then aged seventy-eight, for 22 June 1897, the day of her Diamond Jubilee.

'*Maffick* (mae·fik), *v.* 1900 (no longer used). [Back-formation from *mafficking* (=the place-name *Ma·feking* treated joc. as a pres. pple.).] *intr.* A journalistic word, used to designate the extravagant behaviour of the London crowds on the relief of Mafeking (17 May 1900); also *transf.*'

—Extract from the Shorter Oxford English Dictionary.

'Osborne, 6.45 p.m.

My beloved mother the Queen has just passed away, surrounded by her children and grandchildren.

[signed] Albert Edward'

—Telegram sent to the Lord Mayor and read out from a window of the Mansion House on 22 January 1901.

1. Diamond Jubilee at St Paul's.
2. Mafeking Night in Piccadilly Circus.
3. Outside Buckingham Palace.

TWENTIETH CENTURY LONDON

Edwardian Promenade

'We all feel motherless to-day,' wrote Henry James from London to a friend in Paris in 1901. 'We are to have no more of little mysterious Victoria, but instead fat vulgar dreadful Edward.' Many of the old aristocracy shared this prejudice against the new King whose reign was beginning in his sixtieth year. Edward's amours, his gambling and the influence of what were sneeringly called his 'race track set' were regarded with foreboding. With a shudder, Society anticipated an era in which parvenu families—perhaps even of foreign extraction—would creep into Debrett, and fortunes made in American rail, on the Rand, and on Australian sheep stations would found dynasties in Park Lane.

But the less reactionary soon agreed that Edward was doing much to restore London's lost gaiety. The Season began to regain some of the glamour that had shrivelled in the last years of Victoria's widowhood. The Court found a new lustre.

On his move from Marlborough House, the King's orders for Buckingham Palace were brief–'Get this tomb cleaned up.' Regency furniture and the treasures of Brighton Pavilion saw the light again; staircases and galleries were recarpeted in blue; chandeliers were wired for electric light. Queen Victoria's sedate daytime 'Drawing rooms' at which no refreshments were served were replaced by

levées and receptions to match the new surroundings. His mother had permitted no talking; Edward encouraged gossip, and expected to hear laughter.

Any hint of the feared vulgarity was absent–anyway in the eyes of Queen Marie of Rumania. 'Nothing is more irreproachably perfect in every detail,' she wrote, 'than the King of England's Court and household, a

sort of staid luxury without ostentation, a placid, aristocratic ease and opulence which has nothing showy about it.'

The tone was set by the first Court of the reign, above, held in March 1902. About seventy debutantes were presented. To cut down on the insufferably long standing time, the King streamlined the formalities. When they came up to the red-covered dais in the

3

4

5

Throne Room, ladies simply curtsied, first to him, then to Queen Alexandra. Distinguished foreign visitors were briefly presented by the wives of their ambassadors. It remained a splendid occasion. In attendance were eight dukes and nine duchesses, eleven marquesses and their countesses, thirty-seven earls, eleven viscounts and thirty-eight lords. The Right Honourables and Messieurs and Mesdames were too numerous to count. One innovation for such occasions was an orchestra playing Gilbert and Sullivan over-tures and light music—Edward's choice despite pleas by the Master of the King's Musick for something more serious.

At State Balls tiaras glittered in built-up coiffures, sweeping trains passed up the wide marble staircases, and a still undepleted Empire provided exotic uniforms. Not even the Czar's receptions in St Petersburg, it was said, could equal these events.

A similar gaiety infected the Season, the two months which started with the Private View at the Royal Academy at the end of May and ended with the Royal Garden Party in the latter part of July. The opera, or the first night of a play (like the one at the Criterion, far left) was an occasion for a fashion parade with bare-shouldered women and men wearing cloaks over full evening dress. Top-hats were *de rigueur* and special metal racks were fitted under the seats to accom-modate them. The Eton and Harrow match was watched from the roofs of private coaches drawn up on the boundary at Lord's. In the tea interval, top left, every fellow hoped that his sister would attract approving glances as she strolled with him under her parasol. At the Flower Show, held in the Temple Gardens, left, roses were delicately sniffed and, apparently, even a hat was raised in their honour. Orchids from Leopold Rothschild's hothouses were reported to draw 'excited interest'. Just discernible on the rear coach, bottom left, is a Maharajah. His turban and glittering costume vied, said the social columns, with the dresses of the women who bravely sat on the boxes as the Four in Hand Club came spanking into Hyde Park.

These were some of the brief glories of the new century. In times to come, men who were young then were to look back on the eight years of Edward's reign as the dying fall in an age of peace, privilege and prosperity.

1. After the theatre—at the opening of the Season.

2. First court of the new reign, in 1902.

3. Tea interval at Lord's—July 1901. Harrow won.

4. The Royal Horticultural Society Flower Show.

5. In a valiant endeavour to keep the spirit of coaching alive in the face of the threat from the motor car, the Four in Hand Driving Club paraded in Hyde Park. Lord Lonsdale (with two Indian Maharajahs), Lord Shrewsbury, and Lord Londonderry (with the young Duchess of Marlborough) were among the drivers of twenty-three coaches in July 1902.

Hotels and Restaurants in The New Era

In the heyday of Edwardian extravagance, hotels learnt to be prepared for anything. They would flood a courtyard and engage Caruso to sing while dinner was served on gondolas. Waiters were dressed as eskimos at a banquet to celebrate Peary's discovery of the North Pole. A fountain at the Savoy gushed champagne for a party given by Krupp.

London's smartest and more enterprising hotels ceased to be simply places at which to stay. They catered for banquets, receptions, private parties and balls. Cannon Street Station Hotel drew a large revenue from company meetings. Bars were opened where people could gather, and at the Carlton a balcony was built and lined with palms for intimate rendez-vous.

The palm balcony was the idea of César Ritz who went to the Carlton in the Haymarket after running the Savoy and before the hotel to which he gave his name was opened in 1905. This Swiss hotelier had a passion for making people comfortable—he pioneered baths for every room—and had an eye for detail. At the Carlton he ordered a costly stairway for the dining-room simply to allow women to make dramatic entries, and at the Ritz he insisted on diffused lighting from alabaster bowls to flatter their looks.

The combination of gaiety with utility made hotels big business, and in 1903 the Savoy spent a million pounds, doubling its size, adding 200 rooms, and moving the main entrance from Savoy Hill to the Strand. A rubber roadway was laid so that sleeping guests should not be disturbed by horse traffic. Seven years later it added two storeys and remodelled the Embankment façade. In Piccadilly two small hotels were demolished to make room for the Ritz, which also cost a million. M. Ritz who, with his chef, Escoffier, had created a reputation for perfection, lived just long enough to see the building finished. He described it with typical modesty as 'a small house to which I am very proud to see my name attached'.

Among restaurants a new and growing need was being answered. The wealthy were already well catered for at Frascati's in Holborn, Romano's in the Strand, Rule's, or the Trocadero, which opened its famous Long Bar in 1901; the poor could buy a Penny Breakfast and Fivepenny Dinner at Lockhart's or Pearce and Plenty; writers and painters chose between the Café de l'Europe and the red plush of the Café Royal; the fashionable sipped tea at Stewart's in Bond Street, or Rumpelmeyer's down St James's. But what was wanted now was a middle-priced 'respectable' restaurant where a woman on her own could go for a light lunch if she were working in an office or up in town for a day's shopping.

Earliest among the chain teashops was the Aerated Bread Company which had opened its first teashop in the Strand in 1861. This was followed by Lyons which started their first teashop at 213 Piccadilly in 1894. By 1910 there were ninety-eight Lyons teashops in London with their marble-topped tables and uniformed waitresses who fifteen years later became known as Nippies. Following their success with the Trocadero, Lyons went a stage further in 1909 with the first Corner House, in Coventry Street, and in the same year opened the Strand Palace Hotel. Both were designed to provide what they called 'luxury catering for the little man'.

5

6

8

7

9

1. Opened in 1905, the Ritz was the first steel-constructed building in England, though the decoration remained firmly Louis XVI. A touch of the Rue de Rivoli in Paris came to Piccadilly with its pavement colonnade.

2. Largest among flourishing Edwardian hotels in the City was De Keyser's Royal Hotel on the Embankment at Blackfriars. It had foreign clientele, predominantly German and French. Sir Polydore de Keyser arrived from Belgium as a waiter and remained to become Lord Mayor of London in 1887. His 400-room hotel was opened in 1874. It was demolished to make way for Unilever House in 1932. On the left is the City of London School.

3. With its striped blinds and delicate ironwork balconies the Savoy retained a Riviera-like appearance until this river façade was altered in 1910. The hotel had been built by Richard D'Oyly Carte, the opera impresario,

in 1889. From rooms here, Whistler and Monet drew the Thames.

4. The Gondola Dinner at the Savoy in 1905 cost George A. Kessler, the Wall Street financier, £3,000. Caruso's fee was £450. There were 12,000 carnations, 100 doves, and a number of swans which were killed by blue chemical dye in the water of the flooded courtyard. Guests included Rejane and Edna May, star of *The Belle of New York*.

5. Edwardian London did not surrender completely to imperial palaces. Many visitors preferred intimate, personally run hotels like the Cavendish, Jermyn Street. The white-bearded man by the hotel bus is Sir William Eden (father of Lord Avon). Partly hidden is the legendary Rosa Lewis, proprietress and friend of Edward VII, who took over the Cavendish in 1902.

6. The first Lyons teashop in Piccadilly. The catering company was the idea of Montague Gluckstein. As a traveller in the tobacco firm of Salmon and Gluckstein, he knew the difficulty of finding good, cheap meals. Because of their tobacco association, the partners formed the new company under the name of an acquaintance, Joseph Lyons.

7. Bohemian eating – the Café Royal. Among the famous patrons, seen here in the gilded splendour of the Domino Room, are William Nicholson, James Pryde, the sprawling, bearded Augustus John, and George Moore, walking out right. The Café Royal was opened in 1865 by Daniel Nichols, a bankrupt Paris wine merchant.

8 *and* 9. Popular eating – two of the A.B.C. teashops.

345

From a Pin to an Elephant

After a look round the London shops in 1906, Gordon Selfridge asserted that England knew how to make things, but did not know how to sell them. Two years later, the dynamic executive of Marshall Field's department store in Chicago came back to rectify this. He brought with him an American architect's plans for a store with the largest possible open plan shopping area. 'I want departments, not compartments,' said Selfridge.

Ignoring a trade depression, and hostility from established store owners, Selfridge invested £300,000 of his own money in the enterprise. He settled on a site in Oxford Street, and declared war on building regulations, fire restrictions and legal inertia. Generous compensation was scattered to buy up old leases, and when that failed, as with one jeweller, he simply built around him.

There was a crisis when his financial partner backed out – building came to a halt for three months – but Selfridge quickly raised a £250,000 guarantee over a handshake at a week-end house party. The best buyers and sales experts were recruited, and a staff of 1,200 engaged. A window dresser was brought over from Chicago. Thousands were spent on advertising. Despite all prophecies of doom, Selfridge's opened its doors to a fanfare of trumpets in March 1909, only ten months after building started.

Strolling through the 130 departments in answer to the slogan, 'Why not spend a day at Selfridge's?' the public were delighted to

Our Mammoth Stores
Shopman. 'Excuse me, Madam, but am I not right in presuming you come from the Toy Department?'
Lady. 'Certainly. Why?'
Shopman. 'Would you very kindly direct me to it? I'm one of the assistants there and I've lost my way.'

find goods displayed with taste and as if in an exhibition. But Selfridge's buccaneering methods were not calculated to be popular with his rivals. London was not, after all, exactly without experience of how to run stores.

With residential expansion westwards, shops had started to move in the middle of the previous century from their traditional centre round St Paul's Churchyard. They had opened along Holborn and Oxford Street, and specialization in one sort of goods had been changed for the convenience of customers in Knightsbridge, Kensington, and Bayswater. The conception of a general store, selling a variety of things, had also been influenced by such middle-class co-operative groups as civil servants (the Civil Service Stores in the Strand, 1868) and the services (Army and Navy, Victoria Street, 1872).

Shoolbred's was the first big store selling to the general public, and by the 1860s had a staff of 600 at its Tottenham Court Road premises. Ten years later William Whiteley, 'The Universal Provider', was setting a pace in Westbourne Grove which John Barker, Tom Ponting, Peter Jones, and Charles Digby Harrod (son of the founder) soon had to follow. Whiteley faced a near riot from local butchers when he began to sell meat in addition to millinery and fancy goods, but his initiative soon enabled him to boast, 'We can supply anything from a pin to an elephant'. (Once challenged, Whiteley's borrowed an elephant from a circus and delivered it in four hours.)

But until the turn of the century many stores were, like Harrods, only terraces of intercommunicating shops. Then, on the high tide of Edwardian prosperity and facing increased competition with each other, several began rebuilding their premises as stores. Their complexity prompted *Punch's* comment, bottom left; their glamour provided George Edwardes with a setting for *Our Miss Gibbs* at the Gaiety, with Gertie Millar as a 'Garrod's' salesgirl. It was Harrod's claim that it pioneered shopping by telephone, special shopping trains from the country, and a free country delivery. Naturally, too, goods were supplied 'on account' to approved customers.

The original grocer's shop acquired by H. D. Harrod, a tea retailer in the City, was 105 Brompton Road, in the middle of the row seen below. He lived over his shop. The flat-roofed extensions with plate glass windows were built out over the front gardens of the terrace of private houses which stretched south to New Street (now Hans Crescent). With an additional four and a half acres acquired in 1911, the terrace was swallowed up in the present island site.

5

1. A 'Yankee folly' was how some shopkeepers regarded Selfridge's grandiose plans for his Oxford Street Store. 'Is it to be a shop or – er – a Greek temple?' asked Samuel Waring (of Waring and Gillow) and dropped out as a partner in the scheme.

2. The Duke Street corner seven months before the store opened. The far end is the present main entrance. Selfridge doubled the store's size by 1934.

3. In 1912 Marks and Spencer, originally from Leeds, opened their Edgware Road bazaar (slogan: 'Don't ask the price, it's a penny'), forerunner of some thirty London branches by 1914. Woolworth's (established in England, 1910) were formidable competitors until M. & S. found its modern formula.

4. *Punch* looks at the new stores, 1911.

5. Harrod's as it looked until 1901 and the big rebuilding.

6. The store in 1906 from Montpelier Street.

7. Harrod's greatest innovation was the moving staircase installed in 1898. A forty-foot conveyor belt carried customers to the first floor 'without any of those unpleasant thrills which lifts always succeed in giving nervous persons'. As an added precaution an attendant was on duty at the top with free brandy.

6

7

London Moves Outwards

In 1901 London's first electric tram clanged and swayed from Hammersmith to Kew. Four years later the first electric underground train on the District Line ran from Ealing to Whitechapel. In that same year – 1905 – the first fleet of motor buses, 200 of them, were coughing and shuddering their way through the streets. The horseless carriage, it was agreed, had come to stay.

It was just as well, for London was bursting out of its old confines. In the previous fifty years, the population had almost doubled – from 2,363,000 to 4,536,000. Congestion was pushing people deeper into the suburbs, with the result that between 1851 and the beginning of the new century the residents of the Greater London area beyond the County boundary had multiplied by five. The City remained the centre where people continued to work, but they made their homes farther out. In the decade up to 1911, the population of the County dropped for the first time, while numbers in Greater London increased by 484,000.

Golders Green exemplifies what happened. Although the electrified Metropolitan Railway was already turning the area between Kilburn and Harrow into a popular dormitory, Golders Green was the first place outside the County limits reached by the electrified Underground. How the junction of North End Road and the muddy Finchley Road looked in 1904 may be seen below. The only visible buildings are a broken-down cottage (site of the present Tube station entrance) and the tower of the Crematorium half a mile to the north. But, even as this photograph was being taken, the Tube was burrowing under Hampstead Heath. The traffic barrier of the Northern Heights was being breached. The tunnel emerged in 1905, and two years later the Hampstead Line was opened from Charing Cross to Golders Green terminus.

This was the enterprise of Charles Tyson Yerkes, yet another Chicago financier with London aspirations, who developed three London Tube systems, and for their electricity built Lot's Road Power Station in Chelsea (to Whistler's fury). He transformed this part of north-west London, and the pattern was to be repeated all round Greater London as the Tube and railways extended.

People followed the Tube. Speculative builders went to work. Within three years Golders Green land values had increased six times over. Streets cut across meadows, and rows of houses sprang up in turnip fields. Even as they were being built, the new suburban houses were sold or, as in the uncompleted road, centre right, quickly let. In the seven years after the opening of the Tube, 3,611 houses were built at Golders Green, the population rose by 14,000, and Henrietta Barnett, wife of a Whitechapel clergyman, had started her idealistic community, Hampstead Garden Suburb, for all people regardless of age, class, or income.

Nearer in, the tram and the bus were also helping the daily traveller. Some local authorities, like Woodford, tried to oppose trams as a threat to their social status, but the progressive L.C.C. swept through local prejudice. It took over all private tramways and electrified 189 miles of line so that the working man could be got to and from his newly created municipal home for as little as 1d. for 3½ miles.

1

2

3

4

In 1908–9, 32,000,000 were carried on cheap workmen's fares. Buses (at about 1d. a mile) were the middle-class transport, an alternative and adjunct to the Tube. By 1911 there were twenty-three routes serving districts as far out as suburban Barnes, Ealing, Dollis Hill, Highbury, East Ham, and Norwood. One printed slogan – 'The best way to see London is from the top of a bus' (a saying of Mr Gladstone) – was uncontestable, but the tired commuter was more likely to be attracted by 'We Carry You All the Way'. By now the horse bus was all but extinct. The last 'General' ran in 1911, and five years later the last independent horse bus made its final run.

1. Golders Green crossroads in 1904, looking north.

2. As it was to become – from the same viewpoint.

3. The suburb as an Underground poster idyllically pictured it in 1908, complete with a verse from William Cowper's *Sanctuary*.

4. Hampstead Garden Suburb, looking north-east, showing the Central Square with the Institute in the middle and the flanking Church of St Jude and Free Church, all designed by Sir Edwin Lutyens. From here radiate the key roads, tree-lined and 40 feet wide, with houses 50 feet apart and without separating hedges. Only eight houses (in neo-Tudor or William and Mary style) were permitted on each of the 317 acres. Shops were kept to the perimeter, and all noise forbidden. But, slightly disillusioned by the outcome of her communal scheme, Dame Henrietta Barnett wrote in 1928: 'I wonder if enough of the residents make real attempts to know intimately the classes which do not belong socially to their own?'

5. 'Let' signs in every window of houses even before the road is completed.

6. In January 1905, there were only 20 motor buses operating in London, but this had increased to 200 by the end of the year, and to 1,000 by 1908. This 'B' Type bus, at Victoria in 1914, was part of a fleet of over 2,500.

7. One of London's earliest electric trams. The picture was taken at Shepherd's Bush in 1903 two years after the opening of London's first electrified routes – Lambeth to Tooting and Hammersmith to Kew.

5

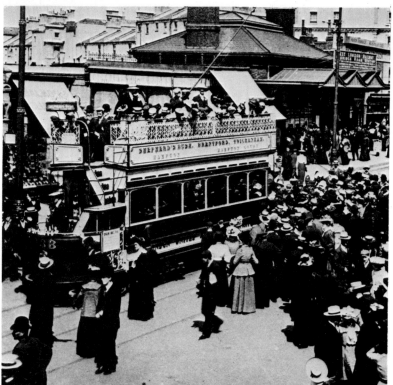

6

7

Kingsway and Aldwych

In the move outward, central London was not completely forgotten. After a postponement of over sixty years, a road joining the Strand and Holborn finally took shape with the opening of Kingsway in 1905. Like Regent Street, a comparable north-south link, it involved large-scale demolition. Twenty-eight acres had to be cleared. Old thoroughfares like Wych Street (page 76) disappeared, and with them the Globe Theatre, Olympic, Opera Comique, and old Gaiety. The Strand was widened by the demolition of a warren of houses backing on to Hollywell Street. A truncated Drury Lane lost its importance as the main artery up to Holborn.

The scheme had the double advantage of easing traffic and getting rid of the slums round Clare Market. Kingsway (named in honour of Edward VII) was given a double access-exit off the Strand by the felicitous idea of a crescent-shaped Aldwych. It was so named from the Danish word for 'old town' as this was the reputed site of the tenth-century Danish occupation (page 16). Eight architects were invited to submit an overall plan for the crescent, but this chance of a unified Aldwych gave way to buildings by different architects, one of whom, A. Marshall Mackenzie, designed the Waldorf Hotel (1908) and Australia House (1918). The main block, Bush House, by the Americans, Helmle and Corbett, was not finished until 1935.

1. Aldwych in 1906. Both the Waldorf (now Strand) Theatre, left, and the Aldwych Theatre were opened in the previous year, and were given identical exteriors by the architect, W. G. R. Sprague. The Waldorf Hotel went up in the gap between them.

2. Kingsway under construction. View looking south shows the tram subway, and to its left, the Holborn-Aldwych extension of the Piccadilly Line.

3. In 1921 Bush House and India House were still to be built. Sentinel, at the ends of the inner perimeter of the crescent, are, left, the new Gaiety (1903, closed 1939) and, right, Australia House.

4. Pre-1900 map showing the area to be cleared. The entire block east of St Mary-le-Strand was the first to be demolished. The Improvements Committee of the L.C.C. cited the architectural 'apathy' shown in the building of Shaftesbury Avenue and Charing Cross Road as the reason why 'every effort should be made to secure that the great thoroughfare from Holborn to the Strand should, in addition to utility, possess beauty and civic dignity, as some of the grand thoroughfares in certain continental cities'.

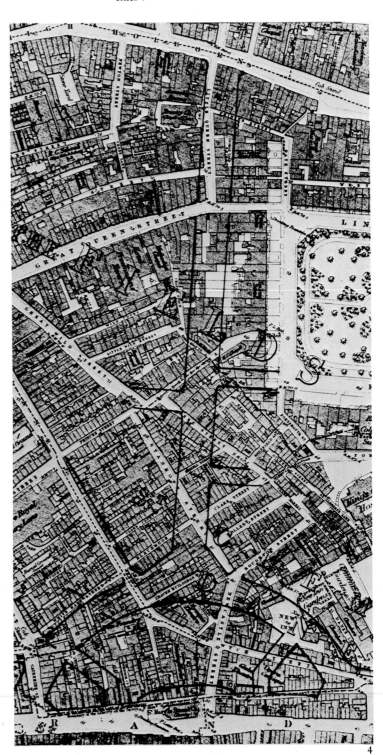

The Sidney Street Affair

Streets acquire immortality by strange chance. Cock Lane (the ghost), Berners Street (the hoax), Cato Street (the conspiracy), and Hilldrop Crescent (Crippen) – all have fame beyond their merits. So does Sidney Street (the siege). The bizarre events of a few hours on a cold January morning in 1911 gave this ill-favoured Stepney thoroughfare a legendary place in London history.

In the previous month, three policemen had been killed in Houndsditch. They were shot down while attempting to arrest a gang of Russian-speaking anarchists who were burgling a jeweller's. The intensive search for the fugitives particularly caught the public imagination because one of them, Peter Piatkow, had the alliterative alias of 'Peter the Painter'.

Before dawn on 3 January, the police surrounded a house – No 100 – in Sidney Street, in a second floor room of which they had discovered that at least two of the foreigners were hiding. At about 7.30 a.m. an officer knocked on the front door. He was answered by a burst of fire from an opened window. A sergeant collapsed, shot through the lungs and foot.

For the next six hours the armed men kept the besiegers at bay by shooting with fast-firing automatics at every person and thing they saw. To deal with them, authority rallied 400 policemen, some armed with sporting guns, a squad of Scots Guards with rifles from the Tower, the Fire Brigade (which lost one man killed) and a detachment of Royal Engineers. There was even a proposal to blow in the side of the house with a field gun. This was later to provoke the derisive suggestion that perhaps the Army should also have used its airship.

Melodrama was given added thunder by the arrival of the Home Secretary in the person of Winston Churchill who came to watch (but not, he insisted, to direct) operations in a top-hat and fur-collared overcoat. His cautious curiosity was recorded, below, in one of the most famous Press photographs ever taken.

During a morning of mounting tension, rooftop grandstands were let for 10s. a head; an old lady tried in vain to supply the soldiers with tea; a cat and a dog were shot dead; and a reporter got a bullet through his overcoat. All this was filmed by an enterprising cameraman for a matinée showing in the variety bill at the Coliseum.

Rumour, inspired by the Press, had it that the mysterious Peter the Painter was one of the armed men who died when, in a Wagnerian climax, the house caught fire at 1 p.m. But when the two charred bodies were examined, it was found that neither was his. This far from killed speculation. He passed, like the whole Sidney Street saga, into legend. Variously, he was said to have escaped disguised as a woman, died on the *Lusitania*, fled to France, Germany and Russia (there to become a leading Bolshevik). No one has ever been able to discover the truth.

1. Sidney Street. Rooftop view looking south from the direction of the Mile End Road towards the Commercial Road. The cross marks the besieged house.

2. Churchill, the Home Secretary, at the scene.

1

2

Music Hall at its Height

Edwardian London saw the full flourishing of the music hall. To those who had joined in choruses over a tankard in the 'free and easies', the smoky, convivial taverns of sixty years before, the Golden Age was past. They talked nostalgically of the old Canterbury, London's first music hall, in the Westminster Bridge Road; of George Leybourne, the original Champagne Charlie; of the expansive old-time chairman and the punitive 'hook' for removing an unpopular act. Now the scope of 'the halls' was extending to justify the new name of 'variety theatres'. Now respectability and numbered and reserved seats were replacing the gilt and the red plush, the gaslit glory of the Bedford and the Old Mo'.

The Tivoli, the Oxford, the Met, and other famous Victorian music halls still drew crowds, but they were being joined by larger, more impressive theatres – the vast Coliseum (1904) with a stage large enough to put on a chariot race, and the Palladium (1910), only slightly smaller and seating 2,338. In the West End there were ten variety theatres, and sixty more in the suburbs and outer London. Catering for a new public – a great middle-class audience up in town for the day – Sir Oswald Stoll, builder and proprietor of the Coliseum, lurked in the shadow of a box during the first house Monday, monitoring the acts for any hint of blue joke. Even so, the music hall was not easily to lose a reputation for vulgarity, and there was some raising of eyebrows when Edward VII paid a private visit to the Empire, Leicester Square, in 1909. This was not simply because of the stage entertainment. Its Promenade was notorious, and for years the reformer, Mrs Ormiston Chant, had been trying to get it closed. It was a campaign that was not to succeed until the first world war when the women who made it a rendez-vous were held to offer too great a temptation to soldiers on leave.

The new variety wooed the new public with elaborate acts and artists who once would never have dreamt of appearing. Ballet was on the bill of the Alhambra. Sarah Bernhardt came to the Coliseum. Beecham conducted excerpts from *Tannhäuser* at the Palladium. Barrie wrote a one-act play for the Hippodrome. Audiences came to expect spectacle (Water Lions and Diving Nymphs in a glass tank) and even sport (a country cricket match on stage in 1908). And with the new reign came royal approval – the first Royal Command Performance in 1912. 'The Cinderella of the Arts goes to the ball at last!' was Stoll's reaction to King George V's command. But on the great night two outstanding music-hall favourites were missing – Albert Chevalier and Marie Lloyd.

1

2

3

4

5

6

7

8

9

10

1. The Alhambra Theatre of Varieties at the turn of the century. For many years it presented a programme of music-hall turns and ballets. Decorated in Moorish-Spanish style to suit its name, the Alhambra on the east side of Leicester Square opened as the Royal Panopticon in 1854 and survived in various forms until replaced by the Odeon cinema in 1937.

2. Drinks on the tables in front of a largely male audience. Bowler hats on heads. Waiters moving about. On stage a dancer-singer. This typical Victorian music hall is The Middlesex – the Old Mo – Drury Lane in 1890. Derived its nickname from the original theatre, the Great Mogul. Survived as a music-hall until 1919. It was on the site of the present New London Theatre.

3. The Empire Promenade, 1902. When, eight years earlier, protests by Mrs Ormiston Chant led the management to put up restrictive trellis, some young men-about-town pulled it down. Their leader was Winston Churchill, accompanied by fellow-cadets from Sandhurst. Afterwards they triumphantly carried pieces of the partition into Piccadilly.

4. Albert Chevalier, 'The Coster Laureate'. He took a whole page in *Era* opposite the review of the Command Performance to complain against his exclusion.

5. Marie Lloyd, also excluded (probably because of her irrepressible vulgarity) hit back with a poster outside her theatre – 'Every performance by Marie Lloyd is a performance by Command of the British Public.'

6. Mrs Ormiston Chant.

7. In the transition from pothouse to palace, Edwardian music halls sought new prestige. When the Victoria Palace (1911) replaced the Royal Standard, previously a tavern, a statue of Pavlova (now lost) was placed on the dome.

8. The Coliseum (1904) was fitted with three revolving stages, one inside the other, seventy-five feet across, and the most complicated in the world.

9. To outdo his rivals, Walter Gibbons lavished £250,000 on the Palladium (1910). Like the Victoria Palace and the Coliseum, the Palladium was designed by the prolific Frank Matcham, who was responsible for twenty theatres in London alone.

10. At the first Royal Variety Performance at the Palace in July 1912, 142 artists appeared in the final tableau. Among the legendary names were:
Front row: Cinquavelli, 'The Human Billiard Table' (in bowler); Charles Coburn, 'Two Lovely Black Eyes' (white tie); Wilkie Bard (check blouse); Vesta Tilley, 'Algy, The Piccadilly Johnny' (military uniform); the ventriloquist Arthur Prince (naval).
Next row: Fred Emney Snr. (dame); Harry Tate, 'Motoring' (tweed coat, without famous ginger moustache); Kate Carney (picture hat); T. E. Dunville (wide parting); Harry Lauder (black tam o'shanter).
Back row: Harry Champion, 'Any Old Iron' (top-hat, white muffler); Marie Loftus, 'The Sarah Bernhardt of the Music Halls' (white hat); Harry Randall and Tom Stuart (heads inclined together); George Robey, 'The Mayor of Mudcumdyke' (peering over specs); Gus Elen, 'Never Introduce Your Donah to a Pal' (swarthy, slightly lower); Ella Retford, 'Hi! Hi! Hi! Mr. Mckie' (in white); Barclay Gammon, the pianist.
Other famous artists taking part included Chirgwin, Fanny Fields, Little Tich, Alfred Lester, Clarice Mayne, Anna Pavlova, Cissie Loftus, and Harry Claff.

The Last Years of Peace

On an untroubled summer day the tinkling music of the barrel organ sets button boots stamping on the cobbles of the quiet suburban backwater. *Adeste Fideles*, *Lula lula lu*, or perhaps Leslie Stuart's *Soldiers of the Queen* may bring down a few coppers from upstairs windows. As we look into that happy cul-de-sac (1), and glance round London between 1911 and 1913 the tranquillity has a prophetic irony. Catastrophe is so close.

Elegant in top hats, and carrying parasols, members of the Ranelagh Club at Barnes crowd round the plane of Claude Grahame-White (2) who has just flown from Hendon on a June afternoon in 1911. The first Englishman to hold an official pilot's licence, this pioneer aviator had acquired land at Hendon to open London's first aerodrome. At a time when Britain has fifty-seven certified pilots, there is much talk about the aeroplane opening up new horizons. But at Hendon this same year Grahame-White is to demonstrate to Members of Parliament the threat of aerial bombing by dropping small bags of flour on the outline of a battleship painted on the grass.

For women a war has already broken out. The Suffragettes are fighting a militant campaign for the vote, and in 1912 they found a martyr in Emily Wilding Davison who threw herself under the King's horse in the Derby. At Victoria Station where her body was brought from Epsom, four of her fellow Suffragettes dressed in black, purple and white stand sentinel around her coffin (3). Emily Davison is the champion of so many women who, like the three 'typewriters' (4), are now working alongside men in offices, and are claiming equal rights.

Such radical ideas are unlikely to cross the mind of the nanny in Hyde Park (5), who is very much part of the social hierarchy. On an autumn afternoon she has brought her two

5

6

small charges to Rotten Row. Snug in suede leggings and angora fur coats, they sit on a seat over which she has carefully spread a wool shawl. Nanny is a symbol of unchanging life and unquestioned values. She earns £25 a year all found, and has her own small sitting-room and bedroom in the house in Rutland Gate. Meals brought up, of course.

Contemplating a pleasant afternoon at Lord's, a gentleman emerges from his club after a good lunch (6). The porter has already hailed a motor taximeter cab. It should get him to St John's Wood far quicker than one of the horse cabs which by 1912 are being driven off the streets. By this date there are only 400 hansoms left in London as compared with 7,600 at the start of the century. No good, now, for the passengers to challenge the fare or offer to toss the cabby double or quits. The new taximeter contraption is inflexible.

The craze for roller skating which on several occasions swept London was seen for the last time in 1913. The enthusiastic 'rinkers' (7) are dancing a tango at Queen's Club, Earl's Court. By this date, Queen's is one of the few remaining rinks in London still making a profit.

Waterloo Station is thronged with holiday-makers, and a family (8) is ready for the perfect holiday at Ventnor. Perhaps it is not too fanciful to see slight apprehension in the eyes of the mother, an uneasy premonition that nothing will ever be quite the same again. The following summer the station will be a harrowing mêlée of khaki and troop trains. The destination will not be the Isle of Wight, but Gallant Little Belgium. This photograph was taken in July 1913.

7

8

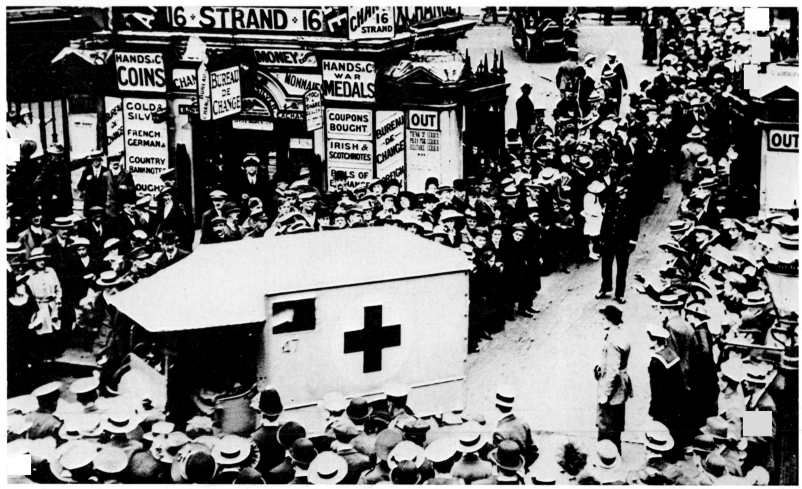

'Good-Bye, Piccadilly . . .'

The hot summer evening was turning to twilight. Looking out of his window at the Foreign Office, Sir Edward Grey mused, 'The lamps are going out all over Europe. We shall not see them lit again in our time.' Luckily he had with him a journalist, J. A. Spender of the *Westminster Gazette*, to record this oracular pronouncement for posterity. At the Oval stumps were drawn for the day. Jack Hobbs's Benefit Match would have to be transferred to Lord's: the Army was commandeering the ground immediately. 'It's all up,' said Mr Asquith to his wife in the Prime Minister's Room in the House of Commons. That was the end of Bank Holiday Monday, 1914. The next day war was declared.

Everyone said the boys would be home by Christmas. But they were not. Nor for four Christmasses to come. The quixotic gallantry with which they volunteered soon hardened into disillusion. Enthusiasm stimulated by propaganda quickly died. The Grand Patriotic Chorus of a Hundred Voices singing, 'Goodbye, Piccadilly . . .' at the Coliseum could achieve only so much. Spy-mania blended with wild rumour. Very early on the allied Russian Army was said to have passed through London by night. Almost treason to suggest that a route to the Western Front from Archangel, via Leith and Blackfriars, was unduly circuitous. Why, a friend of a friend had seen the snow on their boots!

Anti-German feeling grew. A delegation from the City marched on Westminster demanding, 'Intern all Germans!' Hatred mounted with the news from Flanders and rising casualty figures; at the sight of refugees from Gallant Little Belgium arriving at Victoria; with the nightly agony of partings as the men went back to the Front from dimly lit stations. War neurosis prompted normally placid girls to pin white feathers on supposed 'slackers'. Once, it was said, they even gave one to a V.C. who was on leave, and sitting in mufti in Hyde Park.

In September 1915, the first Zeppelin over the City dropped a bomb near the Guildhall. Thirty-nine people were killed in the first of many nightly raids. Two years later the Germans flew twenty planes up the Thames. It was a mid-morning in July, and because they were low and in perfect formation, many assumed they were Royal Flying Corps machines. They left children dead in a destroyed East End infants' school.

The end when it came on Monday, 11 November 1918, took everyone by surprise. Maroons sounding like cannon-fire boomed out suddenly at eleven o'clock, and, almost incredulously people passed on the news –

'The War is over!' Six hundred and seventy Londoners had been killed in the air raids, and hundreds of thousands who had marched away never returned to hear the cheering or claim their medals. Their memorial was the Cenotaph, the Grave of the Unknown Warrior in Westminster Abbey, the Roll of Honour in the office entrance hall.

1. 'It's Your Duty, Lad' says the poster, and to martial music from the gramophone, a volunteer steps forward to join up. There is more apprehension than pride in the eyes of the woman who watches, and the boy with his arm on the parapet is in tears. This is Trafalgar Square early in 1914 when Lord Kitchener was making his appeal, first for 100,000 men aged 19 to 30, then for 200,000 more up to 35. Of these 42,000 were raised in London.

2. Volunteers, many in their summer straw hats, march through the gardens of the Temple on their way to training depots. Within a few weeks they will be wanted to replace the men of the British Expeditionary Force lost in the retreat from Mons.

3. Farewells on Waterloo Station before departure to the Front.

4. After the big battles, casualties arrived back from France, and solemn crowds watched the ambulances taking the wounded from the London stations to Millbank or Roehampton. The scene is at Charing Cross after the Battle of the Somme in July 1916 when, as well as 19,000 killed, there were 57,000 casualties.

5. Violent anti-German demonstrations following the sinking of the *Lusitania* in May 1915, with the loss of 1,198 non-combatants. Especially in the East End, shops with German-sounding names were wrecked. Above, a Poplar tobacconist – A. Schoenfeld – has his windows smashed six days after the disaster.

6. Zeppelin over Leytonstone, 1916, caught by search-lights.

7. In the garden of a south London suburb a boy, just under two, welcomes the peace. Twenty-one years later he was in uniform for the Second World War.

5

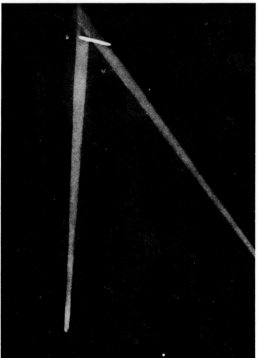

6

7

Hullo, London . . . !

Wearing earphones, and jabbing a crystal with a 'cat's whisker', a small band of wireless enthusiasts picked up London's first broadcast. It was beamed from the roof of Marconi House in the Strand, and they had to be within a radius of twenty miles to hear: 'Hullo, hullo . . .'. 2LO calling . . . 2LO calling . . . This is the British Broadcasting Company . . . 2LO . . . Stand by for one minute . . .'

Those who stood by that night and the next – 14 and 15 November 1922 – heard news of the General Election, results which included the defeat of Winston Churchill by a Prohibitionist and brought the end of Lloyd George's wartime government.

From a small studio, draped in seven layers of butter-muslin to reduce echo, came the first improvised news bulletins (fog and billiard scores), talks ('How to catch a Tiger'), and music (Schubert's 'Unfinished' Symphony by an orchestra of seven, and apologies while a piano was moved).

The following March, John Reith, the B.B.C. General Manager, with a staff of twenty-eight, a cleaner, office boy, and commissionaire moved into Savoy Hill. Up on the doorway went a handprinted postcard proclaiming, 'WIRELESS BROADCASTING COMPANY'. Radio was born.

1. At a microphone slung on rubber, contained in a box, and moved on a heavy trolley, actors broadcast *Passing of the Third Floor Back* in 1926.

2. Improving on the elementary crystal set, a four-valve loudspeaker apparatus was advertised seven months ahead of the first London broadcast.

3. In this corner building on Savoy Hill, a street between the Strand and the Thames, the BBC had its first headquarters. It remained here until Broadcasting House was opened in Portland Place in 1932.

4. The great moment. In a suburban drawing-room the family waits expectantly while father tunes in. So little was understood about sound waves that, hearing wireless for the first time in 1923, the Archbishop of Canterbury asked if the window had to be kept open. Within a year there were several hundred thousand listeners; by the end of the fourth year nearly 2,000,000.

1

Wireless Music, Song, & Speech in the Home.

Everything in the Air is yours with certainty if you use
"BURNDEPT" WIRELESS APPARATUS.

Catalogue Free.

BURNDEPT, LTD., Aerial Works, Blackheath Village, London, S.E. 3.
London Showrooms: 228, SHAFTESBURY AVENUE, NEW OXFORD STREET.

LIVERPOOL:
10, South John Street.

MANCHESTER:
4, Corporation Street.

LEEDS:
48, Great George Street.

2

3

4

1921–Protest

With the docks idle in the post-war slump of 1921, and with 15,000 unemployed, Poplar Borough Council took the most extraordinary action in the history of local government. They refused to levy the rates. This was illegal, but logical; the people simply could not pay. The L.C.C. (owed £270,000 for services) sued; the Lord Chief Justice pronounced it anarchy; and the outcome of *Rex* v. *Poplar* was that the whole council–twenty-four men and six women (one expecting a baby)–were sent to prison. They were given an exultant send-off with flowers from Bow Town Hall. In Brixton they flippantly ignored rules, and demanded that the women members be brought from Holloway for a council meeting. Nightly, Poplar's unemployed came and sang outside the walls, and George Lansbury, labour leader and politician, replied with speeches shouted from behind his cell bars. After six weeks and some face-saving compromises by Whitehall, the appeal judges released them. Their action led to an equalizing of the burden of rates all over London.

Accompanied by 400 unemployed dockers, Poplar's mayor, Sam March with his mace-bearer, George Lansbury and other councillors set out from the East End for the Law Courts, 29 July 1921. Lansbury is walking immediately under the central placard.

1926–Strike

Anarchy and a threat to the Constitution. A demonstration of working class solidarity. Whatever the true political implication, the General Strike of 1926 was treated by a great many Londoners as a bit of a lark. It was summed up by L. S. Amery as 'the mildest mannered revolution that ever tried to coerce a constitutional government'. If you weren't an idle East End docker, or among the millions of trade unionists striking on behalf of the miners, you could enjoy yourself–be late for work, slip off to the Oval, play the loyal defender of 'King and Country'. In response to the appeal by Baldwin, thousands of 'plus-four boys' brought improvisation to the paralysed public services. They manned trains and trams, and climbed into the driving seats of buses which had a police guard and barbed wire across the bonnets to prevent sabotage. Up went facetious signs– 'The driver of this bus is a Guy's Hospital student. The conductor is a Guy's Hospital student. Anyone interfering with either will be a Guy's Hospital patient'. In this lighthearted vein, the strike lasted nine days. Then the T.U.C. called it off. The miners were left to fight alone. The lark was over.

Volunteers manned the buses. By the fifth day of the strike, 529 were running.

1922. Golders Green semi-detached.

1924. Liberty's mock–Tudor.

1929. Becontree Housing Estate.

1931. Shell-Mex House, Embankment.

1932. Broadcasting House, Portland Place.

1933. Battersea Power Station.

1934. Senate House, Bloomsbury.

1935. Sun House, Hampstead.

1936. Peter Jones, Chelsea.

1938. Finsbury Health Centre.

1937. Dolphin Square, Pimlico.

1939. Wembley uniformity.

Building between the Wars

Between the two World Wars the population of Greater London rose by 1,200,000. The L.C.C., local boroughs, and speculative builders were faced with the almost insoluble problem of fulfilling the vain political promise of 1918 and providing homes 'fit for heroes to live in'. Increasingly overcrowded in inner London, working-class families were given new homes in the flats and 'cottage estates' built by the L.C.C. at Downham, Hendon and Becontree. The Becontree Estate at Dagenham, Essex, covered four square miles. With 25,000 homes accommodating 112,000 people it was the largest housing estate in the world.

The middle-income man found his refuge in gabled, double-fronted houses, built to a monotonous pattern, which went up in their hundreds of thousands from Golders Green (offered in 1922 for £250 down, £550 to pay) to Sidcup. Naturally the homeless were not over-concerned with aesthetic objections to 'ribbon development' along new arterial roads. Mock-Tudor houses with little gardens backing on to railways were better than nothing. Until the Green Belt scheme called a

halt in 1935, London's rural fringe was murdered. But by then there was no going back on the uninspired layouts of 'Subtopia' as revealed in a 1939 aerial view of the South Kenton area of Wembley.

For the first few years after the war, monumental buildings remained derivative in style. The Port of London Authority building (1922) in Trinity Square with its giant Corinthian portico; County Hall (page 329) with Piranesi influences (completed 1933); Liberty's (1924) with half-timbering and twisted Elizabethan chimneys; all these consciously borrowed from the past.

A break came in 1929 with Charles Holden's bold London Transport headquarters in Broadway, its severity offset by sculpture by Epstein, Gill and Moore. This use of Portland stone and a diminishing tower was to be repeated by Holden for the Senate House of London University in Bloomsbury. Also in the early thirties came Shell-Mex House on the Embankment and Broadcasting House. These four buildings were austere and quite alien to anything London had seen before. Battersea Power Station was a revelation to those who had always assumed that an industrial building must be ugly, while

across the river Dolphin Square caused interest as the largest self-contained block of flats in Europe.

London achieved another European record in 1935 with the building of the Trocadero Cinema, Elephant and Castle, which held 5,000 people. The talkies brought an extraordinary boom in 'super' cinemas. The Alhambra and Daly's were converted into the Odeon and Warner's; the New Victoria was built; the suburbs acquired Granadas, Regals, and Gaumonts. By 1932 there were 250 cinemas in London.

By the mid-thirties, European influences were being felt. The time was ripe for Maxwell Fry's Sun House in Frognal Way, Hampstead, with windows of a size rarely attempted in London private houses; for Peter Jones (eleven years in time, but a thousand years in thought, ahead of Liberty's) with wide-open selling space, and vertical windows cunningly arranged in horizontal bands; and for Finsbury Health Centre in which the architects, Lubetkin and Tecton, projected themselves twenty years into the future to create the kind of building which was to become familiar in London, but not until after the Festival of Britain.

The Battle of London

At tea-time on a gloriously fine Saturday afternoon – 7 September 1940 – 400 German planes came over London and bombed a virtually undefended city. After dark another armada of 250 bombers followed, helped to their targets by fires already blazing every mile along both sides of the Thames. By dawn, 430 civilians had been killed, and 1,600 carried wounded from the debris of their homes. A dazed, bleeding woman declined brandy from the cupboard of her gutted kitchen. 'Oh no,' she said, 'we are keeping that for an emergency.'

This was the start of the Battle of London – Goering's blow 'right into the enemy's heart' – the blitz that had been expected for a year. The photograph, left, shows a Heinkel 111 flying north over London on the first day of the battle. It was taken from another German bomber in the wave of 400 planes that came over that Saturday. Below are the docks which were heavily damaged, and slightly to the right of the port wing tip is Tower Bridge.

For fifty-seven nights without let-up the Luftwaffe attack continued. Every night during that September and October, bombers were over, at least 200 strong. They dropped 10,000 bombs. London was caught off-balance. Defence was impossible, devastation enormous. The death roll: 9,500. Then, in the middle of September, a Special Commission was set up to ensure that social services continued to function. Some 14,000 Army Pioneers, hundreds of skilled technicians, and civilians were organized into a great emergency repair team.

By the end of September 177,000 people were taking shelter nightly in the Underground stations. Yet even at the height of the bombing, six out of ten Londoners preferred their own beds to shelters. Ordeal toughened their resistance, and, the first shock over, they settled down to a siege which was to last, intermittently, until May. Ahead were the doodlebugs and rockets. But the bomb shock and expected hysteria never came. Only twenty-three neurotic cases were admitted to hospital. By this, the first mass civilian attack in history, the Germans hoped to force a quick surrender. It failed.

1. A German bomber over London, 7 September 1940.

2. Holborn ablaze, 16 April 1941.

3. St Clement Danes, 10 May 1941.

4. Elephant and Castle Underground shelter, 11 November 1940.

5. Firefighters at work. Before September 1940, four-fifths of London's auxiliary firemen had never fought a fire.

6. Rescue of a girl in Endell Street, Holborn, a few minutes after a bomb had fallen.

7. Balham High Road, October 1940.

8. Clearing up on a morning after.

3

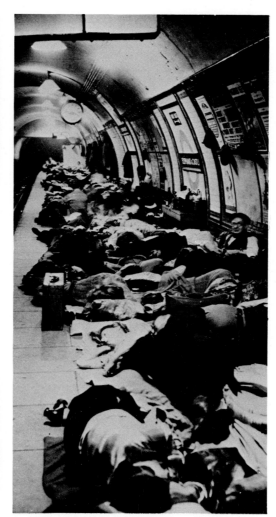

4

5

6

7

8

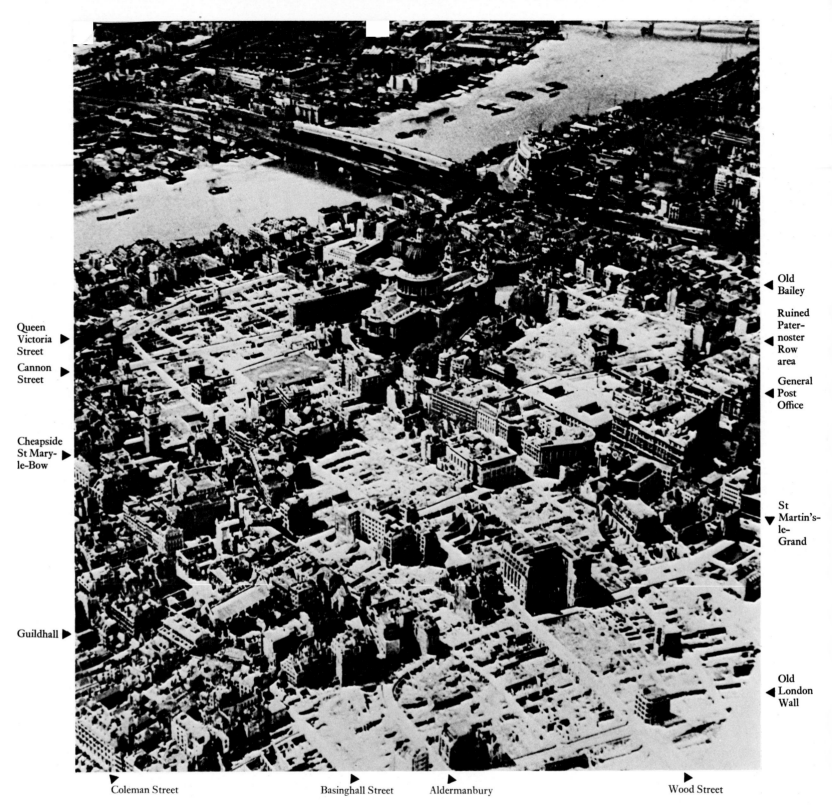

Queen
Victoria
Street ▶

Cannon
Street ▶

Cheapside
St Mary-
le-Bow ▶

Guildhall ▶

◀ Old
Bailey

◀ Ruined
Pater-
noster
Row
area

◀ General
Post
Office

▼ St
Martin's-
le-
Grand

◀ Old
London
Wall

▼ Coleman Street ▼ Basinghall Street ▼ Aldermanbury ▼ Wood Street

After the Last All-Clear

Around St Paul's 164 acres lie in ruins. This is the scene of desolation after the last air raid on the City which took place (and killed 100 people) in March 1945. In five years the area to the north-east of the cathedral had been turned into a modern Pompeii. In the dispiriting catalogue of architectural destruction are nineteen City churches. Ten of the sixteen by Wren were gutted and reduced to shells in a single night. Nineteen halls of the Livery Companies are irreparably damaged. Fire bombs on Paternoster Row have sent 5,000,000 books up in flames. St Paul's suffered a direct hit through the choir, but the cathedral still stands proud amongst the rubble thanks to the disposal of a delayed-action bomb in 1940. Further east, and outside our view, the Tower has received fifteen direct hits, and nearby All Hallows (from which Pepys watched the Fire) is gutted. Another fine medieval church, Austin Friars, is a land-mine victim and totally demolished. Of St Lawrence Jewry, the most sumptuous of Wren's churches, nothing remains of the superb carved panelling or the vestry ceiling painted by Sir James Thornhill.

Bow Bells have been destroyed, although the spire still stands. A temporary roof is visible on Guildhall replacing the burnt one; but inside the wooden statues of Gog and Magog are nothing but ashes. Outside the City, the Elizabethan Middle Temple Hall is badly damaged. Another roof–on Westminster Hall–had been hit, but not destroyed. But the Commons has gone in one of the seventeen attacks on the Houses of Parliament. More than a third of the City's square mile is a devastated wilderness soon to have the look of a romantic ruin and be given unexpected beauty by pink, flowering weeds.

South Bank Festival – 1951

Only slowly did London cut back its flowering weeds. Housing had an obvious priority over the rebuilding of offices and public undertakings. Money was short, and restrictions were severe. Six years after the war the only big public building to have gone up in the contemporary style was the Festival Hall, and the Pimlico estate – to be called Churchill Gardens – the one outstanding scheme for council flats. Then in 1951 came the Festival of Britain. It gave post-war architecture a new impetus, and was to have an incalculable influence on style.

On the twenty-seven acres of South Bank between Waterloo Bridge and County Hall, the exhibition was designed to show Britain's modern achievements in science, art and sociology. A Labour-inspired idea, its initial reception was cool. A Conservative weekly claimed: 'The only two people I have heard who really want the Festival of Britain are Mr Herbert Morrison [Deputy Prime Minister] and Mr Gerald Barry [Director General]. There may be others, but I should be surprised if they amounted to five per cent of the population.' As with the 1851 Great Exhibition, there was much pouring of cold water on an event which the public was ultimately to enjoy.

Compared with the wedding-cake splendours of former exhibitions, Festival buildings were hard for the general public to take. Sir Hugh Casson commissioned the most advanced architects, designers and artists to represent such intangible concepts as Love of Country, Love of Freedom, Pride in Craftmanship, and Fair Play. Faced with a twisted bronze by Reg Butler, entitled 'Female Figure in Repose' or Henry Moore's 'Reclining woman', the visitor had to take comfort from such advice as: 'Some people fail to see its beauty, but they'll learn in time.' This sort of condescension was as off-putting as the technological 'themes' in such exciting buildings as the Dome of Discovery, and the rendering of cloudy abstractions like 'Land is the blanket of man's birth, his launching ground to the stars'.

Less intimidating by far were the Festival Pleasure Gardens. Battersea Park had been decked out with frivolities to remind Londoners of the lost glories of Vauxhall and Ranelagh. On landing from the river, visitors found themselves in a fanciful world of curious inventions, brightly illuminated grottoes, a baroque riverside theatre and a tree walk, a suspended pathway that wound its way through from tree to tree.

Down river from the Festival was a practical demonstration of how a brave new London was shaping. In their exhibition of 'living architecture' on the Lansbury Estate

in Poplar, the L.C.C. was showing its pilot scheme for community living.

After the austerity years, there was a tremendous response, instinctive rather than intellectual, to the Festival buildings with their clean lines, vivid colours, and streamlined, unfussy style. Bewildered, but stimulated, the 8,500,000 visitors to 'Morrison's Folly' left South Bank with a feeling that a new spirit was stirring.

1. Henry Moore's 'Reclining Woman'.

2. In the aerial view of a model of the site, below, the Skylon and Dome are on the far side of the railway bridge. To the left are the Shot Tower, an ironical little model of the 1851 Crystal Palace, the Lion and Unicorn pavilion, and the Festival Hall.

3. Two contrasting symbols of the exhibition – the Skylon (designed by Powell and Moya), tall, slim, and aspiring, with, next to it, the great earthbound Dome of Discovery (Ralph Tubbs). With its saucer-shaped dome of aluminium, 365 feet in diameter, supported by forty-eight diagonal tubular struts, the Dome was by far the largest and most impressive building.

Destruction and Vandalism

The house being pulled down, left, happens to be Devonshire House, Piccadilly. Designed by William Kent, it was a beautiful Georgian building. It could as easily be Dorchester House or Grosvenor House or any of the historic private houses that have been levelled and replaced by offices or hotels. The date of demolition happens to be 1924. It could as easily be taking place today. When it comes to destroying the past, commercial pressures are stronger than aesthetic sighs. Protests are no match for pneumatic drills.

If some particularly outrageous vandalism is taken up by the Press or in Parliament, a temporary halt may be called. But the 'developers' have a safe line. London, they say, is 'a living city' and 'cannot stand still'. They generally win in the end.

The demolition of the Adelphi in 1936 was London's greatest architectural loss. The Adam brothers' elegant masterpiece was destroyed to make way for a monolithic office block. But here the developer was not the only vandal. The seeds of destruction lay in the public's neglect of the whole Adelphi area during the previous seventy years. Royal Terrace, facing the river (page 222), was mutilated, its façade ruined by heavy detail, the pilasters smothered in 1872. In 1908 Robert Street was given an extra storey, and, as the skyline shows, right, John Street had lost its classic elevation.

Even a Government Preservation Order is no guarantee of rescue. The Grange at Fulham, left, is a classic example. This early Georgian house where Samuel Richardson lived while writing *Pamela*, and where Burne-Jones had his studio, was acquired by Fulham Council (1938 and 1954). War neglect rendered it partially derelict, and though it was given a Preservation Order (1954) it was only a matter of time before this could be replaced by a Dangerous Structures Notice (1956). Demolition followed in 1957. Council flats went up on the site, so that it could be argued that a victory had been won for people's needs over antiquarian sentiment.

Plausible reasons for demolitions are not hard to find. Dry-rot can make restoration costs almost prohibitive. Old construction standards may fall short of modern requirements. A building's 'association' with a famous person may seem a trivial factor to set against progress. Only rarely are big financial sacrifices made by landlords (as happened with the Nash terraces in Regent's Park) to preserve something beautiful. Photographic records of the many acts of vandalism that have so changed the face of London in the last forty years are difficult to find. Execution is too often performed quickly, behind tall hoardings, to forestall public outcry.

5

10

7

8

9

1. The end of Devonshire House.

2. Allowed to fall into ruin – the Grange, Fulham, as it looked during two years of futile protests and public enquiry. Sometimes, it seemed, there was a deliberate failure to prevent children breaking in.

3. The house as it was in Richardson's day.

4 *and* 5. In 1908 Epstein sculpted eighteen figures for the British Medical Association building in the Strand. Their nudity was criticized – 'a form of statuary which no careful father would wish his daughter and no discriminating young man his fiancée to see,' said the *Evening Standard*. When the Rhodesian Government bought the building, it seized on the excuse of a falling piece of masonry in 1937 to 'amputate' the figures, leaving the present mutilated frieze.

6. Although Vivien Leigh protested from the gallery of the House of Lords, the St James's Theatre, King Street (opened 1835), was demolished to make way for offices in 1957. But the GLC now insists on no central London theatre demolition without replacement.

7. The ruins of the Adelphi – the site of the central block – seen from the Embankment with John Street behind.

8. An unconscious act of vandalism in 1933 caused a public outcry. When Faraday Building, the Continental and International Telephone Exchange, was completed in Queen Victoria Street, the top storey, as may be seen, right, obstructed the river and Bankside view of St Paul's. To preserve the cathedral's dominating position in the City an elaborate scale of building heights has since been laid down.

9. Intricate cast-iron pillars and brackets supporting one of the balconies of the Coal Exchange, Billingsgate. After four years of vain protests, the Exchange was demolished for road-widening in 1962. Opened by the Prince Consort in 1849, the domed rotunda with its tiers of galleries showed the Victorians' aesthetic use of cast iron. Walter Gropius called it 'a landmark in the history of early iron construction'.

10. The Crystal Palace at Sydenham was gutted by fire in 1936. The destruction of Paxton's 1851 building (to which two towers were added) was officially accepted as an accident. Nothing to the contrary has ever been proved. But the company running the Crystal Palace was not doing well, and doubts were raised.

The City Rebuilt

With a suddenness which is all the more dramatic for the initial delay, a new London has taken shape during the last decade. The skyline is transformed by tall buildings like the Post Office Tower and the office blocks on Millbank and at St Giles Circus. Traffic, the creeping menace, is eased by underpasses at Blackfriars, Euston, and Hyde Park Corner. Victorian terraces have been swept away and replaced by high flats. A new road and riverside development plan is taking shape between Blackfriars and the Tower, and almost unbelievably after a hundred years of talk, the National Theatre is nearing completion on the South Bank.

Nowhere has the concentration of new buildings been more impressive than in the City, which for nearly fifteen years after the war appeared to be dragging its feet. It seemed that no advantage was being taken to develop the bombed sites, and that selfish business interests were blocking enlightened progress.

The first important development came in 1959 with the creation of Route 11 (now London Wall), a new road, 600 yards long, linking Moorgate and Aldersgate Street. With underground car parks, pavements eighteen feet above road level with shops and public houses, this street of glass and grace has been

flanked by five office blocks, 200 feet high. Their dramatic appearance, especially at night, may be seen top right.

The most dilatory phoenix of all was the Barbican. Bedevilled by labour disputes, it was not until the late 1960s that the flats on the north side of London Wall became widely available. This housing scheme, designed to bring back 6,500 residents into the City, is dominated by three 43-storey towers like the one, above left. With its own shops, restaurants, library, art gallery, theatre, cinema and concert hall, the Barbican, when the plan is completed, will be a self-contained community within the City.

The problem of people and traffic decided the City to replace London Bridge. Rennie had not envisaged modern needs – 3,000 vehicles at peak times and 20,000 pedestrians in the rush-hours. Impetus was lent by the discovery that the old bridge was sinking at the not exactly dramatic rate of an inch every eight years. Deflecting romantic demands for a bridge with houses on it like the Tudor one, the City Engineer designed the slim, three-spanned bridge seen above. Capable of taking six lines of traffic, and with forty-one feet of pavement width, it was opened in March 1973 after five years' work.

The Guildhall, centre of the City's civic life, is now in a 'precinct' – surrounded by carefully placed, boldly designed modern

buildings and St Paul's, centre of the City's spiritual life, is being cocooned in another precinct.

The proposals for the St Paul's area were suggested in 1956 by Sir William (now Lord) Holford. The aerial view, opposite above, shows how the devastated area round the cathedral has been transformed, and the way Holford's idea for Paternoster Place – an open Italian-style piazza – has taken shape with shops on the ground floor of surrounding office blocks. A peaceful pedestrian ambiance all round St Paul's will be completed if his 1968 plan is carried out. This involves taking Cannon Street-Ludgate Circus traffic underground south of the cathedral on the line of Carter Lane, and freeing Ludgate Hill of through traffic.

It is expected that by 1980 all but seventy of the 677 acres in the City's 'Square Mile' will have been completely rebuilt.

1. Barbican tower block, and demolition of old buildings on the corner of London Wall and Aldersgate Street.

2. Office blocks flanking London Wall.

3. New London Bridge – artist's impression. Rennie's 1831 bridge was sold for £1,025,000 and transported, block by block, to Lake Havasu, Arizona.

4. New buildings round St Paul's by 1970.

5. Elevated roundabout on Western Avenue Extension at White City, under construction 1968.

6. Vickers Tower, Millbank (1963), London's most elegant skyscraper.

4

(a) Barbican flats 1969; (b) St Alphage House 1961; (c) Forty Basinghall Street 1967; (d) Guildhall precinct 1970; (e) Cheapside; (f) Watling Street; (g) Cannon Street Gateway House 1956; (h) Bank of England Extension (curved building east of St Paul's) 1959; (i) St Augustine's Tower with new Choir School 1967; (j) Financial Times 1959; (k) Memorial garden; (l) Ralli House 1965; (m) St Paul's vista; (n) College of Arms, Queen Victoria Street; (o) Carter Lane; (p) Ludgate Hill; (q) Juxon House 1966; (r) Paternoster Place 1961–1967; (s) GPO site; (t) St Martin's-le-Grand; (u) London Wall.

5

6

London Today

Looking down on the part of London which follows the curve of the Thames from Westminster to the City, one has a curious impression of tranquillity. Time appears to have stopped in a sunlit city that is noiseless and unpeopled. It might have inspired Wordsworth's reflection that 'the very houses seem asleep; And all that mighty heart is lying still'. To add to this feeling of changeless calm, Westminster Abbey stands in the foreground, immutable for the last thousand years.

All this, of course, is deceptive. Look more closely, and one sees that in the early 1970s London is undergoing a great many minor changes. It could hardly be otherwise in the centre of a city which now consists of 720 square miles and a population of 8,000,000. A photograph like the one on the right becomes out of date almost as soon as it is taken. Already a new St Thomas's Hospital has gone up to replace the demolished Victorian buildings on the far side of Westminster Bridge. On the open site beyond Waterloo Bridge, the National Theatre is now being completed. In the far distance one can just discern a London Bridge which has since been shipped to America.

Farther east, work has started on the redevelopment of the disused docks. Five thousand semi-derelict acres are to be turned into housing estates with riverside parks and lakes. This undertaking, already beset by controversy over what is really wanted, is expected to take until the end of the century. Covent Garden, just out of view beyond the upper left-hand edge of the picture, is due to be radically altered when the market moves to Battersea and takes over a vast new building at Nine Elms. Over this, too, battles have still to be fought.

Outside the City, most of the post-war changes in this part of London have taken place on South Bank, helped by bombs, the Festival, and slum clearance. A dominating feature is the Shell Building beyond County Hall, an example of big-business architecture. But the Festival Hall strikes a happier note and is at the nucleus of a group of buildings worthy of the arts for which they are designed. The heavy, unlovely block in Whitehall shows how style and proportion can be disregarded. It houses Government offices, something one would guess without being told. Immediately in front of it, Inigo Jones's delicate Banqueting Hall shows it up by contrast.

A slight haze hangs over the City, but even so it can be seen that the old square mile has acquired a new face. The skyline has been transformed by multi-storey offices. St Paul's still manages to dominate the landscape, but

it is a close-run thing. Of these dozen or so towering buildings the two to the left of St Paul's are high-point flats, part of the Barbican scheme to restore life to the City which is virtually deserted at night.

However much the London of today differs from the images we have seen of it in past centuries, the changes in the centre are not very revolutionary. Some pleasant things from the past disappear. There is occasional vandalism. But the changes never have an overall concept. To the despair of planners, there is rarely much enthusiasm and not enough money to bring about anything radical. Warnings that posterity will blame this generation for not being bolder cuts little ice. People seem almost to prefer congestion in the streets and discomfort in travel to seeing old things discarded.

But even the most complacent see that there is one menace that cannot be ignored. London can stand no further increase in traffic. Something has to be done to prevent more congestion. Heavy traffic must somehow be stopped from using narrow unsuitable streets.

Planners have produced maps on which the City and Westminster appear like citadels at the centre of a beleaguered fortress. Surrounding it are two 'ringways' and a 'motorway box' to act as defences against the daily invasion. But the proposed last-ditch 'box' to deflect through traffic would need very considerable demolition of houses and amenities. An eight-lane, thirty-seven mile motorway carving its way through Islington, Hampstead, Chelsea and Blackheath seemed too big a price to pay. It was countered by philosophical arguments and financial objections. Despite Government approval, and initial acceptance, it has been rejected by the Greater London Council. Temporarily, anyway, the scheme has been put on the shelf, but, in the hope of reducing the number of private cars, there is serious talk of providing free public transport on an increased scale.

Because there is so much gentle procrastination of this sort, it is possible to visualize the historical past even if London today is greatly changed in detail. And, as if demanding not to be forgotten, history keeps breaking through. Excavation for a new riverside road at Blackfriars turns up the Norman foundations of Baynard's Castle. Construction of a car park under New Palace Yard reveals a fifteenth-century fountain. Part of the ancient Palace of Westminster is discovered during demolition in Downing Street. The past remains very much with us, and in the mind's eye we are still able to see the lost eighteenth-century London of the Buck brothers, Kip's London, Hollar's London, and the London of Wyngaerde. It is a great heritage.

371

SOURCES OF ILLUSTRATIONS

The source for every picture is given as follows: the page number followed by the number of the caption which refers to the picture. There follows a description of the picture; painting is taken to mean oil painting, while drawing is used for all other mediums; engraving is used to describe copper, line and steel engraving. All pictures from the *Illustrated London News* are taken to be wood engravings and are therefore not described. The names of artists and engravers are given when they are known and, as many of the prints were originally published as book illustrations, every effort has been made to identify the books in which they first appeared.

The following abbreviations are used:

BM   British Museum
DAG   Dulwich Art Gallery
DE   Department of the Environment
G   Guildhall. Museum, Library and Art Gallery
GLC   Greater London Council
ILN   *Illustrated London News*
LM   London Museum
LTB   London Transport Board
M & M   Mander & Mitchenson Theatre Collection
NMM   National Maritime Museum
NMR   National Monuments Record
NPG   National Portrait Gallery
PJ   Peter Jackson Collection
PL   Pepys Library, Magdalene College, Cambridge
PLA   Port of London Authority
PRO   Public Record Office
RT   Radio Times Hulton Picture Library
SI   Syndication International
SM   Science Museum
V & A   Victoria & Albert Museum

5. King Lud and his sons. Engraving by J. T. Smith, 1795, from his *Antiquities of London & Environs*. PJ.

6–7. *The Times*.

8. (1) Drawing by A. Forestier. LM. (2) Map drawn by Peter Jackson.

9. (1) LM. (2) G. (3) Bust in the Castello di Aglié. German Archaeological Institute. (4) Portrait on coin. BM.

10–11. (1) BM. (2) Drawing by Alan Sorrell. LM. (3, 4, 5, 8) G. (6) Photograph by Bill Mackenzie. (7) BM. (9) From *London in Roman Times* published by the London Museum, 1946.

12–13. (1, 5) G. (2) From ILN 29 May 1869. PJ. (3, 4) LM. (6) G. By permission of the Roman & Mediaeval London Excavation Council. (7) Reuter.

14–15. (1) Electrotype of original medal. LM. (2, 3) Portraits on coins. BM. (4) Drawing by Alan Sorrell. LM.

16. (1) MS drawing. Cott. Tib. B.v.(1) f.40v. BM. (2) G.

17. (1) Map drawn by Peter Jackson. (2) MS drawing. Ee. 3. 59. Cambridge University Library. (3) Detail from Bayeux tapestry.

18–19. (1) Detail from Bayeux tapestry. (2) G. (3) Engraving by George Vertue (1742) from the original survey made by Haiward and Gascoyne in 1597. PJ. (4) DE. (5) MS drawing. Cott. Claud. B.iv, f.9. BM.

20–1. (1, 2) PJ. (3, 5) NMR. (4) MS drawing. Royal 2a. xxii, f.220. BM.

22. (1) Engraving by C. Grignion. PJ. (2) G. (3) MS drawing. Nero D.i, f.169v. BM.

23. (1) Engraving in Pinkerton's *Iconographia Scotica* from a drawing formerly in the College of Arms. PJ. (2) Engraving by Wise from Wilkinson's *Londina Illustrata*, 1814. PJ. (3) PJ. (4) MS drawing. Royal 14 C. vii, f.136. BM.

24. (1) MS drawing. Cott. Nero D ii, f.183. BM. (2) MS drawing. Royal 14 C vii, f.121. BM. (3) PRO.

25. (1) MS drawing. Royal 14 C vii, f.2. BM. (2) MS drawing. Royal 13 A iii, f.14. BM. (3) MS drawing. Cott. Nero D ii, f.18. BM. (4) MS drawing. Add. 42,130, f.164v. BM.

26–7. (1, 2) MS drawings. Cott. Nero D ii, f.194 and 193v. BM. (3) Drawing by Alan Sorrell. DE. (4, 5, 6) DE.

27. (1) MS drawing. Add. 28,162, f.10v. BM. (2) MS drawing. Lansdowne 451 f.127. BM. (3) MS drawing. Bodley, 264, f.83. Bodleian Library, Oxford.

28. (1) MS drawing. Royal 17 D vi, f.93v. BM. (2) MS drawing. MS. No. 61. Corpus Christi College, Cambridge. (3) Engraving from Urry's edition of Chaucer's works, published in 1721.

29–31. (1) NPG photograph. (2) MS drawing. Royal 1 E iv. BM. (3, 4, 5) MS drawings. From Froissart's *Chroniques de France et d'Angleterre*, c.1460. Royal 18 E i, ff.165v, 172, 175. BM.

32. (1) MS drawing. Harl. 1319, f.53v. BM. (2, 3, 4, 5) MS drawings. Harl. 4380, ff.181v, 184v, 186v, 197v. BM.

33. (1) Engraving by J. Bryant, 1805, from Smith's *Antiquities of Westminster*. PJ. (2) Engraving by Hawkesworth after Billings, 1835, from Britton and Brayley's *Westminster*. PJ. (3) DE.

34. (1) Engraving by J. T. Smith. 1807, from his *Antiquities of Westminster*. PJ. (2) Etching by Hollar from Dugdale's *St Pauls*. PJ. (3) NMR. (4) MS drawing. Royal 2 B vii, f.37v. BM.

35. The earliest printed view of London. Woodcut from Richard Pynson's 1510 edition of *Cronycle of Englonde*. Reproduced in the London Topographical Society Record, Vol. I, 1900.

36–7. (1) Drawing by H. W. Brewer, 1887, in the possession of *The Builder* and reproduced by their kind permission. (2) Engraving by S. Rawle, 1802. PJ. (3, 4) NMR.

38–9. (1) MS drawing. Royal 15 E ii. f.265. BM. (2) Drawing by John Carter. G. (3, 4) NMR. (5) Woodcuts from *The Present State of London* by Thomas De Laune, 1681. PJ.

40–1. (1) Leathersellers' Company. (2) MS drawing. From the Wrothesley Manuscript. G. (3) MS drawing. Mercers' Company. (4) Engraving by J. T. Smith, 1812, from his *Ancient Topography of London*. PJ. (5) Engraving published by Bowles & Carver. PJ.

42. MS drawing. MS No. 236. University Library, Ghent.

43. (1) MS drawing from *Dictes and Sayings of the Philosophers*. MS No. 265, f.viv. Lambeth Palace Library. By kind permission of His Grace the Archbishop of Canterbury. (2) Facsimile of the original in the Bodleian Library reproduced in *Facsimiles Illustrating the Labours of William Caxton . . .* by

F. C. Price, 1877. PJ. (3) From ILN 30 June 1877. PJ.

44. (1) Anon. painting. NPG. (2) Drawing. Municipal Library, Arras. (3) DE.

45. St Pauls before 1561. Photograph of unidentified engraving. Courtauld Institute of Art.

46–7. (1) MS drawing. Harl. 1498. BM. (2) Woodcut from tract printed by Wynkyn de Worde, 1509. BM. (3) Etching by Hollar, 1654. PJ. (4) Aquatint. PJ. (5) Photograph by Kerry Dundas. Gordon Frazer. (6) NMR.

48–55. Drawings by Anthony van den Wyngaerde, c.1550. Ashmolean Museum, Oxford.

56. (1) Part of the Westminster section of the 'Agas Map' copied by J. T. Smith for his *Antiquities of Westminster*. PJ. (2) Sport and General. (3) Engraving by George Vertue, published in *Vetusta Monumenta*, 1725. PJ. (4) DE.

57. MS drawing. Royal 16 F ii, f.73. BM.

58–60. College of Arms.

60. Tiltyard. Detail from Faithorne and Newcourt's map, 1658. Facsimile published by The London Topographical Society. PJ.

61. (1) Drawing from Anthony Anthony's Roll of King's Ships, 1546. PL. (2) RT. (3) Drawing, temp. Henry VIII. Cott. Aug. A iii, f.23. BM.

62. (1) Drawing by Hans Holbein. Offentliche Kunstsammlung, Basle. (2) Self portrait, 1543. Holbein. Wallace Collection.

63. (1) Woodcut book illustration. PJ. (2) PRO. (3) Painting after Holbein. NPG.

64–5. (1) MS drawing. Cott. Dom. A xvii, f.177v. PJ. (2) Map drawn by Peter Jackson. BM. (3) MS drawing. Harl. 1498 f.76. BM. (4) MS drawing. Sloane 2435 f.44v. BM. (5) Photograph taken in 1886 for the Society for Photographing Relics of Old London. PJ. (6) Engraving by Howlett after Whichello, 1820, from Wilkinson's *Londina Illustrata*. PJ.

66. (1) Water colour copy made for the Society of Antiquaries by S. H. Grimm in 1785 from a picture painted about 1547 at Cowdray and destroyed by fire in 1793. Society of Antiquaries. (2) Woodcut illustration from Foxe's *Book of Martyrs*. PJ.

67. (1) Anon. painting. NPG. (2) Woodcut heading a broadside entitled *A Conference between the Lady Jane Grey and F. Fecknam a Romish Priest*. BM. Library Pressmark, 816. m. 22. (107).

68. (1, 3) Woodcut illustrations from Foxe's *Book of Martyrs*. PJ. (2) NMR.

69. Queen Elizabeth in a triumphal car. MS drawing. Sloane 1832 f.7v. BM.

70–1. Photograph of engraved copper plate in private possession. Key map showing modern features drawn by Peter Jackson.

72–3. (1, 2, 3, 4) Drawings from a sketchbook made by one of the Heralds. BM. MS Eggerton 3320. (5) Painting by Gwilym Stretes. Warwick Castle.

74–5. (1, 2) Paintings attributed to Cornelis Bol. (1) John Evelyn, Esq. (2) DAG. (3) Copy of John Norden's Map of Westminster, 1593, published in J. T. Smith's *Antiquities of Westminster*. PJ. (4) Photograph in Westminster Public Library of a pen and ink drawing the present whereabouts of which is unknown.

76–7. Cheapside. Engraving by Basire. PJ. (1) Engraving by J. T. Smith, 1812, from his *Ancient Topography of London*. PJ. (2) Photograph taken in 1876. Source as **64–5** (5). (3) Engraving from a drawing by Schnebbelie, 1815, from Wilkinson's *Londina Illustrata*. PJ. (4) V & A. (5) Photograph taken in 1883. Source as **64–5** (5). (6) PJ.

78–9. (1, 2, 3, 4) Engravings by F. Hulsuis from *A Thankfull Remembrance of God's Mercie*, 1627. BM. (5) Source as 66 (2). (6) BM. (7, 8) Anon. paintings. NPG.

80. (1) Engraving in the Crowle Pennant. BM. (2) Engraving by J. Storer, 1804, from *Select Views of London and its Environs*. PJ. (3) Engraving from 1716 edition of Dugdale's *St Pauls*. PJ. (4) Drawing. Courtauld Institute of Art. (5) Engraving by Wise after a drawing by Schnebbelie, 1813, from Wilkinson's *Londina Illustrata*. PJ.

81. (1) Woodcut on title page of *The Life . . . of Charles Courtney*, 1612. BM. (2, 3, 4) Woodcuts from *A Caveat . . . for Common Cursetors*, 1567. By Thomas Harman. BM.

82–4. (1) Drawing attributed to Hollar. BM. (2) Detail from 'Agas'. See **99** (5). (3) Anon. engraving. PJ. (4) Engraving by J. T. Smith, 1807, from his *Antiquities of Westminster*. PJ. (5) Engraving by J. Woods after a drawing made in 1835 by R. W. Billings from Britton & Brayley's *Westminster*. PJ. (6) MS drawing. Add. 28,330 f.29. BM. (7) Wood engraving from a photograph. PJ. (8) Photograph by Donald McLeish.

85. Anon. painting. The Duke of Richmond.

86–7. (1) Anon. painting. NMM. (2) Painting by John de Critz, 1613. NPG. (3) Miniature by Nicholas Hilliard. NMM. (4) Engraving by Michael van der Gucht. PJ. (5) Anon. English woodcut. Late 16th cen. BM. (6) Drawing from *Fragments of Ancient English Shipwrighty*. Late 16th. cen. PL.

88–9. (1) BM. (2) Woodcut. Plate from Derricke's *The Image of Ireland*, 1586. Drummond collection of Library of University of Edinburgh. (3) MS drawing by Robert Adams, 1588. King George III Topographical Collection (K.Top.vi.17). BM. (4) Painting attributed to Cornelil Bol. John Evelyn, Esq. (5, 6) Painting by unknown artist, c.1588. NPG.

90–1. (1) Engraving by Francis Hogenburg, 1569. PJ. (2) Painting attributed to Adrian Thomas Key. NPG. (3, 4) Copies of drawings made by Hugh Alley, citizen and plumber, in 1598. 'Crowle Pennant' Vol. X. Nos. 18 and 41. BM. (5) Anon. engraving from a Dutch painting. PJ. (6) Water colour by T. H. Shepherd, copied from an old drawing. Crace Collection, Portfolio xvii, 46. BM.

92. (1) LM. (2) Map drawn by Peter Jackson.

93. PRO. Ref. MPB/I.

94–5. Facsimile, published by the London Topographical Society, of the unique example of the original edition in the King's Library, British Museum. PJ.

96–7. (1) Detail and continuation of above. (2) Etching by Edward William Cooke after his own drawing. Plate from *Views of the Old & New London Bridges*, 1833. PJ. (3) Engraving by John Norden. PJ. (4) Detail from Hollar's View. See **124–5**.

98–9. (1) Engraving, apparently unique, inserted in the manuscript journal of

Abram Booth, an agent of the Dutch East India Company, *c.*1600. Library of the University of Utrecht. MS No. 1198 Hist. 147. (2) Drawing made by Arend van Buchel of Utrecht in his commonplace book, it being a copy of one made by his friend Johannes de Witt who had visited London about 1596. Source as (1). MS No. 842 (Var. 355) f.132. (3) BM. (4) Map drawn by Peter Jackson. (5) Detail from a facsimile of Agas's *Civitas Londinum* made by Edward J. Francis from the Guildhall Library copy, published in 1874. PJ.

100–1. (1) Engraving by Houbraken from a painting by Zucchero. Plate from Birch's *Heads of Illustrious Persons*, 1739. PJ. (2) Miniature by Nicholas Hilliard. NMM. (3) Detail from the map attributed to Augustine Ryther, *c.*1633. (4) Detail from Visscher. See **94–5**. (5, 6, 7, 8) Anon. paintings. DAG. (9) Detail from *Civitas Londini* by John Norden, 1600. Royal Library, Stockholm.

102. (1) Detail from Agas. See **98–9** (5). (2) From the First Folio, 1623. BM. (3) G. (4) PJ. (5) Pencil drawing, partly traced over in ink, by Hollar, Iolo Williams' Collection.

103. (1) Painting by Joris Hoefnagel, 1590. Hatfield House. (2) Painting by Marcus Gheeraerts, 1600. Col. F. J. B. Wingfield-Digby.

104. Society of Antiquaries of London.

105. (1) NMR. (2) BM. (3) Detail from Agas. See **98–9** (5).

106–7. (1) MS drawing. Royal 18 A xlvii, f.1. BM. (2) Photograph by Edwin Smith. (3) Engraved title page by Renold Elstrack. PJ. (4) Engraved title page by William Hole. BM.

107. (1) Anon. painting. Corpus Christi College, Cambridge. (2) Drawing by Wyngaerde. See **48–55**.

108. (1) MS drawing. Add. 35325 f.37v. BM. (2) Engraving by 'S H'. Plate from *The Archs of Triumph, erected in honour of the High and Mighty Prince James the first, etc.* (1603) Crace Collection. Port. xxxviii, 39. BM.

109. Engraving by Francisco Delarame. Royal Library, Windsor Castle. Reproduced by Gracious Permission of HM The Queen.

110–11. (1) Anon. engraving, 1606. PJ. (2) BM. (3) Aquatint by W. Read. Published 1 Nov. 1822, in *La Belle Assemblée*. PJ. (4) Engraving by J. T. Smith from his *Antiquities of Westminster*, 1804. With map reconstruction by Peter Jackson. PJ. (5) Engraving by G. Dale from a drawing by W. Capon. From Wilkinson's *Londina Illustrata*. 1819. PJ. (6) Anon. engraving, 1606. PJ.

112–13 (1) Detail from engraving by Hoefnagel in Braun's *Civitates Orbis Terrarum*. 1572. BM. (2) Engraving from Smith's *Antiquities of London*, 1791. PJ. (3) Etching by Hollar, 1665. PJ. (4) Engraving from Evelyn's *Sylva*, 1670, after De Caus, 1615. BM. (5) Engraving by Howlett from a drawing made in 1585 by Treswell. From Wilkinson's *Londina Illustrata*. PJ. (6) Painting after Cornelius Johnson. NPG.

114. (1) Painting by Daniel Mytens. Duke of Norfolk. (2) Detail from an etching by Hollar after Meyssens, reproduced in *Wenceslaus Hollar and his views of London*, by Arthur M. Hind. (3, 4) Engravings from J. T. Smith's *Sixty-two Additional Plates to Smith's Antiquities of Westminster*, copied from Hollar's etchings. PJ.

115–17. (1) Drawing by Van Dyck. Devonshire Collection, Chatsworth. Reproduced by permission of the Trustees. (2) Drawing by Inigo Jones. Royal Institute of British Architects. (3, 4) Drawings by Inigo Jones. Source as (1). (5) Anon. engraving. PJ. (6) Anon. drawing. PL. (7) Detail from etching by Hollar. See **136**. (8) Drawing by Inigo Jones. Worcester College, Oxford. (9) Photograph by Teddy Schwarz. (10) Etching by Hollar. PJ.

118–19. (1) Etching by Hollar. (Only known impression.) BM. (2) Photograph taken by York & Son. *c.*1900. PJ. (3) NMR. (4) Engraving by Sutton Nicholls from Strype's edition of Stow's *Survay of London*, 1754. PJ. (5) Lithograph by George Scharf from a drawing by B. Howlet, 1817. PJ.

120–1. (1) Etching by Hollar. PJ. (2) Etching by Hollar. PJ. (3) Engraving by George Vertue, from Maitland's *History & Survey of London*, 1739. PJ. (4) Woodcut from broadside entitled *The Malignant's treacherous & bloody plot against the Parliament . . .*, 1643. BM. (5) Anon. drawing. LM. (6) Etching by Hollar. Source as **80** (1).

122–3. (1) Anon. engraving. PJ. (2) Painting by Edward Bower. By Gracious Permission of H M Queen Elizabeth The Queen Mother. (3) Anon. contemporary etching. PJ. (4) Painting by Gerard Soest. NPG. (5) Detail from engraving by H. Terasson, 1713. PJ.

124–5. Etching by Hollar, 1647. Facsimile published by The London Topographical Society. PJ.

126–7. (1) Painting by Sir Peter Lely. City Museum & Art Gallery, Birmingham. (2) Engraving by D. Smith, 1810. PJ. (3) Great Seal of the Commonwealth, designed by Thomas Simon. BM. (4) Engraving. No. 858 in the BM Collection of Personal and Political Satires. (5) Etching by Hollar, 1647. PJ.

128–9. (1) Painting attributed to I. Fuller. Vivian E. Cornelius, Esq. (2) Anon. contemporary engraving. PJ. (3) Painting by John Michael Wright. By Gracious Permission of H M The Queen. (4) Etching by Hollar from John Ogilby's *A Brief Narrative of his Majestie's Solemn Coronation*, 1662. PJ.

130–1. (1) Detail from anon. painting. Duke of Roxburghe. (2) Detail from anon. engraving entitled *Her Maj. Royal Palace and Park of St James's*, published in 1715. (Ref. Crace. Port. xii, 2.) PJ. (3) Detail from John Kip's view. See **194–5**. PJ. (4) Painting by Simon Verelst, *c.*1670. Arnold Wiggins, Esq. (5) Photograph by E. P. Olney.

132–3. (1) Engraving by George Vertue, 1747, based on a plan made about 1670. PJ. (2) Pen and ink drawing by Kip or Knyff, *c.*1695. Crowle Pennant. iv. 8. BM. (3) Etching by Hollar. PJ. (4) Engraving from a drawing by Hollar. From Wilkinson's *Londina Illustrata*. PJ.

134. (1) Detail from Hollar's view. See **136**. (2) Anon. engraving published in 1814, by J. Nichols. PJ. (3) Engraving by Sawyer from Wilkinson's *Londina Illustrata*, 1809. PJ. (4) Painting by Sir Peter Lely. Earl of Jersey. (5) Painting by William Sheppard. NPG. (6) Detail from Ogilby and Morgan's Map, 1676.

135. (1) Painting by John Hayls, 1666. NPG. (2) Anon. drawing. PL. (3) Anon. engraving published by Tho. Taylor, 1714. PJ.

136. Etching by Wenceslaus Hollar, *c.*1658. Facsimile published by The London Topographical Society from the unique impression in the BM.

138–9. (1) Etching by Hollar, 1658, from Dugdale's *St Pauls*. PJ. (2) Engraving from Wilkinson's *Londina Illustrata* after the etching by Hollar in Dugdale's *Monasticon*, 1673. PJ. (3) PJ. (4) Anon. drawing. NMR.

140–1. (1) Woodcut from a broadside entitled *A Looking-glasse for City and Countrey*, 1630. Broadsides No. 303. Society of Antiquaries. (2) Engraved reproduction from a woodcut original. PJ. (3, 4, 7) Engravings by John Dunstall. LM. (5, 6) Anon. engravings. PL.

142–7. (1) Anon. engraving. PJ. (2) Painting by unidentified Dutch artist. LM. (3) Entry from John Webb's Hearth Tax receipt book (No. 4) Ref.E.179/252/32 PRO. (4) Detail from engraving from Bockler's *Architectura Curiosa Nova*, 1662. SM. (5) Etching by Hollar, 1666. PJ. (6) Etching by Hollar. Facsimile published by The London Topographical Society. (7) LM. (8) PJ. (9) Anon. engraving published in 1676. PJ.

148–9. (1) Photograph by Teddy Schwarz. (2) Anon. engraving. Crace Collection. Port. vi, 277. BM. (3) Engraving from Harrison's *History of London*. PJ. (4) Engraving by T. White after T. Malton, 1768. PJ. (5) Detail from engraving of St Mary-le-Bow by N. Yates and J. Collins after R. Thacker. *c.*1680. PJ. (6) Engraving by W. Sherwin. Crace Collection. Port. xxii, 43. BM.

150–1. (1) Painting by Johann Baptist Closterman, *c.*1695. Royal Society. (2) Drawing by Thomas Wyck, *c.*1673. G. (3) Drawing. All Souls Collection, Vol. 2, No. 13. Photograph Courtauld Institute of Art. (4) Engraving by Charles Burt after J. Buckler. PJ. (5) Photograph Courtauld Institute of Art. (6) Engraving by Edward Rooker after S. Wale and J. Gwyn, 1755. PJ.

152–3. (Panorama of the City Churches). Detail from engraving, probably by J. Kip, printed and sold by I. Smith in Exeter 'Change, *c.*1720. PJ. (1) Engraving by N. Yates and J. Collins after R. Thacker, *c.*1680. PJ. (2) Engraving by B. Cole. PJ. (3) Aquatint by Thomas Malton, 1798. From Malton's *A Picturesque Tour through the Cities of London & Westminster*. PJ. (4) Photographic reproduction from G. H. Birch's *London Churches of the 17th and 18th centuries*, 1896. PJ. (5) Engraving by J. Harris, 1714. PJ. (6) Engraving by T. Bowles after J. Donowell, 1761. PJ.

154–5. (1) Engraving by P. Vanderbank. PJ. (2) Anon. engraving. PJ. (3, 4, 5, 6) Details from engraved broadside. PL.

156. (1) Watercolour drawing by C. H. Matthews, 1784. PJ. (2) Engraving by Simpson. PJ. (3) Anon. engraving. PJ.

157. (1) Etching by Francis Place. NMM. (2) DE. (3) Etching by Hollar, 1667. PJ. (4) Anon. engraving. PL.

158–60. (1) Painting after Lely. NPG. (2) Engraving by Sutton Nicholls from Strype's edition of Stow's *Survay of London*, 1754. PJ. (3) Detail from Faithorne and Newcourt's Map, 1658. See **60**. (4) Engraving by Schiavonetti after S. Harding, 1792. PJ. (5) Crace Collection. Port. xii, 2. BM. (6, 7) Source as (2). (8) Painting by Cornelius Jonson. Viscount De L'Isle, V.C. Penshurst Place. (9) Detail from anon. engraving in Crace Collection. Port. xxix. BM. (10) Detail from engraving in Sandford's *History of the Coronation of . . . James II*, 1687. PJ.

161. (1, 2, 3, 4) All contemporary anon. engravings. PJ.

162–3. (1) Anon. contemporary etching. PJ. (2) Engraving by Mark Anthony Haudroy, published by Thos. Bowles. PJ. (3) DE. (4) Drawing by Thomas Wise. DE.

164. (1) Detail from an engraving by H. Mutlow of a map of Deptford drawn by John Evelyn. PJ. (2) Pen and ink drawing. Evelyn Collection, Christchurch, Oxford.

165. (1) Engraving by J. Kip after Thomas Badslade, 1717. (Proof with lettering hand written.) PJ. (2) Painting by Sir Godfrey Kneller, 1695. Duke of Bedford. (3) Painting by unknown artist. *c.*1670. NMM.

166–7. (1) Anon. engraving entitled *Her Maj. Royal Palace and Park of St James's*, published *c.*1715. (Ref. Crace. Port. xii, 2.) PJ. (2) Painting by unknown artist. DE. (3) Detail from an engraving by J. Kip after L. Knyff, *c.*1707. PJ.

168–9. (1) Engraving by W. H. Toms after T. Lawranson, 1771. PJ. (2) DE. (3) Detail from west wall, Painted Hall, Greenwich. DE. (4) DE.

170–1 (1) Painting by Peter Tillemans. DE. (2) Engraving by J. T. Smith after Sandby, 1805. From Smith's *Antiquities of Westminster*. PJ. (3) Explanatory details by Peter Jackson superimposed on an engraving from Britton and Brayley's *History of the Ancient Palace & late Houses of Parliament at Westminster*, 1835. PJ.

172. (1) Photograph by Henry Dixon for the Society for Photographing Relics of Old London, 1886. PJ. (2) Detail from Kip's view. See **194**. PJ. (3) Engraving by J. Cole. PJ.

173. (1) Anon. drawing. BM. (2) The original Lion's Head now at Woburn House. Duke of Bedford. (3) G.

174. (1) Engraving from Robert Morden's *A Book of the Prospects of the most remarkable places in and about the City of London*. *c.*1700. PJ. (2) Pen and ink drawing. Add. MS 10403. BM. (3) Engraving by J. Green after S. Wale from *London and its environs*, published by R. & J. Dodsley, 1761. PJ.

175. Engraving from *Trivia or the Art of Walking the Streets of London* by John Gay, 1716. PJ.

176–83. Buck's Panorama of the Thames. Engraving by Samuel and Nathaniel Buck, published in 1749. PJ. (1) Engraving by W. H. Toms after H. Gravelot, 1738. PJ. (2) Engraving by Rooker after P. Sandby, 1766. PJ. (3) Aquatint by Thomas Malton, 1795. From his *Picturesque Tour* . . . . PJ. (4) Anon. engraving published 1793 by N. Smith. PJ. (5) Anon. engraving. PJ. (6) Drawing by Canaletto. BM. (7) Engraving by L. P. Boitard, 1757. PJ.

184–5. (1) Detail from an aquatint designed to be made into a fan. PJ. (2) Wood engraving from Hone's *Every-day Book*, 1826. PJ. (3) Detail from Rocque. See **196**. (4) Anon. drawing. PJ. (5) Detail from the original broadside. PJ.

186. (1) Engraving after Hogarth. PJ. (2) Detail from Dutch engraving entitled *De Verwarde Actionisten Torenbouw tot Babel*. PJ. (3) Detail from satirical broadside published by Carington Bowles, 1720. PJ.

187. (1) Bow porcelain figure. V & A. (2) Anon. painting. LM. (3) Governors and Company of The Bank of England.

188–9. (1) Soane Museum. (2) NPG. (3) Royal Academy. (4) Engraving by Rawle from *European Magazine*. PJ. (5) PJ.

190–2. (1) Engraving by J. Kip after L. Knyff, *c.*1707. PJ. (2) Painting by Bartholomew Dandridge. NPG. (3) Painting by Knapton. Devonshire Collection. Chatsworth. (4) Wood engraving from *The Builder*, 28 Oct. 1854. (5) Drawing by William Kent. Duke of Devonshire. (6) PJ. (7) Engraving by Cole from Maitland's *History of London*, 1756. PJ. (8) Engraving by Walker after Donwell. PJ. (9) Robert Atkinson & Partners. (10) DE.

193. (1) Anon. engraving published by J. Smith, 1714. PJ. (2) Detail from **166–7** (1).

194–5. Part of engraving by John Kip entitled *A Prospect of the City of London, Westminster, and St James's Park. c.* 1710. PJ.

196–7. Part of *A Plan of the Cities of London and Westminster* . . . . Engraved by John Pine from the survey taken by John Rocque, 1746. Facsimile published by The London Topographical Society. (Waywiser) Detail from 18th. cen. map reproduced in *London 200 Years Ago*, by W. Crawford Snowden.

198–9. (1) Warburg Institute. (2) Engraving by Pearce Tempest after Marcellus Laroon, 1711. PJ. (3) Pen and wash drawing by Marcellus Laroon, 1735. Witt Collection, Courtauld Institute of Art. (4) Engraving by P. Angier after P. Brookes. PJ.

200–3. (1) Photograph by A. F. Kersting. (2) Detail from Rocque. See **196–7**. (3) Engraving by W. Woolnoth after Elmes. PJ. (4) Engraving by H. Fernell after Hogarth. Plate 8, *Rake's Progress*. PJ. (5) Engraving from Hughson's *Walks through London*, 1816. PJ. (6) Engraving from Maitland's *History of London*, 1756. PJ. (7) Royal College of Surgeons. (8) Detail from engraving published by Bowles, 1725. Wellcome Historical Medical Museum. (9) Anon. engraving. Source as (8). (10) Engraving from a painting by William Bellers, 1753. LM. (11) Mezzotint after Reynolds. PJ. (12) Lithograph by T. C. Wilson from a drawing by Rowlandson. Source as (8). (13) Engraving by Priscott after Nebot. PJ. (14) Engraving by T. Jefferys. Part of plate from the *Gentleman's Magazine*, Vol. xvii, p.284. June 1747. PJ. (15) Engraving by Grignion and Canot after Vale, 1749. PJ.

204–5. (1) Engraving by Boitard, 1747. PJ. (2, 3) Frontispiece engraved by J. June, and title page. Wilmarth S. Lewis Collection, Farmington, Connecticut. By arrangement with Peter Murray Hill, Ltd. (4) Anon. engraving. PJ. (5) Painting by J. Wollaston. NPG. (6) Frontispiece to Jonas Hanway's *Reflections*, 1761. BM. (7) Painting by N. Hone, 1766. NPG.

206–7. (1, 2) BM. (3) Detail from a view of Vauxhall Gardens, aquatint by F. Jukes, engraved by R. Pollard after the drawing by T. Rowlandson, 1785. PJ. (4) Engraving by Charles John Smith, 1836. PJ. (5, 6) PJ.

208–11. (1) Anon. engraving published by T. Harrison. PJ. (2) Engraving by J. Lodge. PJ. (3) Engraving by Valois. PJ. (4) Anon. engraving published 1767. PJ. (5) Anon. engraving. Published by T. Bowles. PJ. (6) Anon. engraving. PJ. (7) Engraving by Jefferies after Ryley. From the *Newgate Calendar*. PJ. (8) Anon. engraving. PJ. (9) Anon. engraving published by Matthew Darly, 1779. BM. (10) Aquatint by Thomas Malton from his *Picturesque Tour* . . ., 1792. PJ. (11) Anon. engraving published by J. Corn, 1785. PJ. (12) Engraving from the *Malefactor's Register*. PJ. (13) Anon. engraving. PJ. (14, 17) Details from an engraving published with *The Report on the Fleet and the Marshalsea, etc.*, 1729. PJ. (15) Anon. engraving from the *Newgate Calendar*. PJ. (16) Engraving by Hogarth, 1747. Plate 11 of Industry & Idleness. PJ. (18) Detail from Rocque. See **196–7**. (19, 20) Anon. engravings. PJ.

212–13. (1) Engraving by J. June, 1747. PJ. (2) Detail from Rocque. See **196–7**. (3) Etching by John Wykeham Archer from his *Vestiges of Old London*, 1851. PJ. (4) Painting by Samuel Scott. G. (5) Etching by Piranesi 'at Rome'. Published 1766. PJ.

214–15. (1) Painting by Canaletto. Duke of Buccleuch & Queensbury. (2) Lord Fairhaven. (3) Painting attributed to Canaletto. Governors and Company of The Bank of England.

216. (1) Painting by Samuel Scott. Duke of Bedford. (2) Anon. drawing. PJ.

217. (1) Painting by Stephen Slaughter, 1736. NPG. (2) Anon. engraving. BM. (3, 4) Engraving by Green after Wale. PJ.

218–21. (1) PJ. (2, 3) The Grosvenor Estate. (4) NPG. (5) Earl of Cadogan. (6) Engraving by Sutton Nicholls from Strype's edition of Stow's *Survay*, 1754. PJ. (7) Aquatint by Thomas Malton from his *Picturesque Tour* . . ., 1792. LM. (8) Engraving by Muller after Eyre, 1750. PJ. (9) Etching by J. P. Malcolm from his *Anecdotes of the Manners and Customs of London*, 1808. PJ. (10) Detail from an aquatint by R. Earlom, drawn and etched by Robert Smirke, Jnr., published 1801 by J. & J. Boydell. PJ. (11) Engraving by Sutton Nicholls, 1719. BM. (12) Aquatint from Ackerman's *Repository of Arts*, Vol. x, pt. 57, 1813. PJ. (13) Drawing by T. H. Shepherd. Crace. Port. xxix, 99. BM. (14) Woodcut from *Town & Country Magazine*, Feb. 1771. PJ. (15) Source as (7). (16) Anon. engraving published by Boydell, *c.*1751. PJ.

222–3. (1) Engraving by Pasterini after Adams, 1770. From *The Works in Architecture of Robert and James Adam*. PJ. (2) Aquatint by Thomas Malton from his *Picturesque Tour* . . ., 1792. PJ. (3) Engraving by and after J. Storer from Cole's *Residences of Actors*. PJ. (4) Photograph by A. F. Kersting. (5) Photograph by Eileen Tweedy.

224–5. (1) Engraving by Muller after Wale. PJ. (2) Anon. engraving published by John & Carington Bowles, *c.* 1752. PJ. (3) Painting by Canaletto. National Gallery. (4) Anon. engraving. PJ.

226–7. (1) Painting by Zoffany. Towneley Hall Art Gallery & Museum, Burnley. (2) Painting by Zoffany. (3) Engraving by Martini after Ramberg. PJ.

228–9. (1) Engraving by Beglie, 1776. *From The Works in Architecture of Robert and James Adam*. PJ. (2) Anon. engraving 1778. V & A. (3) Engraving by White after Parkinson. PJ. (4) Etching by J. Sayers. PJ. (5) Anon. engraving. V & A. (6) Watercolour by Edward Dayes, 1795. Henry E. Huntington Library & Art Gallery, California.

230–1 (1) Engraving by Heath after Wheatley, 1790. PJ. (2) Anon. engraving. LM. (3) Engraving after Bran, 1780. PJ. (4) Watercolour by Robert Dighton. Royal Library, Windsor Castle. Reproduced by Gracious Permission of H M The Queen.

232–3. (1) Engraving attributed to Gravelot. From *Town and Country Magazine*, 1772. PJ. (2) Photograph Teddy Schwarz. (3) Trade card engraved by Evans after Lock. PJ. (4) Aquatint from Ackerman's *Repository of Arts*, April 1809. PJ. (5) Trade card engraved by Skelton. PJ. (6) Detail from engraving *c.* 1750. PJ.

234. (1) Stipple engraving by Bartolozzi after Rigaud, 1785. Honourable Artillery Co. (2) Aquatint by Jukes after Brewer. Source as (1).

235. Detail from aquatint of Hanover Square by Pollard and Jukes after Dayes. PJ.

236–8. (1) Aquatint by J. Black after T. H. Shepherd, 1822. LM. (2) Etching published by G. Humphrey, 1824. PJ. (3) Engraving published 1 Jan. 1818. PJ. (4) Aquatint after T. H. Shepherd. LM. (5) Aquatint by T. Sutherland after Augustus Pugin, 1817. PJ. (6) Aquatint from Ackerman's *Repository of Arts*, Vol. vi, pt. 34, 1811. PJ. (7) Engraving by Cleghorn after T. H. Shepherd. From *Metropolitan Improvements*, 1827. PJ. (8) NMR. (9) Photograph. Edwin Smith. (10) Anon. lithograph. PJ.

239. (1) PJ. (2) Aquatint by W. H. Pyne from his *Costume of Great Britain*, 1808. PJ. (3) Etching by Rowlandson after Woodward. PJ.

240–1. (1) Detail from the plan. BM. Maps. England. Canals. 1265 (23). (2, 3, 4) Engravings after T. H. Shepherd, 1828. From *Metropolitan Improvements*, PJ. (5) Etching by H. Browne, published 1815 by R. Wilkinson. PJ. (6) Lithograph by E. Duncan, 1838. PJ.

242–3. (1) Broadside. BM. (2) PJ. (3) Anon. aquatint. PJ. (4) Painting by Stothard. Governors and Company of The Bank of England. (5) Anon. etching dated 1798. PJ. (6) Aquatint by I. Hill after C. A. Pugin. NMM.

244–5. (1) Etching by G. Cruikshank, 1820. PJ. (2) Aquatint by Dubourg, 1821. From *An Impartial Historical Narrative of those Momentous Events which have taken place In This Country, etc.* PJ. (3, 4) Etchings by Richard Dighton, 1820. PJ. Site maps by Peter Jackson.

246–7. (1) Engraving by W. Radcliff after T. H. Shepherd, 1829. From *Metropolitan Improvements*. PJ. (2) Engraving by Barrett after Ryley. From *European Magazine*. PJ. (3) Detail from map of London engraved by Neele. From Lambert's *History of London*, 1806. PJ. (4) Detail from the variant sheet B.1. from Horwood's Plan of London. PJ. (5) Detail from same map as (3) above. (6) Engraving by Sparrow after Schnebbelie, 1810. From Hughson's *Description of London*. PJ. (7) Photograph. E. P. Olney. (8) NMR.

248. (1) Proof soft-ground etching to which a watercolour wash has been applied to indicate where an aquatint ground was to be laid. By John Augustus Atkinson. PJ. (2) Etching by Alfred Croquis. PJ.

249. (1) Engraving by Higham after Parris. PJ. (2) Engraving by Rawle from *Prospectus. View of London and the surrounding country, taken . . . from an observatory purposely erected over the Cross of St Paul's Cathedral*, by Thomas Hornor, 1823. PJ. (3) Aquatint published by Ackerman, 1829. PJ.

250–1. (1, 2) Engravings after T. H. Shepherd from *Metropolitan Improvements*. PJ. (3) Handbill. PJ. (4) Lithograph by N. Whittock, 1829. PJ. (5) Stipple engraving by R. Cooper from Wilson's *Wonderful Characters*, 1821. PJ. (6) Aquatint by Thomas Rowlandson. PJ. (7) Aquatint by George Cruikshank, 1826. PJ. (8) Handbill. PJ. (9) Poster. PJ.

252–3. (1) Detail from engraving published by Richard Holmes Laurie, 1823. PJ. (2) Lithograph. LM. (3) LTB. (4) Aquatint by F. Rosenberg after J. Pollard, 1831. BM. (5) Aquatint by C. Hunt after W. Summers, 1833. SM.

254. (1, 2, 3) Aquatints drawn and etched by I. R. and G. Cruikshank from Pierce Egan's *Life in London*, 1821. PJ.

255–7. (1) Painting by W. J. Huggins. PLA. (2, 3) Aquatints by William Daniell, 1804. PLA. (4) Lithograph by W. Parrott. PLA. (5) Engraving by S. Hall, 1834. PJ. (6) Engraving by Willey Reveley, *c.*1796. PJ. (7) Aquatint by J. Phelps after W. Ranwell, 1828, PLA.

258–9. (1) Lithograph by George Scharf drawn in June 1830. PJ. (2) Anon. engraving 1758. PJ. (3, 4) Etchings by Edward William Cooke from *Views of the New and Old London Bridges*, 1833. PJ. (5) Engraving by and after Thomas Higham. PJ.

260. (1) Detail from a broadside. PJ. (2) Photograph from LCC *Survey of London*, Vol. xvi. (3) Detail from cartoon entitled *The Last Day or the fall of the Charleys*. Etching by William Heath, 1829. PJ. (4) From *ILN*, 17 June 1848. PJ.

261. Engraving by Henshall after Marshall. Title page decoration to Henshall's *Illustrated Topography of Thirty Miles Around London*, 1839. PJ.

262–3. Wood engraving by Smyth. Published as a supplement to *ILN*, 11 Jan. 1845. PJ.

264–5. (1) Lithograph by and after William Heath. LM. (2) Lithograph by William C. Smith. PJ. (3) Aquatint by W. H. Pyne, 1805, from his *Costume of Great Britain*. PJ. (4) Aquatint by R. G. Reeve after James Pollard. LM. (5) Lithograph by and after William Heath. PJ.

266–7. Stafford House. Painting by Eugene Lami. Duchess of Sutherland. (1) Lithograph. PJ. (2) Drawing by Eugene Lami. V & A. (3) Lithograph by Thomas Shotter Boys from his *Original Views of London as it is*, 1842.

268–9. (1) Drawing by R. B. Schnebbelie, 1840. LM. (2) Aquatint by C. Hunt after A. B. Clayton, 1834. SM. (3) Wood engraving. PJ. (4) Engraving by H. Griffiths after E. Duncan. PJ. (5) Lithograph by and after J. C. Bourne, 1838, from his *London and Birmingham Railway*. PJ.

270–1. (1) Anon. painting. Museum of British Transport. (2) From *ILN*, 22 April 1865. PJ. (3) Wood engraving from *A Story with a Vengeance* by Reach and Brooks, 1852. (4) From *ILN*, 9 April 1859. PJ. Map of Railways by Peter Jackson.

272–3. (1) Aquatint by R. G. Reeves after James Pollard, 1830. PJ. (2) Engraving by Ellis after Gilbert from *London Interiors*, 1841. PJ. (3) From *ILN*, 24 March 1855. PJ. (4) Wood engraving from *Illustrated Times*, 20 June 1857. PJ. (5) Etching from *The World in Miniature*, Edited by W. H. Pyne, published by

R. Ackerman, 1827. PJ. (6) From *ILN*, 28 Feb. 1863. PJ.

274–5. (1) Photograph taken by W. H. Fox Talbot, 1844. Harold White Collection. (2) Engraving by J. Maurer, 1740. PJ. (3) Map by Peter Jackson. (4) From *ILN*, 4 Nov. 1843. PJ. (5) Painting by John Ballantyne. NPG.

276–7. (1) Lithograph by Traulman after Bonisch. LTB. (2) Detail from a French lithograph by Levilly after Massai. PJ. (3) Engraving by Lacey after Jones from *Mighty London Illustrated*. PJ. (4) From *ILN*, 1 April 1843. PJ. (5) Wood engraving from *Illustrated News of the World*, 3 April 1858. PJ. (6) From *ILN*, 8 Jan. 1870. PJ.

278–9. (1) Wood engraving from *Historic Times*, 1849. PJ. (2) From *ILN*, 15 Sept. 1849. PJ. (3) From the *Journal of the London Society*, No. 326. (4) From *ILN*, 20 Jan. 1849. RT. (6) From Cassell's *Old and New London*. PJ. (7) Wood engraving from *ILN*, 4 Oct. 1845. PJ. (8) Felix Barker.

280–3. (1) Lithograph by and after Charles Burton. PJ. (2) V & A. (3) Painting by Henry Windham Phillips. V & A. (4, 5) From *ILN*, 19 July 1851, and 14 Dec. 1850. PJ. (6) Painting by Henry C. Selous. V & A. (7, 8) Lithographs from Dickinson's *Comprehensive Pictures of the Great Exhibition of 1851*. PJ.

284–5. (1) Painting by J. Levin. PJ. (2) Lithograph by C. J. Culliford. PJ. (3) Lithograph published by F. W. Farbrother. PJ. (4, 6) Wood engravings from Mayhew's *London Labour and the London Poor*, 1862. PJ. (5) Wood engraving from *Paul Pry*, 4 Dec. 1848. PJ.

286–9. (1) Lithograph by George Scharf. PJ. (2) Engraving by and after Melville, from *London Interiors*. PJ. (3) Engraving from Payne's *Illustrated London*. PJ. (4) Engraving by Chavanne after T. H. Shepherd from *Mighty London*. PJ. (5) From *ILN*, 7 June 1851. PJ. (6) Handbill. PJ. (7) Handbill. PJ. (8) Etching by George Cruikshank. PJ. (9) Handbill. PJ. (10) Engraving by Radclyffe after Moore, from *London Interiors*. PJ. (11) Chromolithograph. (12) From *ILN*, 19 Aug. 1843. PJ. (13) From *ILN*, 10 May 1851. PJ. (14) Handbill. PJ. (15) Wood engraving after a drawing by M'Connell from *Twice Round the Clock* by George Augustus Sala, 1857. PJ.

290–3. (1) Kensington Public Library. (2) Wood engraving from *ILN*, 9 Aug. 1856. PJ. (3) Engraving from Tallis's *Illustrated London*, 1851. PJ. (4) Photograph taken in 1856. V & A. (5) Drawing by Lanchenick, 1863. V & A. (6) Engraving by Prior after Andrews for the Stationers' *Almanack*, 1870. PJ. (7) Central Press Photograph. (8) Wood engraving from the *London Journal*, 1859. PJ. (9) PJ. (10) Lithograph by and after Charles Rivière from *Vues de Londres*. PJ. (11, 12, 13, 14) PJ. Aerial View of Kensington. Aerofilms.

294–6. (1) Etching by George Cruikshank, 1829. PJ. (2) Detail of map by B. R. Davies, 1843. PJ. (3) Detail of map published by G. Jones, 1815. PJ. (4) Holland & Hannen & Cubitt, Ltd. (5) Engraving from Tallis's *Illustrated London*, 1851. PJ. (6) From *ILN*, 6 Sept. 1851. PJ. (7) From *ILN*, 24 March 1866. PJ. (8) GLC. (9) NMR. (10, 11) GLC.

297. (1) PJ. (2) Wood engraving from *Illustrated Times*, 29 June 1861. PJ. (3) From *ILN*, 25 Jan. 1862. PJ. (4) From *ILN*, 29 June 1861. PJ.

298–9. (1) From *ILN*, 25 June 1842. PJ. (2) Painting by J. Knight. NPG. (3) Painting by unknown artist. NPG. (4) From *ILN*, 7 Feb. 1852. PJ. (5) Engraving from Cassell's *Old and New London*. PJ. (6) From *ILN*, 5 June 1858. PJ. (7) From *ILN*, 2 June 1860. PJ. (8, 9) Wood engravings from *Illustrated Times*, 16 Oct. 1858. PJ.

300–1. (1) Woodcut from *Lloyd's Steam-boat Excursion Guide*. PJ. (2) Detail from supplement to *ILN*, 23 Aug. 1851. PJ. (3) Wood engraving reproduced in *Down the River to the Sea* by Leonard G. Lane. (4) Wood engraving from a drawing by William M'Connell from Sala's *Twice Round the Clock*, 1857. PJ. (5) From *ILN*, 11 April 1846. PJ. (6) Engraving by George Cooke after Samuel Prout, 1826, from *Views in London and its Vicinity*. PJ. (7, 8, 9) From *ILN*, 14 Nov. 1857; 24 Aug. 1861; 14 Sept. 1878. PJ.

302–3. (1) Lithograph by W. Simpson after E. Walker, 1852. PJ. (2, 3) Water colour drawings by George Scharf. BM. (4) From *ILN*, 28 Feb. 1852. PJ. (5) Engraving by Sands after Allom. PJ. (6) Wood engraving from the *Graphic*, 16 Jan. 1875. PJ. (7) Engraving by H. Melville after T. H. Shepherd from *London Interiors*, 1841. PJ. (8) From *ILN*, 19 April 1879. PJ.

304–5. All pictures from *ILN* of following dates. All PJ. (1) 4 Aug. 1866. (2) 21 Dec. 1867. (3) 26 Jan. 1867. (4) 9 Aug. 1862. (5) 11 June 1864. (6) 9 Dec. 1865. (7) 30 Jan. 1875. (8) 25 March 1876.

306. (1, 2, 3) From *ILN*, 2 Feb. 1861; 7 April 1860; 13 Sept. 1862. PJ.

307. (1) Etching by George Cruikshank, 1835. PJ. (2) *The Times*. (3) From *ILN*, 15 June 1867. PJ.

308. (1) From *ILN*, 30 Nov. 1850. PJ. (2) From *ILN*, 14 Dec. 1850. PJ. (3) Wood engraving from *Punch*, 9 Nov. 1850. PJ. (4) PJ.

309. (1) From *ILN*, 17 Oct. 1857. PJ. (2) Wood engraving. PJ. (3) Wood engraving. Salvation Army. (4) PJ.

310–11. (1) Wood engraving from *Illustrated Times*, 28 Feb. 1857. PJ. (2) From *ILN*, 15 Feb. 1868. PJ. (3) From *ILN*, 9 March 1867. PJ. (4, 5, 6, 7, 10) Wood engravings from photographs. From Mayhew's *London Labour and the London Poor*, 1861. PJ. (8) Wood engraving after a drawing by Gustave Doré. From *London. A Pilgrimage*, by Doré and Blanchard Jerrold, 1872. PJ. (9) From *ILN*, 28 Sept. 1867.

312–13. (1) Source as 310–11 (8). (2) Wood engraving. PJ. (3) PJ. (4) Wood engraving. Felix Barker. (5) Wood engraving from *Historic Times*, 1849. PJ. (6) Wood engraving after a painting by William Macduff, 1862. PJ. (7) From *ILN*, 9 Sept. 1871. PJ. (8) Wood engraving after a drawing by H. W. Brewer. PJ.

314–15. (1) From *ILN*, 17 April 1869. PJ. (2) From *ILN*, 22 June 1867. PJ. (3) Engraving by H. Adlard after O'Connor. PJ. (4) From *ILN*, 23 June 1866. PJ.

316–17. (1, 3, 4, 5) LTB. (2) PJ. (6) Painting by William Maw Egley, 1859. Tate Gallery. (7) Painting by William Powell Frith, 1862. Royal Holloway College.

318–19. (1) Painting by Ford Madox Brown, 1852–65. City Art Gallery,
Manchester. (2) Drawing by Max Beerbohm. City Museum & Art Gallery, Birmingham. (3) Wood engraving from the *Graphic*, 19 May 1877. PJ. (4) Painting by William Powell Frith, exhibited 1883. Major A. Rolph Pope.

320–1. (1) Photograph taken about 1881 by York & Son. PJ. (2) Wood engraving from *The Cleopatra Needle*, published by *Engineering*, 1878. PJ. (3) Wood engraving from the *Graphic*, 27 Oct. 1877. PJ. (4) From *ILN*, 21 Sept. 1878. PJ. (5) PJ. (6) Wood engraving from a drawing made on 12 Jan. 1878. PJ. (7) PJ.

322–3. (1, 2, 3) PJ. (4, 5) NMR. (6) Engraving. Plate from Cassell's *Old And New London*. PJ. (7) LTB.

324–5. (1, 2, 3, 6) Wood engravings from the *Graphic*. PJ. (1) 13 Feb. 1886; (2, 3) 19 Nov. 1887; (6) 26 Nov. 1887. (4) Photograph James Klugmann Collection, Communist Party Library, London. (5) Illustration from Cassell's *Illustrated History of England*. PJ. (7) Half-tone reproduction from *ILN*, 7 Sept. 1889. PJ.

326–7. (1) Wood engraving from the *Graphic*, 7 June 1890. PJ. (2, 4, 7) Wood engravings from *The Penny Illustrated Paper*, 1888. PJ. (3, 5) Wood engravings from *Illustrated Police News*, 1888. BM. (6) Photograph reproduced in *Living London* by George R. Sims, 1903. PJ.

328. (1) Wood engraving from the *Graphic*, 4 Jan. 1879. PJ. (2) From *ILN*, 2 Nov. 1878. PJ. (3) Wood engraving from the *Engineer*, 1889. PJ. (4, 5) Wood engravings from the *Graphic*, 1 Sept. 1883. PJ.

329. (1) Painting by H. Jamyn Brooks. GLC. (2) PJ. (3) Elevation by Ralph Knott.

330–1. (1, 2) PJ. (3, 4) *Evening News*. (5, 6) Maps by Peter Jackson. (7) Pencil drawing by J. P. Emslie dated 29 July 1885. PJ.

332–3. (1) Engraving by Higham after Moore, 1832. PJ. (2) Lithograph by T. W. Lee. Music cover for *Pal-o-Mine Waltz*. PJ. (3, 4, 5) From *ILN*, 11 March 1893. PJ. (6) Wood engraving from *Clubland* by Joseph Hatton, 1890. PJ. (7) From *ILN*, 24 Feb. 1894. PJ.

334–5. (1) From *ILN*, 18 Sept. 1880. PJ. (2) Wood engraving from the *Graphic*, 24 Feb. 1872. PJ. (3) Painting by John O'Connor, 1884. LM. (4) Painting by W. L. Wyllie. G. (5) *Evening News*.

336–7. (1) Painting by William Logsdail. G (2) From *ILN*, 18 Feb. 1882. PJ. (3, 4) PJ. (5) Cartoon by Max Beerbohm, 1911. *The Times*.

338–9. (1) Photograph by Alfred Ellis, 1895. PJ. (2–8) M & M.

340. (1) Painting by Oswald D. Smiles, 1897. Miss Kay Robertson. (2) Illustration by W. Small and Frank Dadd from the *Graphic*, 26 May 1900. PJ. (3) Line drawing from the *Graphic*, 1900. PJ.

341. Site of New National Theatre, South Bank. Central Press.

342–3. (1) Drawing by Fortunino Matania reproduced in the *Sphere*, 1905. M & M. (2) Drawing by G. Amato reproduced in *ILN*, 22 March 1902. PJ. (3) Drawing by S. Begg reproduced in *ILN*, 20 July 1901. PJ. (4) Drawing by Frank Craig reproduced in the *Graphic*, 1 June 1901. PJ. (5) Drawing by Frank Craig reproduced in the *Graphic*, 14 June 1902. PJ.

344–5. (1, 2, 3) PJ. (4) Drawing by Fortunino Matania. Savoy Hotel. (5) Photograph from Rosa Lewis's scrapbook in the possession of Mrs Daphne Fielding. By courtesy of Eyre & Spottiswoode. (6) PJ. (7) Painting by Sir William Orpen. Musée d'Art Moderne, Paris. (8, 9) Drawing by Hugh Thompson from *Highways and Byways in London*, by Mrs Cook, 1907. PJ; illustration from *Living London*, by George R. Sims, 1903.

346–7. (1) Advertising card. PJ. (2) Selfridges. (3) Marks & Spencer. (4) Drawing by A. Wallis Mills from *Punch*, 6 Dec. 1911. PJ. (5, 6) Harrods. (7) Illustration from *Living London*, by George R. Sims, 1903. PJ.

348–9. (1) Postcard. PJ. (2, 3, 6, 7) LTB. (4) Aerofilms. (5) Illustration from *Living London*, by George R. Sims, 1903. PJ.

350. (1) M & M. (2) PJ. (3) Aerofilms. (4) From *Old Time Aldwych, Kingsway, and Neighbourhood* by Charles Gordon. PJ.

351. (1) RT. (2) Press Association.

352–3. (1) Aerofilms. (2) Wood engraving from a drawing by Joseph Pennell. Illustration to an article, London Music Halls, in *Harper's New Monthly Magazine*, Vol. lxxxii. PJ. (3) Illustration from *Living London*, by George R. Sims, 1903. PJ. (4, 5) M & M. (6) Drawing by Phil May reproduced in the *Sketch*, 24 Oct. 1894. PJ. (7, 9, 10) M & M. (8) RT.

354–5. (1, 4) *Evening News*. (2) SI. (3, 5, 6, 7, 8) RT.

356–7. (1) Central Press. (2) Photograph by I. M. Cooke. (3) Drawing by Frank Dadd, 1915, reproduced in *The Great War*, published by Amalgamated Press, 1916. PJ. (4) Imperial War Museum. (5) Press Association. (6) Postcard. PJ. (7) Felix Barker.

358. (1, 3) BBC. (2) Advertisement from *ILN*, 29 April 1922. PJ. (4) Drawing by W. R. E. Stott from *ILN*, 29 April 1922. PJ.

359. (1) *Evening News*. (2) SI.

360–1. Golders Green semi-detached. Felix Barker. Liberty's mock-Tudor. Liberty. Becontree Housing Estate. GLC. Shell-Mex House. NMR. Broadcasting House. Jack Scheerboom. Battersea Power Station. Teddy Schwarz. Senate House. Jack Scheerboom. Sun House, Peter Jones, Dolphin Square. *Architectural Review*. Wembley Uniformity. Aerofilms.

362–3. (1, 4) Imperial War Museum. (2, 3, 6) SI. (5, 7) RT. (8) Central Press.

364. Keystone Press.

365. (1) SI. (2, 3) Architectural Press.

366–7. (1) Etching by Job Nixon reproduced in *Disappearing London* published by *The Studio*, 1927. PJ. (2) GLC. (3) Aquatint by and after T. Rickards. PJ. (4) RT. (5) Kent Barker. (6) Central Press. (7) NMR. (8) City Corporation. (9) *Architect's Journal*. (10) RT.

368–9. (1) Julian Holland. (2) *Evening News*. (3) Drawing by Frank Weemys. Mr Harold Knox King. (4) Aerofilms. (5) G. Maunsell's Partners. (6) John Mowlem & Co.

370–1. Aerofilms.

INDEX

This is a selective index, and makes no claim to be comprehensive. Many individuals, places and streets mentioned briefly are not included. Architects and artists are generally omitted, but can be found either in captions or in the Sources of Illustrations.